Good Victims

OXFORD STUDIES IN GENDER
AND INTERNATIONAL RELATIONS

Series editors: Rahul Rao, University of St Andrews, and Laura Sjoberg,
Royal Holloway University of London

Windows of Opportunity: How Women Seize Peace Negotiations for Political Change
Miriam J. Anderson

Women as Foreign Policy Leaders: National Security and Gender Politics in Superpower America
Sylvia Bashevkin

Gendered Citizenship: Understanding Gendered Violence in Democratic India
Natasha Behl

Gender, Religion, Extremism: Finding Women in Anti-Radicalization
Katherine E. Brown

Enlisting Masculinity: The Construction of Gender in U.S. Military Recruiting Advertising during the All-Volunteer Force
Melissa T. Brown

The Politics of Gender Justice at the International Criminal Court: Legacies and Legitimacy
Louise Chappell

Cosmopolitan Sex Workers: Women and Migration in a Global City
Christine B. N. Chin

Intelligent Compassion: Feminist Critical Methodology in the Women's International League for Peace and Freedom
Catia Cecilia Confortini

Complicit Sisters: Gender and Women's Issues across North-South Divides
Sara de Jong

Gender and Private Security in Global Politics
Maya Eichler

This American Moment: A Feminist Christian Realist Intervention
Caron E. Gentry

Troubling Motherhood: Maternality in Global Politics
Lucy B. Hall, Anna L. Weissman, and Laura J. Shepherd

Breaking the Binaries in Security Studies: A Gendered Analysis of Women in Combat
Ayelet Harel-Shalev and Shir Daphna-Tekoah

Scandalous Economics: Gender and the Politics of Financial Crises
Aida A. Hozić and Jacqui True

Building Peace, Rebuilding Patriarchy: The Failure of Gender Interventions in Timor-Leste
Melissa Johnston

Rewriting the Victim: Dramatization as Research in Thailand's Anti-Trafficking Movement
Erin M. Kamler

Equal Opportunity Peacekeeping: Women, Peace, and Security in Post-Conflict States
Sabrina Karim and Kyle Beardsley

Gender, Sex, and the Postnational Defense: Militarism and Peacekeeping
Annica Kronsell

The Beauty Trade: Youth, Gender, and Fashion Globalization
Angela B. V. McCracken

Global Norms and Local Action: The Campaigns against Gender-Based Violence in Africa
Peace A. Medie

Rape Loot Pillage: The Political Economy of Sexual Violence in Armed Conflict
Sara Meger

Critical Perspectives on Cybersecurity: Feminist and Postcolonial Interventions
Anwar Mhajne and Alexis Henshaw

Support the Troops: Military Obligation, Gender, and the Making of Political Community
Katharine M. Millar

From Global to Grassroots: The European Union, Transnational Advocacy, and Combating Violence against Women
Celeste Montoya

Who Is Worthy of Protection? Gender-Based Asylum and US Immigration Politics
Meghana Nayak

Revisiting Gendered States: Feminist Imaginings of the State in International Relations
Swati Parashar, J. Ann Tickner, and Jacqui True

Out of Time: The Queer Politics of Postcoloniality
Rahul Rao

The Other #MeToos
Iqra Shagufta Cheema

Gender, UN Peacebuilding, and the Politics of Space: Locating Legitimacy
Laura J. Shepherd

Narrating the Women, Peace and Security Agenda: Logics of Global Governance
Laura J. Shepherd

Capitalism's Sexual History
Nicola J. Smith

The Global Politics of Sexual and Reproductive Health
Maria Tanyag

A Feminist Voyage through International Relations
J. Ann Tickner

The Political Economy of Violence against Women
Jacqui True

Queer International Relations: Sovereignty, Sexuality and the Will to Knowledge
Cynthia Weber

Feminist Global Health Security
Clare Wenham

Bodies of Violence: Theorizing Embodied Subjects in International Relations
Lauren B. Wilcox

Good Victims: The Political as a Feminist Question
Roxani Krystalli

Good Victims

The Political as a Feminist Question

ROXANI KRYSTALLI

OXFORD
UNIVERSITY PRESS

Oxford University Press is a department of the University of Oxford. It furthers
the University's objective of excellence in research, scholarship, and education
by publishing worldwide. Oxford is a registered trade mark of Oxford University
Press in the UK and certain other countries.

Published in the United States of America by Oxford University Press
198 Madison Avenue, New York, NY 10016, United States of America.

© Oxford University Press 2024

All rights reserved. No part of this publication may be reproduced, stored in
a retrieval system, or transmitted, in any form or by any means, without the
prior permission in writing of Oxford University Press, or as expressly permitted
by law, by license, or under terms agreed with the appropriate reproduction
rights organization. Inquiries concerning reproduction outside the scope of the
above should be sent to the Rights Department, Oxford University Press, at the
address above.

You must not circulate this work in any other form
and you must impose this same condition on any acquirer.

Library of Congress Cataloging-in-Publication Data
Names: Krystalli, Roxani, author.
Title: Good victims : the political as a feminist question / Roxani Krystalli.
Description: First edition. | New York : Oxford University Press, [2024] |
Series: Oxford Studies in Gender and International Relations |
Includes bibliographical references and index.
Identifiers: LCCN 2023054373 | ISBN 9780197764541 (pbk) |
ISBN 9780197764534 (hb) | ISBN 9780197764565 (epub)
Subjects: LCSH: Women—Crimes against—Colombia. | Victims—Colombia. |
Social justice—Colombia. | Feminist theory—Colombia.
Classification: LCC HV6250.4.W65 K797 2024 | DDC 362.8808209861—dc23/eng/20240105
LC record available at https://lccn.loc.gov/2023054373

DOI: 10.1093/oso/9780197764534.001.0001

Contents

Acknowledgements   ix

1. The Political as a (Feminist) Question   1
2. Making Victims: Histories of Violence and Bureaucracies in Colombia   33
3. Living Ethics and Methods as Questions: Dilemmas of Narrating Victimhood   69
4. Making the (Good) State: Bureaucrats of Victimhood   102
5. Victim Professionals and Professionalized Victims   132
6. 'Victim' as Distinction   164
7. The Future of Victimhood   192

Bibliography   229
Index   249

Acknowledgements

'The question is this and only this', said the Greek poet-diplomat Georgios Seferis in a dialogue with Stratis Thalassinos. 'What will we have done? . . . What will we have done with our freedom, with our love, with our suffering? It's a question that will always press in on us, a cycle from which we will never be able to break out. . . . The question will always be there: What did you take? What did you give?'

These questions about giving and generosity, about the duties that flow from freedom, from love, and from loss have accompanied me over the course of researching the politics of victimhood. The questions are a weight and a source of lightness. It is in that spirit of simultaneous lightness and anchoring gratitude that I proceed to thank the many people who have supported me while carrying out this work.

My students have sharpened my sense of conviction about why and how I do this work. Thanks to the 2020–2023 student cohorts of Feminist Theories in Global Politics, The Politics of Nature and Place, Critical Approaches to Peacebuilding, and a series of other lectures and seminars for broadening our collective imaginations of what the study of international relations can be. The doctoral and other postgraduate students I have worked with warrant a special thanks for reminding me of the delightful reciprocity of teaching and learning alongside, with, and from others.

This book began as a PhD dissertation, buoyed by the patient and wise advice of Kimberly Theidon, Alex de Waal, and Dyan Mazurana. I am thankful to them for showing me how to teach, write, and think in community. Thank you, Kimberly, for reminding me to bring ánimo (zest, courage) to everything I do and for inspiring boldness. Thank you, Dyan, for welcoming me into your home and garden, and for insisting on feminist questions. Alex, you provided the encouragement I needed at every turn. Thank you for teaching me how to direct attention to what matters.

At Oxford University Press, I am immensely grateful to Angela Chnapko for her guidance and leadership, to Laura Sjoberg and Rahul Rao as series editors, and to the production team led by Emily Benitez for supporting this book. Gigi Clement shepherded this book to publication with care and patience. My thinking greatly benefited from the generosity of anonymous peer reviewers whose insights strengthened the manuscript.

Earlier versions of parts of Chapters 3, 4, and 5 have appeared in *International Feminist Journal of Politics*, *Current Anthropology*, and *Political and Legal Anthropology Review*, as indicated in the respective chapters. I am grateful to the editors of those journals for the permission to revise those sections for publication in this book, and to peer reviewers for helping me think more deeply about these questions.

Grants and fellowships have funded different parts of this project. The National Science Foundation, the United States Institute of Peace, the Social Science Research Council, the World Peace Foundation, the Henry J. Leir Institute, the Harvard Program on Negotiation, and the Fletcher School PhD fund supported research in Colombia. The Folke Bernadotte Academy and University of St Andrews Centre for Peace and Conflict Studies funded a book workshop and research assistance respectively. I am thankful to these institutions for enabling in-depth engagement with the questions and communities at the heart of this research. All views expressed here are mine and do not necessarily reflect the positions of the funding institutions. My cohort of SSRC 'fellow fellows,' and the life-altering guidance of the wondrous Amy Ross, made a difference to my experience in ways that transcend the financial support I received.

The greatest gift of the research process has been thinking *with* others, rather than merely *about* the subjects of my inquiry. What started out as the Laboratory for the Anthropology of the State in Colombia has given me phenomenal compañer@s de camino. The insights and friendship of Valentina Pellegrino, Sebastián Ramírez, María Fernanda Olarte-Sierra, Erin McFee, Ana María Forero, Felipe Fernández Lozano, Juana Dávila, Emma Shaw Crane, Gwen Burnyeat, and Charles Beach have (re)oriented my life compass again and again. Thank you, friends, for the wisdom and the laughter.

In Colombia, Angelika Rettberg generously facilitated my Visiting Scholar affiliation at Universidad de Los Andes, and has been an inspiring companion for thinking about peace and justice. Also at Universidad de Los Andes, I extend my thanks to Laura Wills and Ana Teresa Chacón for their hospitality. Meeting Lucero Vargas and Paula Monroy in 2010 changed the course of my research and my life, and I am thankful for their continued generosity. Gonzalo Sánchez, María Emma Wills, and Oscar Valencia were invaluably supportive, especially in the early stages of this research. Michael Weintraub and Angélica Zamora, thank you for welcoming me into your homes, institutional and otherwise. Spending time with Tiffany Kohl, Rebecca Hammel, Angela Lederach, Sarah Richardson, Luca Urech, Adriana Rudling, Julia Zulver, Shauna Gillooly, Jabob Bathanti, and Devin Finn was a gift, and I am grateful for every late night and overcaffeinated morning. Catalina Vallejo, querida mía—thank you for the songs, the dancing, the books, the joy.

I am indebted to my former colleagues at the Feinstein International Center, as well as to students, faculty, and administrators at the Fletcher School, for making the completion of this research possible under impossible circumstances. Elizabeth Stites, you paved the way and made it easier for those who come after you. I remain in your grateful admiration. My deep thanks to Bridget Conley, Kim Howe, and Kim Wilson, whose wit and wisdom have been invaluable companions for me not only at work, but in all of life.

Lisa Wedeen, Timothy Pachirat, and Fred Schaffer's workshops at the Institute for Qualitative and Multi-Method Research taught me more about how to do this kind of work than I can express. Conversations with fellow participants at the annual conferences of the International Studies Association, International Feminist Journal of Politics, American Anthropological Association, Conflict Research Society, and Latin American Studies Association, as well as at a series of workshops, enriched the project, as did the tireless mutual support of various PhD cohorts at the Fletcher School. A deep thanks to those who channel generosity towards building and sustaining these communities. Special thanks to Neha Ansari, Sophia Dawkins, Phoebe Donnelly, Torrey Taussig, and Andrea Walther-Puri, who cheered and carried one another along.

I finished this book at the University of St Andrews, where my colleagues have supplied abundant inspiration and encouragement. My life in Scotland would not be the same without marveling at the light with you, walking by the sea, sharing a meal, or occasionally raising an eyebrow in a Teams meeting. Special thanks to John Anderson, Nick Barnes, Ryan Beasley, Adam Bower, Nick Brooke, Mathilde von Bülow, Ariadne Collins, Jasmine Gani, Caron Gentry, Kristen Harkness, Katharina Hunfeld, Tony Lang, Peter Lehr, Jaremey McMullin, Laura Mills, Phillips O'Brien, Muireann O'Dwyer, Mateja Peter, Rahul Rao, Malaka Shwaikh, Henning Tamm, and Ali Watson, all of whom held space, asked questions, filled in for me when I needed help, or made life a little gentler when they could. Gurch Sanghera and Tim Wilson provided thoughtful and generous feedback on a grant application, and

I am grateful for their accompaniment. Gillian Fleming, Lynne MacMillan, Sharon McPherson, Gail Reid, and Joyce Walsh have literally and figuratively kept the lights on, and for that, our email exchanges, and much else, I am very grateful. Thanks to David Garland for administrative support with workshop planning, and to the excellent Grace Chalmers and Jess Macleod for their meticulous research assistance with putting the finishing touches on the book.

Erin Baines, Helen Kinsella, María Fernanda Olarte-Sierra, Paulo Ravecca, and Shambhawi Tripathi: your collective wisdom on a windy week in Scotland helped this book find its grounding. Thank you for the poems, the courage, the vulnerability you inspire; thank you for befriending the ghosts and for benevolently haunting these pages. Dipali Mukhopadhyay, you could not be there, but you *were* there, and you are here. My thanks to the Folke Bernadotte Academy for making a book workshop possible, and to these companions for bringing their magic to the space we created together.

The gifts of friendship transcend any effort to pin them to the page. Several people have expanded my imagination of the possible and my vocabularies of care. Those vocabularies are the shadow bedrock on which this book is built. For that, and much else, deep thanks to Helen Berents, Marie Berry, Steve Bloomfield, Caitlin Hamilton, Aida Hozić, Naeem Inayatullah, Angela Lederach, Zoe Marks, Dipali Mukhopadhyay, Rahul Rao, Paulo Ravecca, Philipp Schulz, Laura Shepherd, Annick Wibben, and Nicole Wegner. To the people who teach me that researching political violence requires attentiveness to that which sustains life, I am gratefully indebted to the clarity of your conviction. Thank you, Yolande Bouka, Kate Cronin-Furman, Anjali Dayal, Jonneke Koomen, Milli Lake, Shiera Malik, Olivia Rutazibwa, Ami Shah, and Abbey Steele. Many of these forms of accompaniment have been woven and sustained from afar, over hastily written emails and delirious WhatsApp messages. I am grateful for the ways these people and relationships make the world feel both bigger and smaller.

A constellation of love anchors my life in ways that spill beyond the boundaries of the university. Thank you, Evangelia Avloniti, Niki Boehm, Emily Burnor, Erin Frey, Rachel Gordon, Kate Graeff, Meghan Johnson, Tais Jost, Iarla O'Halloran, Elizabeth Stahl, and Amy Tan. May we keep showing up for each other.

Over the course of writing this book, I became seriously ill in ways that have reshuffled my life. I owe a debt of gratitude to the National Health

Service in Scotland. Its doctors, nurses, and (hilarious) phlebotomists are a national treasure that I hope to dedicate my life to honouring and preserving.

When I used to line up my stuffed animals on the stairs of my childhood home in order to teach them, my father joked that I would be an academic when I grew up. Neither he nor I could have fully appreciated then what that meant, and neither he nor my mother lived to see this book be published. I have felt my parents' presence, and their loss, while working on this project. They sacrificed greatly to make a life possible for their daughter that never would have been accessible to them. My gratitude for that is never-ending.

Malachy Tallack, walking beside you is my life's greatest joy. Thank you for responding with such care to my exclamations that 'I have Thoughts', for reading every word of everything I write, and for trusting me with your love. Everything shines brighter because of you. Agnes, Roger, Rory, Chloe, Thea, and Malin, thank you for the love, the birds, the dancing.

This work took shape through walks on the Andes in Colombia, and beside the Allan water and the river Eden in Scotland. It crystallized between poems and essays, between moss and light. These have been as essential ingredients to my process as the kindness of the humans listed above.

I extend my most sincere gratitude to my interlocutors in Colombia. You have taught me nearly everything I know about peace and politics, about violence and justice, about sourcing and seeing beauty and joy *during* and *through* loss, not just after it. Your generosity, your kindness, your courage, and your conviction are bright lights in a world of darkness. I hope to be a worthy ally to your efforts to make peace and justice meaningful realities in the lives of people affected by violence.

1
The Political as a (Feminist) Question

Origin Stories

When Victor was twenty-two years old, his older brother was forcibly disappeared in the eastern Antioquia region of Colombia. In the immediate aftermath, his family worked to register his disappearance and begin the search process. 'My mother wanted to talk to the paramilitaries', Victor told me on a July afternoon in 2013. 'None of the rest of us thought it was a good idea, but she kept saying, "If they took him, they know where he is".' Because of threats against the whole family, Victor and his four siblings were displaced to Bogotá. Their mother remained in Antioquia, refusing to leave the land from which her son had been disappeared. In Bogotá, Victor started working with one of the non-governmental organizations advocating for family members of the disappeared. 'The thing is, we are not good victims', Victor said. 'No somos buenas víctimas'.[1] Victor's pronouncement sowed the first seeds of inquiry for this book: What does it mean to be a good victim?

A year later, in June 2014, Sergio Jaramillo, the high commissioner for peace in Colombia, declared in his address to the Colombian Senate that 'this is the era of the victims'.[2] Since then, on occasions ranging from the participation of selected victim delegates in the Havana peace talks to presidential elections, state officials, newspaper headlines, and representatives of international organizations alike have heralded 'the time of the victims', 'the hour of

---

[1] Interview with family member of disappeared person, July 2013. Style guides often suggest italicizing words that appear in a language other than English. I have chosen not to do that because 'I've come to understand the practise of italicizing such words as a form of linguistic gatekeeping; a demarcation between which words are "exotic" or "not found in the English language," and those that have a rightful place in the text: the non-italicized'. Khairani Barokka, 'The Case against Italicizing "Foreign" Words', *Catapult*, February 11, 2020, https://catapult.co/stories/column-the-case-against-italicizing-foreign-words-khairani-barokka.

[2] Office of the High Commissioner for Peace in Colombia, 'El tiempo de las víctimas', June 9, 2014, https://www.funcionpublica.gov.co/eva/admon/files/empresas/ZW1wcmVzYV83Ng==/archivos/1462299931_1c28b3e9306b3b7e4820233b2b2c4bf8.pdf.

the victims', 'the moment of the victims'.[3] In these formulations, 'the victims' are imagined and narrated as an undifferentiated collective.[4]

As of January 2023, the Colombian state had officially recognized 9,423,138 individuals as victims of the armed conflict.[5] Yet, not all victims are created equal. In the lives of people like Victor and others who identify as victims, there are good victims, photogenic victims, desirable victims—and, conversely, complicated victims, hidden victims, forgotten victims, abandoned victims. In their stories, an adjective always accompanies and modifies victimhood. The adjectives contain, reflect, and create hierarchies, simultaneously setting and fracturing the boundaries of solidarity and shaping the scripts of claim-making during transitions from violence.

The questions that initially motivated this research emerged from the contrast between these two stories. What does it mean to be (or not be) a 'good victim'? How do transitional justice mechanisms, as well as the individuals who vie for recognition as victims, create, reinforce, and contest hierarchies of victimhood? And, crucially, what are the implications of these hierarchies for theories and experiences of peace and justice during transitions from violence?

'There is a bias', the political ethnographer Timothy Pachirat claims, 'to the way we present our work—which we often call our arguments, rather than our stories—that causes us to write deductive intentionality backwards into the research process'.[6] A question is born—in the passive voice, in the researcher's head, as though in a vacuum. 'It doesn't help at all that many ethnographies are written as though the researcher had known from the start what the research question would be', Pachirat continues.[7]

---

[3] Nelson Camilo Sánchez León, 'El momento de las víctimas en La Habana', Dejusticia, June 16, 2014, https://www.dejusticia.org/column/el-momento-de-las-victimas-en-la-habana/; Catalina Oquendo, 'Los exsecuestrados de las FARC que buscan llegar al Congreso de Colombia', El País, January 31, 2022, https://elpais.com/internacional/2022-01-31/los-exsecuestrados-de-las-farc-que-buscan-llegar-al-congreso-de-colombia.html.

[4] Critiquing the humanitarian response in Kosovo in the late 1990s, Didier Fassin wrote: 'Humanitarian organisations were for the victims, all the victims, yes; there were no good or bad victims, it went without saying'. Didier Fassin, 'Heart of Humaneness: The Moral Economy of Humanitarian Intervention', in Contemporary States of Emergency, edited by Didier Fassin and Mariella Pandolfi (Zone Books, 2010), p. 283.

[5] Unidad para la atención y reparación integral a las víctimas, https://www.unidadvictimas.gov.co. This number includes only those people the Colombian state officially recognizes as victims. That number excludes people who identify as victims but either did not come forward to register as such with the state or did not succeed in securing official recognition as 'victims'.

[6] Timothy Pachirat, Among Wolves: Ethnography and the Immersive Study of Power (Routledge, 2018), p. 34.

[7] Pachirat, Among Wolves, p. 84.

In the thirteen years that I have been working in Colombia as an academic researcher and practitioner in the fields of humanitarian action, gender analysis, and transitional justice, I have told the story of how this project began, just as I did in the preceding pages, many times. Through repetition in grant applications to fund fieldwork, presentations at conferences and workshops, through publications and informal conversations, the story of this project became a script. The more readily the script rolled off my tongue, and the more fluent I became in telling this story to audiences nodding kindly, the more I worried that the questions became frozen in space and time. Each repetition, each performance of the story of research, locked the narrative in, potentially robbing the questions of their dynamism and their capacity to keep pace with the changes in both the lives of my interlocutors and my own curiosity.[8] Through each retelling, I was crafting a fiction about how a research project moves across time and space, as though the journey from grant proposal to 'the field' to publication could ever leave questions, methods, ethical dilemmas, and analytic frames unaffected by encounters.

Rewriting a more textured story of the trajectory of this inquiry about the politics of victimhood in Colombia requires accounting for three shifts in the project over time. First, the growing ecosystem of fascination with victimhood in Colombia, and the ethical and methodological concerns associated with that gaze, prompted me to reorient my attention towards bureaucracies. Second, I became attuned to the legacies of not only violence, but also mechanisms of transitional justice and the hierarchies these mechanisms contained and created. And third, I wanted to know more about the meanings of the political in the recurrent chorus about 'the politics of victimhood'. Though the narration of these shifts may appear deceptively tidy on the page, these changes were the product of slow fermentation and (often anxiety-producing) reflection in conversation with my interlocutors in Colombia. Since 'research produces us, our selves as researchers',[9] the stories of the research at the heart of this book intertwine with my stories of self. I tell these stories side by side here because they shape and are shaped by each other. I have aged and changed with the questions this book explores. The questions have changed, and they have also changed me.

---

[8] I am grateful to Pilar Riaño-Alcalá, whose reflections on the evolution of storytelling about one's relationship to research at the 'Oral Historians Working in/on Political Violence' workshop, generously convened by Erin Jessee and Leyla Neyzi in Glasgow in June 2022, prompted me to think further about this point.
[9] Laura Shepherd, 'Research as Gendered Intervention: Feminist Research Ethics and the Self in the Research Encounter', *Crítica Contemporánea Revista de Teoría Política* 6 (2017): 6.

Bureaucracies of Victimhood

The landscape of humanitarian, justice, research, and policy engagement in Colombia had changed significantly between the time I first arrived in Bogotá as a humanitarian practitioner in 2010 and my return there to officially start my research on this project in 2016. By 2016, 'seemingly everyone wanted to talk to a victim'.[10] Prompted by ethical concerns about the narrative obligations that the growing interest in the Colombian armed conflict placed on people who identified as victims, I became curious about other ways to investigate the politics of victimhood.[11]

Writing about the state of American anthropology in the late 1960s, Laura Nader expressed concern about the ways that scholars directed the anthropological gaze at 'the poor, the ethnic groups, the disadvantaged'.[12] While she acknowledged the significance of knowledge generation about these groups, she also called for an understanding of the experience of poverty, marginalization, or suffering through the study of powerful institutions that produce or exacerbate it. Nader called this reorientation 'studying up'.[13] Banks, law firms, police departments, bureaucratic documents, and government professionals play an important part in creating and perpetuating inequalities and injustices in the world. 'It is appropriate', Nader concluded, 'that a reinvented anthropology study powerful institutions and bureaucratic organisations ... for such institutions and their network systems affect our lives and also affect the lives of people that anthropologists have traditionally studied all around the world'.[14]

Victims do not merely exist; they are also made, not only through acts of violence during war, but also through acts of bureaucratic affirmation during 'the-time-of-not-war-not-peace'.[15] In that spirit, I started turning my attention to how the agencies, professionals, and documents of the Colombian

---

[10] Roxani Krystalli, 'Narrating victimhood: Dilemmas and (in)dignities', *International Feminist Journal of Politics* 23, no. 1 (2021): 127. I elaborate on this point in Chapter 3.

[11] Feminist researchers in other contexts have observed similar dynamics. With reference to northern Uganda, Erin Baines writes: 'It was the specificity of a woman's victimhood that attracted international researchers like myself, and journalists, writers, documentary makers, photographers, aid workers, religious charities, travellers, and a host of other people to do their work'. Erin Baines, *Buried in the Heart: Women, Complex Victimhood and the War in Northern Uganda* (Cambridge University Press, 2017), p. xiii.

[12] Laura Nader, 'Up the Anthropologist: Perspectives Gained from Studying Up', Distributed by ERIC Clearinghouse (1972): 5.

[13] Nader, 'Up the Anthropologist', p. 1.

[14] Nader, 'Up the Anthropologist', p. 9.

[15] Carolyn Nordstrom, *Shadows of War* (University of California Press, 2004), p. 165.

state and its transitional justice apparatus shape the politics of victimhood. I call this constellation of agencies, professionals, documents, and encounters 'bureaucracies of victimhood' because the category of 'victim' defines not only the people who vie for recognition as such, but also the professional ecosystem that attends to them. Whole floors of bureaucratic buildings in Colombia were named 'Victims', and professionals described themselves as working on the 'victims' team'. 'Victims' was the word written onto business cards, printed onto high-visibility vests, and featuring on calendars, bookmarks, notebooks, and T-shirts. Victimhood, more than the broader frame of transitional justice, defined the day-to-day work of the bureaucratic encounters I studied.

Where a researcher presumes studying 'up' to be depends on that researcher's interpretation of power. 'Who is "up" there?', the anthropologist Liisa Malkki asked in her correspondence with Allaine Cerwonka about the limits of categories like 'elites' and 'ordinary people'.[16] 'The state', of course, is not the single, undisputed site of power that is always 'up' there, nor are 'the victims' 'down' and powerless. And, indeed, neither entity is monolithic or monophonic.[17] A more meaningful interpretation of studying up in the Colombian context requires spelling out the forms of power that are of interest to this analysis.

State bureaucracies of transitional justice have the power to confer the status of 'victim', to distinguish between people they recognize as victims (and the experiences and harms that give rise to that recognition) and the rest of the population, as well as to direct attention, remedies, and resources to those who successfully secure victim status. The Colombian state exercises

---

[16] Allaine Cerwonka and Liisa H. Malkki, *Improvising Theory* (University of Chicago Press, 2007), p. 88.

[17] On the polyphony and heterogeneity of the state in Colombia, see Julieta Lemaitre, *El estado siempre llega tarde* (Siglo XXI Editores, 2019); Juan Ricardo Aparicio, *Rumores, residuos y estado en 'la major esquina de Sudamérica'* (Ediciones Uniandes, 2015); Valentina Pellegrino, 'Between the Roll of Paper and the Role of Paper: Governmental Documentation as a Mechanism for Complying In compliantly', *PoLAR: Political and Legal Anthropology Review* 45, no. 1 (2022): 77–93; Juan Pablo Vera Lugo, 'The Humanitarian State: Bureaucracy and Social Policy in Colombia' (PhD dissertation: Rutgers University, 2017); Juana Dávila Sáenz, 'A Land of Lawyers, Experts, and "Men without Land": The Politics of Land Restitution and the Techno-Legal Production of "Dispossessed People" in Colombia' (PhD dissertation: Harvard University, 2017); Erin McFee, 'An Ambivalent Peace: Mistrust, Reconciliation, and the Intervention Encounter in Colombia' (PhD dissertation: University of Chicago, 2019); Gwen Burnyeat, *The Face of Peace* (University of Chicago Press, 2022). On the polyphony of those who identify as victims in Colombia, see Angelika Rettberg, *Entre el perdón y el paredón* (Ediciones Uniandes, 2005); Adriana Rudling, 'What's Inside the Box? Mapping Agency and Conflict within Victims' Organisations', *International Journal of Transitional Justice* 13, no. 3 (2019): 458–77.

that power through regulations, bureaucratic documents, encounters between transitional justice professionals and those who seek recognition as victims, state-organized events for victims of the armed conflict, and other instruments. In these various ways, the state apparatus of transitional justice also has the power to influence how people understand and present themselves, as well as how they make sense of their relationships to the state, to the harms they suffered,[18] and to each other in the wake of violence.[19]

The story of the bureaucratic production of the politics of victimhood is necessarily a *story of encounter* between the agencies with power to confer the status of victim and its associated benefits, and people who vie for such recognition.[20] People who identify as victims are important interlocutors in this story, even if they are not the sole protagonists, and even though I treat these interlocutors as knowledge bearers on more than the subject of their suffering.[21] In this context, studying up involves both seeing the state as a key actor in the production and contestation of the politics of victimhood *and* maintaining a curiosity about how people who identify as victims infuse the 'victim' category with their own meanings, challenge, resist, and subvert the interpretations of the state, and actively shape the politics of victimhood.[22]

The first contribution of this book, therefore, lies in highlighting how the politics of victimhood do not only pertain to the people who identify as victims, but are also critical for reimagining the state and bringing a vision of it into being through bureaucratic encounters in the wake of war. This contribution builds on exciting work that is underway in the field termed the 'anthropology of the state' in Colombia and beyond. In Colombia, much of this

---

[18] Importantly for the purposes of choosing to 'study up', state agencies have the 'institutional protections or . . . the socio-economic means to block access to researchers' and are perhaps more likely to exercise this power (to refuse to be studied, or studied in a particular way) than those who identify as victims. Cerwonka and Malkki, *Improvising Theory*, p. 88.

[19] Inspired by Christina Sharpe, I rely on the language of 'the wake', rather than definitely speaking of the 'aftermath' of war, in acknowledgement of the violence that persists in many forms after peace accords. In her book on Blackness, survival, care, and the afterlives of slavery, Sharpe draws attention to how the metaphor of the wake unfolds on different temporal planes without creating sharp or illusory distinctions between past, present, and future. Christina Sharpe, *In the Wake: On Blackness and Being* (Duke University Press, 2016).

[20] I am inspired by Andrea García González's feminist analysis of encounter as method. Andrea García González, 'Desde el conflicto: Epistemología y política en las etnografías feministas', *Antípoda* 35, no. 1 (2019): 3–21.

[21] I elaborate on this point in Chapter 3. This commitment has been inspired by Eve Tuck, 'Suspending Damage: A Letter to Communities', *Harvard Educational Review* 79, no. 3 (2009): 413.

[22] As Fassin and Rechtman write regarding the label of trauma, 'It becomes clear that individuals themselves are not content to behave as passive victims of the labelling process, but are redefining trauma, or even denying it'. Didier Fassin and Richard Rechtman, *The Empire of Trauma: An Inquiry into the Condition of Victimhood* (Princeton University Press, 2009), p. 97.

scholarship concerns itself with questions of how to interpret state presence and absence in the wake of violence,[23] and engages with how imaginations of centres and peripheries affect the project of state-building and shape state–citizen relations.[24] The present analysis complements that work by reflecting on how the project of transitional justice *as a state project* and, specifically, its bureaucracies of victimhood, becomes one pillar of establishing state presence and authority during transitions from violence. It also shows how the moments of disappointment that often inflect bureaucratic encounters affect state–citizen relations in the wake of war. Throughout, my understanding of the state is inspired by the feminist scholar Begoña Aretxaga: 'I attempt to leave the state as both an open notion and an entity, the presence and content of which is not taken for granted but is the very object of inquiry'.[25]

This contribution also builds on the interdisciplinary body of work on social suffering, which has highlighted how injury, trauma, pain, and suffering that result from political violence, health inequities, and other causes can generate subjectivities.[26] The suffering associated with violence is one of the pillars that give rise to the victim subject. I extend this argument by looking at how the victim subject itself, and the bureaucratic encounters surrounding it, contribute to producing the state and its relationship to citizens during transitions from violence. In the chapters that follow, I show that ideas about 'good victims' are entwined with conceptions of the 'good state'.

I deliberately frame the above as contributions to ongoing conversations, rather than as scholarship that fills the proverbial 'gap in the literature'. The fiction of the gap in the literature remains persistent in academic storytelling. 'While much literature examines X', this story goes, 'We know little about Y' or 'Few studies have examined Z'.[27] In this story, the 'we' often remains

---

[23] Teo Ballvé, *The Frontier Effect: State Formation and Violence in Colombia* (Cornell University Press, 2020); Winifred Tate, 'The Aspirational State: State Effects in Putumayo', in *State Theory and Andean Politics*, edited by Christopher Krupa and David Nugent (University of Pennsylvania Press, 2015); Lemaitre, *El estado siempre*.

[24] Margarita Serje, *El revés de la nación* (Ediciones Uniandes, 2011); María Clemencia Ramírez, 'The Idea of the State in Colombia: An Analysis from the Periphery', in *State Theory and Andean Politics*, edited by Christopher Krupa and David Nugent (University of Pennsylvania Press, 2015); Lugo, 'The Humanitarian State'.

[25] Begoña Aretxaga, 'Maddening States', *Annual Review of Anthropology* 32 (2003): 396. On the same page, Aretxaga continues: 'By thinking about the state in this way, I want to emphasise the power it still conveys; its social and political presence can hardly be ignored'.

[26] Arthur Kleinman, Veena Das, and Margaret Lock, *Social Suffering* (University of California Press, 1997), p. ix.

[27] Paulo Ravecca and Elizabeth Dauphinee call this 'fortress writing', which 'portrays the researcher and the research as invulnerable, inoculating the inquiry against anticipated challenges and pre-empting critique. This form of writing, itself a product of power relations, ... erases the political conditions of knowledge production. It also conceals the inescapable partiality of the social scientist's

undefined, implying an omniscient academic who has read every book and form of knowledge in every language, and who can confidently identify The Gap.[28] The imagined gap in the literature is a convenient fiction because it highlights opportunities for a unique contribution. In the political economy of academic success, uniqueness and innovation are treasured prizes, and the rewards are often publication, critical acclaim, or a place in the canon. 'We are taught to use others' shortcomings—real, perceived, or otherwise—as the launching sites for our own work', Jasmine Brooke Ulmer writes.[29]

Alternative launch sites exist. There are rewards for contributing to, extending, or building on conversations that are already underway. These are the rewards of *thinking with* others, and of tackling intellectual and political problems and inequalities as collectives, rather than individuals. 'Instead of reinforcing the figure of a lone thinker', the feminist scholar María Puig de la Bellacasa argues in her reflections on writing with care, 'the voice in such a text seems to be saying: *I am not the only one*. . . . It builds relation and community, that is: possibility'.[30]

The Effects of Hierarchies and Legacies of Transitional Justice

My interest in understanding the politics of victimhood is not a typological endeavour. Paying attention to others' expectations of this project, especially when those did not resonate with my own, was particularly generative for refining the scope of inquiry. I took notes each time a peer reviewer or audience member at a conference asked whether I was coining the concept of a 'good victim' or creating a typology of victims. (The answers were no and no.) I am not suggesting that 'good victims' 'are a "type" of victim group that

---

point of view, making a plain notion of objectivity or veracity seem plausible'. Paulo Ravecca and Elizabeth Dauphinee, 'Narrative and the Possibilities for Scholarship', *International Political Sociology* 12, no. 2 (2018): 127.

[28] Donna Haraway names this 'the god trick of seeing everything from nowhere'. Donna Haraway, 'Situated Knowledges: The Science Question in Feminism and the Privilege of Partial Perspective', *Feminist Studies* 14, no. 3 (1988): 581.

[29] Jasmine Brooke Ulmer, 'Pivots and Pirouettes: Carefully Turning Traditions', *Qualitative Inquiry* 26, no. 5 (2020): 454.

[30] María Puig de la Bellacasa, '"Nothing Comes without Its World": Thinking with Care', *Sociological Review* 60, no. 2 (2012): 203.

should be identified and added to the remit of the field of transitional justice'.[31] Nor am I interested in coining a term or classifying different types of hierarchies, 'pinned to the page like so many colourful butterfly wings'.[32]

Rather, my interest is oriented at the lasting effects of these hierarchies, of these ideas about 'good victims', on political subjectivities and relationships. When Victor spoke about family members of the disappeared not being 'good victims', his concern was with the consequences of this adjective for people's search for justice. The suffering of 'good victims' is more likely to be believable and grievable,[33] with material, social, emotional, and political effects. 'Good victims' are more likely to be included—and rendered archetypal—in transitional justice initiatives. They are likely to be invited to be part of spaces and encounters that are limited, in that they are not available to the majority of people recognized as victims in Colombia (or to the broader population), and they require judgments on the part of gatekeepers regarding who is worthy of access. In an analysis of what she calls victim-based identity, Tami Amanda Jacoby argues that 'being recognised as a victim is a right and even arguably a privilege not equally bestowed on all injured people'.[34] The passive voice here—'being included', 'being recognised'—is deliberate because, although these processes of inclusion and recognition are hardly passive, there is no single actor at the helm of them. State officials, people who identify as victims, leaders of human rights and social justice organizations, media, and members of the general public all participate in different ways in creating, reinforcing, and contesting hierarchies, as well as in making their effects felt. People who challenge ideas about 'well-behaved victims'—or those whom others view as 'trouble-making victims'—may struggle to receive attention, access resources, and form relationships that are essential for navigating the bureaucracy of victimhood during transitions from violence.

Therein lies the second contribution of this book: it takes up the call to study the legacies not only of violence, but also of the transitional justice mechanisms set up in its wake. Feminist work across fields shows how performances of injury, loss, trauma, or suffering establish one's initial

---

[31] Baines, *Buried in the Heart*, p. 7. Baines powerfully continues: 'Rather, I work towards a conceptualisation of justice that unsettles categories, and makes possible the praxis of judgment, one in which the polity deliberates over what it means to be a human being in the face of violence'.

[32] Kimberly Theidon, *Intimate Enemies* (University of Pennsylvania Press, 2012), p. 26.

[33] Judith Butler, *Frames of War: When Is Life Grievable?* (Verso Books, 2016), pp. 14–15. A life is grievable 'if it would be grieved if it were lost'. Butler argues that 'grievability is a presupposition for the life that matters'. Butler, *Frames of War*, p. 16.

[34] Tami Amanda Jacoby, 'A Theory of Victimhood: Politics, Conflict and the Construction of Victim-Based Identity', *Millennium* 43, no. 2 (2015): 517.

eligibility for protection or assistance.[35] In the context of Colombia, this important work has examined how individuals must act in order to be seen as worthy of inclusion in land restitution programmes,[36] the Victims' Registry,[37] or mechanisms for humanitarian assistance and reparations.[38] This book complements and extends this body of work by examining the lasting effects, rather than initial goals, of performances of victimhood and the hierarchies that emerge in the process of seeking legibility and recognition within the bureaucratic realm of transitional justice encounters.

The 'Victim' Subject as a Political Subject

The phrase 'the politics of victimhood' recurred in my fieldnotes and in the literature I reviewed on this subject. Researchers working in different contexts worldwide appear to agree that victimhood can be political,[39] and I wanted to know more about this political content. I have followed this curiosity by resisting the urge to define politics myself and, instead, inquiring about the meanings my interlocutors attached to 'the political' and its associations with victimhood.

---

[35] Miriam Ticktin argues that the claims of individuals who experienced violence 'must be mediated by embodied performances that make them recognisable . . . as worthy of compassion'. Miriam Ticktin, *Casualties of Care* (University of California Press, 2011), p. 13.

[36] Dávila, 'Land of Lawyers'; Jemima García-Godos and Henrik Wiig, 'Ideals and Realities of Restitution: The Colombian Land Restitution Programme', *Journal of Human Rights Practice* 10, no. 1 (2018): 40–57.

[37] Angélica Franco Gamboa, 'Daño y reconstrucción de la cotidianidad en covíctimas y sobrevivientes de minas antipersonal', *Nómadas*, no. 38 (2013): 115–31; Fredy Alberto Mora-Gámez, 'Reparation beyond Statehood; Assembling Rights Restitution in Post-conflict Colombia' (PhD dissertation: University of Leicester, 2016).

[38] Catalina Vallejo, 'Pricing Suffering: Compensation for Human Rights Violation in Colombia and Peru' (PhD dissertation: University of Virginia, 2019).

[39] Marie Berry, *War, Women, and Power: From Violence to Mobilization in Rwanda and Bosnia-Herzegovina* (Cambridge University Press, 2018); Alex Vandermaas-Peeler, Jelena Subotić, and Michael Barnett, 'Constructing Victims: Suffering and Status in Modern World Order', *Review of International Studies* 2022: 1–19; Vincent Druliolle and Roddy Brett, *The Politics of Victimhood in Post-conflict Societies* (Palgrave Macmillan, 2018); Jelena Golubović, '"One Day I Will Tell This to My Daughter": Serb Women, Silence, and the Politics of Victimhood in Sarajevo', *Anthropological Quarterly* 92, no. 4 (2019): 1173–99; Cheryl Lawther, '"Let Me Tell You": Transitional Justice, Victimhood and Dealing with a Contested Past', *Social & Legal Studies* 30, no. 6 (2021): 890–912; Robert Meister, 'Human Rights and the Politics of Victimhood', *Ethics & International Affairs* 16, no. 2 (2002): 91–108; Lilie Chouliaraki, 'Victimhood: The Affective Politics of Vulnerability', *European Journal of Cultural Studies* 24, no. 1 (2021): 10–27; Clara Eroukhmanoff and Alister Wedderburn, 'Introduction: Constructing and Contesting Victimhood in Global Politics', *Polity* 54, no. 3 (2022): 841–48.

Empirically investigating notions of politics, rather than defining them a priori, is complicated. To begin with, the word 'política' in Spanish is polysemic, potentially referring to what English speakers would understand as both 'policy' and 'politics'.[40] Ambiguities can be fruitful for research because they fuel further inquiry. When an interlocutor spoke of the 'política' surrounding the victim category or of being a political subject [sujeto politico], I had to ask: What kind of política are we talking about? Where is it observable? What subjects does it generate?

These questions were inspired by Veena Das's investigations of the political. 'For me the political is not set apart', Das said in an interview with Kim Turcot DiFruscia: 'It is closely related to the way in which one's being in the world is engaged'.[41] Das continues: 'Politics become the arena in which a lot of people can engage in actions of claiming for themselves particular forms of dwelling in the world.... I understand the political through these questions: What are the ways that the world claims you? And how do you respond to this kind of claim, from the position that you are in?'[42]

The denial and simultaneous omnipresence of politics further complicate the exploration of these questions. On the one hand, researchers are often told that an institution or an individual is apolitical, not interested in politics, or 'eschews political mandates'.[43] Wherever these researchers happen to be looking for politics and the political, they will not find it. Over here, there is 'just' bureaucracy, just a process, just a bureaucratic form, just a meeting, just people doing their work. 'Just' is an illusory term that minimizes interest and curiosity; it is one of the words that wraps an environment, concept, or activity 'in a protective blanket, making it almost immune to bothersome questioning'.[44]

Alongside the denial of politics, the anthropologists Jennifer Curtis and Jonathan Spencer have expressed concern about what they term 'the new ubiquity of the political'.[45] In their words, 'There has been an expansion of

---

[40] My inquiry was further complicated by the fact that 'victimhood' itself does not have a direct translation into Spanish (or at least one that circulated in Colombia among my interlocutors). People would speak of the 'política de la categoría de la víctima' or 'estatus de víctima' or 'política de ser víctima'—the politics of the victim category, the victim status, of the politics of being a victim—to describe what I translate into victimhood.

[41] Kim Turcot DiFruscia, 'Listening to Voices: An Interview with Veena Das', Altérités 7, no. 1 (2010): 141.

[42] Turcot DiFruscia, 'Listening to Voices', p. 141.

[43] Ticktin, Casualties of Care, p. 7.

[44] Cynthia Enloe, The Curious Feminist (University of California Press, 2004), p. 2.

[45] Jennifer Curtis and Jonathan Spencer, 'Anthropology and the Political', in The Sage Handbook of Social Anthropology, edited by John Gledhill and Richard Fardon (Sage, 2012), p. 169. Thanks to Gwen Burnyeat for thinking with me about how to draw out this point.

the category of the political itself, which has become so diffuse and nebulous in recent usage that more or less everything might count as political'.[46] They argue that 'the cost of this theoretical freedom is twofold: a loss of acuity in the analysis of actually existing politics, and an inability to engage with our informants' own ideas about what might and might not count as political'.[47]

I am sympathetic to the need for acuity in the analysis of concepts. Claiming that 'the political is everywhere' can make 'politics disappear'.[48] At the same time, the phrase 'actually existing politics' seems to suggest that there is a predefined, knowable, limited universe of what politics is and could be. This understanding is at odds with the interpretive approach in this book. Rather than defending the narrowness of the concept of politics, I am interested in the varied meanings with which people imbue it. I am intrigued by 'the contingency, unpredictability, and fragility of action' that makes up politics and political life.[49] This approach requires investigating the political as a question, not a declaration: What is at stake for people who identify as victims when they claim to be political subjects? What does it mean to understand the victim subject as a political subject, and the political subject as shaped through victimhood?

The third contribution of this book is that it highlights the possibilities of politics *through*, rather than after or in opposition to, the status of 'victim'. Scholars and practitioners of peacebuilding and transitional justice alike have been sceptical about these possibilities. This scepticism often arises from the view that claim-making on the basis of suffering may obliterate politics by locking subjects into a 'suffering slot' that can become reductive.[50] Illustrating these concerns, the political theorist Wendy Brown has argued that wounded attachments, referring to 'the logics of pain' that inform the creation of identities based on a premise of suffering, can wholly swallow subjects.[51] According to Brown, a politics premised on pain is possible, but ultimately limited and circular because 'it can hold out no future . . . that triumphs over this pain'.[52]

---

[46] Curtis and Spencer, 'Anthropology and the Political', pp. 168–69.
[47] Curtis and Spencer, 'Anthropology and the Political', p. 169.
[48] Roxani Krystalli and Cynthia Enloe, 'Doing Feminism: A Conversation between Cynthia Enloe and Roxani Krystalli', *International Feminist Journal of Politics* 22, no. 2 (2020): 294.
[49] Helen Kinsella, *The Image before the Weapon: A Critical History of the Distinction between Combatant and Civilian* (Cornell University Press, 2011), p. 191.
[50] Michel-Rolph Trouillot, 'Anthropology and the Savage Slot: The Poetics and Politics of Otherness', in *Global Transformations*, edited by Michel-Rolph Trouillot (Palgrave Macmillan, 2003), p. 33.
[51] Wendy Brown, 'Wounded Attachments', *Political Theory* 21, no. 3 (1993): 390–410.
[52] Brown, 'Wounded Attachments', p. 406.

While remaining attentive to these concerns, I also show that the politics of victimhood is more than a politics premised on pain and suffering—and, further, I argue that pain and suffering can enable, rather than merely foreclose, particular practices of politics and manifestations of the political. The politics of victimhood is also a practice of labour and care, a lesson in solidarity and its limits. It is a politics that simultaneously broadens and disciplines understandings of what counts as violence, when that violence begins and ends, and what forms it takes. It is a politics that articulates (victim) subjects into being, and also shapes the remaking of states during transitions from violence.

Questions and Aims

Following these three shifts in my engagement with the politics of victimhood over the past decade, the central questions that now animate this book are: What kind of politics is—or, indeed, are—the politics of victimhood? And how does the label of 'victim' shape how people understand themselves as political subjects in relation to one another, the harms they suffered, and the state during transitions from violence?

It is possible to draw a dotted, not-quite-straight line between the questions this book explores and the questions I began to articulate when I first noticed the contrast between the narratives of 'good victims' and 'the era of the victims' a decade earlier. Tracing the changes of the questions and my relationship to them allows for a fuller account of the research process. I am not sure if this is necessarily a more honest account, in part because I believe that stories of research are full of fictions. Speaking of fictions of research does not mean that these accounts lack academic rigour, or that they are wholly untrue. After all, fiction has a complex relationship to truths. Literature, according to Naeem Inayatullah, highlights 'the limits of the theory/fiction, politics/art, scientific/mythological ... dichotomies'.[53] In critically revisiting my own fictions of research, I call into question the linearity that defines many stories about the research process. The straightforward account of

---

[53] Naeem Inayatullah, 'If Only You Could See What I Have Seen with Your Eyes: Staging an Encounter between Social Science and Literature' (unpublished essay, 2001), p. 2, https://citeseerx.ist.psu.edu/viewdoc/download?doi=10.1.1.602.1126&rep=rep1&type=pdf. I am also inspired by Shambhawi Tripathi's approach to challenging binary imaginations of fiction and reality. Shambhawi Tripathi, 'But Where Is the Magic? Emotional-Relational Humans and Their Untold Stories in International Relations', *Millennium* 51, no. 1 (2023): 157–83.

research whose questions, methods, and analytic frames remain unchanged through encounters across space and time is an invented account. My goal is to make peace with the reinventions, the zigzags, the pivots: to narrate, sometimes uncomfortably, the multiple threads and dilemmas that have shaped the research and the-self-as-researcher along the journey of this project.

This book, then, has two related aims: First, drawing from in-depth research in Colombia and informed by feminist methodologies, it analyses the politics of victimhood during transitions from violence. This exploration is primarily focused on understanding what kind of politics the status of 'victim' enables and forecloses. Second, the book reckons with the ways in which the researcher is implicated—ethically, methodologically, narratively, emotionally—in the creation, performance, and contestation of these politics through the research process.

Considering these aims in tandem allows for a more meaningful acknowledgement of what the political theorist Paulo Ravecca describes as 'the situated interplays between objects of inquiry (political processes, regimes, discourses, etc.) and the knowing subject (the scientist and the discipline)'.[54] It also prompts researchers and writers to consider how our inquiry, our research gaze, and our storytelling create subjects on the page. 'Good victims' do not only become visible through bureaucratic categories, interactions with state agencies, or contestations within social movements. They also come into being through researchers' questions, narrations, and silences.[55] I am interested in an account of the politics of victimhood that treats these politics as also enmeshed in the researcher's investigation of them.

The Argument

Two stories about the politics of victimhood emerged in response to these questions. According to one story, 'good victims' are patient, pleasant, obedient, and diligent. They behave professionally, but do not expect rewards for this behaviour. They are productive and entrepreneurial, but resist making victimhood itself the currency of that entrepreneurship. They remain in ongoing conversation with 'the state', but ultimately do not place their

---

[54] Paulo Ravecca, *The Politics of Political Science: Rewriting Latin American Experiences* (Routledge, 2019), p. 222.
[55] Golubović, 'One Day', p. 1188.

expectations of assistance, well-being, or reparation entirely in the state's hands. They are poor enough to be believable as subjects of need, but not so poor that their reliance on the status of 'victim' and resources associated with it may trigger suspicion. In this view, people recognized as victims become political subjects when they shed the identity of 'victim', recover the agency that many perceive them to have lost, and build subjectivities on a premise other than suffering.

The second story converges with the first in acknowledging that 'victim' is a label that shapes claim-making, understandings of self, and relationships with the state, but offers a different view of the political within these processes. It sees the very labour of victimhood—the labour associated not only with receiving official recognition as a victim, but with continuing to advocate on behalf of and care for those who identify as such—as a form of political work. This type of politics resists focusing on the individual, instead broadening the frame to bring collectives (and their various fragmentations) into view. Some of the political work involves holding the state accountable to its mandate of reparation. In this story, politicization and victimhood are both ongoing processes, rather than shaped by singular events. This understanding of the politics of victimhood pays attention to the less visible, more continual acts of violence that underpin life in the shadow of armed conflict, even though these acts sometimes do not give rise to official 'victim' status. Cast in this light, victimhood resists the false antagonism between past, present, and future and offers a different view of subjectivity and time.[56] According to this story, the victim subject is already a political subject, brought into being through violence, bureaucratic encounters, struggle, labour, contestation, and interactions with others who identify as victims, dispute claims to victimhood, confer the official status of 'victim', or designate access to resources.

It would be tempting to ascribe the first story to state officials within bureaucracies of victimhood and the second story to people who identify as victims. However, such a designation would be misleading. The nuances of the argument lie in the fact that these stories emerged from and found resonance among different actors within the constellation of victimhood. What the anthropologist Lina Buchely calls 'bureaucratic activism' interrupts an understanding of 'the state' as a unified, coherent whole with a single view of

---

[56] Thanks to Paulo Ravecca for prompting me to spell out this point.

victims or the politics associated with them.[57] Simply put, while some state officials developed a narrative of victimhood that is in line with the first story, others spoke passionately against such a view. I also do not pretend that there is a single notion of 'victim politics' among people who identify as victims—or, as the feminist historian Florencia Mallon writes, that 'subaltern politics has a unity and solidarity of its own'.[58] The encounter and collision between the two stories, and the surprises that emerged from noticing who embraced and developed which story at different points in time, are part of the process of producing the politics of victimhood.

The Language of Victimhood and the Intricacies of Agency

I treat 'victim' not as a passive synonym for victimization or a mere description of having suffered harm, but as a political status and a potential site of power that different actors vie for, reject, wield, or contest.[59] 'The simple fact of having experienced adversity', the victimologist Mijke de Waardt aptly notes, 'is a necessary but insufficient condition for being classified as a victim'.[60] A fuller understanding of victimhood considers the ways in which people identify as victims in their own lives and imbue that word with meaning, hopes, and fears.[61] It takes into account the acts through which they 'self-stage' as victims in order to be legible as subjects of assistance or protection,[62] as well as the official and unofficial processes of conferral of the status of 'victim' on some people and not others. These considerations, in turn, can illuminate the political meanings and contestations of power that

---

[57] Lina Buchely, *Activismo burocrático: La construcción cotidiana del principio de legalidad* (Ediciones Uniandes, 2015).

[58] Florencia Mallon, 'The Promise and Dilemma of Subaltern Studies: Perspectives from Latin American History', *American Historical Review* 99, no. 5 (1994): 1497.

[59] Laura Acosta, 'Victimhood Dissociation and Conflict Resolution: Evidence from the Colombian Peace Plebiscite', *Theory and Society* 50 (2021): 679.

[60] Mijke de Waardt, 'Naming and Shaming Victims: The Semantics of Victimhood', *International Journal of Transitional Justice* 10, no. 3 (2016): 433. As Diana Meyers writes in her exploration of different victim paradigms, critical engagement with the politics of victimhood requires moving beyond the view 'that victims are just people whose rights have been violated'. Diana Meyers, 'Two Victim Paradigms and the Problem of "Impure" Victims', *Humanity* 2, no. 2 (2011): 256.

[61] Myriam Jimeno, 'Lenguaje, subjetividad y experiencias de violencia', *Antípoda: Revista de Antropología y Arqueología* 5 (2007): 169–90.

[62] Mats Utas, 'West-African Warscapes: Victimcy, Girlfriending, Soldiering: Tactic Agency in a Young Woman's Social Navigation of the Liberian War Zone', *Anthropological Quarterly* 78, no. 2 (2005): 430.

THE POLITICAL AS A (FEMINIST) QUESTION   17

inflect claims, actions, and relationships. In this sense, victimhood does not merely describe a condition of being, but also acts of doing.

My framing of victimhood as a political status is gratefully indebted to Bridget Conley's reflections on naming the actors affected by atrocities. She argues that 'the critical work is not to define the *subject*, but to understand the *work* of claiming rights'.[63] Like Conley, I posit that 'the political subject... does not describe a finalised condition, but rather forms the grounds of contestation'.[64] The framing of victimhood as a site of power is inspired by Roxanne Lynn Doty's understanding of power as 'productive of meanings, subject identities, their interrelationships, and a range of imaginable conduct'.[65] In her analysis of US interventionist policy in the Philippines, Doty clarifies that she is not primarily interested in power as something 'that social actors possess and use'.[66] Similarly, in this book, the power of victimhood cannot be understood as a yes/no referendum that distinguishes those who have it from those who do not. What is of analytic interest here is how the power the victim category can carry—the power to direct attention and resources, to distinguish and prioritize subjects and experiences in the wake of war, to validate certain kinds of political claims—shapes meanings, identities, relationships, and experiences of peace and justice during transitions from violence.

To engage with these nuances of the language of victimhood, I have chosen not to refer to 'the victims' as a descriptive category in my own narrative. Instead, depending on the context, I refer either to 'people who identify as victims', meaning that the interlocutors in question do not necessarily have official victim status, or 'people recognized as victims', meaning that they have successfully registered as such with the Colombian state.[67] While these references are certainly clunkier than the shorthand of 'the victims', it is my hope that they are also less likely to obscure the contestations and politics of victimhood that are at the heart of this inquiry.[68]

---

[63] Bridget Conley, 'Who Is the Subject of Atrocities Prevention?', *Global Responsibility to Protect* 6, no. 4 (2014): 430.

[64] Conley, 'Who Is the Subject', p. 430.

[65] Roxanne Lynn Doty, 'Foreign Policy as Social Construction: A Post-positivist Analysis of US Counterinsurgency Policy in the Philippines', *International Studies Quarterly* 37, no. 3 (1993): 299.

[66] Doty, 'Foreign Policy', p. 299.

[67] Interlocutors regularly volunteered, often without my prompting, whether they had registered as victims or not with the Colombian state. Some of the spaces in which I conducted my observations were open exclusively to those the state officially recognized as victims. I discuss these nuances in Chapter 3.

[68] The key exceptions to this practice are instances in which I quote interlocutors who refer to 'the victims' as such, or when I cite laws and policies that use this language. In those cases, I critically examine whom my interlocutors (or the laws and policies in question) imagine as 'the victims' and

Some readers might wonder, as audiences at academic conferences have asked in the past, whether 'survivor' might perhaps be a more suitable term for this exploration. The complexities of naming invite scholars to revisit our assumptions about the bearers and manifestations of agency, the sources of power, and the binaries of categorization. Feminist scholarship across disciplines has engaged meaningfully with these dilemmas.[69] Based on research with people who identify as survivors in a range of contexts, some scholars have asserted that 'more positive and powerful attributes are associated with "survivors" than "victims"'.[70] These more positive attributes often relate to ideas about agency, a concept with which existing literature on victimhood has a complicated relationship.

As the philosopher Diana Meyers writes, 'Being victimized is understood as excluding agency—that is, as entailing shameful albeit blameless passivity'.[71] To the extent that agency enters the picture for people who identify as victims, it is often framed as a future aspiration, with agency imagined as a state that lies beyond or after victimhood.[72] The feminist scholars Anne-Kathrin Kreft and Philipp Schulz conclude that 'a dichotomous

---

explore the effects of the monolithic reference to this category. Consistent with both feminist and interpretive methodologies for researching violence, I refer to my interlocutors as they wish to be described. As such, references to 'victim leaders' or 'human rights defenders' in the footnotes reflect these individuals' preferred identification—acknowledging that the categories are dynamic and the boundaries between them are porous, such that the same people may identify as 'victim leaders' in one context and 'human rights defenders' in another. For more on this point, see Richard Georgi, 'Peace through the Lens of Human Rights: Mapping Spaces of Peace in the Advocacy of Colombian Human Rights Defenders', *Political Geography* 99 (2022).

[69] Clare Hemmings and Amal Treacher Kabesh, 'The Feminist Subject of Agency: Recognition and Affect in Encounters with "the Other"', in *Gender, Agency, and Coercion*, edited by Sumi Madhok, Anne Phillips, and Kalpana Wilson (Palgrave Macmillan, 2013); Philipp Schulz, *Male Survivors of Wartime Sexual Violence: Perspectives from Uganda* (University of California Press, 2020); Sarah Gharib Seif, 'Beyond the "Jihadi Bride": Interrogating the Colonial, Racialised, and Gendered Narratives of Women Who Joined IS' (PhD thesis: University of St Andrews, forthcoming).

[70] Kaitlin Boyle and Kimberly Rogers, 'Beyond the Rape "Victim"-"Survivor" Binary: How Race, Gender, and Identity Processes Interact to Shape Distress', *Sociological Forum* 35, no. 2 (2020): 323. Regarding the victim-survivor naming dilemmas, see also Jennifer Dunn, '"Victims" and "Survivors": Emerging Vocabularies of Motive for "Battered Women Who Stay"', *Sociological Inquiry* 75, no. 1 (2005): 1–30.

[71] Meyers, 'Two Victim Paradigms', p. 258.

[72] Rudling elucidates this logic in her critical discussion of 'resilient victims', who are framed as 'individuals who overcame the passivity associated with being the recipients of harm and adversity, recovering their agency'. Adriana Rudling, '"I'm Not That Chained-Up Little Person": Four Paragons of Victimhood in Transitional Justice Discourse', *Human Rights Quarterly* 41, no. 2 (2019): 433. See also Huma Saeed, 'Victims and Victimhood: Individuals of Inaction or Active Agents of Change? Reflections on Fieldwork in Afghanistan', *International Journal of Transitional Justice* 10, no. 1 (2016): 168–78.

understanding of victimhood and agency ... persists, where individuals are understood to occupy *either* a victim *or* an agent space'.[73]

Building on Schulz and Kreft's important claim that victimhood and agency 'not only *intersect*, but can, at times, also be *co-constitutive*',[74] I offer a different view of the relationship between agency and victimhood than some of the literature on survivors proposes. I hesitate to assume that the label of survivor is singularly associated with agency in every context and, conversely, that victimhood is antithetical to agency or synonymous with powerlessness.[75] Instead, I highlight the agency that the contestations and claim-making surrounding the category of 'victim' can enable. Rather than always and necessarily obliterating the self and the political, then, I see the category of 'victim' and claims to victimhood as potentially generative of subjectivities and political possibilities alike.

Agency becomes a more meaningful concept if scholars move away from seeing it as something one can have or lack, and move towards framing it in terms of *how* people exercise agency: Who do acts of agency enable people to be in the world? What are these people able to feel, think, say, do, and desire as a result of exercising agency in particular directions? What might some of the surprising sources of agency be, and what are the limits some people face in exercising it? Engaging with these questions further highlights the potential resonances between the concept of agency and the label of 'victim', as well as the links between political subjectivities, agency, and victimhood. Inspired by Erin Baines's powerful analysis of complex victimhood in northern Uganda, I think of agency as 'including moments of the political' and as part of 'the ongoing process of negotiating personhood'.[76] Thinking of agency in this way means that the concept is not singularly associated with the label of 'survivor' or 'victim' and, instead, holds open possibilities for both terms, depending on the context.

Ultimately, I also rely on the term 'victim' here because it has been the prevailing term that governs both policy discourses and my interlocutors' descriptions of themselves in Colombia. 'Victim', rather than 'survivor', is the

---

[73] Anne-Kathrin Kreft and Philipp Schulz, 'Political Agency, Victimhood, and Gender in Contexts of Armed Conflict: Moving beyond Dichotomies', *International Studies Quarterly* 66, no. 2 (2022): 2.
[74] Kreft and Schulz, 'Political Agency', p. 1.
[75] As Sumi Madhok, Anne Phillips, and Kalpana Wilson write, 'We seek here to shift the focus away from simpler oppositions of agent or victim'. They also note that 'discourses on agency are heavily saturated with associations linking them to racialised as well as gendered hierarchies and a long history of attachment to only certain kinds of persons and actions'. Sumi Madhok, Anne Phillips, and Kalpana Wilson, 'Introduction', in *Gender, Agency, and Coercion*, pp. 3–4.
[76] Baines, *Buried in the Heart*, p. xvi.

category that has shaped the transitional justice vernacular in Colombia, in part because of the legal connotations and potential benefits associated with the category. I am committed to describing people in the terms by which they know themselves and to understanding the meanings they attach to these labels.[77] This approach means also paying attention to the moments in which people reject the term 'victim' in favour of other identifications, or to shifting (self-)identifications in different contexts and spaces. I make the case here for arriving at an understanding of 'victim' that does not always elide or occlude political action. Such an understanding is open to the generative potential of claims to victimhood and the ways those claims help the individuals who make them, as well as scholars of violence and justice, understand and reimagine 'the political' in the wake of violence.

Context and Stakes of Investigating Victimhood

Motivating this inquiry is the recognition that the politics of victimhood are not merely rhetorical matters. 'If the process of naming the violence presents such a challenge', Veena Das claims, 'it is because such naming has large political stakes'.[78] Put another way, contests over 'good victims' are so prevalent and salient *because* of the stakes associated with the status of victim during transitions from armed conflict. The extensive scholarship on the 'moral currency' associated with victimhood highlights that recognition as a victim potentially confers access to a range of benefits and resources.[79] The 'era of the victims' encompasses legal, material, and policy implications, not only in Colombia, but also in other contexts facing transitions from violence.[80] In

---

[77] Lisa Wedeen suggests this is a key feature of interpretivism: 'Interpretivists are particularly interested in language and other symbolic systems', studying the meanings people assign to phenomena and words (and how those meanings shape people's words), rather than taking terms at face value. Lisa Wedeen, 'Ethnography as Interpretive Enterprise', in *Political Ethnography: What Immersion Contributes to the Study of Power*, edited by Edward Schatz (University of Chicago Press, 2009), pp. 80–81. For more on feminist methodologies for researching violence, see Annick T. R. Wibben, *Researching War: Feminist Methods, Ethics and Politics* (Routledge, 2016).

[78] Veena Das, *Life and Words: Violence and the Descent into the Ordinary* (University of California Press, 2006), p. 205.

[79] Diane Enns, *The Violence of Victimhood* (Penn State University Press, 2012), p. 19.

[80] Jessie Barton Hronešová, 'The Uses of Victimhood as a Hegemonic Meta-narrative in Eastern Europe', *Journal of Contemporary European Studies* 2022: 1–17; Erica James, *Democratic Insecurities: Violence, Trauma, and Intervention in Haiti* (University of California Press, 2010), pp. 25–26; Elissa Helms, *Innocence and Victimhood: Gender, Nation, and Women's Activism in Postwar Bosnia-Herzegovina* (University of Wisconsin Press, 2013); Alyson Cole, *The Cult of True Victimhood* (Stanford University Press, 2006).

this sense, the moral status of victimhood is not merely moral; the category of victim has 'gained powerful symbolic currency *and* significant material stakes'.[81]

In the context of Colombia, these stakes are wide-ranging. In the letter of the laws and policies discussed at length in Chapter 2, people recognized as victims of the armed conflict are eligible for reparation in its individual, collective, material, and symbolic forms, including access to compensation for harms suffered. They are also eligible for participation in forums for public policy creation, in which they are invited to put forth proposals for the government to consider, as well as comment on government policy towards peace and justice. Additional rights include preferential access to education, health, professional training, and a range of other social benefits. The government created a series of institutions to attend specifically to those recognized as victims of the armed conflict, while mandating other state entities incorporate into their programming differential attention for those with victim status. The peace process between the government and the FARC, which culminated in the 2016 peace accord, included mechanisms for direct and indirect participation in the proceedings of some people recognized as victims. There are also provisions for direct and indirect participation of victims in the truth-telling and justice mechanisms the 2016 peace accord created, including the Commission for the Clarification of Truth and the Special Jurisdiction for Peace. In conflict-affected contexts, both in Colombia and beyond, in which many citizens have few avenues through which to participate in public policy or to fully access benefits like health and education, the potential benefits associated with recognition as a victim gain particular significance.

It is important to note, however, that these are the benefits for which those recognized as victims of the armed conflict are eligible in the letter of the laws and policies. The analysis in the empirical chapters that follow elucidates two important caveats: First, the promise of justice, as envisioned and enshrined in laws and policies, does not always correspond to the fulfilment of that promise in the lives of those who identify as victims or who vie for official recognition as such. Second, beyond the official realm of law and policy, the category of victim also shapes—in the sense of both enabling and fracturing—relationships, social movements, understandings of self, and

---

[81] Ballvé, *The Frontier Effect*, p. 139, emphasis mine.

claim-making in ways that transcend formal, official spaces and processes, and which are essential for understanding the political stakes of this status.

At the same time, although the laws and policies are written for 'the victims', one needs to be a *particular kind of victim* to access the full benefits associated with the category. Of the millions of individuals the Colombian state officially recognizes as victims, sixty were selected to participate in the Havana peace talks.[82] As of 2021, only 12 percent of those eligible for compensation had actually received any in the ten years the reparation programme had been active.[83] The Colombian Truth Commission, which issued its final report in June 2022 after four years of work, relied on thirty thousand testimonies of people implicated in or affected by the conflict. These numbers serve as reminders of the limits of speaking of 'the victims' in a context in which not all those who identify or are recognized as victims can access all forms of justice. As the anthropologist Jelena Golubović writes with reference to Bosnia, 'Moral victimhood is not simply a resource, it is a *scarce* resource'.[84] In many different kinds of transitions from violence, being a 'good', 'photogenic', or 'desirable' victim matters for access to spaces, institutions, and resources. The adjectives that modify victimhood have a direct bearing on people's experiences of justice.

Mijke de Waardt and Sanne Weber have argued that Colombia is 'the international showcase for integrating lessons learned regarding local meanings of justice and victim participation'.[85] The transitional justice program for those recognized as victims in Colombia is far larger, in terms of both the harms that are eligible for inclusion in the category and the number of individuals who hold victim status, than any other country in the world.[86] In part because of its wide approach to those recognized as victims, a series of actors have hailed the transitional justice program in Colombia as

---

[82] Roddy Brett, 'The Role of the Victims' Delegations in the Santos-FARC Peace Talks', in *The Politics of Victimhood in Post-conflict Societies*, edited by Vincent Druliolle and Roddy Brett (Palgrave Macmillan, 2018), p. 293.

[83] Comisión de Seguimiento y Monitoreo a la Implementación de la Ley 1448 de 2011, 'Octavo Informe de Seguimiento al Congreso de la República 2020–2021' (Bogotá, 2021), p. 243.

[84] Golubović, 'One Day', p. 1176.

[85] Mijke de Waardt and Sanne Weber, 'Beyond Victims' Mere Presence: An Empirical Analysis of Victim Participation in Transitional Justice in Colombia', *Journal of Human Rights Practice* 11, no. 1 (2019): 210.

[86] Kathryn Sikkink, Phuong N. Pham, Douglas A. Johnson, Peter J. Dixon, Bridget Marchesi, and Patrick Vinck, 'An Evaluation of Comprehensive Reparations Measures in Colombia: Accomplishments and Challenges' (Carr Center for Human Rights Policy and Harvard Humanitarian Initiative, 2015), p. 3.

innovative,[87] ambitious,[88] exemplary, and historic.[89] These accolades suggest that scholars and practitioners alike may be looking to Colombia to understand what other transitional justice processes can learn from its approach to victimhood. If Colombia, indeed, becomes an archetypal case for states dealing with victims of mass violence, it will remain important to look beyond legal definitions and technocratic processes to shed light on the politics of victimhood that come into being through, and sometimes in opposition to or clashes with, bureaucracies of transitional justice.

In the classroom, as a feminist teacher of world politics, I tell students that critique (and critical scholarship) is about more than flaw-finding.[90] The point of critique is to see power at work, which requires curiosity about the manifestations, inequalities, harms, and rewards that flow from different forms of power. Critique can be a generative invitation to imagine worlds that address these workings of power more meaningfully and equitably. This premise intrigues feminist students, as it intrigues me. It is, after all, full of promise—the promise of imagining and rebuilding, rather than merely tearing down. Students then ask me: 'Okay, then, but how? How do we get to more than flaw-finding?'

I have carried their question with me as an accountability compass while writing this book. Getting to more than flaw-finding requires acknowledging that the same institutions, processes, and concepts that scholars critique are also ones in which people deposit hope: the hope of justice, of reparation, of coming to terms with a violent past, and perhaps even of imagining a more peaceful, just future. 'Bureaucracy', according to the anthropologist Monique Nuijten, 'is a hope-generating machine'.[91] My analysis of the transitional justice program in Colombia proceeds from the premise that it is important to honour the places into which people deposit their hope, and to recognize that which is historic and ambitious, the significant and the innovative.

---

[87] Kristian Herbolzheimer, 'Innovations in the Colombian Peace Process' (Noref: Norwegian Peacebuilding Resource Center, 2016), pp. 1–10.

[88] Nicole Summers, 'Colombia's Victims' Law: Transitional Justice in a Time of Violent Conflict?', *Harvard Human Rights Journal* 25, no. 1 (2012): 224; Virginia Bouvier, 'Gender and the Role of Women in Colombia's Peace Process' (UN Women and US Institute of Peace, 2016), https://www.unwomen.org/-/media/headquarters/attachments/sections/library/publications/2017/women-colombia-peace-process-en.pdf?la=en&vs=17.

[89] 'Remarks by UN Women Executive Director Phumzile Mlambo-Ngcuka at the Peace Talks Table with the Government of Colombia and FARC-EP in Havana', UN Women, July 2016, https://www.unwomen.org/news/stories/2016/7/speech-by-executive-director-in-cuba.

[90] Rachelle Chadwick, 'The Question of Feminist Critique', *Feminist Theory* (2023).

[91] Monique Nuijten, 'Between Fear and Fantasy: Governmentality and the Working of Power in Mexico', *Critique of Anthropology* 24, no. 2 (2004): 211.

Enshrining the rights of victims in Colombian law and policy and setting up institutional processes to fulfil the state's obligations that are associated with those rights are important steps towards justice. It is possible, I believe, to hold multiple truths in one embrace: a transitional justice program can be ambitious *and* limited, hope-fuelling *and* disappointing. From bureaucrats to people who identify as victims, many of my interlocutors have lived at the intersection of these truths, and it is that coexistence and multiplicity that I have sought to represent in my analysis of their experiences.

Dilemmas of Belonging, or, Why Is This a Feminist Book?

Situating an inquiry within broader academic conversations raises questions of disciplinary membership and kinship. These frames influence one's sense of belonging. Though they often work by activating different emotions, from fear to hope, and from a sense of obligation to excited curiosity, both disciplinary membership and a sense of kinship shape what scholars choose to read and cite, how we write, how we relate to our questions and interlocutors, what we research, and, ultimately, 'whom we want to be taken seriously by'.[92]

Considering the question of kinship *alongside* the question of disciplinary membership is a hopeful practice, one that invites me to think about scholarship not only through the vein of fearful, obedient obligation—to cite certain orthodoxies, to anticipate and respond to certain criticisms, to conform to certain disciplinary expectations[93]—but also through the generous, imaginative lens of the potential for community, of shared curiosity and supported exploration. It is important, in other words, to define work not only by what it is not or by what it stands in opposition to, but also by what it is and what it aspires to be. What this work *is* comes into being through relations with ideas, with other humans, with the places from which the work originated. In which traditions does this book belong and how comfortably does it sit within them? In what ways is this a feminist book, and why might this designation matter?

---

[92] Krystalli and Enloe, 'Doing Feminism', pp. 289–90.
[93] In thinking about these points, I have benefitted from the excellent work of Roland Bleiker and David Duriesmith. Roland Bleiker, 'Forget IR Theory', *Alternatives* 22, no. 1 (1997): 57–85; David Duriesmith, 'Negative Space and the Feminist Act of Citation', in *Rethinking Silence, Voice, and Agency in Contested Gendered Terrains*, edited by Jane Parpart and Swati Parashar (Routledge, 2018), pp. 66–77.

To explore these questions, I return to the entwinement of the story of research with the story of self-as-researcher. Throughout my life as an academic and a practitioner until this point, I have been 'the gender person', whatever that meant to whoever labelled me as such in a given space.[94] 'Oh, Roxani does gender', mainstream international relations (IR) scholars at academic conferences or practitioner colleagues would say, often accompanied by an ambiguous hand gesture. I have learned that 'doing gender', even if initially intended by my interlocutor as a slight or articulated as though the content of the work were a total mystery, is an identification that resonates with me and a label I claim with joy.

At a basic level, being a 'gender person' has meant being legible as someone who asks questions explicitly about gender and explores them in ways that were attentive to gendered power. Often, it has also meant being what Sara Ahmed calls 'a feminist killjoy' because 'we become a problem when we describe a problem'.[95] The best moments of being the gender person have been the ones in which the definite article softens into an indefinite one: when I am *a* gender person among many others who care about these issues. At its best, being a gender person has meant being in community with other feminists, others who insisted on noticing, understanding, and addressing the problems of inequalities, injustices, and violence in the world.[96] That sense of community and of the possibilities of the worlds we could bring into being by thinking about and acting on gender justice has fuelled both the work of being a gender person and my joy in doing this work.

Being a gender person among gender people brought this book into being. Yet this book represents a different kind of endeavour than the ones that led to my being labelled as a gender person in the first place. It proposes a feminist approach to the politics of victimhood that does not focus primarily on the stories of women as protagonists or on a gender analysis of violence as the main analytic frame—but which, nonetheless, proceeds from a feminist sensibility.[97] What does it mean to approach research on the politics of victimhood with a feminist sensibility?

---

[94] For more reflections on what it means to be a 'gender person', see Joyce Wu, '"Doing Good and Feeling Good": How Narratives in Development Stymie Gender Equality in Organisations', *Third World Quarterly* 43, no. 3 (2022): 634–50. I have also treasured Henri Myrttinen's critical analysis of 'Gendermen' and 'gender champions': Henri Myrttinen, 'Stabilising or Challenging Patriarchy? Sketches of Selected "New" Political Masculinities', *Men and Masculinities* 22, no. 3 (2019): 563–81.
[95] Sara Ahmed, *Living a Feminist Life* (Duke University Press, 2017), p. 39.
[96] Shepherd, 'Research as Gendered Intervention', p. 11.
[97] In so doing, I respond to feminist calls to direct curiosity at sites that may not, at first glance, lend themselves as readily to feminist analysis as, for example, the important studies of wartime

I see feminism—in the study of world politics, in the academy more broadly, and beyond—as an unfinished, ongoing project of insistence on investigating the political. Echoing Lola Olufemi's proposition that 'feminism is a political project about what *could be*',[98] feminist investigations are aspirational in that they remain attuned to the possibilities and ways of being and existing in relation that emerge through diverse notions and practices of politics.[99] What Cynthia Enloe calls 'feminist curiosity'[100] is what prompted me to ask what kind of politics the 'politics of victimhood' is, and what possibilities of existence in the wake of violence may emerge under the banner of victimhood.

The aspirational dimension and sense of possibility are important to this analysis because this book challenges the idea that victimhood is necessarily an 'anti-politics'.[101] Feminist scholars of world politics pay attention to moments others tell us that something is decidedly not political, or that a concept or practice obscures and elides the political, or that politics cannot be found wherever we happen to be inquiring about it.[102] I thus join curious feminists in investigating the political as a question. In practice, this feminist curiosity materializes into inquiry about the meanings, hopes, and practices that people attach to victimhood as a form of politics.

'I think of feminism as a building project', Sara Ahmed suggests. 'If our texts are worlds, they need to be made out of feminist materials'.[103] The analytic frames on which this book relies are gratefully indebted to and build on key pillars of interdisciplinary feminist thought. Feminist theories of harm in

---

sexual violence or women's peacebuilding work. See Enloe, *The Curious Feminist*, p. 240; Carol Cohn, *Women and Wars* (Polity Press, 2013).

[98] Lola Olufemi, *Feminism Interrupted* (Pluto Press, 2020), p. 1.

[99] The plural form—possibilities, ways of being—is essential to the argument here. Feminist scholars have emphasized that there is no single feminist approach to research or one answer to the question 'What is *the* feminist methodology?' Sandra Harding, 'Is there a feminist method?', in *Feminism and Methodology: Social Science Issues*, edited by Sandra Harding (Indiana University Press, 1989), pp. 1–14; Marysia Zalewski, 'Distracted Reflections on the Production, Narration, and Refusal of Feminist Knowledge in International Relations', in *Feminist Methodologies for International Relations*, edited by Brooke Ackerly, Maria Stern, and Jacqui True (Cambridge University Press, 2006), pp. 42–61.

[100] Enloe, *The Curious Feminist*, p. 42.

[101] I borrow this term from James Ferguson's discussion of how development actors, in conjunction with state bureaucracies, produce 'anti-politics' in the populations they seek to serve. James Ferguson, *The Anti-politics Machine: 'Development'. Depoliticization and Bureaucratic Power in Lesotho* (Cambridge University Press, 1990), p. 256.

[102] Cynthia Enloe, *Seriously! Investigating Crashes and Crises as Though Women Mattered* (University of California Press, 2013), p. 40.

[103] Ahmed, *Living a Feminist Life*, p. 14.

the field of transitional justice and feminist anthropological critiques of category creation have deepened my thinking about distinctions among forms of violence and the subjectivities associated with them.[104] Feminist reflections have sharpened my understanding of both the concepts and practices of politics and agency,[105] and feminist scholarship on labour and care made me attuned to the labour of victimhood.[106]

In addition to feminist curiosity in generating a question and feminist interpretive frames for exploring that question, there are other features of research that can render a project feminist. A researcher may do feminism[107] through methodological commitments to reflexivity,[108] or through citational practices that critically engage with which voices the researcher treats as sources of authority.[109] Feminist work also unfolds through approaches to theory generation that treat research interlocutors as creators of knowledge and as potential theorists themselves,[110] rather than 'the theories dominating the people', whereby 'the people come to life only to the degree that they illustrate or support the abstract academic arguments behind the study'.[111]

Like politics and power, the question of feminist research is most useful *as a question*. Genuine inquiry makes room for dilemmas, for moments of failure, for the anxiety of whether one belongs. Declaring this book to be feminist, in the way I feel compelled to do when attempting to belong (in a book series, in a field of study, in an academic community) requires the

---

[104] Fionnuala ní Aoláin, 'Exploring a Feminist Theory of Harm in the Context of Conflicted and Post-conflict Societies Emerging Paradigms of Rationality', *Queen's Law Journal*, no. 1 (2009): 219–44; Sally Engle Merry, *The Seductions of Quantification* (University of Chicago Press, 2016).

[105] Sumi Madhok, *Rethinking Agency: Developmentalism, Gender and Rights* (Routledge, 2013); Baines, *Buried in the Heart*; Das, *Life and Words*; Kreft and Schulz, 'Political Agency', p. 2.

[106] María Puig de la Bellacasa, *Matters of Care: Speculative Ethics in More Than Human Worlds* (University of Minnesota Press, 2017); Joan Tronto, *Moral Boundaries: A Political Argument for an Ethic of Care* (Routledge, 1993).

[107] I prefer the formation of 'doing feminism', rather than 'being a feminist', both because feminist work in research and beyond is *work* that requires doing and because as, bell hooks suggests, 'The shift in expression from "I am a feminist" to "I advocate feminism" could serve as a useful strategy for eliminating the focus on identity'. bell hooks, *Feminist Theory: From Margin to Center*, 3rd ed. (Routledge, 2014), p. 32.

[108] Kim England, 'Getting Personal: Reflexivity, Positionality, and Feminist Research', *Professional Geographer* 46, no. 1 (1994): 80–89; Roxani Krystalli, 'Feminist Methodology', in *Gender Matters in Global Politics: A Feminist Introduction to International Relations*, 3rd ed., edited by Laura J. Shepherd and Caitlin Hamilton (Routledge, 2022), pp. 34–46.

[109] Ahmed, *Living a Feminist Life*, pp. 15–16.

[110] bell hooks, *Teaching to Transgress* (Routledge, 1994), p. 64; Clare Hemmings, *Why Stories Matter: The Political Grammar of Feminist Theory* (Duke University Press, 2011); Laura Rodríguez Castro, *Decolonial Feminisms, Power, and Place: Sentipensando with Rural Women in Colombia* (Palgrave Macmillan, 2021).

[111] Christine Sylvester, *War as Experience: Contributions from International Relations and Feminist Analysis* (Routledge, 2013), p. 53.

performance of a kind of certainty that is at odds with the dilemmas that fuel feminist curiosity and motivate feminist work. This is where proving disciplinary membership and being motivated by a sense of kinship collide when it comes to making sense of belonging: to earn membership, one feels pressure to provide proof. Kinship, on the other hand, is a practice of mutual recognition, a sense affirmed by feeling.

The sense of what makes a book feminist, then, necessarily involves the reader. My intention here is to invite, trust, and inspire feminist readings of this text.[112] Feminist students, scholars, and practitioners in the fields of peace and conflict, political violence, and transitional (in)justice are an important part of my answer to 'whom I want to be taken seriously by'.[113] These actors and audiences are sources of inspiration, analytic insights, methodological approaches, curiosity, and—most importantly—community. 'It is in these affective connections that I find solace, even purpose', the feminist scholar Laura Shepherd writes. She goes on: 'They enable me in ways that I cannot fully comprehend. Being a feminist, being an academic: These are relational identities for me, subject-positions that cannot exist—not only philosophically, but also in a material, embodied sense—without others, but not others against whom to define myself but others with whom I can navigate those insecurities and explore the silences in the account that I give of my self'.[114]

The same dilemmas about belonging, kinship, and constructing or proving a self in the world have shaped my understanding of the interdisciplinary roots and aspirations of this book. Perhaps fuelled by the estrangement I have felt in certain corners of the field of IR, I have at times denied my affiliation. 'I am not an international relations scholar', I have told myself and others at various points. Denial, or dis-identification, can be fruitful for arriving at who one is, especially if one reflects on the sources of her estrangement.[115]

---

[112] For helping me arrive at this sense of trust, and for inviting me to frame feminism as necessarily engaging the reader, I am gratefully indebted to wise and gentle nudges from Erin Baines, Helen Kinsella, María Fernanda Olarte-Sierra, Paulo Ravecca, and Shambhawi Tripathi.
[113] Krystalli and Enloe, 'Doing Feminism', p. 289.
[114] Shepherd, 'Research as Gendered Intervention', p. 11.
[115] These sources include having felt alienated by mainstream IR's insufficient engagement with the everyday, affective, embodied, relational aspects of world politics, with world politics beyond war, and with notions of care and joy. I have also sometimes felt estranged by the disciplinary voices that render themselves archetypal through particular kinds of academic writing. As the citations in this book indicate, there are, of course, communities that meaningfully engage with each of the issues I have named here, and which model different ways of being and writing. The existence and care of these communities, and the ways they blur tidy distinctions between 'mainstream' and 'critical' work or definitive declarations of what the field of IR is, make my own work possible.

They can also be what Eve Tuck and K. Wayne Yang call 'moves to innocence', referring to gestures that seek to absolve one of guilt and complicity in unequal and unjust power structures.[116] The materiality and relationality of my existence in academia tell a different story than my dis-identification with IR. The signature at the bottom of my emails locates me at a School of International Relations, and so does the label on my office door. Students of IR populate the classrooms in which I teach, even if those same students at the end of the semester often declare that 'this', the work we did together, was not what they had imagined IR to be.

Ultimately, proving whether a piece of scholarship, or indeed a whole scholar, 'belongs' to IR or to another discipline is not the question that animates my work. Instead of seeking or finding a single disciplinary home, or assuming that any academic discipline offers a pure and innocent relationship to power,[117] I am more at home in interdisciplinarity—or in being 'a joyful undisciplined discipline-jumper and genre jumper'.[118] Roland Barthes has persuasively argued that 'interdisciplinary work ... is not about confronting already constituted disciplines (none of which, in fact, is willing to let itself go)'. Rather, 'To do something interdisciplinary, it's not enough to choose 'a subject' (a theme) and gather around it two or three sciences. Interdisciplinarity consists in creating a new object that belongs to no one'.[119]

This does not mean that interdisciplinary work is untethered. There are intellectual debts, inspirations, and relations of care, kinship, and community that enable interdisciplinary work to go on. My debts and relations stem from and extend to the fields of anthropology, transitional justice, feminist theory, narrative international relations, critical humanitarianism, and political theory, which have offered generous theoretical frames, methodological inspirations, and analytical prisms with which to think and make sense of the experiences narrated in this book. Rather than belonging in or to IR, this book is for all those who find it a fruitful companion, regardless of their

---

[116] Eve Tuck and K. Wayne Yang, 'Decolonization Is Not a Metaphor', *Decolonization: Indigeneity, Education and Society* 1, no. 1 (2012): 1. Tuck and Yang write about settler moves to innocence, primarily beyond/outside the context of academia, though the concept travels to performances of purity, innocence, and lack of complicity within the academy as well.

[117] For more on these 'attachments to innocence' and the ways they 'obscure the multiple registers on which oppression and violence operate', see Paulo Ravecca and Elizabeth Dauphinee, 'What Is Left for Critique? On the Perils of Innocence in Neoliberal Times', *Las Torres de Lucca, Revista internacional de filosofía política* 11, no. 1 (2022): 37–38.

[118] Si Transken, 'Poetically Teaching/Doing the Profession of Social Work as a Joyful Undisciplined Discipline Jumper and Genre Jumper', *Critical Social Work* 3, no. 1 (2002): 1.

[119] Roland Barthes in *Writing Culture: The Poetics and Politics of Ethnography*, edited by James Clifford and George Marcus (University of California Press, 1986), p. 1.

situatedness. It is through the lens of companionship that I wish to think, and I am excited by the possibilities and communities that this lens can bring into being.

Structure of the Book

Chapter 2 interweaves the three historical accounts that form the backdrop of this research. I offer a brief history of violence in Colombia, an account of the 2016 peace process between the government and the FARC, and an analysis of the development of the institutional framework of transitional justice in the country. A full review of the history of the Colombian armed conflict is beyond the scope of this book. Instead, the chapter focuses on key turning points that shaped the transitional justice process, which remarkably took shape before a formal peace accord had been concluded. I pay particular attention to the emergence of an institutional framework and bureaucracy of victimhood in Colombia, analysing both laws and policies pertaining to those recognized as victims and the normative shifts that allowed them to come into force. These include a shift from mobilization around the mantle of displacement towards the category of 'victim', and a transition from the language of disasters and development to the register of rights.

Chapter 3 discusses the ethical, methodological, and narrative dilemmas of researching the politics of victimhood. The chapter is deliberately organized around questions, as this is how research dilemmas are lived. These questions correspond to different phases of the research process, highlighting that ethical and methodological dilemmas do not only pertain to the research design and fieldwork, but also to the processes of analysis and writing. Among the dilemmas I examine are questions about where to direct the research gaze, how to ground the inquiry in time and place, how to investigate victimhood without placing the narrative burden exclusively on those who suffered harm, and how to navigate the complicated expectations of loyalty among different interlocutors. Throughout the chapter, I emphasize that discussions of feminist research methods and ethics are inseparable from each other, from the findings of the research, and from the politics of victimhood.

Chapter 4 focuses on the life histories of the professionals who populate the bureaucracy of victimhood in Colombia. This chapter proceeds from an attentiveness to how 'the state' haunts those who embody it or seek its attention. The ghosts introduced in this chapter reappear throughout the book.

The chapter traces the tensions and contradictions professionals embody and navigate in the process of being, becoming, and being seen like a state during transitions from violence. I pay particular attention to the acts of dissonance that mark the daily lives of transitional justice professionals, and I analyse the emotions they express in making sense of their work. Through their narratives, my interlocutors sketch what it might mean to be a 'good state official' in the context of transitional justice. I connect these ideas of the 'good state (official)' to the notion of the 'good victim' and the politics and bureaucracies of victimhood.

Chapter 5 pays attention to contrasting expectations of professionalization pertaining to people who identify as victims and the bureaucrats who work with them. Engaging with feminist literature on care, affective and invisible labour, and audit culture, I ask: What counts as labour? Who benefits from the labour of victimhood, who gets recognized for it, who uses it, and to what end? And crucially, which forms of labour do *not* get counted? I also discuss the many ways in which ideas about professionalization are part of the politics of victimhood and explore the ways in which both those who identify as victims and bureaucrats participate in the production, contestation, and subversion of the professionalization script. The chapter concludes by analysing how the labour of victimhood—and its many affective, invisible, unrecognized, or unpaid dimensions—informs the concept of the 'good victim'.

Chapter 6 investigates the complex relationship between transitional justice, victimhood, and forms of violence not directly linked to the armed conflict and its bureaucracies. How do the politics of victimhood reflect and reinforce divisions in the violence that matters? I answer this question by focusing specifically on how bureaucracies of victimhood engage—or fail to sufficiently reckon with—broader dynamics of patriarchy and poverty. I pay close attention to how Colombian transitional justice professionals attempt to implement a framework of differential attention to people recognized as victims, and to the fragmented subjectivities that come into being through these efforts. I also analyse the implications of the distinctions between different vectors of identity (such as gender and race) and types of harms (such as conflict-related sexual violence versus other forms of gendered violence) for socio-political mobilization, and for how individuals and collectives understand their experiences through the prism of different frames of violence and subjectivities.

Chapter 7 looks towards the future of the victim category. What does it mean to be, in the words of one of my interlocutors, a 'country of victims'?

Building on interdisciplinary feminist literature on pain, politics, and time, I analyse different imaginations of the future of victimhood among state officials and those who identify as victims. I pay particular attention to how these accounts frame politics and the political. This includes a discussion of state narratives about overcoming the condition of victimhood through self-reliance and entrepreneurial productivity, and the ways in which these narratives illuminate concerns about welfarism and notions of citizenship. The chapter then turns to how people who identify as victims interpret the political not as a future aspiration that lies beyond and after victimhood (or that is achievable through economic transactions with the state), but as a set of practices born *through* the victim category and mobilization around it. Inspired by Anna Lowenhaupt Tsing's notion of the 'anti-ending',[120] and by feminist research that complicates the notion of when violence truly ends, the chapter resists tidy narrative closures and, instead, focuses on the questions that remain open and contestable about the politics of victimhood.

---

[120] Anna Tsing, *The Mushroom at the End of the World: On the Possibility of Life in Capitalist Ruins* (Princeton University Press, 2015), p. 278.

2
Making Victims
Histories of Violence and Bureaucracies in Colombia

Fictional Beginnings

'All beginnings are fictions', said the National Centre for Historical Memory official seated across from me at the café of Cine Tonalá.[1] Speaking over the lunchtime din, this official identified a key challenge in narrating the events of the Colombian armed conflict: When did the violence begin? 'One of the most complicated issues in Colombian historiography', Eduardo Pizarro has written, 'is to determine when the armed conflict that the country has endured in the last decades began properly. In 1930? In 1946? In 1948? In 1958? In the 1980s?'[2] This question is not merely a matter of historiography. The start date of the armed conflict has implications for which conflict-affected individuals are recognized as victims, affecting their access to justice in the form of eligibility for reparations, participation in truth-seeking mechanisms, and encounters with those recognized as perpetrators.

Different institutions have determined different start dates for the armed conflict for the purposes of their work.[3] This variation affects the legibility of different populations as claimants in the eyes of the state. The periodization of violence also shapes the rights and justice options these individuals have, depending on whether they are seen as victims of the armed conflict or of 'ordinary violence', relegated to the system of 'ordinary', rather than transitional,

---

[1] Interview with National Centre for Historical Memory official in Bogotá, January 2018.
[2] Pizarro in Comisión Histórica del Conflicto y sus Víctimas, *Contribución al entendimiento del conflicto armado en Colombia* (Ediciones Desde Abajo, 2015), p. 16.
[3] Most reports of the National Centre for Historical Memory take 1958 as the starting point of the armed conflict. The Victims' Unit set 1985 as the starting point of official victim recognition for the purposes of reparation. The Land Restitution Unit took January 1, 1991, as the starting point for claims. And when the government and the Revolutionary Armed Forces of Colombia (FARC) announced they had reached a peace agreement in 2016, headlines worldwide reported the end of a fifty-two-year conflict, placing the start point to coincide with the establishment of the FARC as an armed group in 1964.

Good Victims. Roxani Krystalli, Oxford University Press. © Oxford University Press 2024.
DOI: 10.1093/oso/9780197764534.003.0002

justice.[4] The fact that different Colombian institutions and scholars have used different date ranges for their work also makes it difficult to compare data on the scale of the conflict. In short, who was a victim of the Colombian armed conflict in the eyes of the state depended in part on when different institutions of that state thought that the conflict in question began.

Three additional issues emerge when attempting to craft a brief account of the Colombian armed conflict, and its associated peace and justice processes. One is the challenge of continuity, about how to represent ruptures or turning points without erasing the consistent threads and legacies of violence that run through the centuries.[5] Which violence is presumed to flow from the previous wave, and which marks a break or a new era? Another is the issue of multiplicity. This is not just a question of the existence of many causes, ideologies, alliances, strategies and tactics, and effects of violence over time. Rather, it is that the various threads cannot be understood in a vacuum, meaning that accounts that separate so-called political violence from criminal activity, colonial violence from contemporary violence, or human rights violations from military campaigns, fail to reflect how people experience both violence and politics in their everyday lives. The final issue relates to narrating time. Violence shuffles time. It reorients—and challenges—one's sense of progress or forward motion. Though the chapter appears to proceed 'forward' through the pages, tracing a journey from conflict to peace, people have made and experienced peace *alongside* violence—and people continue to feel the effects of violence in the post-accord time of alleged peace. The coexistence of violence, peace, justice, and injustice can be difficult to narratively represent,[6] but remains a defining feature of how people experience and make sense of these phenomena.

In developing this account of three interlocking histories (of violence, peace, and transitional justice institutions in Colombia), I have struggled with scale and scope. The 2011 Victims' Law, which created the legal and institutional framework that most directly affected the lives of my interlocutors, recognized as victims those who suffered conflict-related harms after January 1, 1985. However, an account that zooms in (too) narrowly on the time period that the institutional framework in Colombia designates as

---

[4] The language of ordinary and transitional justice reflects the terms my interlocutors used. I discuss these issues in depth in Chapter 6.

[5] Robert Karl, *Forgotten Peace: Reform, Violence, and the Making of Contemporary Colombia* (University of California Press, 2017), p. 233.

[6] Marie Berry and Trishna Rana, 'What Prevents Peace? Women and Peacebuilding in Bosnia and Nepal', *Peace and Change* 44, no. 3 (2019): 321–49.

relevant to the lives of people recognized as victims risks reinforcing the same hierarchies that are analytically at the core of this inquiry. Such a focus takes as a given that the violence (and victimhood) that matters is the one that state institutions determine, potentially obscuring continuities and legacies of violence over the decades. It also erases the ways in which time itself, and the classification of violence into 'armed conflict' and 'not armed conflict', becomes a vector of hierarchy among people who suffered harms. For this reason, I proceed with a wider, admittedly more unwieldy, account that dates back to the early days of independence from colonial rule and traces the turning points of violence and victimhood over time.

Independence from Colonial Rule and Nineteenth-Century Conflicts

In July 1810 Bogotá declared its independence from Spanish colonial rule, which dated back to the 1500s. It would take nearly an additional decade to liberate the rest of what was then known as New Granada and is now known as Colombia from colonial rule. The principal clashes in the aftermath of independence were about the degree of centralization in governance. Followers of Simón Bolívar, who was known as 'the liberator' and whose supporters were known as Bolivarians (and subsequently as the Conservatives), favoured a model of centralized governance from the capital. Liberals wanted more autonomy for the various regions and territories of the newly independent country. After independence and over the course of the nineteenth century, political affiliation in the form of identifying as a Liberal or a Conservative 'became deeply ingrained, passed on from one generation to the next'.[7]

The clashes between Liberals and Conservatives resulted in six civil wars during the nineteenth century, as well as the turn-of-the-century Thousand Days' War (1899–1902). Some of the key factors affecting the nature of these conflicts included 'the position to be assigned to the church in its relations with the state; the abolition or nonabolition of slavery; the nature of political organization—federal or centralist; and, in general, matters very similar to those that often divided Latin American oligarchies in this period'.[8]

---

[7] Shoultz in Abbey Steele, *Democracy and Displacement in Colombia's Civil War* (Cornell University Press, 2017), p. 62.
[8] Gonzalo Sánchez, 'La Violencia in Colombia: New Research, New Questions', *Hispanic American Historical Review* 65, no. 4 (1985): 790.

Many contemporary narratives of peacebuilding in Colombia refer to the 2016 peace accord ending 'decades' of conflict, not centuries. The implication is that the armed conflicts and political confrontations in the aftermath of Colombia's independence are out of the frame, that they belong to a different, separate era of history. At the same time, these clashes illuminate the origins and forms of contemporary violence. The resonance of political identity and party affiliation planted the seeds of subsequent conflicts. A common factor linking subsequent violence in Colombia to this earlier stage was that 'ideological management was exercised in both cases by segments of the ruling class, through political parties'.[9]

Many of the contested issues in Colombia in the immediate aftermath of independence, such as concerns over landownership, governance, agrarian reform, or labour, would come to underpin future struggles. The centrality of land issues in the Colombian armed conflict dates to the early 1900s, when the barriers to campesino landownership led to clashes with landowners and with the central state, which campesinos felt protected the interests of landowners over their own.[10] This period was also marked by emergent campesino socio-political organization, which did not neatly map on to being aligned with one party or another.[11]

In the 1940s, many campesinos sided with presidential candidate Jorge Eliécer Gaitán. Gaitán was a fervent supporter of economic redistribution and favoured increased political participation for disenfranchised rural populations. Gaitán's loss in the elections triggered a wave of violence against campesinos. On April 9, 1948, during his second bid for president, Jorge Eliécer Gaitán was assassinated in Bogotá. The assassination kicked off a series of riots and clashes known as the Bogotazo, which marked the start of the period known as La Violencia.

---

[9] Sánchez, 'La Violencia', p. 790.
[10] I retain the Spanish language of 'campesino' over the English translation of 'peasant' or 'rural farmer'. The translation of 'peasant' does not fully capture the set of meanings with which people infuse the word campesino in Spanish. As Angela Lederach writes in her beautiful ethnographic exploration of peacebuilding in Montes de María, 'When asked what it means to be a campesino, people in the Alta Montaña often begin by describing the human and nonhuman relationships that are central to their identity and sense of self: "To be a campesino is to breathe pure air, to wake up to the birds singing, to cultivate and harvest the land, to walk peacefully through the countryside with one's burro [donkey]. It's that. For me, that is what it means to be a campesino"' (interview, April 2017). Angela Lederach, '"The Campesino Was Born for the Campo": A Multispecies Approach to Territorial Peace in Colombia', *American Anthropologist* 119, no. 4 (2017): 599–600.
[11] Steele, *Democracy and Displacement*, p. 63.

From La Violencia to violencias in the Twentieth and Twenty-First Centuries

The start of La Violencia—capital and singular—was defined by electoral, partisan violence, the height of which took place after Gaitán's assassination in 1948. A key difference between La Violencia and the periods that preceded it was that citizens, in particular campesinos, became involved in the fighting.[12] Historical accounts of conflict often privilege the activities of armed actors over the actions of civilians, many of whom resisted or collaborated with these armed actors, and led their own initiatives for peace. Maintaining a focus on civilians as actors, and on the socio-political struggles that affected violent confrontations, is essential for understanding the causes and effects of the Colombian armed conflict.[13] During La Violencia, which stretched until the mid-1960s, conflicts centred on redistribution, labour politics, and agrarian reform.[14] There is wide variation in the estimated death count during La Violencia, highlighting that numbers have been part of the contested terrain of the armed conflict throughout Colombian history.[15]

The rise of leftist guerrillas was a defining feature of the armed conflict in the 1960s and 1970s. The Revolutionary Armed Forces of Colombia (FARC), the oldest guerrilla force in Latin America, was established in 1964. Other guerrillas, such as the National Liberation Army (ELN), the Popular Liberation Army, and the 19th of April Movement (M-19), also formed during the 1960s and 1970s. The Cold War and the Cuban Revolution had a profound impact on events in Colombia during this period, influencing the emergence of guerrillas, models of governance, and state-citizen relations. Clashes between communist and capitalist ideologies, and their implications for landownership, poverty alleviation strategies, approaches to

---

[12] Sánchez, 'La Violencia', pp. 790–791.
[13] Lederach, 'The Campesino', p. 590; Karl, *Forgotten Peace*. See also Oliver Kaplan, *Resisting War: How Communities Protect Themselves* (Cambridge University Press, 2017). On the conceptual and practical challenges of distinguishing combatants from civilians, see Kinsella, *Image before the Weapon*.
[14] Frank Safford and Marco Palacios, *Colombia: Fragmented Land, Divided Society* (Latin American Histories, 2002), p. 346.
[15] Safford and Palacios claim that La Violencia resulted in between eighty thousand and four hundred thousand deaths, while Gonzalo Sánchez places his estimate at one hundred thousand to three hundred thousand. Few accounts provide estimates of the magnitudes of other harms that did not result in death. Safford and Palacios, *Colombia*, p. 345; Sánchez, 'La Violencia', p. 792; Steele, *Democracy and Displacement*, p. 69.

socioeconomic inequalities, and governance of rural territories, shaped the confrontations between guerrilla groups and the state.[16]

Narcotrafficking and the consolidation of paramilitarism have defined the armed conflict since the 1980s. According to the Commission for the Clarification of Truth, Coexistence and Non-Repetition (henceforth, the Truth Commission), 'the most intense period of the war was from 1996 to 2010', resulting in violations against 75 percent of those registered as victims.[17] In the 1980s, the United States 'enthusiastically embraced counternarcotics operations'.[18] In her excellent ethnography of how US drug policy shaped US-Colombian relations and the nature of the violence, the anthropologist Winifred Tate emphasizes that understanding the conflict or the guerrillas solely through the prism of drugs can lead to a mischaracterization of the violence and the political projects that underpin it. Tate also underscores that any analysis of narcotrafficking needs to reckon with the role of the United States during this phase of the Colombian armed conflict. The United States was, among others, a market and destination for drugs, a producer of militarized policy and discourses about violence in Colombia, an actor influencing justice outcomes through extraditions, and a party involved in aerial eradication of crops.[19] The conflict in Colombia is more than a 'war on drugs'. Understanding the 'war on drugs' as a component of the conflict requires broadening the frame to shed light on the role of a range of actors beyond Colombia, including foreign states and corporations.

In addition to narcotrafficking, another defining feature of the armed conflict in the 1980s and beyond was the rise and consolidation of right-wing paramilitary groups, which have perpetrated a range of violations against civilians and guerrilla groups.[20] Some paramilitary groups formed

---

[16] For more on the history, ideologies, and activities of some of these armed actors, see María Clemencia Ramírez, *Between the Guerrillas and the State: The Cocalero Movement, Citizenship, and Identity in the Colombian Amazon* (Duke University Press, 2011); María Victoria Uribe and Juan Felipe Urueña, *Miedo al pueblo: Representaciones y autorrepresentaciones de las FARC* (Editorial Universidad del Rosario, 2019); Ana Arjona, *Rebelocracy* (Cambridge University Press, 2016).

[17] Comisión de la Verdad (CEV), 'Convocatoria a la paz grande', in *Hay futuro, si hay verdad: Informe final de la Comisión para el Esclarecimiento de la Verdad, la Convivencia y la No Repetición* (CEV, 2022), p. 45.

[18] Winifred Tate, *Drugs, Thugs, and Diplomats: US Policymaking in Colombia* (Stanford University Press, 2015), p. 38.

[19] Tate writes that 'throughout its history, the FARC has maintained that it is a political and military organization oriented toward the overthrow of the state in defense of the rural poor'. She continues: 'The FARC's economic relationship to the coca trade transformed over time' and 'drug profits clearly financed the FARC's military expansion and its escalating attacks'. Tate, *Drugs, Thugs*, pp. 49–51; 54–55.

[20] For more on paramilitaries, their connections to other armed actors, the state, and civilians, see Centro Nacional de Memoria Histórica, *Paramilitarismo: Balance de la contribución del Centro*

in opposition to guerrillas and to the perceived communist threat; others were oriented at protecting illicit business interests; yet others claimed to offer protection against extortion and other forms of violence.[21] Though the precise nature of the relationship between paramilitaries, the Colombian armed forces, and state institutions remains hotly contested, the Truth Commission has concluded that 'political and economic elites consolidated a tendency to delegate security, and therefore, violence to private parties. This happened... generally in powerful sectors that have used weapons to protect privileges and take away rights from the most vulnerable and unprotected'.[22] This is no longer La Violencia, capital and singular, but a period of violencias in the plural, in many senses continuing until the present day.

Counting and Narrating Harms

'The apparently simple question of what to count', when it comes to measuring violence and its effects, 'is a fundamental dimension of the power of quantification to shape public knowledge', according to the feminist anthropologist Sally Merry.[23] Building on Merry's important work to highlight 'the extensive interpretive work that goes into the construction of indicators',[24] this section synthesizes relevant data on the scale of the Colombian armed conflict. I rely primarily on the final report of the Colombian Truth Commission, published in 2022, because of the magnitude of its data synthesis effort and the salience of the methodological reflections of the commissioners, each of which I discuss below.

I start from the premise that numbers about violence matter. They matter to those involved in documentation of harms, from academics to human rights organizations seeking to shed light on the scale and effects of violence.[25] Numbers also matter to decision-makers and bureaucrats who

---

Nacional de Memoria Histórica al Esclarecimiento Histórico (CNMH, 2018); María Teresa Ronderos, *Guerras recicladas* (Aguilar, 2014); Mauricio Romero, *Paramilitares y autodefensas: 1982–2003* (Temas de Hoy, 2003).

[21] Centro Nacional de Memoria Histórica, *Paramilitarismo*, p. 41.
[22] CEV, 'No matarás', in *Hay futuro, si hay verdad*, p. 578.
[23] Merry, *The Seductions of Quantification*, p. 107.
[24] Merry, *The Seductions of Quantification*, p. 1.
[25] Noelle Brigden and Anita Gohdes, 'Transparency Intersections in Studying Violence: The Politics and Ethics of Data Access across Methodological Boundaries', *International Studies Review* 22, no. 2 (2020): 250–67.

delimit the universe of those recognized as victims and the reparations and other benefits to which they will be entitled. Underscoring the relevance of numbers to activists, Diane Nelson argues that numbers can 'reveal disproportionate suffering, and provide tools to resistance movements confronting racist exclusion and ecological destruction'.[26]

Actors who are positioned in relation to violence in different ways, and with different power to shape remedies, imbue the numbers with different meanings. They often disagree on 'where to lump and split, what to include and what to leave out, how many categories to use, and what the criteria for these categories should be'.[27] These interpretative disagreements have been observable among—and sometimes within—different institutions of the Colombian state, which have relied on different categorization and periodization of harms. As a result, databases and registries of harms have not always been integrated or consistent with each other, complicating comparison of sources, as well as the bureaucratic pathways of people affected by violence.[28]

Acknowledging this challenge, and building on other institutions' attempts at data synthesis about the Colombian armed conflict, the Truth Commission, in partnership with the Special Jurisdiction for Peace and Human Rights Data Analysis Group, integrated 112 databases from forty-two institutions of the Colombian state, as well as data supplied by human rights organizations, victims' associations, and civil society groups.[29] To arrive at its final report, the commission synthesized the statistical data referenced above and conducted over fourteen thousand interviews to hear the testimonies of people recognized as victims, witnesses, and actors responsible for violence. The commission also engaged with an additional thirty thousand people who participated in organized dialogues aimed at truth-seeking both in Colombia and in the diaspora.[30] 'We should not lose sight', the authors of the Truth Commission's final report write 'of something that seems evident, but on which we ought to insist: The war is usually counted in numbers of victims and effects, in figures and percentages, in general estimates that try to rationalize the horror, but behind each of these pieces of data there is a

---

[26] Diane Nelson, *Who Counts? The Mathematics of Death and Life after Genocide* (Duke University Press, 2015), p. 3.
[27] Merry, *The Seductions of Quantification*, p. 14.
[28] Jairo Rivas, 'Official Victims' Registries: A Tool for the Recognition of Human Rights Violations', *Journal of Human Rights Practice* 8, no. 1 (2016): 116–27.
[29] A full list of these databases and organizations can be found in CEV, 'Hasta la guerra tiene límites', in *Hay futuro, si hay verdad*.
[30] CEV, 'Hallazgos y recomendaciones', p. 40.

unique and unrepeatable world; in war, they lose this person, this family, this community'.[31]

The institutional language of documenting harms has varied in Colombia, referring to 'victimizing acts', crimes, or violations.[32] The Truth Commission final report focuses on violations of human rights and international humanitarian law, acknowledging that this is not always the language that people affected by those violations use. In the context of the Colombian armed conflict, these violations included homicide, massacres, selective assassination, extrajudicial killings, and attacks on the right to life, indiscriminate attacks, forced disappearance, threats, kidnapping, arbitrary detention, torture, cruel, inhumane, or degrading treatment, sexual violence, forced recruitment of children and adolescents, forced labour, forced displacement, land dispossession, confinement, attacks on protected assets, and pillage and extortion.[33] Nine out of ten victims of the conflict were civilians.[34]

The report also refers to 'responsible actors', rather than perpetrators, and acknowledges that sometimes more than one actor was responsible for harms, or the responsibility could not be conclusively determined. Responsible actors included state armed forces, paramilitaries, guerrilla groups, and 'third parties', ranging from local narcotrafficking gangs to multinational corporations in extractive industries. Highlighting the complexity of synthesizing and interpreting this data, the tome of the Truth Commission final report that analyses the types of harm and the actors responsible for them is 1,144 pages long.

'The war left a country of victims', the final report declares, labelling the scale of victimization as being 'of biblical proportions', with over nine million people officially recognized as victims.[35] When it comes to experiences of violations, the final report affirms what earlier scholarship and documentation efforts in Colombia had established: Many of the recognized victims of violence suffered more than one kind of harm in the context of the armed conflict. To illustrate, people who suffered forced displacement also commonly experienced land dispossession, threats against life and property, and physical violence. Forced displacement is by far the most common form of

---

[31] CEV, 'Hasta la guerra', p. 56. One tome of the final report, titled *When the Birds Don't Sing*, is dedicated exclusively to testimonies and life histories of the violence in the words of the individuals, communities, and natural environments that experienced it.
[32] I critically reflect on this language in Chapter 6.
[33] CEV, 'Hasta la guerra', p. 30.
[34] CEV, 'No matarás', p. 573.
[35] CEV, 'No matarás', p. 573.

conflict-related harm in Colombia, with the Truth Commission reporting 7,753,964 registered victims between 1985 and 2019.[36] Displacement was one of the forms of violence that affected nearly every municipality across Colombia.[37]

Approximately 450,000 people lost their life due to the armed conflict in Colombia between 1985 and 2018.[38] Paramilitaries were responsible for 45 percent of those cases, the FARC for 21 percent, other guerrillas for 6 percent, and agents of the state for 12 percent. Some forms of violence, such as sexual violence, were committed, to varying extents, by all armed actors engaged in the conflict,[39] while the perpetration of other forms of violence differed significantly across armed actors.[40] For example, forced disappearances were primarily a systematic practice of the Colombian armed forces and paramilitary groups, whereas kidnapping was primarily associated with the FARC.[41]

The violence also had a territorial dimension.[42] Three Andean mountain ranges run along the length of Colombia, and the territory stretches from the Pacific and Caribbean coastlines to the Amazonian rainforest. An analysis of this political geography reveals how different climates and relationships to land have structured the lives of communities, as well as their experiences of violence and the state alike.[43] In the words of the Truth Commission final report, 'Important parts of the national territory and its inhabitants were excluded from the processes of democratic formation and the production of wealth and well-being.'[44] The report continues: 'The project of the state at the national level imagined its geography as fragments governed by a hierarchy that assigned predominance to some territories over others, converting whole regions to marginal or peripheral spaces, and throwing their populations, both in rural and urban areas, to informality and or to

[36] CEV, 'Hasta la guerra', p. 1000.
[37] Steele, *Democracy and Displacement*, p. 115.
[38] CEV, 'Hasta la guerra', p. 986.
[39] CEV, 'Hasta la guerra', p. 994.
[40] Francisco Gutiérrez-Sanín and Elisabeth Jean Wood, 'What Should We Mean by 'Pattern of Political Violence'? Repertoire, Targeting, Frequency, and Technique', *Perspectives on Politics* 15, no. 1 (2017): 20–41.
[41] CEV, 'Hasta la guerra', p. 988.
[42] For more on territorial dimensions of violence and peace, see Serje, *El revés de la nación*; Angela Lederach, *Feel the Grass Grow: Ecologies of Slow Peace in Colombia* (Stanford University Press, 2023); Laura Rodríguez Castro, '"We are not poor things": Territorio Cuerpo-Tierra and Colombian Women's Organised Struggles', *Feminist Theory* 22, no. 3 (2021): 339–59.
[43] Steele, *Democracy and Displacement*, pp. 58–60.
[44] CEV, 'Colombia adentro', in *Hay futuro, si hay verdad*, p. 28.

integrate into illegalized economies as a mechanism of survival and social advancement. The violence of the armed conflict has concentrated principally in these same territories'.[45] To reflect these territorial dimensions of the violence and its effects, the final report contains a tome organized by geographic region. Importantly, the Truth Commission declared that 'the territory and nature were victims of the armed conflict', who 'suffered multiple harms and were desecrated by the violent actions of armed groups in association with economic or political sectors who benefitted from the armed conflict'.[46]

In addition to the territorial dimensions, the violence had gendered, racialized, and ethnic components, in terms of both the nature of harms and the populations who experienced them. The Truth Commission report underscores that campesinas, as well as Afro-Colombian and Indigenous women, suffered disproportionately in the conflict.[47] Certain forms of violence, such as forced disappearance, were gendered by primarily targeting men, with the effects reverberating across the family and community. Other forms of violence, such as sexual violence, primarily targeted women and girls, while homophobic and anti-trans violence unfolded both in the context of the armed conflict and beyond it. In an important attempt to name and acknowledge the structural roots of violence, as well as their manifestations, the Truth Commission emphasized that patriarchy, colonial legacies, and racism all affected the forms, targeting, and effects of the violence.

Towards a Victim-Centred Peace Process?

Against this backdrop, there were sixteen different attempted peace negotiations with guerrillas and paramilitary groups between 1984 and 2016.[48] The formal peace talks that resulted in the 2016 peace agreement took place between appointed negotiators of the government of Colombia and the FARC in Havana, Cuba. These negotiations, and the resulting agreement, applied only to the government and the FARC, as opposed to other armed

---

[45] CEV, 'Colombia adentro', p. 28.
[46] CEV, 'Resistir no es aguantar', in *Hay futuro, si hay verdad*, p. 11.
[47] CEV, 'No es un mal menor', in *Hay futuro, si hay verdad*, p. 306.
[48] Eduardo Pizarro, *Cambiar el futuro* (Debate, 2017), p. 27.

actors, though negotiations with the ELN have intermittently unfolded since the 2016 accord.[49]

The parties to the Havana talks set a defined, limited agenda, which focused on six thematic points: (1) comprehensive rural reform and development; (2) political participation; (3) end of the conflict (including cessation of hostilities and laying down weapons); (4) solution to the problem of illicit drugs; (5) victims; (6) ratification, implementation, and verification mechanisms.[50] Each of these points mapped on to the six thematic pillars (also known as chapters) of the 2016 peace agreement.

One of the notable features of the Havana peace talks was the negotiators' commitment to engage with 'civil society actors'.[51] In practice, this engagement unfolded through various channels, including encouragements for Colombians to electronically submit proposals for the peace negotiators to consider.[52] The negotiators also called for the organization of national and regional forums in Colombia to discuss the progress of the peace accords and solicit public input, including specifically from people who identified as victims, on various points of the agreed agenda. These measures aimed to build a bridge between Colombia and Cuba, and between the high-level negotiators at the peace table and the broader base that had mobilized for peace in Colombia through the years.

These consultative mechanisms allowed for the participation of groups in the formal and official peacebuilding process who had not always been adequately represented at the official peace table.[53] This was particularly the case for women. Representatives of civil society groups focusing on women's experiences, gender issues, and feminist causes participated in regional working groups and dialogues on monitoring the peace process.[54] The

---

[49] As of December 2022, the newly elected President of Colombia, Gustavo Petro, had appointed a new team of government negotiators to recommence talks that had started and stalled several times in the previous years.

[50] Pizarro, *Cambiar*, pp. 2–4.

[51] The language of 'civil society' is the language used in the accord and documentation of the peace process. I share Laura Shepherd's concern about the risks of homogenizing actors with varied political agendas under the umbrella of 'civil society'. I also share Shepherd's curiosity about how 'civil society' is constructed discursively as both a subject and a spatial domain. Laura Shepherd, *Gender, UN Peacebuilding, and the Politics of Space: Locating Legitimacy* (Oxford University Press, 2017), pp. 132–33.

[52] The negotiators received 9,306 proposals through the electronic submission mechanism. Roddy Brett, 'La voz de las víctimas en la negociación: Sistematización de una experiencia' (United Nations Development Program, 2017), p. 12.

[53] Virginia Bouvier, 'Gender and the Role of Women in Colombia's Peace Process' (UN Women and US Institute of Peace, 2016), p. 19.

[54] Not all associations of women work explicitly on gender issues, and not all of them embrace the language of feminism to describe their work. For more on these nuances, see Julia Zulver, *High-Risk Feminism in Colombia* (Rutgers University Press, 2022).

engagement of the peace process with gender issues was formalized in June 2014, when, in a joint communiqué, the government and FARC announced the creation of a gender sub-commission. Its mandate was 'to review and guarantee, with the support of national and international experts any peace agreements that are reached and to ensure that they have an adequate gender focus'.[55] Of the 578 stipulations of the final peace agreement, 130 have an explicit gender perspective, leading to the gender sub-commission being praised as one of the exemplary innovations of the Colombian peace process.[56]

The creation of the gender sub-commission was first announced in a communiqué on discussion principles related to Point 5 of the agenda, which was the item labelled 'Victims'. However, the work of the gender sub-commission went beyond equating victimhood with femininity to examine the experiences of women combatants, LGBTQ individuals affected by conflict, and other issues. As part of its mandate, the gender sub-commission invited delegations to visit Havana and share the 'perspectives and proposals of women's groups—... not as victims, but as peacebuilders'.[57] This indicates a consciousness on the part of the commission not to limit public engagement with the peace process to the remit of (feminized) victim identity.[58]

The June 2014 communiqué that announced the creation of the gender sub-commission also declared that there would be mechanisms for the direct participation of victim delegations in the peace process in Havana. Although the negotiating parties were the ones to issue that communiqué, it was civil society actors, human rights defenders, and victims' associations who had actively campaigned to guarantee the engagement of people recognized as victims of the conflict in the official peace process. In the words of Father Francisco (Pacho) de Roux, a Jesuit priest who has over forty years of experience in peacebuilding and who was subsequently selected to preside over

---

[55] Alto Comisionado para la Paz, 'Declaración de principios para la discusión del Punto 5 de la agenda: 'Víctimas'—comunicado conjunto', June 7, 2014, p. 3. For more on the sub-commission, see Lina Céspedes-Báez, 'En los confines de lo posible: Inclusión del enfoque de genero en el acuerdo de La Habana', *Utopía u oportunidad fallida: Análisis crítico del acuerdo de Paz*, edited by Lina Céspedes-Baéz and Enrique Prieto-Rios (Editorial Universidad del Rosario, 2017), pp. 295–326.

[56] *Special Report of the Kroc Institute and the International Accompaniment Component, UN Women, Women's International Democratic Federation, and Sweden on the Monitoring of the Gender Perspective of the Implementation of the Colombian Peace Accord* (Kroc Institute, 2018), https://kroc.nd.edu/assets/297624/181113_gender_report_final.pdf.

[57] Bouvier, 'Gender', p. 22.

[58] On the nuances of framing participants in peacebuilding beyond the 'woman as victim' trope, see María Martín de Almagro, 'Producing Participants: Gender, Race, Class, and Women, Peace and Security', *Global Society* 32, no. 4 (2018): 395–414.

the Colombian Truth Commission, 'There was a great pressure on the part of the victims in Colombia, asking to be heard.... What I find interesting is that the [negotiating] parties understood that they ought to listen to victims of all sides'.[59]

Actors who directly participated in the talks and international commentators alike have constructed the narrative that 'the victims' were at the centre of the peace in Colombia.[60] The then UN high commissioner for human rights, Navi Pillay, said that victims' direct participation in the Havana peace talks was unprecedented and 'Colombia could become a global example of listening to the victims'.[61] To fully appreciate and assess these statements, I rely on Roddy Brett's detailed accounts of *which* victims participated in the official peace process, *how* they participated, and *what effect* this participation had on the process and actors. Brett's account is particularly instructive because it emerged in response to a request 'of the members of the delegations of victims to the peace talks' to document their experiences.[62]

A key challenge in facilitating the direct participation of selected victims in the official peace talks was the question of representation. The communiqué announcing the first victims' delegation expressly stated that 'this delegation will be composed in such a way that it ensures the plural and equal representation of different victims, as well as different victimizing acts, without pretending that one delegation could represent the millions of victims with which the armed conflict has left us'.[63] In practice, the United Nations, the Centre for Thought and Follow-up to the Peace Dialogue of the National University, and the Episcopal Conference of the Catholic Church were tasked with selecting the participants. Representatives of these institutions selected a total of sixty individuals who participated in the peace talks as part of five separate delegations.[64]

---

[59] Brett, 'La Voz', p. 13.

[60] Herbolzheimer, 'Innovations'. This narrative is in keeping with scholarly and policy discussions on victim-centred peacebuilding and transitional justice. See, illustratively, Jemima García-Godos, 'Victims in Focus', *International Journal of Transitional Justice* 10, no. 2 (2016): 350–58; Simon Robins, 'Failing Victims', *Human Rights and International Legal Discourse* 11 (2017): 41–58.

[61] Navi Pillay, 'Colombia puede convertirse en un ejemplo global al escuchar a las víctimas', *La Semana*, August 14, 2014, https://www.semana.com/opinion/articulo/colombia-puede-convertirse-en-un-ejemplo-global-al-escuchar-las-victimas/399178-3/

[62] Brett, 'La Voz'; Brett, 'Role of Victims' Delegations'.

[63] Alto Comisionado para la Paz, 'Comunicado Conjunto', August 2014.

[64] The sixty victim delegates came from twenty-five different departments across Colombia. There were thirty-six women and twenty-four men, and the participants ranged in age from nineteen to seventy-eight years. Brett, 'La Voz', p. 28.

To arrive at the final selection, these organizations collectively developed a set of criteria, which aimed to balance (a) forms of victimization; (b) geographical region; (c) demographic groups; and (d) victims of all (often multiple) armed actors, as well as seeking to 'maximise the heterogeneity of victims'.[65] Despite the fact that the negotiating team took care to think imaginatively about the composition of victim delegations, the fact that only sixty victim delegates participated directly in the peace talks out of a universe of (at the time) eight million was a source of deep dissatisfaction for people who identified as victims.[66]

These concerns about representation weighed on the minds of the selected victim delegates. For reasons related to security and to the privacy of the peace process, the delegates received very little notice that they had been selected to travel to Havana. They often had to make a decision about whether to attend in the span of a few hours and were not allowed to discuss with anyone else that they would be participating in the peace process.[67] These requirements ran counter to the practices of many victims' associations and civil society organizations. Asking delegates to momentarily set aside the principles of collective action and consultation in decision-making that underpinned the work of their organizations caused internal conflicts and tensions within these groups.

In terms of the nature of participation at the peace table, each selected victim delegate had fifteen minutes to make remarks. Some of the delegates told personal stories about their experiences during the conflict, including detailed accounts of the harms they suffered; others presented specific proposals for the peace negotiators to consider regarding victim-related issues; yet others made proposals that related to the peace process more broadly. In addition to this formal component of participation at the peace table, victim delegates had more informal interactions with negotiators and other actors during breaks.

A particular source of frustration for victims' delegates was that direct participation in the negotiations was limited only to the agenda item pertaining specifically to victims' issues and 'amounted to ten days during eighteen months of negotiations'.[68] Beyond that, victim delegations were not invited

---

[65] Roddy Brett, 'Victim-Centred Peacemaking: The Colombian Experience', *Journal of Intervention and Statebuilding* 16, no. 4 (2022): 482.
[66] Brett, 'Victim-Centred Peacemaking', p. 483.
[67] Brett, 'La Voz', p. 44.
[68] Brett, 'Victim-Centred Peacemaking', p. 489.

to participate in talks related to the other agenda items, implicitly limiting their expertise to the remit of victimhood itself, rather than soliciting their insights on other aspects of the conflict and peace. In the words of a female participant in the victims' delegations to Havana, 'How are we going to guarantee the fundamental rights of victims . . . if we went to Havana and that's it, nothing else? They are talking about our rights and in this country it's always the victim who presents their testimony of pain and the rest is done by the experts, by historians. This is not the way'.[69]

Despite the limited scope of their engagement, Brett's research suggests that the victim delegations had a profound impact on the peace talks. 'The arrival of the victims in Havana produced a qualitative leap and transformed the process', de Roux said.[70] A UN negotiator echoed: 'Through my point of view, I could perceive that the victims brought the reality to the table. . . . It was powerful because until then, very technical issues were being discussed, and suddenly the victims arrived with their stories of suffering and violence'.[71] A third interviewee of Brett's added: 'I believe that participation of the victims gave more legitimacy to the process'.[72] I propose treating these narratives as both sincere reflections on the ways in which direct victim participation in peace negotiations can be transformative for the talks and actors engaged in them, *and* as reminders that peace negotiators often treat victims as 'moral beacons', potentially obscuring the full texture of their experiences and their complexity as actors.[73]

The experience of victim participation in the peace process was meaningful for many of the selected delegates, who appreciated having access to a key forum to tell their story. Some of them also cherished meeting others with similar experiences and forming potential bonds of solidarity. A few delegates found meaning in the experience of meeting individuals whom they considered to be the perpetrators of the harms they suffered and appreciated having the chance to 'confront those directly responsible for their suffering',[74] despite the emotional difficulty of these encounters. For some, participation in the Havana talks fomented faith in a peace process towards which they had previously been sceptical.[75]

---

[69] Brett, 'Victim-Centred Peacemaking', p. 486.
[70] Brett, 'La Voz', p. 55.
[71] Brett, 'La Voz', p. 59.
[72] Brett, 'La Voz', p. 63.
[73] Rudling, 'I'm Not That Chained-Up', p. 424.
[74] Brett, 'Victim-Centred Peacemaking', p. 484.
[75] Brett, 'La Voz', p. 62.

However, participation also carried real risks for the selected victim delegates, 'the majority of whom suffered death threats relating to their participation' after their return from Havana.[76] Brett reports that 'approximately 7% of all [victim delegation] participants were forcibly displaced to avoid potential repercussions; for some this represented their second or third displacement. Although the organisers aimed to establish effective security protocols, such measures were inadequate'.[77] Threats also included reputational harms, with several delegates facing social media attacks and encountering much criticism, including from others who identified as victims, some of whom rejected the premise of negotiating directly with actors who had caused harms.[78] The process of participation and testimony was emotionally taxing, requiring victim delegates to revisit and publicly narrate painful experiences. This aspect of the experience does not negate that participation in the peace process was potentially meaningful for some of the victim delegates, but it requires recognizing that meaning often comes at significant and lasting costs.

Some scholars have rightly worried about the instrumentalization of 'the victims' and of the narrative of 'victim-centred peace'.[79] 'Throughout the negotiations', the legal scholar Nadia Tapia Navarro observes, 'victims were increasingly invoked by other actors to either support the negotiations or reject them'.[80] She reminds scholars and practitioners that a claim to be acting in the name or interest of 'the victims' comes with particular moral and political authority, and that different actors deploy that authority in ways that merit critical investigation. However, I distance this synthesis of victims' participation in Havana from the view that 'the victims' became 'phantom actors',[81] who 'only had visibility when integrated in the discourse of others to justify support or rejection towards the negotiations'.[82] Such a narrative potentially underestimates the different ways people who identified as victims exercised agency in narrating their experiences, made claims in front of the negotiators, and derived meaning from their role in the peace process.

---

[76] Brett, 'Victim-Centred Peacemaking', p. 486.
[77] Brett, 'Victim-Centred Peacemaking', p. 486.
[78] Brett, 'Victim-Centred Peacemaking', p. 486.
[79] Nadia Tapia Navarro, 'The Category of Victim "from Below": The Case of the Movement of Victims of State Crimes in Colombia', *Human Rights Review* 20 (2019): 303.
[80] Tapia Navarro, 'The Category', p. 303.
[81] Marya Hinira Sáenz Cabezas, *La paz en primera plena* (Universidad Nacional de Colombia, 2017), p. 139.
[82] Tapia Navarro, 'The Category', pp. 306–7.

The 2016 Peace Agreement between the Government and the FARC

On August 24, 2016, after four years of talks, the parties announced from Havana that a final agreement had been reached. Rather than providing a full summary of all provisions of the 297-page agreement, this section focuses on the provisions related specifically to people recognized as victims of the armed conflict, which called for the creation of a Comprehensive System of Truth, Justice, Reparation, and Non-Repetition. The Comprehensive System consists of five components, all of which have to be implemented in a way that takes gender, as well as a differential and territorial approach, into account. It is essential to underscore that, as discussed below, the peace accord did not *create* the transitional justice system in Colombia; rather, it bolstered and complemented an already existing legal and institutional infrastructure that pre-dated the peace talks.

The first component called for the establishment of the Commission for the Clarification of Truth, Coexistence, and Non-Repetition. This was a temporary, extrajudicial body whose mandate was 'to establish the truth about what happened and to clarify violations and breaches and provide a full explanation to the whole society regarding the complexity of the conflict; to promote acknowledgment of the victims and of the responsibilities of those directly and indirectly involved in the armed conflict; and to promote coexistence in the territories to ensure non-repetition'.[83] Following the extensive data synthesis and consultations detailed earlier, the Truth Commission issued its final report in 2022.

Second, the peace accord established the Special Unit for the Search of Missing Persons in the context of and due to the armed conflict. This is a 'high-level special unit of a humanitarian extrajudicial nature', aiming to 'direct, coordinate and contribute to the implementation of humanitarian measures through the search and identification of all missing persons in the context of the conflict who remain alive, and for those who have died, if possible, the location and dignified return of the remains'.[84] As of January 2023, the Special Unit considered 99,235 people to have been disappeared in the

---

[83] Alto Comisionado para La Paz, 'Agreement on Victims of the Conflict: Comprehensive System of Truth, Justice, Reparation, and Non-Repetition', 2016, https://www.peaceagreements.org/wgenerateAgreementPDF/1547, p. 7.

[84] Alto Comisionado para La Paz, 'Agreement on Victims', p. 7.

context of the armed conflict. The Special Unit is set to have a mandate of twenty years to complete its work.

Third, the peace accord created the Special Jurisdiction for Peace (JEP). This is a tribunal with the aim 'to administer justice and investigate, clarify, prosecute and punish those responsible for serious human rights violations and serious breaches of International Humanitarian Law'.[85] The JEP began its work in 2018 and has a twenty-year mandate. As of January 2023, 13,563 individuals had come before the JEP, over 70 percent of whom were associated with the FARC.[86] The JEP has considered ten separate legal 'macro-cases' so far, with themes ranging from the recruitment of children into armed groups to crimes committed by the state armed forces and paramilitaries.[87]

Fourth, the peace accord called for the strengthening of existing mechanisms for comprehensive reparations. Many of these provisions related to both materially and symbolically strengthening the collective reparations program. Finally, the accord called for guarantees of non-repetition and a commitment to the promotion, respect, and guarantee of human rights. The latter involved a commitment to strengthen protection mechanisms for human rights defenders, as well as education on human rights for all Colombians.

The Colombian Constitutional Court ruled that the peace agreement would have to be subject to ratification through a plebiscite. The plebiscite took place on October 2, 2016. The 'no' side, against the peace accords, won by 50.2 percent compared to 49.8 percent for 'yes'. 'No' prevailed by fifty thousand votes.[88] Turnout was low, with only 38 percent of eligible voters casting a ballot.[89] A factor affecting the outcome was a perception among segments of the Colombian public that the transitional justice provisions of the accord would mean impunity for former combatants.[90] Others resisted the political participation provisions of the peace accord, which would grant the political party of the FARC ten seats in the congressional elections in 2018 and 2022. Yet other contributing factors included the inadequate effort on the part of the state to educate the Colombian public about the contents and meaning of

---

[85] Alto Comisionado para La Paz, 'Agreement on Victims', p. 8.
[86] Jurisdicción Especial para la Paz (JEP), Principales Estadísticas, January 27, 2023, https://www.jep.gov.co/jepcifras/JEP-en-Cifras-enero-27-2023.pdf
[87] JEP, Principales Estadísticas.
[88] Pizarro, *Cambiar*, p. 379.
[89] 'Colombian Voters Reject Farc Peace Deal', *BBC News*, October 3, 2016, https://www.bbc.com/news/world-latin-america-37537252
[90] For more on the referendum, see Andrei Gomez-Suarez, *El triunfo del no: La paradoja emocional detrás del plebiscite* (Icono, 2016).

the peace accord, which is lengthy, written in technical language, and not always accessible. A persistent campaign by the Right, led by former president Álvaro Uribe, also marshalled gendered and religious rhetoric to oppose the peace accord.[91]

After the referendum, President Juan Manuel Santos first agreed to renegotiate certain provisions of the peace accord, but he chose to instead put the revised deal through Congress, rather than subjecting it to a second public vote. The revised peace agreement contained changes to all six thematic chapters of the accord, and the process of negotiating did not include any of the victim delegates who participated in the Havana talks. The Colombian Congress approved the revised accord, which the government and FARC signed in November 2016.

Post-accord, Not Post-conflict: Implementing the Peace Agreement

The Colombian peace talks have received much international praise both for innovations in the process, such as the consultative mechanisms for civil society participation and the creation of the gender sub-commission, and for the comprehensiveness of the final accord.[92] At an address in Havana in July 2016, the UN Women executive director Phumzile Mlambo-Ngcuka said: 'I refer to the example of Colombia all the time. The ambassador can tell you, in New York when we make speeches, we always refer to Colombia as a symbol of hope'.[93] In October 2016, President Juan Manuel Santos was awarded the Nobel Peace Prize for his work on the peace process. Santos accepted the prize, but 'in the name of the victims', rather than in his own name.[94] He also donated the monetary component of the prize to the victims' reparation fund.

Despite these accolades, the lauded 'peace on paper' is different from the everyday reality of fractured, partial peace in post-accord Colombia. Some of what limited the experience of peace related to the applicability of the

---

[91] On the role of gender in the referendum, see Lina Céspedes-Báez, 'Gender Panic and the Failure of a Peace Agreement', *American Journal of International Law* 110 (2016): 183–87.
[92] Pizarro, *Cambiar*, p. 379.
[93] 'Remarks by UN Women Executive Director'.
[94] 'Santos: "Recibo este premio Nobel en nombre de las millones de víctimas del conflicto en Colombia"', *BBC News Mundo*, October 7, 2016, https://www.bbc.com/mundo/noticias-america-latina-37586193.

accord, which only pertained to the Colombian government and the FARC, with other ongoing conflicts not falling under its purview. Further, though more than thirteen thousand FARC fighters have participated in the official process for laying down their weapons, a few dissident FARC factions remain actively engaged in violence, with 161 municipalities across Colombia reporting FARC dissident presence in 2022.[95] Even prior to the peace accord, 'There were already clear signs that neutralizing the FARC would not end Colombia's 52-year armed conflict'.[96] The peace accord also does not directly apply to violence by drug cartels and neo-paramilitaries, and their violence has continued since the 2016 agreement.

Two groups especially affected by the ongoing violence are social leaders / human rights defenders, and former FARC combatants/signatories to the accord.[97] In 2022 alone, there were 189 documented assassinations of social leaders and human rights defenders in Colombia, and an additional 42 assassinations of FARC affiliates and signatories to the accord.[98] Between the signing of the accord and the end of 2022, the UN Verification Mission in Colombia had recorded 355 assassinations of FARC ex-combatants.[99] These realities remind scholars and peacebuilders that, though peace agreements are significant milestones, they do not single-handedly signal the arrival of peace in the lives of people affected by violence.

To monitor the implementation of the 2016 agreement, the Kroc Institute for International Peace Studies is publishing a series of regular reports that rely on qualitative and quantitative indicators of fulfilment. The 2022 report found that, though 'uninterrupted implementation is a positive sign', 'the implementation process faced serious internal and external obstacles'.[100] Of the accord's 578 stipulations, '30% have been completed, 19% are at an intermediate level of completion, 37% are at a minimum level, and 15% have not

---

[95] Indepaz, 'Desafío a la Paz Total', November 2022, https://indepaz.org.co/wp-content/uploads/2022/11/INFORME_GRUPOS_FINAL_NOV28.pdf, p. 12.

[96] Alex Fattal, 'Violence and Killings Haven't Stopped in Colombia Despite Landmark Peace Deal', *The Conversation*, February 2019, http://theconversation.com/violence-and-killings-havent-stopped-in-colombia-despite-landmark-peace-deal-111232.

[97] The naming of these categories reflects Indepaz's documentation and coding.

[98] Indepaz, 'Líderes sociales, defensores de DD.HH y firmantes de acuerdo asesinados en 2022', December 31, 2022, https://indepaz.org.co/lideres-sociales-defensores-de-dd-hh-y-firmantes-de-acuerdo-asesinados-en-2022/.

[99] Misión de Verificación de las Naciones Unidas en Colombia, 'Informe trimestral del secretario general', December 26, 2022, https://colombia.unmissions.org/sites/default/files/infografia_informe_enero_2023.pdf.

[100] Josefina Echavarría Álvarez et al. 'Five Years after the Signing of the Colombian Final Agreement: Reflections from Implementation Monitoring', Kroc Institute for International Peace Studies, 2022, p. 4.

yet been initiated'.[101] Of the 167 provisions that specifically focus on victims' rights, 51 percent are either at a minimum level or have not been initiated at all.[102] The ethnic and gender approaches to peace are particularly lacking in implementation, with only 12 percent of the commitments stipulated by provisions pertaining to gender having been fully implemented at the five-year mark.

Transitions in Government and Effects on the Implementation of the Peace Accord

The electoral climate in Colombia has also affected the implementation of the peace accord and work towards justice. In the final year of President Juan Manuel Santos's administration, the Colombian Constitutional Court ruled that 'the institutions and authorities of the state have the obligation to comply in good faith with what is established in the Final [Peace] Agreement'.[103] The same judgement declared that the accord could not be modified or nullified for three full presidential terms (twelve years), thus effectively guarding the peace agreement from modifications stemming from change in elected administrations. Yet amendments to the text of the agreement are not the only instrument through which administrations can limit its effect. Lacking implementation, underfunding of the mechanisms mandated by the agreement, and legal delays surrounding their authorization can have the effect of slowing or dismantling peace without appearing to do so on paper.

In June 2018, Iván Duque of the right-wing Centre Democratic Party was elected president of Colombia, with the backing of former president Álvaro Uribe (then a senator). Uribe has openly opposed the peace agreement at various moments and has been a vocal opponent of the 2011 Victims' Law as well. During his campaign, Duque stated his intention to revise the peace accord (the Constitutional Court judgement notwithstanding), particularly with regard to the JEP and the provisions governing the punishment of former combatants.[104] Following his

---

[101] Echavarría Álvarez et al., 'Five Years', p. 6.
[102] Echavarría Álvarez et al., 'Five Years', p. 7.
[103] Acto Legislativo 02 de 2017; Sentencia C-630/17 (October 2017), p. 1.
[104] Fabio Andres Diaz, 'Colombia Elects a Conservative Who Promises to 'Correct' Its Peace Accord', *The Conversation*, June 2017, http://theconversation.com/colombia-elects-a-conservative-who-promises-to-correct-its-peace-accord-98273.

election, he promised to 'correct' the agreement without 'tearing it to shreds'.[105]

During Duque's administration, many worried that the 2016 Colombian peace agreement could be facing 'death by bad implementation'.[106] Some of the challenges, particularly regarding the small percentage of recognized victims who had received reparation, were problems during the Santos administration as well. Some, however, were new, or exacerbated under Duque. For example, the Commission for the Follow-up and Monitoring of the Implementation of the Victims' Law found that budget allocations to Afro-Colombian and Indigenous communities had decreased between 25 percent and 43 percent (depending on the ethnic group) during Duque's first year in office.[107] Duque further cut the budgets of entities tasked with implementing key provisions of the accord related to land and rural development, with other peace and justice entities remaining under-resourced as well. Duque's government ultimately failed to gain congressional support to enact legislative changes to the peace accord, but implementation slowed significantly.

Although his attitude to the peace accord and the transitional justice provisions differed from his predecessor's, there was continuity in Duque's rhetorical invocation of 'the victims' as motivating his actions. 'The peace that we long for', he said, 'that demands corrections, will have corrections so that the true victims are at the centre of the process, and so that we guarantee truth, justice, reparation, and non-repetition'.[108] In front of three hundred people recognized as victims of the armed conflict in Barranquilla, Duque declared that in his administration, 'victims will be the protagonists'.[109] Santos, too, had invoked the name of the victims as motivating various

---

[105] Francesco Manetto, 'Iván Duque advierte de que cambiará los acuerdos de paz sin romperlos', *El País*, June 19, 2018, https://elpais.com/internacional/2018/06/18/colombia/1529351991_715042.html.

[106] Vanda Felbab-Brown, 'Death by Bad Implementation? The Duque Administration and Colombia's Peace Deal(s)', Brookings, July 24, 2018, https://www.brookings.edu/blog/order-from-chaos/2018/07/24/death-by-bad-implementation-the-duque-administration-and-colombias-peace-deals/

[107] Contraloría General de la Republica, 'Comisiones de Seguimiento a La Ley de Víctimas y Decretos Leyes Étnicos alertan sobre aumento de nuevos hechos de violencia y precisan que se requiere $115,9 billones para reparar a las víctimas', August 2019, https://apps.procuraduria.gov.co/portal/-Comisiones-de-seguimiento-a-la-Ley-de-Victimas-y-Decretos-Leyes-Etnicos-alertan-sobre-aumento-de-nuevos-hechos-de-violencia-y-precisan-que-se-requiere-_115_9-billones-para-reparar-a-las-victimas.news.

[108] Manetto, 'Iván Duque advierte'.

[109] 'Víctimas serán las protagonistas: Duque—Colombia', ReliefWeb, November 2018, https://reliefweb.int/report/colombia/v-ctimas-ser-n-las-protagonistas-duque

political actions towards the peace accord on many occasions, notably including his Nobel Peace Prize speech.

In 2022, Gustavo Petro and Francia Márquez were elected as Colombian president and vice-president on the promise of 'total peace'. Petro, a former M-19 guerrilla member, and Márquez, an Afro-Colombian feminist and environmentalist, promised a government of 'life and peace'.[110] The platform of total peace involves 'resurrecting the transformative spirit of the 2016 accord', restarting peace talks with the ELN, developing 'collective surrender and plea-bargaining benefits for paramilitary successor groups', entering political dialogue 'with political and economic elites who have historically opposed and felt side-lined by past peace policies', and investing in education for peace, tolerance, and reconciliation.[111]

'Victim' Antecedents: From the Language of Disasters to the Register of Rights

It may seem surprising, given the prominence of the language of victimhood in the peace-and-justice process in Colombia, that the frame of 'victim' has gained resonance only relatively recently. The language of 'victim', the historian Nicolás Rodríguez Idárraga argues, has been in circulation since the 1950s to passively describe the experience of harm, 'but without the moral charge that it was accorded later'.[112] Tracing the antecedents of the term 'victim' sheds light on important shifts in the institutional framework in Colombia, including the shift from the frames of humanitarian disaster and development to the registers of rights and transitional justice, and the evolution of government narratives about how to classify the violence.[113]

The discourse of development, rather than the register of rights or justice, had been the dominant frame through which to make sense of and respond to the experiences of people affected by violence throughout the

---

[110] '"Este es el gobierno de la vida, de la paz, y así será recordado": Presidente Petro', Presidencia de la República, August 7, 2022, https://petro.presidencia.gov.co/prensa/Paginas/Este-es-el-Gobierno-de-la-vida-de-la-paz-y-asi-sera-recordado-Presiden-220807.aspx

[111] Sebastian Guerra and Steve Hege, 'Colombia's New Administration Raises Hopes for 'Total Peace', United States Institute of Peace, July 12, 2022, https://www.usip.org/publications/2022/07/colombias-new-administration-raises-hopes-total-peace

[112] Nicolás Rodríguez Idárraga, 'La naturalización de la violencia: Damnificados, víctimas y desarrollo en la segunda mitad del siglo XX colombiano' (PhD dissertation: University of Montreal, 2017), p. 17.

[113] Aparicio, *Rumores, residuos y estado*.

1980s.[114] Rodríguez argues that 'the discourse of development was formally felt in Colombia since the end of the 1940s, with the arrival of an economic mission organized by the International Bank for Reconstruction and Development'.[115] Within the development paradigm, the same institutions that tended to those affected by so-called natural disasters, calamities, or other emergencies would also tend to those affected by violence.[116] The people affected by violence were known as 'damnificados', which Rodríguez translates as 'survivors' and others translate as 'affected', 'damaged', 'hurt', or 'victimized' people.[117] A response predicated on an imaginary of emergency or disaster can involve 'precisely trying to alleviate suffering without regard to the political identities or actions of those in need'.[118] This is not to suggest that, prior to the emergence of 'victim' as a category for socio-political mobilization, people did not make claims or leverage their identities. Rather, it is to note that between the 1940s and 1980s in Colombia, there was no meaningful differentiation between the institutional responses to harms resulting from violence and other harms.

In the 1990s and early 2000s, the category of 'the displaced' was the main referent for describing conflict-affected populations.[119] Socio-political mobilization on the part of those who had suffered harm was crucial for the emergence of the frame of displacement. In the late 1980s, Colombian activists began to label their experiences of migration as 'internal displacement', framing them as a consequence of political violence, rather than of urbanization.[120] The goal was to 'de-naturalize' displacement, connecting it initially to the language of disaster and subsequently to the register of rights,

---

[114] Rodríguez Idárraga, 'La naturalización', p. 219.

[115] This is one of the institutions that now comprise the World Bank Group. As Rodríguez notes, the Colombian mission was the first of its kind, 'sent by the Bank to an underdeveloped country'. Rodríguez Idárraga, 'La naturalización', p. 131.

[116] I am sceptical about the language of 'natural' disasters, although I use it in this case because it reflects dominant discourse at the time about which I am writing. As Calhoun writes, 'In important senses it is misleading to speak of 'natural disasters'. Disasters often occur precisely because we have meddled with nature and they kill and injure on a large scale because of risks we take in relation to nature'. Craig Calhoun, 'A World of Emergencies: Fear, Intervention, and the Limits of Cosmopolitan Order', *Canadian Review of Sociology/Revue Canadienne de Sociologie* 41, no. 4 (2004): 382.

[117] Rodríguez Idárraga, 'La naturalización', p. iii.

[118] Calhoun, 'A World of Emergencies', p. 392.

[119] For an extensive account of the emergence and use of the category of 'displaced' in Colombia, see Roberto Vidal-López, *Derecho global y desplazamiento interno: Creación, uso y desaparición del desplazamiento forzado por la violencia en el derecho contemporáneo* (Pontificia Universidad Javeriana, 2007); Dávila Sáenz, 'A Land of Lawyers'.

[120] Kristin Sandvik and Julieta Lemaitre, 'From IDPs to Victims in Colombia: A Bottom-Up Reading of Law in Post-conflict Transitions', in *International Law and Post-conflict Reconstruction Policy*, edited by Matthew Saul and James Sweeney (Routledge, 2015), p. 256.

with the hope that these linkages would invite a response on the part of the Colombian state.[121] Support from both Colombian non-state entities and international organization representatives helped the issue of displacement gain attention in the early 1990s.

In 1997, the Colombian Congress passed Law 387, a crucial piece of legislation that 'required the government to prevent and address internal displacement; enshrined IDPs' rights to protection from discrimination; recognized all civil and political rights previously recognized in international law; and provided immediate humanitarian aid for a three-month period, as well as assistance with economic stability and return or resettlement'.[122] The law openly acknowledged the connections between forced displacement and violence in Colombia. Interestingly, five clauses made reference to the language of 'victim', though the law neither defined 'victim' as a category nor linked it to instruments of international human rights and humanitarian law. Instead, the provisions primarily referred to 'victims of this phenomenon' (displacement) or 'victims of this situation'.[123] Though people who had been displaced had commonly suffered other forms of harm too, it was under the mantle of displacement that they mobilized and became visible to the law and institutional frameworks.

The implementation of Law 387 was challenging. Between 1997 and 2004, IDPs would resort to filing petitions before the Colombian Constitutional Court in order to compel the state to address their needs and claims. After a series of intermediate judgments, the Constitutional Court combined the petitions of over five thousand IDPs into a structural judgement in 2004. Through Judgement T-025 of 2004, the Constitutional Court declared 'an unconstitutional state of affairs' when it came to the situation of the internally displaced in Colombia.[124]

Through its language in Judgement T-025 and in subsequent actions, the Constitutional Court declared that the government's actions towards the displaced 'violated both the Constitution and Colombia's international human rights obligations'.[125] The development-centred discourse did not necessarily give way to the language of rights; rather, the two discourses coexisted in ways that created both opportunities and challenges for people affected by

---

[121] Rodríguez Idárraga, 'La naturalización'.
[122] Sandvik and Lemaitre, 'From IDPs', p. 256.
[123] Law 387 of 1997, Art. 10 (1); Art. 19 (5); Art. 19 (10), Art. (20).
[124] Sentencia T-025 of 2004.
[125] Sandvik and Lemaitre, 'From IDPs', p. 258.

violence.[126] It is important to read the growing circulation of rights discourse as resulting from interactions among differently positioned actors, rather than merely flowing top-down from official documents and decisions by those with formal, legal authority. This interplay requires considering the significance of the actions of the Colombian Constitutional Court, legislature, and administration *alongside* and *in response to* the ongoing mobilization of Colombian NGOs, other grassroots actors, and their allies domestically and internationally.

The Victim Category in the Emergent Transitional Justice Framework

Scholars of Colombia generally trace the setup of a transitional justice system to Law 975 of 2005, known as the Law of Justice and Peace.[127] For many, this was a remarkable development, given that transitional justice processes are typically set up *after* a peace accord.[128] Colombia, instead, chose to put in place a system in the era Lisa Laplante and Kimberly Theidon have called '*pre*-post-conflict'.[129] Another parameter that makes Colombia's transitional justice origins stand out is that such processes in other countries were explicitly set up to engage with victims of violence; in Colombia, however, 'a comprehensive scheme of transitional justice mechanisms was put in place with the aim of achieving a partial peace by focusing primarily on one of the armed actors in the conflict: the paramilitary groups. In this case, TJ processes are clearly linked to demobilization processes'.[130]

Article 5 of the Law of Justice and Peace defined a victim as 'the person who individually or collectively has suffered direct harm such as temporary or permanent injuries that cause some kind of physical, psychological and/or sensory disability (visual and/or auditory), emotional suffering, financial loss

---

[126] Sandvik and Lemaitre, 'From IDPs', p. 253.

[127] Pizarro wrote that 'effectively, the Law of Justice and Peace introduced to Colombia the model of transitional justice, which had gained much prestige at the international level in the last decade'. Pizarro, *Cambiar*, p. 350.

[128] Rodrigo Uprimny and María Paula Saffon, 'Usos y abusos de la justicia transicional en Colombia', *Anuario de Derechos Humanos*, no. 4 (2008): 165–195; Lisa Laplante and Kimberly Theidon, 'Transitional Justice in Times of Conflict: Colombia's Ley de Justicia y Paz', *Michigan Journal of International Law* 28 (2006): 50–106.

[129] Laplante and Theidon, 'Transitional Justice', p. 51.

[130] Jemima García-Godos and Knut Andreas O. Lid, 'Transitional Justice and Victims' Rights before the End of a Conflict: The Unusual Case of Colombia', *Journal of Latin American Studies* 42, no. 3 (2010): 488.

or impairment of their fundamental rights. The damages must be a consequence of actions that have transgressed the criminal legislation, carried out by armed groups organized outside the law'.[131] The law further recognized as victims the first-degree relatives of those who had suffered direct harm. It also made provisions to include the members of the armed forces who had suffered the types of harm listed above or experienced infringement of their rights. According to the law, victims would have the right to access to truth, justice, and reparation. Pizarro has credited the Law of Justice and Peace with the 'birth of the victim'.[132] Although many of the provisions of the law were geared towards a reincorporation process for armed actors, it had a significant impact on the creation, legal recognition, and social circulation of the category of 'victim' as well.

The law came under criticism domestically and internationally. Some of this criticism was geared towards the processes for registering as a victim and accessing justice. 'In order to receive reparations', the legal scholar Nicole Summers noted, 'victims first had to come forward and report the crime and then go through a legal proceeding to establish the legal culpability of that particular crime's perpetrator'.[133] This logistically complicated and emotionally taxing process meant that very few individuals were able to complete it. Only 24 individuals recognized as victims had received reparations payments by 2008, out of the 235,000 individuals who reported harms.[134] For these reasons, some criticized the process 'for having addressed both victims and perpetrators in a single law (and, by implication, for neglecting victims' rights)'.[135]

Additional critiques note that the law may have attempted to address paramilitaries, but left paramilitarism intact, thus potentially planting the seeds for demobilized armed actors to be 'recycled into the conflict'.[136] The reincorporation provisions and related sanctions for those demobilizing applied only to 'armed groups organized in the margins of the law' Tapia Navarro concludes, and 'put pressure on a movement of victims that had no clear organization until then'.[137]

---

[131] Law 975 of 2005, Art. 5.
[132] Pizarro, *Cambiar*, pp. 349–50. Rettberg also refers to the birth of victims as political actors. Angelika Rettberg, 'Victims of the Colombian Armed Conflict: The Birth of a Political Actor', in *Colombia's Political Economy at the Outset of the 21st Century: From Uribe to Santos and Beyond*, edited by Bruce Bagley and Jonathan Friedman (Lexington Books, 2015), pp. 111–140..
[133] Summers, 'Colombia's Victims', p. 224.
[134] Summers, 'Colombia's Victims', p. 224.
[135] Sandvik and Lemaitre, 'From IDPs', p. 259.
[136] Laplante and Theidon, 'Transitional Justice', p. 68.
[137] Tapia Navarro, 'The Category', p. 298.

Recognition of the Existence of an Internal Armed Conflict

The lessons from these previous legislative attempts to address the lives of populations affected by violence informed the process of development of Law 1448 of 2011, the Law of Victims and Land Restitution (commonly referred to as 'Victims' Law'). This is the piece of legislation that delineates the rights of those recognized as victims and governs the institutional framework that most directly shaped the lives and claims of my interlocutors during this research. Juan Manuel Santos 'made victim reparations a key platform of his ... bid for Colombia's presidency, ... stating that "if this law is passed, it will have been worth it to be president" '.[138] The victims and land restitution act was signed into law on June 10, 2011, with the United Nations secretary general Ban Ki-moon in attendance to witness the proceedings.[139]

The 2011 Victims' Law marked the first official recognition on the part of the Colombian state that an internal armed conflict had been unfolding in the country. Until then, prior administrations had used a variety of other terms to describe the violence. Former president Álvaro Uribe (2002–2010) rejected the language of 'armed conflict' in favour of labelling the FARC a terrorist threat.[140] In a BBC interview in 2004, Uribe articulated this position: 'There is no armed conflict here', he said. 'There was armed conflict in other countries when insurgents fought against dictatorships. Here there is no dictatorship; here there is a profound, complete democracy. What we have here is the challenge of a few terrorists'.[141] In 2005, a guidance document of the Office of the High Commissioner for Peace listed terms that Colombian agencies should avoid using in their presentations to international organizations or foreign governments.[142] 'The vetoed terms included "armed conflict", "armed actors", and "actors of conflict" '.[143]

---

[138] Max Counter, 'Producing Victimhood: Landmines, Reparations, and Law in Colombia', *Antipode* 50, no. 1 (2018): 127. For in-depth histories of the buildup to the passage of the Victims' Law and the corresponding debates in the Colombian legislature, see Paula Gaviria Betancur and Laura Gil Savastano, *La agenda de las víctimas en el Congreso 2007–2009: Aprendizajes para la incidencia desde la sociedad civil* (Fundación Social, 2010).

[139] Vera, 'The Humanitarian State', p. 1.

[140] Sandra Borda Guzmán, 'La administración de Álvaro Uribe y su política exterior en materia de derechos humanos: De la negación a la contención estratégica', *Análisis Político* 25, no. 75 (2012): 127.

[141] Heather Hanson and Rogers Romero Penna, 'The Failure of Colombia's "Democratic Security" ', *NACLA Report on the Americas* 38, no. 6 (2005): 23.

[142] Carolina Rodríguez, 'Conflicto armado interno en Colombia? Más allá de la guerra de las palabras', *Magistro* 4, no. 7 (2010): 111–25.

[143] Rodríguez, 'Conflicto Armado', pp. 115–16.

The use of the word "terrorism" to describe the nature of violence and the activities of the guerrilla had normative, political, financial, and legal implications.[144] The terrorist label creates an adversary who is a particular kind of 'other': it suggests a perpetrator who, in the words of the political scientist and expert participant in the Colombian peace negotiations Iván Orozco, is 'always less than human'.[145] By framing the activity of the FARC as 'the challenge of a few terrorists' and declaring that 'here there is no dictatorship', Uribe both emptied the collective struggle of the FARC of its political content and obscured the violence on the part of the Colombian state.[146] Recognizing the political character of the guerrillas would involve acknowledging that 'the guerrillas are not simple bandits, terrorists, or narcoguerrillas, that they are instead rebels with an ideology, resources, and specific aims that are contrary to the existing order'.[147] Instead, the language of terrorism enabled the state to invoke particular responses and form strategic alliances. Thus, 'By aligning the Colombian government's conflict with FARC with the global war on terror, Uribe rendered his government's "counterinsurgency" efforts eligible for US funding'.[148]

Against this backdrop, the clear recognition of the existence of an internal armed conflict in the 2011 Victims' Law marked a significant departure from prior discourse. For combatants in non-state armed groups, particularly within the FARC, the formal recognition of the existence of the armed conflict also contributed to 'opening the channels of communication' that eventually led to the 2016 peace accord.[149]

Definition of 'Victim', Registration Process, and Rights

The Victims' Law defined as victims 'those people who individually or collectively suffered harm due to acts that occurred after January 1, 1985, as a

---

[144] Sophie Haspeslagh, *Proscribing Peace: How Listing Armed Groups as Terrorists Hurts Negotiations* (Manchester University Press, 2021); Anna Meier, 'The idea of terror: Institutional reproduction in government responses to political violence,' *International Studies Quarterly* 64, no. 3 (2020): 499–509.

[145] Iván Orozco, 'Reflexiones impertinentes: Sobre la memoria y el olvido, sobre el castigo y la clemencia', in *Entre el perdón y el paredón: Preguntas y dilemas de la justicia transicional*, edited by Angelika Rettberg (Idrc, 2005), p. 173.

[146] Orozco, 'Reflexiones', p. 173.

[147] Sánchez in Bergquist et al., 'Violence in Colombia', p. 31.

[148] Sandvik and Lemaitre, 'From IDPs', pp. 258–59.

[149] Pizarro, *Cambiar*, p. 376.

consequence of infractions of International Humanitarian Law or grave violations of international human rights norms that occurred within the context of the internal armed conflict'.[150] Spouses, permanent partners, same-sex couples, and first-degree relatives of those who were killed or disappeared are also considered victims,[151] as are those who suffered harm while intervening to assist those who became victims or to prevent their victimization. In a change from the Law of Justice and Peace, individuals can receive recognition as victims independently of knowing, identifying, or otherwise encountering and confronting a presumed perpetrator.[152] Members of the armed forces can be considered victims, but their eligibility for compensation depends on the processes of their respective armed forces. Members of 'armed groups organized outside the law' are not considered victims, except in the case of boys, girls, and adolescents that left the armed group while still being minors.[153]

The law also excludes from consideration as victims 'those whose rights were harmed as a consequence of acts of common criminality'.[154] Over time, this criterion has become particularly difficult to adjudicate, given the challenges of distinguishing between the violence of the armed conflict and what the law terms 'common criminality'. This has been especially challenging for people who were harmed by so-called criminal bands (BACRIM), some of which actively recruited former combatants from demobilized armed groups into their ranks.[155] To address the potential issues that arise from this exclusion, the Constitutional Court decided that the state ought to 'analyse each case individually, applying objective criteria in order to determine if the facts narrated maintained a 'close and sufficient' relationship with the internal armed conflict, thereby avoiding categorization of the perpetrator'.[156]

---

[150] Law 1448 of 2011, Art. 3.
[151] If there are no first-degree relatives or any of the other relations listed under this clause, second-degree relatives are eligible.
[152] Law 1448 of 2011, Art. 3.
[153] Relatives of members of armed groups organized outside the law have the right to recognition as victims if they suffered direct harm in the context of the armed conflict, but cannot claim indirect victim status for harms suffered by a member of these groups. Law and policy on this matter are rapidly evolving, so I encourage readers to check the latest status of this point at the time that they engage with these provisions.
[154] Law 1448 of 2011, Art. 4.
[155] Oliver Kaplan and Enzo Nussio, 'Explaining Recidivism of Ex-Combatants in Colombia', *Journal of Conflict Resolution* 62, no. 1 (2018): 64–93.
[156] Rivas, 'Official Victims' Registries', p. 120.

64 GOOD VICTIMS

Receiving official recognition as a victim means inclusion in the Single Victims' Registry [Registro Único de Víctimas], which is operated by the Victims' Unit and is the basis of eligibility for reparations and other entitlements.[157] To be included in the registry, those vying for recognition as victims have to file a declaration with the Public Ministry.[158] The Victims' Unit designed the form for this declaration, but the law deliberately entrusted the actual process of statement-taking to the Public Ministry.[159] This was in part a trust-building measure, aimed at separating the entities that would analyse statements and make a determination on inclusion in the registry from the entities taking testimonies and interacting directly with those who experienced harm.[160] People who suffered harm prior to the passage of the Victims' Law in 2011 had up to four years to complete their declaration, while those who suffered harms after 2011 must have completed their declarations no more than two years after the event.[161] In addition to taking direct statements from those seeking recognition as victims, there was a process for integrating into the Victims' Registry those who had been part of other such registries prior to 2011.

Once those vying for recognition as victims completed the process of filing a declaration, the data would move to the Victims' Unit for analysis. The Victims' Law presumes 'good faith on the part of the victims' and, in that spirit, calls for the authorities to interpret victims' accounts in good faith as well.[162] This marked a departure from some previous registry efforts and required the state to invest in training officials working on the registry in the new process.[163] The average inclusion rate in the Single Registry of the Displaced Population was 61.1 percent in 2010 (the year before the passage

---

[157] Law 1448 of 2011, Art. 154.
[158] The Public Ministry in Colombia is 'composed of three autonomous entities in charge of protecting civil rights'. The entities are the Office of the Attorney General [Procuraduría General de la Nación], the Office of the Ombudsman [Defensoría del Pueblo], and the difficult-to-translate municipal Personerías, entities tasked with protecting due process, promotion and protection of human rights, environmental conservation, effective provision of public services, and guarantee of citizens' rights. Rivas, 'Official Victims' Registries', p. 120.
[159] For an in-depth, fascinating account of the process (and debates) of designing the format of the declaration, see Mora-Gámez, 'Reparation beyond Statehood'.
[160] Rivas, 'Official Victims' Registries', p. 120.
[161] Law 1448 of 2011, Art. 155. There are exceptions for a force majeure that may have impeded people's willingness or ability to declare in a timely manner, on which the Victims' Unit deliberates on a case-by-case basis.
[162] Law 1448 of 2011, Art. 5; Art. 61; Art. 158.
[163] Rivas, 'Official Victims' Registries', p. 124. Phuong Pham, Patrick Vinck, Bridget Marchesi, Doug Johnson, Peter Dixon, and Kathryn Sikkink, 'Evaluating Transitional Justice: The Role of Multi-level Mixed Methods Datasets and the Colombia Reparation Program for War Victims', Transitional Justice Review 1, no. 4 (2016): 86.

of the Victims' Law); by contrast, 'between 2012 and 2014, under the new guidelines of the Single Registry of Victims, the average inclusion rate for the displaced population rose to 92.9 percent'.[164] Those who are included in the Victims' Registry receive an administrative notice informing them of the success of their petition.

The Victims' Law recognizes that victims have the right to truth, justice, reparation, and guarantees of non-repetition. Article 9 emphasizes the transitional nature of the measures of the law, which have the aim of contributing to 'victims coping with their suffering and having their rights re-established' such that they can 'respond to and overcome the violations' they experienced.[165] The law clarifies that it may be the state that recognizes individuals as victims of the armed conflict, but that recognition is not 'proof of the responsibility of the state or its agents'.[166]

The law outlines a strategy of 'comprehensive reparation', consisting of 'restitution, compensation, rehabilitation/restoration, satisfaction and guarantees of non-repetition, in their individual, collective, material, moral and symbolic dimensions'.[167] In addition to these rights, those recognized as victims have a right to receive humanitarian assistance, which is not considered a form of reparation and does not affect the reparation to which these victims would be entitled.[168] Other rights articulated in the law include the rights to (a) be part of community and institutional dialogues; (b) be a beneficiary of affirmative action (advanced by the state) to protect and guarantee the right to live in conditions of dignity; (c) participate in the formulation, implementation, and monitoring of public policy towards victims; (d) reunification, for those who experienced family separation due to their victimization; (e) return to place of origin or to voluntary, secure, and dignified resettlement; (f) land restitution for those who were dispossessed; (g) information about the routes and means for accessing the rights enshrined in the law.[169]

In addition to what the law terms a 'differential approach', requiring implementing agencies to design their activities in ways that take into account age, gender, sexual orientation, disability, and the needs of Afro-Colombian

---

[164] Rivas, 'Official Victims' Registries', p. 124.
[165] Law 1448 of 2011, Art. 9.
[166] Law 1448 of 2011, Art. 9.
[167] Law 1448 of 2011, Art. 25.
[168] Law 1448 of 2001, Art. 25.
[169] Law 1448 of 2011, Art. 28.

and Indigenous communities,[170] the law articulates a specific 'right for women to live free of violence'.[171] A series of provisions recognize additional rights for boys, girls, and adolescents.[172] Acknowledging the risks that many people recognized as victims continue to face, the law calls for special protection measures, risk assessments, and early warning systems for both those recognized as victims and their family members.[173]

To fulfil victims' right to participation in the design, implementation, and monitoring of public policy, the law called for the creation of Forums for Victims' Participation (Mesas de Participación de Víctimas).[174] The Mesas are organized at the municipal, departmental, and national level, and those recognized as victims can stand for election to be part of them. As part of its provisions aimed at symbolic reparation and memory, the law established April 9 as the annual Day of Memory and Solidary with the Victims and committed the state to organizing events of 'recognition of the harms that victimized Colombians'.[175] The law also created the National Centre for Historical Memory, a public institution, with administrative and financial independence.[176] Among other objectives and activities, the centre would oversee many of the memory functions of symbolic reparation, including creating and maintaining archives related to the armed conflict, and promoting and disseminating research on violence.

Institutional Framework Created by the Victims' Law

The Victims' Law also established the institutional framework that would tend to those recognized as victims. I focus specifically on the Special Administrative Unit for Attention and Comprehensive Reparation of Victims (Victims' Unit), which is responsible for coordinating the National System of Attention and Reparation for Victims and for the implementation of the public policy towards victims.[177] Among other responsibilities, the Victims' Unit collaborates with other government agencies to design

---

[170] Law 1448 of 2011, Art. 13; Decreto Ley 4633 of 2011; Decreto Ley 4634 of 2011; Decreto Ley 4635 of 2011.
[171] Law 1448 of 2011, Art. 25. I analyse the differential approach in Chapters 5 and 6.
[172] Law 1448 of 2011, Arts. 181–91.
[173] Law 1448 of 2011, Art. 31 and 32.
[174] Law 1448 of 2011, Arts. 192–94.
[175] Law 1448 of 2011, Art. 141.
[176] Law 1448 of 2011, Art. 146.
[177] Decreto 4802 of 2011.

this policy, budget for its implementation, administer the Fund for Victims' Reparation, manage the Victims' Registry, coordinate with territorial entities to ensure full implementation, and ensure the use of a differential focus in all activities. In 2018, fulfilling the Victims' Unit objectives required coordination with thirty-nine national-level entities across Colombia.[178] The law specifically calls for the Victims' Unit to implement its activities with a territorial approach, acknowledging that needs and capacities vary across Colombia's regions.[179]

Between 2012 and 2018, the Colombian government allocated 76.9 billion Colombian pesos (COP) (a little over 22 million USD as of 2018) to the implementation of the public policy towards victims.[180] The 2022 report monitoring the implementation of the Victims' Law estimated that an additional 301.3 billion COP would be required to fulfil the promises of the law by 2031, when it is slated to expire.[181] Some of the persistent under-resourcing that has affected the Victims' Unit is due to the fact that budgeting for the Victims' Law unfolded based on the presumption that the universe of people recognized as victims would be about three million people, rather than the over nine million who have official victim status in 2023.

The Victims' Law has received praise for its comprehensiveness. In 2015, a Harvard-led team evaluated the activities of the Victims' Unit, including a quantitative and qualitative analysis of the reparations program in Colombia and benchmarking with forty-five reparations policies in thirty-one countries.[182] The evaluation found that 'the scope of victims the Colombian reparations program aims to serve is far broader and larger than any other reparations program, in both absolute terms and relative to population size. The Victims Unit uses a larger list of victimizing acts than any other country in our database. The Colombian registry ... now includes more than 12.7% of the current population of Colombia [in 2015]; none of the other programs have registered or repaired more than 1% of their populations'.[183]

The Harvard evaluation added that 'the leaders within the Unit are visionary, strongly mission-driven, and highly knowledgeable of the dynamics

---

[178] Comisión de Seguimiento y Monitoreo a la Implementación de la Ley 1448, 'Quinto informe de seguimiento al Congreso de La República 2017–2018', August 2018, p. 29.
[179] Law 1448 of 2011, Art. 172.
[180] Comisión de Seguimiento, 'Quinto Informe', p. 29.
[181] Comisión de Seguimiento y Monitoreo a la Implementación de la Ley 1448 de 2011, 'Noveno informe de seguimiento al Congreso de la República, 2021–2022', August 2022, p. 13.
[182] Sikkink et al., 'An Evaluation', p. 3.
[183] Sikkink et al., 'An Evaluation', p. 3.

of victimization and victims' organizations'.[184] Some Colombian scholars have echoed this praise, with Angelika Rettberg noting that 'the Colombian state has clearly demonstrated the political will to promote and advance the tasks associated with the reparation of Colombian victims'. Rettberg concludes that 'in Colombia, there has been reparation due to the Colombian state, not in spite of it'.[185]

However, scholars have acknowledged that the number of entities involved in public policy towards victims, and the challenges of coordination among them, have been obstacles in the implementation of the Victims' Law.[186] There has also been increasing worry among state officials, scholars, and those recognized as victims alike about the fact that the law may have made promises that are difficult to keep.[187] In 2015, four years into the implementation of the law, Rettberg wrote that 'already currently, demand for reparation exceeds the rhythm and capacity to respond on the part of state authorities. 90 percent of the current universe of victims is still pending reparation'.[188] At a public event in Antioquia in February 2019, the first director of the Victims' Unit to be appointed under the administration of President Iván Duque admitted that only 962,000 of the over eight million people recognized as victims had received reparation.[189] The implication is that 'close to fifty-seven years would be required to provide compensation to the victims that have not had access to this right'.[190]

---

[184] Sikkink et al., 'An Evaluation', p. 2.
[185] Angelika Rettberg, 'Ley de Víctimas en Colombia: Un balance', *Revista de Estudios Sociales*, no. 54 (2015), p. 186.
[186] Pham et al., 'Evaluating Transitional Justice', p. 75; Summers, 'Colombia's Victims', p. 231.
[187] Sikkink et al., 'An Evaluation', p. 2.
[188] Rettberg, 'Ley de Víctimas', pp. 186–87.
[189] Ana María Londoño Ortiz, 'Más del 80% de víctimas de la violencia en Colombia esperan ser reparadas', *RCN Radio*, February 5, 2019. https://www.rcnradio.com/colombia/mas-del-80-de-victimas-de-la-violencia-en-colombia-esperan-ser-reparadas.
[190] Comisión de Seguimiento, 'Quinto Informe', p. 8.

3
Living Ethics and Methods as Questions
Dilemmas of Narrating Victimhood

Glances and Gazes

The purpose of a methods-and-ethics chapter is for the reader to imagine the researcher doing the work: What does researching the politics of victimhood look like on an ordinary Tuesday?[1] Methods at a glance, then, is the story of what the researcher did and how they did it. This story matters because it is the reader's first entry into the world of that research, and it offers a prism for interpreting the analysis that follows.

Beyond the initial glance, though, a more complicated story lurks. In anxious WhatsApp messages exchanged with loved ones while the research unfolds, and in hushed conversations at conferences years after projects have nominally concluded, the dilemmas of research take a different shape. In these spaces, many researchers shed the shiny confidence of methods sections in books and articles and begin to unravel the threads of the dilemmas of the research as a lived, shared, and often messy experience.[2] This story includes much of what formal methodological discussions leave out: 'Pains and pleasures, hopes and horrors, intuitions and apprehensions, losses and redemptions, mundanities and visions, angels and demons, things that slip and slide, or appear and disappear, change shape or don't have much form at all, unpredictabilities'.[3] This more affective story of research makes room for doubts, for critical thinking about directing the research gaze, and

---

[1] An earlier version of parts of this chapter appeared as an article in the *International Feminist Journal of Politics*, where it was the runner-up for the Cynthia Enloe Prize. That article has been significantly revised and expanded into this chapter, with thanks to the editors and peer reviewers of IFJP for shaping my thinking on these topics. Krystalli, 'Narrating Victimhood'.

[2] I am inspired by John Law's invitation to 'imagine what it might be to remake social science in ways better equipped to deal with mess, confusion and relative disorder'. John Law, *After Method: Mess in Social Science Research* (Routledge, 2014), p. 2.

[3] Law, *After Method*, p. 2.

for reflection on what we wish we had looked at more carefully, what we wish we had asked or not asked, what we could have interpreted differently.[4]

The abundance of synonyms for ways of seeing is not a coincidence. The etymology of the word 'theory' can be traced to the ancient Greek 'theorein', which means to see. At its best, theory allows for ways of seeing: seeing connections between life experiences, seeing (and making visible) how power operates, seeing how ideas shape and are shaped by embodied and relational realities. The etymology of 'research', in turn, traces back to 'Old French, re-, meaning "with intensity or force" and *cerchier*, meaning "to search". So "research" means to search with intensity, to search closely, to seek'.[5] This chapter concerns itself with different ways of seeing and seeking, exploring the methodological and ethical dilemmas that have underpinned this study of the politics of victimhood.

Here is the story of this research at a glance: during fifteen months of fieldwork between July 2016 and September 2018, I conducted 157 in-depth, semi-structured interviews and life histories with Colombian state officials in bureaucracies of victimhood, representatives of NGOs and international organizations, and people who identify as victims of the armed conflict.[6] I also observed ninety-eight events that were part of victim-centered programs of transitional justice, including events administered by state institutions and those organized by victims' associations.[7] These events included commemorative acts, such as those associated with the annual Victims' Day or with the completion of a reparations cycle for victims of conflict-related sexual violence; meetings of the commissioners of the Commission for the Clarification of Truth, Coexistence, and Non-Repetition with representatives of victims' associations; congressional oversight meetings for the implementation of the

---

[4] For more on affect in research, and on what feminist researchers often write out of stories about research, see Andrea García-González, Elona Marjory Hoover, Athanasia Francis, Kayla Rush, and Ana María Forero Angel, 'When Discomfort Enters Our Skin: Five Feminists in Conversation', *Feminist Anthropology* 3, no. 1 (2022): 151–69.

[5] Shepherd, 'Research as Gendered Intervention', p. 5.

[6] I conducted all interviews myself in Spanish, and interviewed many interlocutors several times over the course of the research, rather than relying on a one-time encounter. Cited excerpts from interviews are often extensive, and I include the footnote to the interview at the start of each excerpt. All translations (and errors) are my own. The research was approved by the Institutional Review Board at Tufts University (Protocol Number: 1605037).

[7] The write-up of the observations is based on my fieldnotes. I do not cite my fieldnotes in footnotes and instead provide context about the observations in the text itself, except in cases in which I am drawing a composite picture, as I do in Chapter 6 with the reconstruction of the script about sexual violence. In that instance, it is important to understand which distinct events make up the composite script, so I refer to different entries in my field diary.

Victims' Law; and numerous meetings of forums for victims' participation in policy creation.

The above paragraph tells the story of research in quantifiable terms. These types of indicators 'offer forms of information that satisfy the unease and anxiety of living in a complex and ultimately unknowable world'.[8] The research process, however, was full of the kind of complexity that a tidy summary obscures. In his reflections on the treatment of emotions in writing about international relations, Naeem Inayatullah envies novelists for their 'willingness to explore, expose, and display an intimacy with doubt', compared to social scientists, who usually see doubt as a 'dangerous opponent'.[9]

This chapter documents the dilemmas and doubts that became my constant research companions. Ethical and methodological dilemmas pertain not only to the research design and fieldwork, but also to the processes of analysis, theory development, and writing.[10] Mired in power, discussions of research methods and ethics are inseparable from each other and from the findings of research.[11] As such, they do not merely belong in an appendix, tucked at the end of a book, but instead require a conversation about power and the ways in which it operates on different actors engaged in the research process throughout the narrative. What scholars know about victimhood is shaped by what we seek, how we relate to academic knowledge, loss, and justice alike, and whom we treat as a bearer of knowledge, theory, and wisdom.

The goal of this chapter is not to ascertain the single best way to wrestle with ethics and methods when researching violence and victimhood, or to offer a 'pristine way of linking knowledge and ethics'.[12] Such an approach would be antithetical to reckoning with the doubt that I hope to invite into the room as a fruitful companion. Instead, the aim is to 'leave up some scaffolding'[13] that

---

[8] Merry, *The Seductions of Quantification*, p. 4.
[9] Inayatullah, 'If Only You Could See', p. 35.
[10] For more on methods and ethics after fieldwork in politically dynamic contexts, see Eleanor Knott, 'Beyond the Field: Ethics after Fieldwork in Politically Dynamic Contexts', *Perspectives on Politics* 17, no. 1 (2019): 140–53; Kai Thaler, 'Reflexivity and Temporality in Researching Violent Settings: Problems with the Replicability and Transparency Regime', *Geopolitics* 27, no. 1 (2019): 1–27.
[11] Romain Malejacq and Dipali Mukhopadhyay, 'The "Tribal Politics" of Field Research: A Reflection on Power and Partiality in 21st Century Warzones', *Perspectives on Politics* 14, no. 4 (2016): 1011–28; Kate Cronin-Furman and Milli Lake, 'Ethics Abroad: Fieldwork in Fragile and Violent Contexts', *PS: Political Science & Politics* 51, no. 3 (2018): 607–14; Dyan Mazurana, Karen Jacobsen, and Lacey Andrews Gale, *Research Methods in Conflict Settings: A View from Below* (Cambridge University Press, 2015).
[12] Ravecca, *Politics of Political Science*, p. 31; Ravecca and Dauphinee, 'What's Left for Critique?'
[13] I borrow this concept from Timothy Pachirat. He writes: 'Where other modes of research and writing might prize the construction and presentation of a gleaming and flawless edifice, two key criteria for the persuasiveness of an interpretive ethnography are the degree to which the ethnographer leaves up enough of the scaffolding in her finished ethnography to give a thick sense to the reader

allows the reader to understand *how* researchers know some of what we know about victimhood, power, and politics during transitions from violence.

Everyone Wants to Talk to a Victim: (Re)directing the Research Gaze

When the questions in this book first started to take shape, I was a practitioner, working at the intersection of gender analysis, humanitarian action, and peacebuilding. These fields are overlapping, and their boundaries are porous, meaning that the ways in which I made sense of myself, the work, and the self in relation to the work shifted with each project and professional engagement. The key aspect that has brought my work outside the academy together with my scholarly research is that both types of engagement represent an intervention in the lives of people who have experienced gendered violence. The ambiguous connotations of 'intervention' allow both for the possibility of agency, or even delight, *and* for the likelihood that the process of research itself feels like a burden, an imposition, or a cause of harm in the life of research participants.[14]

It was in the capacity of a gender adviser that I first arrived in Colombia in January 2010. My task that year was to support a partnership between an international organization and a Colombian NGO that aimed to incorporate a gender perspective into reconciliation programs for former combatants and people who identified as victims of the ongoing armed conflict.[15] Nearly every word in that sentence was—and, in some settings, still is—either ambiguous

---

of how the building was constructed and the degree to which the finished ethnography includes enough detailed specificity, enough rich lushness, about the social world(s) she is interpreting that the reader can challenge, provoke, and interrogate the ethnographer's interpretations using the very material she has provided as an inherent part of the ethnographic narrative'. Timothy Pachirat, 'The Tyranny of Light', *Qualitative & Multi-method Research* 13, no. 1 (2015): 29.

[14] A version of this sentence first appeared in Roxani Krystalli, Elizabeth Hoffecker, Kendra Leith, and Kim Wilson, 'Taking the Research Experience Seriously: A Framework for Reflexive Applied Research in Development', *Global Studies Quarterly* 3, no. 1 (2021): 3. Severine Autesserre also uses the language of 'interveners' to refer to the heterogeneous group of professionals working in peacebuilding. Severine Autesserre, *Peaceland* (Cambridge University Press, 2014), p. 161.

[15] I choose not to name these organizations here because, at the time that work took place, I was not conducting academic research and my relationships to these interlocutors were not filtered through the prism of consenting to appear in this book as named parties. While I remain in touch with some of them, both the leadership of these organizations and their activities have evolved in ways that make it impossible to receive retroactive consent. Instead, I describe the nature of the work to give the reader a sense of how it shaped the explorations in this book.

or controversial: the meanings of reconciliation varied among different actors, as did perspectives on whether it was a feasible or desirable goal.[16] Designations of who counted as a former combatant also varied, and many of the people whom official processes identified as such suggested that the label 'former' did not accurately describe the complex realities of transitioning out of an armed group. The intricacies of designating victimhood, and of treating it is an entirely separate category from 'former combatant', further complicated the picture.

It soon became apparent that creating workshop guides and delivering trainings, which are quintessential activities in the life of a practitioner, are tasks that privilege taking the above categories for granted and incorporating them into one's vernacular, rather than prodding the meaning of each. Nevertheless, both in that first year and in my subsequent professional engagements in Colombia,[17] I noticed the moments of friction, the ways people resisted the labels we, gender analysts, peacebuilders, humanitarians, and transitional justice professionals, assigned to them. These frictions gave rise to questions, which at the time were not fodder for academic inquiry (though they would eventually sow the seeds of it), but sources of professional anguish and life dilemmas. What did it mean to be part of the 'we' that created hierarchies and tensions whose existence 'we' failed to admit to or meaningfully engage with?[18]

In the thirteen years since that first encounter with Colombia, the salience of these questions has only grown. When I arrived back in Colombia as a PhD candidate in July 2016, weeks before the announcement of the peace accords between the Colombian government and the FARC, the transitional justice industry was in full swing. This process came with international experts, consultants, academic researchers, acronyms, organograms, and a capacity-building workshop for every day of the week.

---

[16] McFee, 'An Ambivalent Peace'.

[17] I have remained engaged in Colombia as a professional since then on various humanitarian and peacebuilding projects related to gender and violence. Beyond the frame of these formal professional engagements, relations of care and accountability connect me to Colombia and to the people whose stories appear in this book.

[18] The quote marks around the 'we' are retrospective informed by years of subsequent postgraduate study and of scribbling 'Who is "we"? in the margins of students' writing. Students and I alike have benefitted from engaging with the feminist poet, essayist, and activist Adrienne Rich's work on the politics of location. Rich wrote, with reference to women's activism in the 1970s, 'The problem was that we did not know whom we meant when we said "we"'. Adrienne Rich, 'Notes Towards a Politics of Location', In *Feminist Postcolonial Theory: A Reader*, edited by Reina Lewis and Sara Mills (Edinburgh University Press, 2003), p. 33.

During preliminary fieldwork, the aim of which was to refine the research questions and methods for this project, I visited state officials, NGO staff, representatives of victims' associations, and former combatants whom I had met during my prior work in Colombia. My interlocutors were generous with their time and insights, and simultaneously overwhelmed by the level of foreign interest in violence and its endings. 'I sometimes have to save a whole day to meet with researchers: Master's thesis students, PhD candidates, professors', Miguel, a high-ranking professional at a justice NGO, told me. 'From Sweden, from Switzerland, from the US, from England. You're still the only Greek, though, don't worry', he laughed. 'Everyone is studying Colombia and wants to interview me. I'm a professional interview subject.'[19]

My interlocutors were acutely aware of the descent of a transitional justice industry upon their lives, of having become the subjects to whom justice is done. This is not to suggest that Colombia did not have its own concepts and mechanisms of justice, or that 'the international' and 'the local' are wholly 'separate and distinct spheres of activism'.[20] Rather, it is to recognize that in the particular moment of this research, the transitional justice industry and its accompanying academic cadre were a palpable presence in the lives of people working towards peace and justice.

This was especially the case for people who identified as victims of the conflict. Seemingly everyone, from journalists to academics and from humanitarian practitioners to other types of advocates, wanted to 'talk to a victim'. Bonus points if the victim in question were Afro-Colombian and a woman, as a Colombian researcher told me, based on the experience of having worked as a fixer for journalists covering the peace process. To this day, I receive requests asking if I can introduce journalists, researchers, or even students studying abroad to a victim of the conflict who can provide a quote about the harms they suffered.

The reliance on victim testimony as a pillar of storytelling, and of memory and justice initiatives after armed conflict, is not unique to Colombia.[21] Given its recurrence in transitional justice mechanisms worldwide, the focus on testimony has become a site of debate about the virtues and vices of (re)

---

[19] Interview with senior official at a justice NGO in Bogotá, July 2016.
[20] Winifred Tate, *Counting the Dead: The Culture and Politics of Human Rights Activism in Colombia* (University of California Press, 2007), p. 11.
[21] Fiona Ross, 'On Having Voice and Being Heard: Some After-Effects of Testifying before the South African Truth and Reconciliation Commission', *Anthropological Theory* 3, no. 3 (2003): 325–41.

telling.[22] Feminist scholars, in particular, have questioned the assumption that storytelling and testimony on the part of people who experienced harm is as liberating as institutional mechanisms might hope.[23] I neither wish to fetishize centering the narratives of victims and survivors of violence as necessarily healing for them, nor to dismiss victim-centered storytelling as always retraumatizing. Instead, I sought then—and continue to seek now—a way to think about storytelling, narrative obligations, and the politics of victimhood that engages meaningfully with the complex dynamics of research fatigue, resists the reduction of an individual or community to the suffering they have endured, and allows for the possibilities of narrative agency over that suffering and the worlds that come into being through it and in its wake. The magnitude of these dilemmas can be daunting. Luckily, I did not have to navigate them alone.[24]

In July 2016, I had coffee with Carlos in his office at a human rights NGO in Bogotá. The coffee came in a cup branded with 'everything for the peace'. When I remarked on it, Carlos told me the cup was part of a broader array of peace process 'swag' that was circulating in Colombia. He got up and showed me his wall calendar, which announced it was July, accompanied by a photo of an Afro-Colombian woman in a straw hat, whom the caption described as a 'woman of resilience recovering from the armed conflict in the Urabá region'. In his office, and in other offices I would visit during my time in Colombia, there were daily planners, bookmarks, coffee cups, vests, lanyards, notebooks, memory sticks—all branded with the promise of justice and peace (figures 3.1 and 3.2). One does not have to look far for the markers

---

[22] Two different views in the 'virtues versus vices' of retelling debate are captured in the texts of Paul Ricoeur and David Rieff. Ricoeur considers memory, produced through the testimonies of victims of violence, a moral imperative. He writes, 'We owe a debt to the victims.... By remembering and telling, we prevent forgetfulness from killing the victims twice'. Paul Ricoeur, *Figuring the Sacred: Religion, Narrative, and Imagination*, edited by Mark I. Wallace, translated by David Pellauer (Fortress Press, 1995), p. 290. By contrast, David Rieff asks, 'What if, at least in some places and on some historical occasions, the human and societal cost of the moral demand to remember is too high to be worth paying?' David Rieff, *In Praise of Forgetting: Historical Memory and Its Ironies* (Yale University Press, 2016), p. 58.

[23] I have been particularly inspired by the work of Jill Stauffer on 'ethical loneliness', which she defines as 'a condition undergone by persons who have been unjustly treated and dehumanized by human beings and political structures, who emerge from that injustice only to find that the surrounding world will not listen to or cannot properly hear their testimony—their claims about what they suffered and about what is now owed to them—on their own terms. So ethical loneliness is the experience of having been abandoned by humanity compounded by the experience of not being heard'. Jill Stauffer, *Ethical Loneliness* (Columbia University Press, 2015), p. 1.

[24] I am grateful to Erin Baines for helping me think about how to soften and (re)frame the dilemmas in this paragraph.

Figure 3.1 Victim-branded notebooks were among the transitional justice 'swag' circulating in Colombia at the time of the research. The front of this notebook, which was gifted to attendees of the 'Victims in the Post-Conflict' event, features the logos of Foro Semana (the media group organizing the event), the Victims' Unit, and the government of Colombia.

of the transitional justice industry; they are visible on clothes and writing implements, on walls and inside kitchen cabinets.

Once Carlos had given me a tour of the peace-and-justice swag, we turned to my question about research fatigue among conflict-affected communities and the burdens of storytelling. 'What you essentially want to ask in your thesis, if I understand correctly, are questions about the production of

LIVING ETHICS AND METHODS AS QUESTIONS 77

Figure 3.2 The back of the notebook reads: '731,282 victims have been compensated with more than 4.92 billion pesos and nearly four million have received some type of attention and assistance. Since the peace process began, rural poverty in Colombia has been reduced by 14%.'

categories through the mechanisms of transitional justice', Carlos told me. 'I understand why you wouldn't want to go asking victims to narrate and narrate. You wouldn't be the first, nor would you be the last, and that's the perversity. If you really want to understand the category of "victim", all you have to do is pull up a chair and sit here and watch me all day. You're the fourth one of you I've met with today. All day long, I explain what things mean. If you're asking for my advice, I say: don't study the victims. Study the people producing them'.[25]

Carlos's prompt helped me imagine a way of implementing Nader's call to 'study up' in the context of the politics of victimhood.[26] An array of actors—state agencies and their officials, human rights NGOs and their reports, international organizations and their consultants, researchers and their questions, victims' associations and their advocacy—continually construct, contest, accord, and perform the category of 'victim'. Rather than asking war-affected individuals to renarrate acts of violence, I would focus on the bureaucratic production of the 'victim' category through state mechanisms of transitional justice.

Methodologically, ethically, and practically, this reorientation had several implications:[27] It meant situating the inquiry at different sites than I had originally imagined as suitable for the study of victimhood, centering the narratives of different interlocutors (such as transitional justice professionals), and observing different kinds of encounters (such as those between transitional justice professionals and people seeking recognition as victims). Each of those decisions came with its own set of dilemmas.

Situating the Inquiry in Place: Locating the Encounter

With thirty-nine different entities dedicated to offering services to those the state recognized as victims in thirty-two administrative departments across Colombia at the time of my research, there were decisions to make about where to locate this inquiry and what this vantage point would reveal and foreclose. Regardless of their institutional positioning, my interlocutors agreed with each other: I must go to 'the territories', speak to victims in 'the regions'. The pattern of framing the rural Colombian periphery as the source of authentic expertise on victimhood recurred throughout my research. At an event titled 'The Victims in the Post-Conflict', which took place in Bogotá in December 2017, a senior Victims' Unit official said: 'We—and by we, I mean the central Colombian state—are learning. What was the first thing we learned? That we need to learn from the territories. The victims there are teaching us. We knew very little. They know so much. They are teaching us'.

---

[25] Interview with human rights NGO professional in Bogotá, July 2016.
[26] Nader, 'Up the Anthropologist'.
[27] I discuss the analytic and theoretical implications in Chapter 1.

In this official's narrative, 'the territories' become a metonymy, standing in for a particular kind of knowledge, subsuming the imagined inhabitants of these areas into an undifferentiated collective of suffering subjects.

In other narratives pointing towards 'the regions' as the appropriate site for understanding victimhood, the humans become more visible—and they are almost always Afro-Colombian, Indigenous, and/or female.[28] Over the course of my research, I observed many state-sponsored commemorative events, as part of programs of symbolic reparation. During these events, people who identified as victims would perform a collective commemorative act, which typically involved elements of music, dance, and theatre. The introduction would consist of state officials and representatives of international organizations thanking the donors and reiterating the significance of what we were about to observe. Introducing an event called *Voices of Life*, which consisted of victims of sexual violence commemorating the harms they suffered through six acts of song and dance, a Victims' Unit official in Bogotá said: 'They dignify us all—these women from the territories'.

Five months later in Medellín, an NGO leader pointed to a group of Afro-Colombian women who were sitting silently on the stage behind her prior to their dance performance and said: 'As a paisa,[29] I can tell you: these women from eastern Antioquia are the essence of what it means to be a Colombian survivor, a resilient heart full of love. They are experts in overcoming'. As these narratives suggest, imaginations of victimhood in Colombia have a location (rural), a skin tone (dark), and a gender (female) (figure 3.3).[30]

The insistence that some purer form of truth about the conflict lives 'out there' in 'the regions' or 'the territories' partly tracks with patterns and settings of violence during the conflict.[31] Many Colombians 'locate rurality as the place violence occurred. This understanding is consistent with victimization statistics considering that rural areas have been disproportionately more affected by wartime violence than cities'.[32] At the same time, imagining the

---

[28] Martha Cecilia Herrera and Carol Pertuz Bedoya, 'Narrativas femeninas del conflicto armado y la violencia política en Colombia: Contar para rehacerse', *Revista de Estudios Sociales*, no. 53 (2015): 150–62; Helen Berents, 'Hashtagging Girlhood: #IamMalala, #BringBackOurGirls and Gendering Representations of Global Politics', *International Feminist Journal of Politics* 18, no. 4 (2016): 513–27.

[29] 'Paiso'/'paisa' is an adjective Colombians use to refer to people from the region of Antioquia.

[30] As the anthropologist Dani Merriman also finds in Colombia, 'Victimhood is commonly represented nationally through images of feminine figures (often mothers) and signs of rural and/or impoverished conditions'. Dani Merriman, 'Contentious Bodies: The Place, Race, and Gender of Victimhood in Colombia', *Transforming Anthropology* 28, no. 1 (2020): 27.

[31] Merriman, 'Contentious Bodies', p. 27.

[32] Acosta, 'Victimhood Dissociation', pp. 693–94.

80   GOOD VICTIMS

Figure 3.3 One of the banners displayed at the offices of the High Advisory for the Rights of Victims, Peace, and Reconciliation in Bogotá illustrated how gender, age, race, ethnicity, and rurality inflect imaginations and depictions of victimhood in Colombia. Partially obscured on the bottom is the logo of the city of Bogotá, which reads, 'Bogotá, better for everyone'.

Colombian periphery as synonymous to suffering reduces the people who live there to the harms they experienced, while also failing to fully represent the urban dimensions of the conflict.[33] These imaginations troublingly point people 'elsewhere', leaving the centre unexamined.

[33] Federico Pérez Fernández, 'Laboratorios de reconstrucción urbana: Hacia una antropología de

Where storytellers and researchers locate the centre—geographically, administratively, politically—is a question of power.[34] This research is concerned with how power manifests and how it hides itself in the wake of violence, and how centres make sense of themselves and produce peripheries in the process. For this reason, fieldwork unfolded primarily in two administrative centres, Bogotá and Medellín, and in two types of entities that had a mandate to exclusively serve people whom the state recognized as victims of the armed conflict. These were the national-level Victims' Unit and its regional, municipal counterparts, called the Office of the High Advisory for Victims, Peace, and Reconciliation in Bogotá and the Municipal Victims' Team in Medellín.[35] As the Colombian capital and anchor of many national bureaucracies, Bogotá represents a fitting site at which to study how state institutions at both the national and municipal level imagine and produce victimhood. The Medellín offices of state entities with victim-centric mandates serve the highest number of registered victims, in part because of the intensity and diversity of forms of violence in the Antioquia region during the conflict. 'Observing the state at one level or area or bureau', the anthropologist Akhil Gupta argues, 'cannot provide knowledge of the state by analogy or exception'.[36] Any study of the multisited politics of victimhood must necessarily move between settings, tracing 'connections and networks operating between and among institutions' and 'exploring power as fluid and relational'.[37] To that end, I also interviewed interlocutors at a variety of state agencies, NGOs, and victims' groups beyond the sites of my primary focus.

The focus on capital cities does not mean that rural actors are absent from the narrative. By accompanying state officials to victim-centred events throughout Colombia, I observed interactions between bureaucrats based at administrative centres and those further afield in places framed

la política urbana en Colombia', *Antípoda: Revista de Antropología y Arqueología*, no. 10 (2010): 51–84; Austin Zeiderman, *Endangered City: The Politics of Security and Risk in Bogotá* (Duke University Press, 2016); John Bhadra-Heintz, *A Tyranny against Itself: Intimate Partner Violence on the Margins of Bogotá* (University of Pennsylvania Press, 2022).

[34] Doreen Massey, *Space, Place and Gender* (John Wiley & Sons, 2013); Sara Koopman, 'Making Space for Peace: International Protective Accompaniment in Colombia', in *Geographies of Peace*, edited by Nick Megoran and Philippa William (IB Tauris, 2014).

[35] Numerous other entities—such as, for example, the Ministry of the Interior, the Ministry of Justice, the Office of the Ombudsman—also had mandates to serve victims within their broader mandate to serve the general population of Colombia.

[36] Akhil Gupta, *Red Tape: Bureaucracy, Structural Violence, and Poverty in India* (Duke University Press, 2012), p. 53.

[37] Tate, *Counting the Dead*, p. 11.

as 'the territories'. These observations allowed me to explore how centres and peripheries imagine the other and how those imaginations, which are themselves not homogeneous, inform tensions and relationships. In all observations, my interest has been in the *encounter* between bureaucracies of victimhood and the actors who seek their attention.

Situating the Inquiry in Time: The Afterlives of Research

Though the book and research alike have been informed by my longer-term engagement in Colombia over the past thirteen years, fieldwork for this project primarily unfolded between July 2016 and September 2018, which corresponds to an important period for the politics of victimhood in the country. Research formally started one month before the Colombian government and the FARC signed a peace accord, while the concluding period corresponded with the last month of the administration of President Juan Manuel Santos and the first month of the administration of Iván Duque. Santos's administration had established many of the key policies and milestones discussed in Chapter 2, while Duque's election caused much worry among people who identified as victims and their allies.[38] In many ways, this was a particularly timely window into the hopes and fears that different people attached to the prospects of peace and justice, and a fruitful period during which to study the politics of victimhood.

While the analytic salience of this time period was an important consideration for this project, it was not the only factor that shaped when research began and ended. The availability of research funding, visas and immigration concerns, caregiving responsibilities, employment duties beyond and outside my PhD studies, love, grief, and ill health all influenced when this research started and ended. Many accounts of the research process—including most of my own in the past—tend to silence these aspects of life, perhaps deeming them too personal, too intimate, too messy, unpredictable, or irrelevant to the goals of the research. The truth is, however, that worries about money, about the frailty of bodies (mine and those I cared about), about love

---

[38] This is not to suggest that Santos's policies were wholly welcome or celebrated among people who identified as victims, or that Duque had no support among victim groups. After all, as noted throughout the analysis, the 'victim universe' in Colombia is fractured and heterogeneous. The point here is that the concluding months of this research corresponded with a notable turning point in the Colombian peace and justice process.

and home, shaped the realities of fieldwork, even if they were seemingly extraneous to the subject matter.

It is tempting to treat these factors merely as obstacles or distractions, entirely separate from the topic of the research. However, my reluctant fluency in grief over the years has shaped my research practices. I believe in the invisible language of loss, the register that bereaved people recognize each other as speaking, even when it is not stated. Though hierarchies inflect it, the shared language of grief is not one of equivalence, nor of entitlement. Having experienced protracted and sudden losses of different kinds in life does not give me automatic permission to investigate the losses of others. Losing a father suddenly is not 'the same as' being a victim or survivor of violence; losing a mother to protracted illness after a lengthy period of caregiving does not cloak me in goodness. Loss, however, can tune inquiry and calibrate responses. It can inform the 'mmm', the sound of empathy.[39] Or, in the words of the poet Kevin Young:

> It's like a language,
>   loss—
> can be
>   learned only
>   by living—there—.[40]

In concrete terms, this research began in earnest once I had amassed enough PhD fellowship and grant funding for the work to be feasible, especially given the precarity of funding in my graduate program at the time, and once I had negotiated with my employer an arrangement that made research alongside other livelihood-supporting work possible. And, though August and September 2018 did coincide with the transition of governments in Colombia, these months also marked the time when I realized my own body was too ill to carry on with the gruelling pace of fieldwork, and that my heart was unwilling to live at a distance from my partner and many communities and places I cared about for much longer.[41]

---

[39] An earlier version of this paragraph first appeared as part of Roxani Krystalli, 'Of Loss and Light: Teaching in the Time of Grief', *Journal of Narrative Politics* 8, no. 1 (2021): 43.
[40] Kevin Young, 'Ledge', Academy of American Poets, April 28, 2023. https://poets.org/poem/ledge.
[41] Again, the dilemmas of research ethics and methods do not only pertain to the 'fieldwork' itself, but also shape the processes of analysis and writing. Like many others, I particularly felt the burdens of grief, illness, caregiving, and living at a distance from some of my homes and communities while working on this book during the Covid-19 pandemic. I am inspired by how María Fernanda

What ends when 'fieldwork' ends?[42] In many ways, the relationships that underpin and sustain this work—the relationships that are the sources of accountability and joy alike—continue to this day. Sometimes these continuities manifest in ongoing encounters in formal and official spaces, ranging from briefing the Victims' Unit on some preliminary insights emerging from this work to sharing my reflections on the politics of victimhood with professionals of the Special Jurisdiction for Peace.[43] More frequently, the work lives on through continued care and ephemeral storytelling: through WhatsApp messages, through the exchange of memes and emojis, through questions and tales about births and deaths and marriages and everyday mundanity, shared with the knowledge that a living web of stories, even if told at a distance, is what keeps lives willingly entangled.

This discussion brings into view the limits of the term 'fieldwork', and highlights some possibilities for reimagining it.[44] I think of 'the field' not as geographically bounded (though it is, of course, *located*), and of fieldwork not as temporally marked by singular points of entry and exit, of arrival and departure. The field is 'an almost random assemblage of sites that come into coherence through processes of fieldwork itself: the field as deterritorialized and reterritorialized, as it were, by the questions brought to bear on it in the course of research'.[45] If 'the field' is made and remade through encounter, shaped and reshaped by questions and their subtle transformations, then the story of fieldwork is the meandering story of that encounter, as opposed to a

---

Olarte-Sierra puts the body back into discussions about research. María Fernanda Olarte-Sierra, 'On Bodies and Our Own Bodies: Care and Vulnerability When Teaching about Death and Loss', *Curare Journal of Medical Anthropology* 46, no. 1 (2023): 106–12.

[42] I am grateful to Kate Cronin-Furman, with whom I have thought about this question over the years.

[43] While some scholars understand these activities under the banner of 'dissemination' or 'research uptake', both terms suggest a definitiveness, finality, and unidirectionality of information sharing that does not match my experience of these encounters or the nature of the ongoing exchange between my interlocutors and me.

[44] Berit Bliesemann de Guevara and Morten Boas, *Doing Fieldwork in Areas of International Intervention: A Guide to Research in Violent and Closed Contexts* (Bristol University Press, 2021); Annika Björkdahl, Oliver Richmond, and Stephanie Kappler, 'The Field in the Age of Intervention: Power, Legitimacy, Authority vs the "Local"', *Millennium* 44, no. 1 (2015): 23–44.

[45] Deepa Reddy, 'Caught! The Predicaments of Ethnography in Collaboration', in *Fieldwork Is Not What It Used to Be: Learning Anthropology's Method in a Time of Transition*, edited by James Faubion and George Marcus (Cornell University Press, 2009), p. 90. The reflections in this paragraph build on earlier writing on transparency about fieldwork. Roxani Krystalli, 'When Humans Become Data', in *The Companion to Peace and Conflict Fieldwork*, edited by Roger Mac Ginty, Roddy Brett, and Birte Vogel (Palgrave Macmillan, 2020).

narrative neatly punctuated entirely by analytic or theoretical imperatives or by singular points of the researcher's entry and exit into a fixed domain.

Selecting Interlocutors

The main interlocutors for this study were transitional justice professionals within state bureaucracies and people who identified as victims, some of whom had official victim status. Selecting interlocutors who were officials within bureaucracies of victimhood was a fairly straightforward task, in that I sought to speak to anyone within the transitional justice agencies named above who was willing to speak with me. As the stories of these professionals in Chapter 4 indicate, I engaged with professionals at all levels of the bureaucracy of victimhood, from street-level bureaucrats who dealt with people recognized as victims on a nearly daily basis to high-level officials involved in decision-making and policy creation.[46] Acknowledging that the trajectories of these professionals are not fixed and nor are their positionings, I also spoke to individuals situated within NGOs and international organizations working with and for victims of the armed conflict, many of whom had either worked directly for a state agency in the past or worked closely alongside one at the time of this research. A 'snowball' effect developed over time, whereby one professional would introduce me or refer me to the next, thus building a chain of conversations.

My background as a practitioner in Colombia was helpful in establishing initial connections, as I was familiar with many of these agencies (or the institutions that preceded them) and with the nature of the work that the professionals did in the day-to-day. I was also fluent in the acronyms that permeate this work, and in performing the kind of knowledge that indicates that fluency. As Shepherd writes with reference to her engagement with professionals in the Women, Peace, and Security sector, 'I have learned the power of the knowing nod, as a response to the phrase that begins, 'Well, of course you know...' *Of course <nod>*. This is a benefit of the time I have spent in these spaces, a privilege of the assumption of expertise that structures my own engagement'.[47]

---

[46] Lipsky defined street-level bureaucrats as 'public service workers who interact directly with citizens in the course of their jobs, and who have substantial discretion in the execution of their work'. Michael Lipsky, *Street Level Bureaucracy: Dilemmas of the Individual in Public Services* (Russell Sage Foundation, 1980), p. 3.

[47] Laura Shepherd, *Narrating Women, Peace, and Security* (Oxford University Press, 2021), p. 15.

This background also complicated interlocutors' expectations of me, especially among people who identified as victims. As a practitioner in peacebuilding, humanitarianism, and transitional justice, I had access to resources (programmatic, financial, and otherwise) that I did not have as a PhD candidate. People affected by violence rightly have expectations of the people they trust with their stories.[48] 'I will tell you my story, with the hope that it can do X'. The promise of X varies widely, as does its potential efficacy: I will tell you my story so you can tell the world, I will tell you my story so you can connect me to resources, I will tell you my story in the hope that it will alleviate pain, in the hope of justice. Each of these heavy expectations generates questions: Which world, which resources, what forms of justice, by what means can a story alleviate pain? The questions are part of how interlocutors rightfully hold interveners in their lives accountable. Though these expectations, especially when articulated explicitly, can make interveners uncomfortable, they are also, in my view, justified, considering the power inequalities between interveners and our interlocutors, and the material realities in which these inequalities manifest.

The promise of potential benefits resulting from interlocutors' engagement with interveners is far hazier for academic research, especially early in the researcher's career. At that stage, the benefits of research accrue more readily and favourably for the researcher and the broader state of knowledge than directly for the research participant. To be clear, I am neither suggesting that practitioners can always fulfil expectations to their interlocutors' satisfaction, nor am I cynical about the potential impacts of knowledge creation. Rather, I wish to reflect on how the overlapping identities of scholar/practitioner can complicate the process of research participant recruitment and selection.[49] On the one hand, prior knowledge of a context and the key actors engaged in it can facilitate access; on the other, it is difficult for a researcher to reintroduce herself in different terms and to meaningfully redefine her interlocutors' understanding of how that researcher is situated within power structures.

These considerations, coupled with the concerns I discuss below related to the narrative burdens of telling the story of suffering, shaped my criteria for

---

[48] Chloé Lewis, Alfred Banga, Ghislain Cimanuka, Jean De Dieu Hategekimana, Milli Lake, and Rachael Pierotti, 'Walking the Line: Brokering Humanitarian Identities in Conflict Research', *Civil Wars* 21, no. 2 (2019): 213.

[49] Lewis et al., 'Walking the Line'; Henri Myrttinen and Subhiya Mastonshoeva, 'From Remote Control to Collaboration: Conducting NGO Research at a Distance in Tajikistan', *Civil Wars* 21, no. 2 (2019): 228–48.

the selection of interlocutors who identified as victims. Rather than starting my research participant selection by contacting individuals who identified as victims whom I had met through my work as a practitioner, I chose to establish new relationships.[50] For this aspect of the project, I would primarily engage with elected representatives of the victims' participation forums [Mesas de Participación Efectiva de Víctimas, henceforth 'Mesas'.]

The Mesas were mandated by the 2011 Victims' Law, with the aim of guaranteeing victims' participation in public policy creation. According to the institutional framework laid out in the Victims' Law, 'It is the duty of the state to offer victims of the armed conflict institutional spaces at the national, departmental, district, and municipal levels to guarantee their influence on the development, implementation and monitoring of the policies that affect victims (for example, reparation, prevention, protection), and on how parts of the budget will be allocated to these activities'.[51] In practice, Mesas ranged from twenty-four to twenty-six seats for elected victim representatives, with the legal framework specifying that the representatives needed to correspond to a diversity of harms (e.g., torture, sexual violence, enforced disappearance), as well as a range of vectors of identity and power, including the representation of women, young victims, elderly victims, disabled victims, Indigenous communities, Afro-Colombian communities, LGBTI victims, and members of organizations specifically dedicated to defending the rights of victims of the conflict. Mesas were expected to have at least one meeting a month between the elected representatives and state officials from the various entities that had a mandate to work with victims of the armed conflict.[52] Because facilitating encounters between state agencies and people recognized as victims was central to the aims of the Mesas, these sites were especially well suited to the questions at the heart of this research.

Accessing Mesas required accompanying either an elected victim representative or a state official. I opted to do the latter. It is analytically fruitful to examine how the state controls the spaces in which it, and victimhood,

---

[50] Throughout the fieldwork, I was in touch with some of the individuals who identified as victims whom I had met through my humanitarian/peacebuilding work and conducted interviews and life histories with a selected few among them. I did not, however, rely on them for introductions to others, and my engagement with them primarily consisted of continuing the threads of informal conversations that had been ongoing among us for over a decade.

[51] De Waardt and Weber, 'Beyond Victims' Mere Presence', p. 216.

[52] State agencies were responsible for facilitating the meetings both organizationally and financially, the latter of which included providing lunch and refreshments, as well as transit reimbursements for attendees recognized as victims. Though meetings were typically scheduled to last half a day, they commonly took up the entire day throughout the period of this research.

can be studied. Though elected victim representatives to Mesas also wield power in these contexts, I did not wish to put the burden of securing my access on them.[53] Securing access was not a one-off exchange, but a constant negotiation, consisting of many WhatsApp messages to confirm the time and location of meetings, iterative explanations of the purpose of my research, and multiple bus rides across town only to find a meeting had been cancelled without notice. The state officials I accompanied to the Mesas were facilitators who, by virtue of their role at their respective agencies, acted as liaisons between elected victim representatives and state institutions. Although they were occasionally puzzled that a researcher would be interested in observing the Mesas, they welcomed me when I tagged along.

I identified victim interlocutors through Mesas for two reasons. First, there is an element of choice inherent in running for election to be part of a Mesa: a choice to represent others who identify as victims and to speak on victims' issues. The analysis in Chapter 5 both troubles the illusion of perfect representation and elucidates the question of who gets to speak for whom. However, at a basic level, people who identified as victims and participated in the Mesas had chosen to be public interlocutors on victims' issues in ways that made me more comfortable making them research interlocutors on the same subject. Second, my attendance as an observer at meetings of various Mesas allowed me to learn from these interactions through observation and listening without requiring people who identified as victims to narrate their experience strictly for my benefit.[54] Those who are present at Mesas are *particular kinds* of victims, enacting specific politics. I engage with these interlocutors not as stand-ins for all victims or as metaphors for authentic, pure victimhood, but as individuals situated fractiously within shifting hierarchies.

In my conversations with people who identify as victims and state officials alike, I have also asked about people who suffered harm during the conflict, but who choose *not* to identify as victims or participate in public forums framed around victimhood. Researchers often call these types of interlocutors 'hidden' or 'hard to reach' populations.[55] Although understanding the

---

[53] I sought and obtained their consent to be in those spaces at each interaction.
[54] To complement their perspectives, I have also engaged with members of victims' associations not represented at the Mesas, as well as individuals who identify as victims of the conflict without being members of such groups
[55] Amy Ellard-Gray, Nicole K. Jeffrey, Melisa Choubak, and Sara E. Crann, 'Finding the Hidden Participant: Solutions for Recruiting Hidden, Hard-to-Reach, and Vulnerable Populations', *International Journal of Qualitative Methods* 14, no. 5 (2015): 1–10.

reasons people may distance themselves from private or public identification with victimhood is analytically valuable, I chose not to reach these people directly, not to require them to unhide themselves.[56] Following Veena Das's approach to silence as a form of agency, it bears recognition that for some people affected by violence, silence is indeed one of the *only* forms of agency available.[57] Preserving and respecting the agency involved in rejection and refusal,[58] in choosing not to relate to victimhood, not to know oneself through that frame or become known in the world through that lens, is more important than adding a few more interlocutors to a research project. Rather than interrogating the choices of some conflict-affected individuals who distance themselves from performances of victimhood, I chose to 'leave some stones unturned'.[59]

The Politics of Silences: Anonymity and (In)dignity

Not all silences in this research were consistent with the wishes of my interlocutors. Violence in Colombia has been ongoing after the peace accords, in ways that create continued risks for identifiable interlocutors. As Sarah Parkinson and Elisabeth Wood note in their reflections on transparency about research, 'There is often no way to know whether an activist who judges herself to be safe one day will be criminalized tomorrow, next month, or in five years. Those in this position may not be able to telephone or email a researcher in order to remove their name from a book or online database; they may not know until it is too late'.[60] Echoing the practices of other researchers working in conflict and transitional settings, I anonymize my interlocutors and refer to them by pseudonym. In addition to using

---

[56] For an excellent edited volume on silences in research, see Jane Parpart and Swati Parashar, eds., *Rethinking Silence, Voice and Agency in Contested Gendered Terrains: Beyond the Binary* (Routledge, 2018). See also Lee Ann Fujii, 'Shades of Truth and Lies: Interpreting Testimonies of War and Violence', *Journal of Peace Research* 47, no. 2 (2010): 231–41.

[57] Das, *Life and Words*.

[58] The anthropologist Audra Simpson has powerfully asked: 'What is theoretically generative about . . . refusals? . . . In listening and shutting off the tape recorder, in situating each subject within their own shifting historical context of the present, these refusals speak volumes, because they tell us when to stop'. Audra Simpson, 'On Ethnographic Refusal: Indigeneity, 'Voice' and Colonial Citizenship', *Junctures* 9 (2007): 78.

[59] Liisa Malkki, *Purity and Exile: Violence, Memory, and National Cosmology among Hutu Refugees in Tanzania* (University of Chicago Press, 1995), p. 51.

[60] Sarah Elizabeth Parkinson and Elisabeth Jean Wood, 'Transparency in Intensive Research on Violence: Ethical Dilemmas and Unforeseen Consequences', *Qualitative & Multi-method Research* 13, no. 1 (2015): 25.

pseudonyms, I sometimes omit or abstract other details, including place of work and geographic location.[61]

I was honest about this choice with my interlocutors, some of whom expressed displeasure about it. My conversation with a man I call Hernando illustrates dynamics I encountered with others who identify as victims. Hernando and I first met in 2013 at an event framed around 'pro-peace civil society actors'. At the time, he was leading a small NGO advocating on victims' issues. When I spoke to him five years later, he was one of the elected victim representatives in one of the Mesas in the greater Bogotá area. I have always enjoyed speaking to Hernando, with our conversations moving from Marxist politics to bureaucratic attendance sheets at meetings and from the Colombian culinary affection for potatoes to what counts as political work. At the end of what was scheduled to be our last encounter before I left Colombia, I revisited with him the question of how he would like to be quoted in this research.

'I wanted to talk to you again about how you would like to be cited in this research. We had discussed it a few times and you told me to not worry about it until the end', I began.[62]

'Always worrying, you', Hernando laughed. 'Where did you learn to worry so much? Relax, calm down, friend!'

I continued tentatively: 'There are many options that I have offered to others like you who have helped me understand these issues. For example, I could cite you as a human rights defender. Or as an NGO leader. Or as a representative in one of the Mesas. Or are there other options you prefer?'

'Yes', Hernando said. 'Can you write down my real name? I prefer to be cited by my name'. I told Hernando that was not an option, that I am not permitted to use anyone's real names in this research. 'No me lo permiten'. The passive voice, omnipresent in Spanish, crept into my own speech too. The passive voice, I tell students in my feminist classroom, hides the workings of power. For me, in that moment, it was a convenient hiding.

'Who doesn't permit you?' Hernando asked, putting the actors and agency that I had obscured back into the conversation.

---

[61] The pseudonyms I have relied on in the book are sometimes different from the ones by which I refer to the same officials in other published work, such as journal articles. I have changed pseudonyms across publications in cases in which relying on the same pseudonym would result in two people quoted in the book having the same name, thus potentially causing confusion for the reader. In the case of public events (open to broader audiences across Colombia, not just to selected researchers), I have identified speakers by their names.

[62] Interview with elected victim representative to a Mesa in the greater Bogotá area, August 2018.

'There is a university ethics board that has to approve all research', I responded. 'They approved of mine on the condition that the interviews remain anonymous'.

'Well, if that is the policy of your university, I respect it', Hernando said. 'But what are they afraid is going to happen?'

This is always the uncomfortable point in the conversation: the point at which I articulate the risks that my interlocutors have lived with all their lives. Hernando does not need me to explain to him that the violence is ongoing. This had been his reality before our paths ever crossed. He has spent his life attaching his body and name to causes that may lead to his becoming a target of further violence. Still, his question stood, and I had to answer it. 'They are afraid you might be hurt, that you might be targeted', I said.

He asked: 'That I will be killed?' I nodded silently. 'Tell your university that they have tried to kill me many times already. I have been killed many times already'. Hernando and I both knew that I would not ask who 'they' were in this context. More stones are left unturned.

Angela Lederach had a similar experience in navigating the challenge of anonymity in her conversation with a campesino named Dionisio. 'If you use this interview, I want you to use my name', Dionisio told Lederach, concluding, 'We cannot be silenced anymore'.[63] Paying close attention to her interlocutors' stories, Lederach learned that campesinos' understanding of security did not depend on individualized notions of protection through anonymity, but through a collective centring of voice and community wisdom. Such a reframing, however, was at odds with the research ethics protocols that govern much university-based research. 'In falling back on Western-defined assumptions about security and vulnerability', Lederach reflects, 'my protocols undermined campesino practices of nonviolent collective protection and well-being, which centered *visibility*—rather than *anonymity*—as vital for their security. The experience brought the paternalistic politics embedded within the protocols I had developed to "protect" my "human subjects" into sharp relief'.[64]

---

[63] Like Hernando's, Dionisio's was not an isolated experience: '"Que mi nombre sea registrado (that my name be registered)", Einer Martínez Sierra, a social leader who had endured state-sanctioned violence as a result of his commitment to community work, declared before the start of one interview'. Angela Lederach, '"Each Word Is Powerful": Writing and the Ethics of Representation', In *The Companion to Peace and Conflict Fieldwork*, edited by Roger Mac Ginty, Roddy Brett, and Birte Vogel (Palgrave Macmillan, 2020), pp. 462–63.

[64] Lederach, 'Each Word Is Powerful', p. 464.

Navigating ethical and methodological questions in community, rather than in isolation, reminds researchers that we carry our dilemmas alongside the wisdom of our friends, colleagues, and interlocutors. In retrospect, I regret having pursued a research protocol of full anonymity. This is not a regret I can immediately address in this book. My thinking on this subject evolved too late to pursue a change of protocol at the university whose ethics committee had approved of this research and, as several scholars of research ethics and methods point out, it is often not advisable to change the terms of the engagement with interlocutors while a research project is underway, especially in settings affected by violence.[65] Nonetheless, I record these reflections here to underscore that, even when the ink has dried on a research project, ethics and methods are not settled matters. The questions, doubts, and regrets live on. Looking ahead to my future research, I intend to think more imaginatively alongside my interlocutors about ways to preserve their authorship and voice, including the possibility of naming them in full or in part.

A Different Kind of War Story

For many people who identify as victims, telling the story of their victimization became a script, rehearsed and performed for the benefit of journalists, humanitarian staff, state agencies, and researchers. Over the years, I have seen the tonal shift and embodied change when people get ready to deliver this script. The shoulders drop, and so does the gaze. The researcher presses 'play' on her recorder; the interlocutor presses 'play' on the internalized script, which appears to be performed almost from passive, rote memory.

Calling it a script or a performance does not mean there is anything artificial or less than real about the grave harms people suffered.[66] Instead, I wish to draw attention to the effect of repetitive storytelling about conflict-related violence, to the ways in which people habituate to trotting out a certain narrative identity,[67] and to the stories that might remain in the shadows when

---

[65] Parkinson and Wood, 'Transparency in Intensive Research'.

[66] I follow E. Summerson Carr's definition of scripts as 'semiotic entanglements that . . . set the term of representations'. E. Summerson Carr, *Scripting Addiction: The Politics of Therapeutic Talk and American Sobriety* (Princeton University Press, 2010), pp. 2–3.

[67] On victimhood as narrative identity and a form of narrative currency, see Theidon, *Intimate Enemies*, pp. 113–14.

researchers focus too narrowly on particular harms, sites, or time periods of violence.

The types of violence my interlocutors narrated as part of this research rarely involved a weapon or physical force. Their stories were primarily anchored not in the land from which people had been displaced, but in the bureaucratic offices in which they sought redress. Like narratives of physical violence, stories about navigating bureaucracies of justice are rarely linear, tidy, or chronological.[68] They involve hope and frustration, humour and indignation. These stories are not necessarily easier for people who identify as victims to share with researchers. Indeed, the telling of them seems to foment both a sense of agency over one's own narrative and simultaneous resignation in my interlocutors. I do, however, believe that exploring victimhood through bureaucracies and encounters with the state can allow for a different kind of war story to emerge and for a different understanding of violence, its endings, and its afterlives.[69]

Complicated Loyalties: Entangled Accountability and Compassionate Critique

In settings affected by violence, 'One's presence, one's speech, elide neutrality', Kimberly Theidon states. 'We are, to paraphrase Favret-Saada, already caught'.[70] Many of the dilemmas in this chapter have emerged from the weaving of one life with another, and from the expectations that arise from these webs. Being caught in these webs of relation highlights a series of complex questions around the ethics of critique and the researcher's perceived loyalty to different interlocutors. Ana María Forero aptly summarizes these dilemmas with reference to her ethnographic work with officials of the Colombian military: 'How to not betray the sacred pact between the anthropologist and the other . . . ? How to respect the established complicities? How to represent the disagreements? The tensions?'[71]

---

[68] As the feminist scholar Jenny Edkins argues, the resistance to linearity is not a narrative failure or flaw, but a constituent part of the logic of violence and its remembrance. Jenny Edkins, *Trauma and the Memory of Politics* (Cambridge University Press, 2003).

[69] I am indebted to Carolyn Nordstrom's book by the same name for this phrase. Carolyn Nordstrom, *A Different Kind of War Story* (University of Pennsylvania Press, 1997).

[70] Theidon, *Intimate Enemies*, p. 20.

[71] Ana María Forero Angel, *El coronel no tiene quien le escuche* (Ediciones Uniandes, 2017), p. 7.

94 GOOD VICTIMS

These questions came alive for me at a municipal Mesa I was observing in the Antioquia region in 2018. In addition to the thirteen victim representatives who were in attendance, there were also two Victims' Unit officials, an official of the Office of the Public Ministry, three Municipal Victims Team staff, and Carmen, the facilitator who was running the meeting. A little before noon, during a discussion on victim-centred budgeting for transitional justice programs, the official from the Public Ministry began to unload Styrofoam lunch boxes onto a table in the back. She then lined up cartons of juice in two rows, with guava in the back and 'tropical' in the front. When she was finished, she tapped me on the shoulder: 'The institucionalidad [institutionality] will be eating lunch out at 12:30',[72] she whispered in my ear.

I nodded, uncertain as to what to do with this information beyond acknowledging it. 12:30 p.m. came and went and the discussion on budgeting became heated and ran overtime. 'Ladies and gentlemen, your lunch is getting cold', Carmen announced at 12:55 p.m. in the voice of an aggravated mother. She gestured towards the door and the rest of the state officials began to file out. On her way out, the Public Ministry official tapped me on the shoulder again and said, 'Ready?' Only then did I realize I was expected to have lunch with the institucionalidad too. I gathered my things clumsily and tried to shuffle past the victim representatives who were standing in line for their Styrofoam lunch. 'Oooohh, Señorita Roxani is going to eat with the state', said Arturo, followed by a wolf whistle and giggles among other victim representatives.

At lunch, state officials alternated between discussing their weekend at the finca,[73] the football, or their spouses' latest peculiarity. Mixed in were observations about the Mesa, ranging from commenting on the victim representatives' way of dress, to their mood and posture. I was mostly quiet. It felt inappropriate to participate in this kind of commentary about my interlocutors who identified as victims. Yet there is little room for elective silences in spaces like this.[74] Carmen punched me playfully on the shoulder and said, 'Roxani won't talk. She's too good for gossip'. We all laughed and

---

[72] For a full discussion of the concept of the institucionalidad, see Chapter 4.
[73] A finca is an estate, typically in a rural area, to which some urban dwellers travel for weekends or short holidays away from the city. Upper-middle-class families often own fincas, and they are also available for rent.
[74] I have found Kimberly Theidon's conceptualization of this particularly poignant. She writes: 'One simply cannot observe. You will not be permitted to if you ever intend to open your mouth. There will come a point when you must take a stand. People will remind you that you are far too implicated not to, just as they reminded me'. Theidon, *Intimate Enemies*, p. 22.

returned to the topic of weekend plans, to which I could contribute. When we resumed the afternoon session of the Mesa, the victim representative seated next to me offered me candy. I politely declined. 'Roxani had a big lunch with the state and she does not want our sweets', the woman retorted.

What does it mean to sit *beside* and *among* the state without being *of* it? I had many interactions like the one described above, living in the third person, in the space between silence interpreted as complicity and silence interpreted as judgment.[75] In the eyes of some of my victim interlocutors, particularly the ones who witnessed my interactions with state officials at the Mesas, I was *of* the state enough to be lumped in with it—or, at least, to warrant a joke about the ways in which 'the state' tries to claim different subjects. It did not matter that I was not Colombian, that I was not employed in one of the public service agencies, that I did not wear the shiny, colourful vests that became a metonymy for the state.[76] While I sought to be clear about my independent researcher role at every opportunity, I ultimately did not resist when people spoke of the ills of the state as though I, too, were responsible for creating them. It felt fairer to allow my interlocutors to critique the state in front of me than to excuse myself by denying any meaningful association with it.

Questions of where the researcher's loyalties lie also surfaced among my state interlocutors. My ongoing work alongside human rights advocates and victims' associations was sometimes a source of hesitation. 'You're one of the activist anthropologists, aren't you? One of those who come here to do critique [hacer crítica]?', a senior Victims' Unit official asked me before an interview.[77] I struggled with how to answer this question without, on the one hand, minimizing my critiques, or, on the other, alienating the state officials whose lives I sought to understand.

These dilemmas also shed light on the complexities of participant observation as a method. In the encounters between state officials and those who identify as victims, I was more observer than participant. Unlike other social scientists who have produced valuable accounts of similar phenomena in Colombia,[78] I did not work for a state agency or a victims' group. At the

---

[75] I am grateful to Helen Kinsella for helping me think about this point.
[76] For a powerful analysis of chalecos and the symbolism associated with them, see Ximena Castro-Sardi and Cristian Erazo, 'Sufrimiento y agencia política: Pesquisa sobre la condición de víctima en Bojayá, Colombia', *Athenea Digital* 19, no. 1 (2019): 17.
[77] Interview with senior official at the Victims' Unit in Bogotá, October 2017.
[78] Pellegrino, 'Between the Roll of Paper'; Vera, 'The Humanitarian State'; Dávila, 'A Land of Lawyers'.

same time, as a researcher, through the questions I ask, the stories I craft, the narratives I privilege and silence, and the theories I develop, I *participate* in the creation and contestation of the politics and hierarchies of victimhood.

Though these dilemmas of loyalty, representation, and critique manifested initially during the fieldwork, they continued to surface during the processes of analysis and writing. 'I was analysing texts that I had created through an encounter with another person', Shepherd writes with reference to her research within UN bureaucracies. 'I breathed the same air as these people, they welcomed me into their offices, and we talked beyond the research, sharing small details of our lives. Deconstructing their words. . . felt decidedly wrong, as though I were trying to catch them out, trip them up, or twist their words. As I made notes, I could hear them in my head: "That's not what I meant!"'[79]

Ultimately, I navigated these complexities by choosing not to save the critique for the writing. Rather than treating the writing as a post facto exposé, I sought to engage with my interlocutors by asking them to confront opposing views or unpopular perspectives in the moment of the research. These engagements were not always comfortable for them or for me. Yet they helped me move through the research with a keen awareness that people operate within power structures, which they sometimes explicitly discuss, and with compassion for the dilemmas these power structures create for the individuals who generously shared their time and insights with me. There is a place for generosity in representation of complex interlocutors, and generosity is not antithetical to the kind of critique that remains curious about the workings of power.

Entanglement has long (after)lives. My accountability to bureaucrats and people who identify as victims alike does not end when I 'exit' the proverbial 'field'. The quotations are doing a lot of work here because in relations of true accountability, there is no exit. I carry my interlocutors' voices in my head when I speak and write. They do not always find it comfortable to read my arguments about the state or the politics of victimhood, but it is ethically important to me that they feel I have treated their words with care, that I have not made caricatures of them. Multiple accountabilities—to state officials, to people who identify as victims, to those who oppose the state—tug at the

---

[79] Shepherd, *Gender, UN Peacebuilding*, p. 29.

heart, slow down the writing, and magnify the anxiety. But, crucially, they are also the gift of a life lived and sustained by relations.[80]

Generosity does not mean sanctification. There are neither pure heroes nor perfect villains in this book.[81] As one state official said, 'We are dealing with victims, not with angels'.[82] This statement challenges what the anthropologist Miriam Ticktin calls 'a search for purity, a space outside corruption and contamination, a space emptied of power that can ground both tolerance and action'.[83] Ticktin concludes that 'because innocence is both mythical and ephemeral, we are constantly displacing politics toward the limit of innocence in a never-ending quest'.[84] How, then, to navigate the moments of less-than-angelic humanity? Who is allowed to be a messy, flawed, fully human subject of research? Over the course of this project, I listened to hours of gossip among state officials, as well as among people who identified as victims, sometimes about other victims who they think are unreliable, arrogant, promiscuous, or self-serving. I heard stories of fraud and cheating in many domains, as well as stories of the violence that people who identified as victims have experienced at the hands of other victims.

My nervousness in including these stories is a product of the keen awareness that people who identify as victims of conflict experience ongoing violation in the aftermath of peace accords, not only through direct physical violence, but also through the violence that lives on in bureaucracies of justice and in the social stigmatization of those who have to navigate them. I worry that sharing stories about what a state official called 'badly behaved victims' can undermine already difficult struggles in search of recognition and justice. This worry is shared among fellow researchers of victimhood. 'Analysing the politics of victimhood should not undermine the experiences of victims', Jelena Golubović argues, 'rather, it should make visible the effects of claiming or denying victimhood'.[85] The worry manifests in caveats. I write a vignette, I edit it, I want to tell the reader 'please do not judge this person'.

---

[80] A version of this paragraph appeared in my reply to commentary on Roxani Krystalli, 'Being Seen Like a State: Transitional Justice Bureaucrats and Victimhood in Colombia', *Current Anthropology* 64, no. 2 (2023): 128–46.

[81] In thinking through this point, I have learned from Ravecca and Dauphinee's thoughts about innocence and the 'foreclosure of politics through reification'. Ravecca and Dauphinee, 'What's Left for Critique?', p. 39.

[82] Interview with state official on the Victims' Registry team, October 2017.

[83] Miriam Ticktin, 'A World without Innocence', *American Ethnologist* 44, no. 4 (2017): 578.

[84] Ticktin, 'A World without Innocence', p. 578.

[85] Golubović, 'One Day', p. 1175.

Whom or what does this defensiveness protect? It is my hope that it is a defense of what the sociologist Avery Gordon calls 'complex personhood', which means that 'all people (albeit in specific forms whose specificity is sometimes everything) remember and forget, are beset by contradiction, and recognize and misrecognize themselves and others'.[86] Complex personhood allows for—and necessitates—texture. Analysing how the state and conflict-affected individuals themselves shape notions of 'good victims' requires interrogating the ways in which *I* also sanitize the portrayal of victimhood through my own writing. The selection of which research narratives I share and which I silence is part of the process of validation of certain kinds of victimhood, part of the production of particular kinds of victim subjects. Simply put: If I were to only tell the stories of 'well-behaved victims', I, too, would be quietly reinforcing the same hierarchies of victimhood that I hope to bring to view.

Having suffered violence in the armed conflict or working in bureaucracies aimed at justice does not automatically endow humans with a cloak of goodness. As Florencia Mallon states, 'A leader of a movement can become a collaborator or go home and beat up a wife and children'.[87] The ways in which people who identify as victims embody patriarchy, enact harassment or violence, or behave in ethically questionable ways are an essential piece of understanding the politics of victimhood and the tensions within social movements. They can also illustrate the ways in which power operates not only between 'victims' and 'the state' as monolithic categories, but among those who identify as victims themselves, thus fracturing the illusion of a cohesive, singular, innocent-and-pure victim identity. 'Most subalterns are both dominated and dominating subjects', Mallon reminds us, 'depending on the circumstances or location in which we encounter them'.[88] Rather than orienting narrative efforts towards covering up flaws or flattening the humanity of interlocutors, I attempt to practice curiosity towards the systems and mechanisms that require people affected by or implicated in violence to behave in certain ways in order for their suffering to be believable, for their lives to be grievable, and for them to access justice.

---

[86] I delve into this concept in greater detail in Chapter 4. Avery Gordon, *Ghostly Matters* (University of Minnesota Press, 2007), p. 5.
[87] Mallon, 'The Promise and Dilemma', p. 1511.
[88] Mallon, 'The Promise and Dilemma', p. 1511.

Theorizing Victimhood

People who identify as victims and the professionals whose mandate is to attend to their needs are not merely characters in this story. They are also theorists of their own experiences. 'Within the academy, the word *theory* has a lot of capital', Sara Ahmed claims.[89] Like Ahmed, 'I have always been interested in how the word *theory* itself is distributed; how some materials are understood as theory and not others'.[90] I have observed the dynamic that Ahmed describes during presentations of my research on the politics of victimhood at international academic conferences. Complementing the other sites at which this research unfolded, academic conferences are relevant loci for the investigation of the politics of victimhood, as they are sites of international knowledge creation, as well as settings at which the performance and circulation of expertise are readily observable.[91] 'Your research participants are unusually articulate', a panellist remarked, after I presented a paper on bureaucracies of victimhood. 'You seem to have surprisingly eloquent interlocutors', a colleague at a different academic conference echoed.

My interlocutors are, indeed, eloquent and articulate. The modifiers, however, are telling. How do scholars imagine victimhood or suffering, if the eloquence of those who experience it is 'unusual' or 'surprising'? These reactions highlight 'an enduring juxtaposition: . . . some people and groups have 'theory" and others have "beliefs"; some people and groups export categories of knowledge, while others remain resolutely "culture bound"'.[92]

Scholars working in Colombia, and decolonial feminists in particular, have paved alternative paths to theory generation that are full of promise. 'I question how I can move away from the colonial anthropological/research paradigms of "studying people/places/nature" to *doing knowledge with*', Laura Rodríguez Castro writes in her excellent book about rural women's experiences in Colombia.[93] In the context of my research, 'doing knowledge with' people has meant treating victimhood, the state, and politics alike as emic, rather than etic, categories, and practicing curiosity about the

---

[89] Ahmed, *Living a Feminist Life*, p. 8.
[90] Ahmed, *Living a Feminist Life*, p. 8.
[91] For more on knowledge creation about violence, see Alejandro Castillejo Cuéllar, 'Unraveling Silence: Violence, Memory and the Limits of Anthropology's Craft', *Dialectical Anthropology* 29, no. 2 (2005): 159–80. See also Tshepo Madlingozi, 'On Transitional Justice Entrepreneurs and the Production of Victims', *Journal of Human Rights Practice* 2, no. 2 (2010): 208–28.
[92] Theidon, *Intimate Enemies*, p. 26.
[93] Rodríguez Castro, *Decolonial Feminisms*, p. 67. See also Sara Motta, *Liminal Subjects: Weaving (Our) Liberation* (Rowman & Littlefield, 2018).

meanings my interlocutors attach to these labels. It has also meant resisting the popular academic structure of a stand-alone 'theory' chapter in the book, existing separately from the empirical sections, in acknowledgement that the theory emerges directly from and through the narratives of these interlocutors. As Angela Lederach powerfully states, ' "Writing" understood as a "responsibility" requires an ethical stance—a refusal to edit away the voices and contributions of people like Dionisio, who live and move through the landscapes of memory etched into the territory'.[94]

This kind of writing requires acknowledging interlocutors' contributions as theoretical, rather than as merely confirming or supporting a theory that exists separately from them.[95] Acknowledging research interlocutors as theorists means not only recognizing that they planted the seeds of inquiry, but also that their insights can be theoretical and do the work of theory—the work, in other words, of sense-making—without always requiring theorization 'overlaid' onto them by a scholar. This does not mean that the scholar is absent from the picture, or that there is no room for my own theorization here; nor does it imply that theories that emerge from people with direct experiences of victimhood ought to be reified and unquestioned. What I am suggesting, instead, is that theory is the product of encounter.

I am relatively new to this way of thinking, and I still have a long distance to travel. As is common in many politics and international relations PhD programmes in North America, to the extent that my postgraduate training engaged with research methods at all, it privileged positivist and quantitative methodologies and methods over interpretivist, relational, or qualitative ones. One consequence of this training is that I have had to unlearn a lot of ideas about where theory comes from,[96] about rigour in research, and about how to write in ways that centre interlocutors as knowledge bearers and theorists.[97] In this journey of unlearning and relearning, this book represents a beginning, rather than a fully completed process or an arrival point.

---

[94] Lederach, 'Each Word Is Powerful', p. 458.

[95] Again, I turn to Ahmed: 'Some work becomes theory because it refers to other work that is known as theory. A citational chain is created around theory: You become a theorist by citing other theorists that cite other theorists'. Ahmed, *Living a Feminist Life*, p. 8.

[96] Shiera S. el-Malik, 'A Letter to Baba', *Review of International Studies* 49, no. 4 (2023): 539–46.

[97] I have learned much from Nicola Henry's view of victims as 'agentic bearers of knowledge'. Nicola Henry, 'The Fixation on Wartime Rape: Feminist Critique and International Criminal Law', *Social and Legal Studies* 23, no. 1 (2014): 111.

The Silences That Remain

Dilemmas are lived in questions—and there have been a lot of questions in this chapter. Because ethical and methodological dilemmas are not merely rhetorical, I have sought to concretely address many of these questions by telling the story of how I navigated dilemmas when they arose at different stages of the research process. In this way, the chapter recounts both what I did and how I did it—the story of methods at a glance—and weaves the more complex story of the questions that emerged along the way, ranging over where and how to direct the research gaze, how to think about narrative obligations, what the sources of theory are, and how to represent relationships with interlocutors that transcend the fixed temporal boundaries of a research project.

Silences and erasures remain in this account. Again, it helps to be concrete: some of these ellipses are the product of how my research interests and approaches to methodology, ethics, and other aspects of my relationship to the profession have evolved over time. For example, thanks in large part to Colombian scholars and activists and to the communities I call home in Scotland,[98] I now think, care, and write more about the politics of place and about relationality with nature and the more-than-human. I am more aware of (and interested in) methodologies that go beyond the verbal and beyond discourse to encompass more complex ways of thinking-feeling and existing politically in relation to one another. And, importantly, I now think more about joy—joy as method in and through the research process,[99] joy as a political experience that exists alongside grief, suffering, and victimhood, rather than in denial of them. While I have tried to write some of these lessons, interests, and curiosities backwards into the research account in this book, they appear here mostly as not-fully-explored possibilities, as seeds for future inquiry that I and others can hopefully take up.

---

[98] Rodríguez Castro, *Decolonial Feminisms*; Rogério Haesbaert, 'Del cuerpo-territorio al territorio-cuerpo (de la tierra): Contribuciones decoloniales', *Cultura y Representaciones Sociales* 15, no. 29 (2020): 267–301.

[99] Elina Penttinen, *Joy and International Relations: A New Methodology* (Routledge, 2013).

4
Making the (Good) State

Bureaucrats of Victimhood

> In our yearning for justice and care we reach for the good state.
> —Anna Secor, 'Between Longing and Despair'[1]

Being the State

A woman in a yellow leotard and white ballerina tutu was standing on stilts in the foyer of the Museum of Antioquia. A man in a clown costume was rehearsing dance steps beside her. I had arrived at the first meeting of officials from the Truth Commission with representatives of victims' associations, human rights defenders, and pro-peace advocates in the Antioquia region of Colombia. 'Yes, this is the meeting space. Welcome', the dancing clown said to me.

Inside the hall, helium balloons containing strings of colourful Christmas lights were floating above the stage. Representatives of various organizations were arriving, many of whom were dressed in T-shirts identifying the name of their organization, often accompanied by slogans, such as 'Justice for All' or 'We Want the Truth'. Aspirations for truth, peace, and justice were observable close to the skin.

A bundle of chrysanthemums rested on each seat in the audience, with white lilies on the floor in front of the stage, along with woven tapestries, books, and other offerings. People greeted one another with affection, blowing kisses across the room and getting out of their seats to say hello to those they recognized. Representatives of local NGOs walked around the room handing out gifts. A woman pressed a bookmark into my hand and stood beside me while I read it. The logo of an NGO working in rural

---

[1] Anna Secor, 'Between Longing and Despair: State, Space, and Subjectivity in Turkey', *Environment and Planning D: Society and Space*, no. 25 (2007): 48.

Antioquia was printed at the top, along with an excerpt from its mission and a passage by the Colombian writer Gabriel García Márquez. The mission of the NGO called for 'walking with intergenerational women and men in the utopia of life', supplemented by Márquez's prompt 'to inhabit a world where love is really true and happiness is possible, and where the lineage condemned to one hundred years of solitude finally have a second chance on earth'.[2] Knowing that resources are scarce, I offered to give the bookmark back to her, but she pressed it into my palm and then held my hand in both of hers. 'No, keep it', she insisted. 'It's a gift, you must take care of it'.

A band, complete with trumpets, marched in to usher the six truth commissioners in attendance onto the stage. 'We will have peace', sang a dancing group accompanying the band, followed by 'Truth is memory'. The clown rehearsing in the foyer was now dancing on stage next to the president of the Truth Commission, whom he hugged when the song reached its conclusion. Four of the six commissioners were taking photos of the scene with their cell phones, allowing themselves to be as swept up in the spectacle as the audience.

I had arrived at the event expecting formality and manifestations of 'official' authority: banners with logos, officials in suits, speeches thanking the donors. Instead, I encountered clowns, trumpets, gifts, and affectionate salutations, with commissioners opening their remarks by extending 'a fraternal greeting' or 'a loving greeting' to the attendees. The search for justice is fuelled not only by the wounds of violence, but by the persistence of love. Survival merits dancing.

The president of the Truth Commission, Francisco de Roux, took the microphone to greet the attendees. De Roux had been a Jesuit priest, philosopher, and economist, whose work had been instrumental in Centro de Investigación Popular por la Paz (Center for Popular Research for Peace, CINEP), a non-profit dedicated to promoting peace in Colombia through rigorous research and popular education. In his opening remarks, he reflected on the bewilderment of now being associated with 'the state'. 'None of us', he said, gesturing to the commissioners on the stage, 'has played a political part before, in the sense of being [affiliated] with a political party. What a surprise it is to be the state! The Colombian state!' He took a long pause, then

---

[2] The Nobel website translation of Gabriel García Márquez's Nobel prize lecture offers a slightly different translation of the same text. See Gabriel García Márquez, Nobel lecture, Nobelprize.org. https://www.nobelprize.org/prizes/literature/1982/marquez/lecture/

continued: 'Not the government, but the state. There are so many questions generated in us by this . . . so many doubts'. Another long pause, then: 'We are the state. We are a state institution. We are an institution of a state so violent, so unjust, so . . . stupid at times'. The audience erupted into laughter. 'And now we find ourselves part of it'.

De Roux publicly articulated a set of preoccupations that recurred in my conversations with professionals in bureaucracies of transitional justice: How does being seen like a state shape encounters with people who identify as victims?[3] On a more fundamental level, what does it mean to *become* the state, and how do professionals make sense of that positioning, the power they wield, and the affective dilemmas it generates? Ultimately, how are the politics of becoming, being, and being seen like a state entwined with the politics of victimhood during transitions from violence?

This chapter engages with these questions through the life stories and narratives of professionals who populate these bureaucracies of victimhood. 'To emphasize an obvious point', the anthropologist Tess Lea writes, 'bureaucracies are peopled'.[4] I take up her invitation to 'see bureaucrats as fleshly beings', and engage with Aretxaga's prompt to be curious about how 'the state is constituted . . . through an embodied and sensual effect'.[5] Fittingly then, the pages that follow are full of love and hate, hope and disappointment. They are saturated with professionals' desire to 'incarnate a virtuous state', which 'will be a better state, or *better than* the state, . . . a state different from the one that allowed and even contributed to the victimization and invisibilization'.[6]

Building on the collective wisdom of ethnographies of peace and justice in Colombia,[7] I show that the relationship between state bureaucracies and victimhood is not unidirectional. It is not only the state that makes victimhood by conferring the status of 'victim' through its bureaucracies. Victimhood also makes the state. What Lauren Berlant calls 'the cluster of

---

[3] Cf. James Scott, *Seeing Like a State* (Yale University Press, 1998).
[4] Tess Lea, 'Desiring Bureaucracy', *Annual Review of Anthropology* 50 (2021): 64.
[5] Aretxaga, 'Maddening States', p. 403.
[6] Dávila, 'A Land of Lawyers', p. 50; p. iv.
[7] Juan Pablo Vera Lugo, 'Burocracias humanitarias en Colombia: Conocimiento técnico y disputas políticas en la implementación de la Ley de Víctimas y Restitución de Tierras', *Revista de Estudios Sociales* 81 (2022): 21–37; Aparicio, *Rumores, residuos, y estado*; Buchely, *Activismo burocrático*; Lemaitre, *El estado siempre llega tarde*; Pellegrino, 'Between the Roll of Paper'; Vera, 'The Humanitarian State'; Burnyeat, *The Face of Peace*; Dávila, 'A Land of Lawyers'. I've also learned much from Dipali Mukhopadhyay's powerful work in Afghanistan. Dipali Mukhopadhyay, *Warlords, Strongman Governors, and the State in Afghanistan* (Cambridge University Press, 2014).

promises' of justice through bureaucracies of victimhood drew professionals into those institutions,[8] many of whom would not have otherwise imagined becoming part of 'the state'. These bureaucrats' daily labour and encounters instantiated the state in the eyes of people seeking attention and resources.[9] In the best moments of these encounters, professionals 'gave face' to the state promise of transitional justice,[10] embodying and enacting a version of 'the state as an ideal form: caring, responsive, generous, and abundant, rather than distant, repressive, and extortive'.[11]

In the bureaucrats' self-narrations, the 'good state' derived its goodness from professionals' proximity to victimhood, whether through some bureaucrats' identification as direct or indirect victims of the conflict, their past work alongside people who identified as victims, or their empathetic action in their current post. Proximity to victimhood endows a particular group of professionals with a form of moral authority,[12] certifying their expertise in transitional justice and shaping their relationships with those seeking state attention. This is an intimate expertise, marking a departure from theories of bureaucratic indifference,[13] 'disinterested loyalty to the public good',[14] and impersonal bureaucrats.[15] Victimhood, in this instance, does not only cloak the figure of the victim in imagined moral purity; it also potentially creates a pathway for the state to establish a particular kind of presence, image, and set of relationships during transitions from violence.[16]

---

[8] Lauren Berlant, *Cruel Optimism* (Duke University Press, 2011), p. 23.

[9] I have learned much about embodying and instantiating the state through María Fernanda Olarte-Sierra's work on forensic experts, whose 'knowledge produces the very violence they work on'. María Fernanda Olarte-Sierra, Gina Urazan Razzini, David Garces, and Sergio Rodríguez Vitta, 'Forensic Tales: Embodied Peace and Violence in Colombian (Post) Armed Conflict', *Trajectoria* 4, no. 1 (2023): 4.

[10] Burnyeat argues that Colombian government officials' use of the phrase 'dar la cara' ('giving face') 'denoted the act of government officials "facing" society via diverse face-to-face encounters and assuming responsibility to society "as" the government'. Burnyeat, *The Face of Peace*, p. 2.

[11] Tate, 'The Aspirational State', p. 236. For more on the caring state, see Davina Cooper, *Feeling Like a State* (Duke University Press, 2019).

[12] Tate, *Counting the Dead*, p. 150.

[13] Michael Herzfeld, *The Social Production of Indifference: Exploring the Symbolic Roots of Western Bureaucracy* (Routledge, 1992).

[14] Pierre Bourdieu, 'Rethinking the State: Genesis and Structure of the Bureaucratic Field', in *State/Culture: State-Formation after the Cultural Turn*, edited by George Steinmetz (Cornell University Press, 1999), p. 72.

[15] Max Weber, *Economy & Society*, vol. 2 (University of California Press, 1978), p. 959.

[16] My interest in this chapter is not in adjudicating whether the state was present or absent; rather, I focus on how bureaucracies of victimhood created the potential for establishing *a particular kind of state presence*, even when that potential was not fulfilled. For more on the nuances of state presence and absence, see Ramírez, *Between the Guerrillas*; Ballvé, *The Frontier Effect*.

The 'good state' that the bureaucracies of victimhood bring into being, and the goodness that its officials narrate, experience, and aim to embody, are not merely fantasies or illusions. They do not 'just' represent a 'longing for a good paternalistic state'[17]—though the longing is real, and so are its resulting disappointments. Nor are narratives of 'the good state' merely projected into the future as dreams of what Tate aptly calls 'the aspirational state', which, in her account, is 'revealed less through ongoing encounters, but more so conjured through these possible futures'.[18] Goodness and possibility crucially also unfold in the present tense, underscoring that 'radical imagination is not just about dreaming of different futures. It's about bringing those possible futures 'back' *to work* on the present, to inspire action and new forms of solidarity today'.[19]

Therein too, in the present seeds of goodness and their possibilities, lies the heartache, the hurt of the unfulfilled promise. 'To study social life', Avery Gordon argues, 'one must confront the ghostly aspects of it'.[20] The 'good state' is haunted by its simultaneous coexistence with its ghost twin, the state that disappoints not only the claimants who appear before it, but also the bureaucrats who people it.[21] If it is through proximity to victimhood that these bureaucrats (and the state they embody and represent) gain a form of moral authority, it is through their articulated distance from bureaucratic authority that they cope with the disappointments and frustrations of 'being the state'.[22]

It is significant to this analysis that both bureaucrats' and claimants' encounters with 'the state' are not *always* or *wholly* disappointing. I offer this not as a half-hearted excuse for unfulfilled promises of justice, but as a possible explanation for why bureaucracies of victimhood persist, and why people direct any hope or labour towards them.[23] The frustration comes

---

[17] Aretxaga, 'Maddening States', p. 397. See also Ballvé, *The Frontier Effect*, p. 8.

[18] Tate, 'The Aspirational State', p. 236.

[19] Max Haiven and Alex Khasnabish, *The Radical Imagination: Social Movement Research in the Age of Austerity* (Zed Books, 2014), p. 3.

[20] Gordon, *Ghostly Matters*, p. 7.

[21] For an analysis of haunting in the transitional justice process in Northern Ireland, see Cheryl Lawther, 'Haunting and Transitional Justice: On Lives, Landscapes and Unresolved Pasts', *International Review of Victimology* 27, no. 1 (2021): 3–22.

[22] 'Tracing the shifts in the imaginaries of bureaucratic authority ... allows us to attend to the state in its relationality, connectedness, and instability'. Elif Babül, *Bureaucratic Intimacies: Translating Human Rights in Turkey* (Stanford University Press, 2017), p. 57.

[23] 'People criticize bureaucracy's imperfections because of a profound belief that a higher level of ethical functioning is not just desirable but mandated. This hope, this desire, authorizes bureaucracy's license to continue, despite failures and betrayals, on the basis that it could and should do better'. Lea, 'Desiring Bureaucracy', p. 69.

from the fact that the promise and hope of justice through 'the state' exist in real enough terms to haunt, to cause hurt when they remain unfulfilled or illusory. In her writing about haunting as a frame for understanding social life, Gordon claims that the ghost usually represents 'a loss, sometimes of life, sometimes of a path not taken. From a certain vantage point, the ghost also simultaneously represents a future possibility, a hope'.[24] It is the duality and simultaneity of the ghostly visions of 'the good state' and its disappointing counterpart that complicates the project of being, becoming, and being seen like a state during transitions from violence.

Bureaucrats' Life Stories, or, 'Why Would You Believe Them?'

Investigating bureaucrats' stories with feminist curiosity requires seeing these professionals as textured, complicated 'social actors, rather than ciphers in a machine'.[25] Didier Fassin argues that 'proximity with agents reveals the warmer side of the state, so to speak'.[26] Such a revelation is an ethically and methodologically complicated endeavour, especially when the inquiry is oriented at what de Roux characterized as 'a state so violent, so unjust . . .'. Echoing the interdisciplinary literature on working with figures of authority complicit in complex institutional power dynamics,[27] I have tried to approach these interlocutors beyond strict labels and categories. Through the intimacies of research, I have become entangled in their worlds. 'Entanglement', the anthropologist Anna Tsing claims, 'bursts categories and upends identities'.[28] Bureaucrats of victimhood are not 'repugnant others'.[29] Though they narrate complex relationships to both the violence of the armed conflict and the institutional violence in its wake, they are not quite 'perpetrators'.[30] And though some of them practice care, they are not wholly

---

[24] Gordon, *Ghostly Matters*, p. 64.
[25] Herzfeld, *The Social Production of Indifference*, p. 82.
[26] Didier Fassin, *At the Heart of the State: The Moral World of Institutions* (Pluto Press, 2015), p. x.
[27] Fujii, 'Shades of Truth'; Beatrice Jauregui, 'Intimacy: Personal Policing, Ethnographic Kinship, and Critical Empathy', in *Writing the World of Policing: The Difference Ethnography Makes*, edited by Didier Fassin (University of Chicago Press, 2017).
[28] Tsing, *Mushroom*, p. 138.
[29] Susan Harding, 'Representing Fundamentalism: The Problem of the Repugnant Cultural Other', *Social Research* 58, no. 2 (1991): 373–93.
[30] Kjell Anderson and Erin Jessee, eds., *Researching Perpetrators of Genocide* (University of Wisconsin Press, 2020).

caring professionals. By resisting these labels, I attempt to hold open the space for the professionals' own meanings and processes of sense-making: How do they frame and make sense of their own complicities—and complicities in what, exactly? What is their experience and understanding of power and its limits? Where do they see, find, create, and deny the political? What is their sense of goodness and justice, and how does it orient their work?

I have relied on bureaucrats' life stories to sketch answers to these questions. These start from premises similar to those behind other life stories about violence, namely that 'telling stories involves a negotiation about meaning, life, and relationships',[31] and that 'those stories were meant to be earned through trust and time'.[32] Stories are more meandering than interviews. I could—and, indeed, at times do—ask, 'What does "being the state" mean to you?' But I am more interested in the open-ended 'Tell me how you got here' and in letting my interlocutors define whether 'here' is a physical location in an office with fluorescent lights, or an institutional post, or an era of life. Starting with some version of 'Tell me how you got here'—in Spanish, literally, 'Tell me a story' [Cuéntame]—involves the body, memory, and feeling. Life stories of bureaucrats remind us that 'the life of the state has a corporal grounding'[33] and affective dimensions.[34]

Stories do not pour out unprompted. They are guided, encouraged, coaxed, and contested—by nods, by the 'mm-hmm' of empathy,[35] by raised eyebrows and arms folded across the chest, by verbal cues to elaborate and objections that 'surely, you've thought about . . .'. In reconstructing these life stories, I've narratively preserved my own presence as listener, inquirer, audience, writer/editor, companion, and critic, hoping that this creates space for interlocutors' narration in their own terms without the illusion of unfiltered-ness.

What, then, is the filter? Inspired by Gordon, I have interpreted bureaucrats' stories through the lens of complex personhood. 'Even those who haunt our dominant institutions and their systems of value', Gordon claims, 'are haunted too by things they sometimes have names for and sometimes do not'.[36] Complex personhood demands a lot from us as readers and

---

[31] Baines, *Buried in the Heart*, p. xv.
[32] Sebastián Ramírez, 'Making Home in War: An Ethnography on Reparations and Horizons in the Eve of Peace in Colombia' (PhD dissertation: Princeton University, 2019), p. 23.
[33] Uli Linke, 'Contact Zones: Rethinking the Sensual Life of the State', *Anthropological Theory* 6, no. 2 (2006): 206.
[34] Cooper, *Feeling Like a State*.
[35] Krystalli, 'Of Loss and Light', p. 43.
[36] Gordon, *Ghostly Matters*, p. 6.

audiences for stories, not only in terms of the ethics of inquiry, research, and writing, but also in terms of the ethics of listening and interpretation. When sharing bureaucrats' life stories at conferences and workshops, in published work and in the classroom, I often find that their complex personhood is disbelieved or outright denied. A common reaction is that bureaucrats are predictable, that we all already know who they are, what they wear, what they are like. Another is that bureaucrats are unreliable narrators. The implied, and sometimes articulated out loud question, becomes 'Why would you believe them?' 'Of course they think they are not the state!', a discussant will exclaim with the satisfaction of exposing a convenient lie.

I have tried to replace the predictability and satisfaction with curiosity. Denial and distancing—from 'the state', from formal authority, from power to meaningfully affect experiences of justice—are as analytically important as intimacy and goodness. While keeping a keen eye on the instrumentalization of narratives about the state, power, politics, and victimhood, I refuse to treat bureaucrats' life stories as purely or merely instrumental.[37] I am not a detective in a trench coat, seeking to shine a torch on the singular hidden truth of power. The task, rather, is to openly ask others about their beliefs, and to invest curiosity in the meanings with which they imbue them and the work those meanings do to create state, politics, power, and their associated hauntings during transitions from violence.[38]

Becoming and Unbecoming the State

'I was always very idealistic', Gabriela said, when prompted to reflect on how she joined the bureaucracy of victimhood.[39] 'I wanted to change society, change the world. I still am an idealist, but of a more grounded kind. How did I get here? It was a million years ago—let's see if I even remember'. Gabriela and I had this conversation six months after she had left a senior institutional post in the bureaucracy of victimhood. She still spoke of that post as 'here', and the seven years she had spent at different state institutions felt like a million. Both transitions from violence and being the state warp time and shuffle one's sense of location.

---

[37] Jauregui, 'Intimacy', p. 74.
[38] I'm indebted to Forero's beautiful and ethically complex enactment of these commitments in Colombia for teaching me how to practice this kind of curiosity. Forero, *El coronel.*
[39] Interview with former senior official in the bureaucracy of victimhood, August 2018.

'I joined straight after graduating. There were many of us: anthropologists, lawyers, some political scientists, some sociologists. We grew up with the conflict and we wanted to do something about it. Some had worked in the entities that came before the Victims' Unit,[40] but the big moment was that Santos was elected, and the Victims' Law became a reality. For me, it felt like the right time, like an opportune moment to wear the team shirt for my country, so to speak'. Like memory and truth, 'the state' becomes wearable too. Gabriela's trajectory was common, with many professionals citing some combination of their educational background, the timing of Santos's election, and the 2011 Victims' Law as propelling them towards state institutions of transitional justice.[41]

'I never worked for Avianca or anything like that.[42] Since the early 2000s, all of the jobs I had were of this type', Ximena said, referring to her post at the High Advisory for Victims, where she was a state representative and liaison to Mesas in peri-urban neighbourhoods of Bogotá.[43] In her understanding, something set work with victims apart from other professions. The 'something' became clearer to her over time. With a background in communications, television, and radio, Ximena became a press officer for a municipality on the topic of humanitarian response to displacement in the late 1990s. 'You could say that's how I started entering the world of development, as it was known then, and getting closer to social problems. I slowly realized it is one thing to be in a radio booth interviewing the lady who had an emergency and another to be out there with people, shoulder to shoulder, giving them humanitarian aid, discussing what they lost. From there, with every job I got, I got closer to the war', she said. In Ximena's narrative, proximity to the war and the victims it creates is in the rubbing of shoulders; closeness is tactile, not merely metaphorical. I asked her what she thought the difference was between this work and working for Avianca or, for that matter, the other state institutions she had been part of, such as the Ministry of Health. 'Victims...', she said, taking a long pause. 'It's something different, totally different. This is sacred work'.

Victims, in this account, refer not to the subjects who identify with this status, but to the professional domain of work that comes into being in

---

[40] For a great overview of these entities, see Vera, 'The Humanitarian State'.
[41] Vera uses the same phrase in his own ethnography of the humanitarian sector in Colombia, noting that many saw this time as 'an opportunity to wear the team shirt for our country'. Vera, 'The Humanitarian State', p. 48.
[42] Avianca is Colombia's biggest airline.
[43] Interview with High Advisory for Victims official in Bogotá, April 2018.

response to their existence. 'Suffering ennobles', Rudling argues, and it establishes victims as 'moral beacons . . . , which elevates them well above other members of society'.[44] The ennobling quality of victimhood attaches not only to victim subjects themselves, but also to professionals in bureaucracies of victimhood. The purported sanctity of victimhood, the apparent goodness of the mission to attend to those recognized as victims, draws people to the bureaucracy of transitional justice and sustains their work within it.

Becoming the state and 'getting closer to the war', as Ximena said, require learning, especially for professionals who did not have a background in working directly with people who had experienced harms. I asked Ximena about her process of learning how to do the job. 'The process?' She made a dismissive hand gesture. 'Back then, there was no process. Now we have everything: routes, capacity-building programs, trainings. Back then you go and do the job and learn from the people. I joined an early warning program in the territories with the Office of the Ombudsman. And so we began to go to the regions to look with the local defenders at what the communities were doing, how the communities were dialoguing with the institutions to move forward, despite the enormous difficulties of the panorama of war. I was there. In Montes de María, I learned the country and I learned the war'. A Victims' Unit official echoed the sentiment: 'You learn by doing. You learn from the victims and the territories'.

These narratives raise questions about where the responsibility of teaching and learning about violence and (in)justice lies, and about the processes by which knowledge comes into being. On the one hand, the approach Ximena articulated allows for the possibility of treating people who had experienced harms as 'bearers of essential knowledge'[45] who can affect professionals and the work of bureaucracies. For this possibility to be fully realized, however, professionals and bureaucracies would have to demonstrate that these encounters meaningfully shaped their work. Otherwise, the approach of 'learning from victims in the territories' reallocates the responsibility of training professionals from the state institutions that employed them to people who had suffered harm, who are required to renarrate those experiences without a clear sense of how the retelling might affect their search for justice. Crucially, as discussed in the previous chapter, the gendered and racialized insistence that 'the territories', uniformly imagined, are

---

[44] Rudling, 'I'm Not That', p. 24.
[45] Shepherd, *Gender, UN Peacebuilding*, pp. 142–43.

synonymous with suffering and exist as sites of training and education for people from capital cities reifies a hierarchical and binary relationship between places imagined as centres and those framed as peripheries.[46]

For some professionals, knowledge about victimhood was not the product of training, but of intimate experience. I opened my conversation with Samuel in the way I typically did when meeting these professionals for the first time. Tell me how you got here. How did you begin to work in this sector? Why did you choose to do this kind of work? 'Well, you might say that the sector chose me', Samuel said with a smile. 'On the eve of my thirteenth birthday, my father, who was a lifelong human rights defender, was assassinated'.[47]

The university board that must review what federal regulations term 'human subjects research' had approved two interview protocols for this research: one for those who identify or are recognized as victims of the armed conflict, and one for professionals interacting with them. Samuel's answer defied easy categorization into this binary. Over time, I would get to know eight more transitional justice professionals who publicly identified as victims, and many more who had directly or indirectly experienced victimization in the context of the armed conflict, but did not narrate their relation to the 'victim' label when discharging their professional duties.[48] 'You could say I am a victim-bureaucrat', a Victims' Unit official in Medellín said. The hyphen collapses easy distinctions between 'the state' and 'the victims' and forms a tenuous—sometimes hopeful, sometimes tense—bridge between bureaucrats and the people who seek their attention.

For people like Samuel, the identity of 'victim', memories of the conflict, and professional motivations all shaped the path into the bureaucracy. 'You know, my family was one of inter-generational activism', he said. 'My grandfather was an activist, my father was a human rights defender. I became interested in law and criminology, but my mother worried I would run many risks in this country because of my family. So I left for a bit, went abroad, studied law. But I found it so boring. I needed something to move me from within. And I also believed that this country needed to listen to voices who could speak to the perspective of victimization, which is very powerful. . . . So I decided to work with victims' issues'.

---

[46] Serje, *Revés de la nación*; Ramírez, *Between the guerrillas*; Vera, 'The Humanitarian State'.
[47] Interview with state official in Bogotá, January 2018.
[48] For more on the lives of these professionals, see Krystalli, 'Being Seen'.

For those who had not experienced the violence of the conflict quite so directly, memories of conflict-related events still shaped professional trajectories. 'The massacre of Salado—that impacted me tremendously', a former state official said. 'It changed what I studied, what I wanted to do'.[49] A different official echoed: 'The massacres of Urabá, and then all the disappearances were in the news. I began really paying attention'.[50] When I teach feminist theories in global politics, I ask students to reflect on their earliest political memory. Without predefining politics, I invite them to consider when they first recall encountering 'the political'. The premise of the prompt is that memories are formative, and they shape ideas about who does politics, how, and with what effect. For many professionals in bureaucracies of victimhood who grew up during the armed conflict, albeit at different distances from it, memories of violence and politics alike entered the frame in early childhood and influenced these professionals' ideas about who they would become.

State bureaucracies represent only one pathway for pursuing justice-oriented work. Many of my interlocutors had initially done this kind of work as part of the vast constellation of NGOs and victims' associations in Colombia. Though many of these victims' associations and NGOs were formed in active opposition to state policies on justice and the armed conflict, the transitional justice industry is quite a porous professional universe. Professionals move between organizations and highlight the permeability of the boundaries of 'state' and 'civil society'.[51] These are not easy movements. Prior experience in NGOs and activist groups endowed professionals with invaluable expertise and relationships that at times facilitated their work within state bureaucracies,[52] but the process of transition into state entities was challenging.

Becoming the state comes with relational costs. 'When I left an activist organization to work for the state, my friends said to me, "You are formalizing impunity"', a former senior official at the Victims' Unit shared.[53] Others spoke of a sense of betrayal that haunted them after leaving the world of

---

[49] Interview with former state official in Bogotá, January 2018.
[50] Interview with Victims' Unit official in Bogotá, November 2017.
[51] Veena Das and Deborah Poole, eds., *Anthropology in the Margins of the State* (School of American Research, 2004).
[52] As Tate's research on the state-NGO nexus in the Putumayo region of Colombia has highlighted, connections with well-established NGOs can allow certain 'state officials greater political space'. Tate, 'The Aspirational State', p. 248.
[53] Interview with former Victims' Unit official in Bogotá, November 2017.

professional activism and joining 'the state'—and sometimes after leaving 'the state' too. The effects of becoming the state in the eyes of people who oppose it are lasting. Unbecoming the state is a complicated project. 'It's very unjust', a former senior official said.

> It was very difficult after I left the [Victims'] Unit. First of all, I was exhausted. Dead. Spent. And then, when I was slowly beginning to think about what I will do next and who will I be, I found myself constantly attacked. Why? Because I had been part of the state. I wish I could say to all these people attacking the officials: we do this work with commitment, with our sleeves rolled up. We do it to make the world better. To do that from 'inside' is not easy, you know. And then to deal with this stigma after you leave. Why? Because you tried to make the world better.[54]

In our conversations about these tensions, my interlocutors often had phantom exchanges, rehearsing what they would say to their critics—or, more accurately, critical friends—if they could. 'I want to say to these people, "Wait a minute, I'm still your friend"', Gabriela said. 'I still have the same politics. We are all fighting for the same things'.[55] In these narratives, the mark of 'the state' is imagined to be indelible on a professional trajectory and life story. 'Obviously, I am not the person to pity', a former state official who subsequently joined the private sector said.[56] 'Thank God, I have everything I need, all the privilege you could imagine. I found another job, my colleagues are nice, everything is good. But you can still notice something, especially in certain circles: my hands are still contaminated for having been an official of the Colombian state'. These interlocutors are often aware that 'the state' is not singularly a pollutant, nor is the NGO or activist sphere entirely pure, but this knowledge does not always ease the judgment they encounter when moving between worlds.

The anthropologist María Victoria Uribe, who had been part of the Grupo de Memoria Histórica, commented on a notable peculiarity in the trajectories of these professionals. 'How strange it is', she said, 'that this recruitment happens in a mostly right-wing country like Colombia, in which the historical rejection of the communist individuals that oppose the political system and those that have been considered close or related to the Left

---

[54] Interview with former senior official at the Victims' Unit in Bogotá, August 2018.
[55] Interview with former senior official in the bureaucracy of victimhood, August 2018.
[56] Interview with former state official in Medellín, April 2018.

is evident'.[57] She concludes this reflection with a question: 'How could one understand that the Colombian state hires people ... from the same armed groups that have declared war on it or from the territories that have historically been abandoned to their own luck?'[58] A possible explanation for this paradox lies in the different kinds of expertise these professionals embody and carry with them, and the ways that expertise creates a particular image of the state during the transition from violence. Proximity to the violence of the conflict, and the victim experiences and claims that emanated from it, endows professionals not only with a potentially relevant form of expertise, but also with the legitimacy to carry out their work on transitional justice. However, doing that work from within the state, and *as* the state, also highlights the contrasts with other institutional locations and positionings.

Diego's pathway to the bureaucracy of victimhood was unusual, but not unique. He had spent seventeen years in the Popular Liberation Army (EPL), a Marxist-Leninist guerrilla group. 'I was raised in a paisa, conservative, religious family', he said.[59] 'They are Uribistas now. The EPL hooked my brother first.[60] In the 1970s, it was individual recruitment like that. I was next, and I think it was because I saw it as a rupture with the religiosity of my family. I didn't see it that way then, of course, but I see it now'. Though his life within the armed group unfolded nearly four decades before our conversation, he spoke of it in the present tense: 'It is a para-society, a para-family. We call ourselves 'uncle' and 'nephew'. We dream of a future among ourselves. And we gave life as an organization to people who had nothing, who were marginalized. We gave them a uniform and an opportunity to belong. We gave them a role and a weapon. We gave life to people. We also gave death'.

Diego told this story while wearing one of the fluorescent vests that had become a metonymy for the state.[61] I asked how he went from wearing the uniform of a guerrilla to the uniform of the state. 'Well, over time I noticed that war is shit, and it wasn't going anywhere. So if I wanted to live, I had to leave the group. I convinced a lot of people to demobilize with me; it wasn't just a question of leaving alone. My first job was with a foundation because the director had also been [in the] EPL. That was important—if he hadn't given me that first job, who knows where I would be now. Then the mayor's

[57] Uribe in Krystalli, 'Being Seen', n.p.
[58] Uribe in Krystalli, 'Being Seen', n.p.
[59] Interview with High Advisory for Victims official in Bogotá, May 2018.
[60] Ejército Popular de Liberación (EPL), created in the 1960s.
[61] The vests of the state became a metonymy, a symbol, and a material presence during the transition from armed conflict in Colombia. See Lederach, *Feel the Grass Grow*.

office, then victims' issues for the municipality, working on reconciliation with ex-combatants'.

Reflecting on the differences in working for different non-state entities, and on his impressions when first starting to work with the state on victims' issues, Diego said: 'Look, our model of attention to victims is good, but it lacks political content. Do you understand me?' His 'our' was 'the state', with which he now identified. 'Having political content means talking about power. We barely ever talk about power. We have a lot of data, databases, variables, processes. But we barely ever talk in our institutions about what is political about victims and about working with them. Being in the EPL or in any NGO, we talked about power all the time'. In Diego's experience, being the state with a mandate to attend to victims could often be reduced to acronyms, indicators, and processes, which, in the words of Sally Merry, can fly 'under the radar of social and political analysis as a form of power'.[62]

Many of these stories highlight continuities and ruptures—of motivations, convictions, relationships, loyalties, and solidarities alike. For Carmen, joining the bureaucracy represented a rupture with her own past. 'I was different from some of the others on the Victims' Team', Carmen told me.[63] 'I realized this immediately when I joined. Most of them are militant leftists. I went to a private university, my friends are all in a high economic stratum,[64] I voted 'no' in the referendum, I used to be with the Democratic Center Party'.[65] I had many questions: Why did she join the state bureaucracy to work with victims, if it was so radically different from her background? Would she vote 'no' again? 'Never! Never, never, never', she emphasized, laughing. 'This job has changed me. It's more than a job, it's a whole life, with my heart set [con el corazón puesto]. I took the job because my dad, who is on the left of this country, said to me, "Go work with victims for a bit and see what you think". My mum is on the right. She cannot figure out why I do what I do. She

---

[62] Merry, *The Seductions of Quantification*, p. 5.
[63] Interview with Municipal Victims' Team official in Antioquia, February 2018.
[64] Stratum is a system of socioeconomic classification in Colombia. It manifests in the classification of buildings and neighbourhoods, particularly in large metropolitan regions such as Bogotá, where areas are marked from one (the lowest) to six (the highest). The concept and practice are related to socioeconomic class, but do not fully map on to it. For more, see Ana Marcos, 'Los estratos en Colombia: Eres el lugar en el que vives', *El País*, April 22, 2018, https://elpais.com/internacional/2018/04/20/colombia/1524176587_818282.html.
[65] The Democratic Center is a political party in Colombia, cofounded in 2014 by former president Álvaro Uribe, former vice-president Francisco Santos Calderón, and former minister of finance Óscar Zuluaga. Though self-described as a centrist party, its stance has been right-wing and conservative. This has included opposition to the 2016 peace accords and party politicians actively supporting Donald Trump's re-election campaign in the 2020 US presidential race.

says to me all the time, "Ay ay ay, my daughter, you've changed". I regret profoundly this vote in the referendum. It haunts me every day'.

It is tempting to read these stories like a typology—the idealistic bureaucrat, the victim-bureaucrat, the unlikely bureaucrat. Typologies can be helpful for illuminating different pathways and motivations to join the bureaucracy of victimhood. I am, however, more interested in reading these life stories *as* stories, with curiosity about the visions of the state and victimhood that they bring to light. Revisiting them a few years after I first heard them, I am newly attentive to the 'hauntings, ghosts and gaps, seething absences, and muted presences'.[66] Hauntings and ghosts are not merely rhetorical devices or theoretical frameworks imposed on experiences; rather, they recurred in the language and sense-making processes of professionals within bureaucracies of victimhood.

Some of the haunting is in the pronouns: The 'we' of the state is—and, crucially, is seen as—different from the 'we' of those who work on justice and victims' issues outside the state. In this instance, it matters little that the 'we' of the state is as multifaceted, shifting, and fragmented as its professionals, or that the space between 'state' and 'non-state' can be porous, calling into question the conceptual and practical relevance of the binary imagination. Becoming part of the state and its pronouns can often mean being in conflict with those who, often with very good reason, are fearful of, sceptical about, or critical of the state and its interventions. The state's 'we' haunts across time horizons, leaving its mark on relationships and reputations even after people have left state bureaucracies.

Hauntings and longings coexist. Nowhere is this more evident than in the meanings with which people invest bureaucracies of victimhood. These are affective investments: Samuel needed to 'be moved from within'. Ximena wanted to sit shoulder to shoulder. Professionals speak of wearing the team shirt, and of putting their heart into their work. They are spurred by personal experience or formative memories of violence and injustice, and fuelled by a desire for meaning, a longing to do work that matters. Victimhood is not incidental to this longing; on the contrary, what Rodríguez calls the 'moral charge' of victimhood anchored and oriented the work.[67]

The weight of meanings that different actors pin onto the status of 'victim' is significant to this story. 'Victim' is more than a label that makes people

---

[66] Gordon, *Ghostly Matters*, p. 21.
[67] Rodríguez, 'La naturalización', p. 17.

legible to 'the state' as particular kinds of subjects who can, in turn, make rights-based claims. It becomes a symbolic terrain, proximity to which can grant goodness by association. Victimhood is also imagined as a school, a site of education and learning, a moral compass that orients people's work and gives their (not just professional) lives meaning. This reality is not dissimilar to how the livelihoods, professional identities, and sense of purpose of other humanitarians working in 'regimes of care'[68] are linked to the existence of suffering, violated subjects.[69] What is particular about professionals in bureaucracies of victimhood, however, is that their livelihood and professional identity also derives from being part of *state* entities—in the same state that has been, simultaneously, violator and duty-bearer of transitional justice. The process of inquiring about how these professionals make sense of that complex positioning reveals more ghosts.

Ghosts of the State

Becoming the state means having to become fluent in a bureaucratic vernacular of victimhood. 'There is a technical vocabulary of victims', Antonio said.[70] 'My friend and I have a list and we add whatever the term of the moment is. For example, 'articulate'. The state is always 'articulating' and 'interlocuting' with the victims. When I first joined, I had to learn the acronyms, of course, the routes, the flow charts, but also the vocabulary'.

The term 'institutionality' [institucionalidad] was a cornerstone of the vernacular of victimhood. Many professionals would speak of being part of the institucionalidad, rather than relying on the language of 'the state'. I preserve institucionalidad in its Spanish form here because it does not neatly map on to an English translation; it refers to more than a single institution, and the clunky language of 'institutionality' does not quite capture the meanings of institucionalidad. When I asked a legal researcher who was a former state official to explain the nuances, she said, 'We have an awful lot of institutions in Colombia, but the institucionalidad is more than institutions. It is more abstract than a single entity. It is a gigantic ghost of the Colombian state'.[71]

---

[68] Ticktin, *Casualties of Care*, p. 3.
[69] Fassin and Pandolfi, *Contemporary States of Emergency*.
[70] Interview with Victims' Unit official in Bogotá, September 2017.
[71] Interview with former state official in Bogotá, March 2018.

Though it defies easy conceptualization, the institucionalidad makes itself known and felt in the lives of people who constitute it and seek its attention. It is both material *and* difficult to pin down. 'The Mesa called the institucionalidad on Friday night', a liaison to one such Mesa said to me on a Monday morning. The dual metonymy of Mesa and institucionalidad makes both entities ungraspable: Who called whom? In my conversations with bureaucrats, the institucionalidad was simultaneously a collective subject and an abstract place, at which people showed up, demanded, complained. The ghostly quality of the institucionalidad means that the diffuse incarnations of 'the state' sometimes remain a mystery even to the people who bring that state into being. This was sincerely a mystery, in that few state officials could concretely point to all manifestations of the institucionalidad when it came to the bureaucracy of victimhood. At the same time, rhetorical reliance on 'the institucionalidad' was a convenient mystery too, in that the un-pin-down-able quality of the institucionalidad, and its treatment as an abstract, collective subject, could more readily absolve any individual bureaucrat of a sense of meaningful accountability.

María Fernanda said, 'I think that going into defining something that one is part of is hard, but I'm going to try. When I speak of institucionalidad, what I am referring to is the possibility that an issue is recognized as problematic from the framework of a public policy agenda. This means that there are organizations that become responsible for it, tasks, budgets, practices, protocols, and routes. In our case, there is an institucionalidad for victims'.[72] She continued: 'Look at the issues don't have an institucionalidad behind them. Take the issue of forced recruitment [of people into armed groups]. It is massively important, but without a dedicated institucionalidad, it does not receive enough attention. Without institucionalidad, the issue loses its political charge. The victims don't get attention if there's no institucionalidad'.

The institucionalidad, then, is intricately linked to understandings of the politics of victimhood, and state power and authority to shape them. According to this account, politicization of the 'victim' subject occurs *through* the state and, specifically, through its bureaucratic mechanisms. 'What the institucionalidad does', a Victims' Unit official said, 'is that it converts victims to subjects of state attention, and that is how they enter our lives and can access resources'.[73] The existence of an institucionalidad, with its staff and

---

[72] Interview with Ministry of Interior official in Antioquia, March 2018.
[73] Interview with Victims' Unit official in Bogotá, December 2017.

acronyms and budgets and flow charts, is some of how 'the state' assumes responsibility over an issue and begins to enact mechanisms to address it. Power and authority, in this instance, refer to the capacity to effect change, to respond to an issue that 'the state' has identified as a public policy problem.

The possibility of exercising that power and authority, in turn, drew some professionals to bureaucracies of victimhood. 'I believe profoundly in the work of the state, and I think it is the most important work', Daniela began.[74] We were sitting in her office in a municipal entity in Antioquia, surrounded by ferns. Declaring that she was 'the gardener around here', she'd frequently get up mid-conversation to pick a dead frond off a plant or empty a glass of water into a nearby pot. She had worked for seven different state entities with a mandate to assist the displaced and, subsequently, those recognized as victims of the conflict. Given the many candid criticisms of the state that she had shared over time, I was surprised by her profound belief in state work. She said: 'I would never change it for anything. I know all the difficulties, but I also know all the possibilities. And I know too that the state is not the same everywhere, that it is not homogenous. There are many states, and many spots of resistance within the state'.

'One does not have to be the president to affect change from within the state. The president probably does less in a day than I do in my little office most days', Daniela laughed. 'The thing is, the difference is, that many of us who work on the matter of victims do not do it out of obligation. It became a passion, and we try to correct problems. I work with the institucionalidad because I wanted to resolve problems through it. We, as the state, can affect communities through the re-establishment of their rights in ways other entities cannot'. Passion and power go hand in hand in Daniela's understanding of her work.

I asked her to explain further, to shed light on what, in her opinion, 'the state' could do vis-à-vis people recognized as victims that other entities could not. 'Victim is a card for calling and directing the attention of the state to a particular subject. . . . That is why the institucionalidad matters. The victim does not exist only for the state, of course', she conceded. 'But what the state can do *as a state* for victims is enormous'. Others echoed this sentiment. 'I manage privileged information because I am part of the state', a senior state official said. 'That information can help victims, so they see me as their connection to power'.[75] Power here refers to the state's ability to confer statuses

---

[74] Interview with Municipal Victims' Team official in Antioquia, February 2018.
[75] Interview with senior state official in Medellín, February 2018.

and determine the distribution of resources on the basis of them. This is an account of power that is *necessarily* state-centric, which is a different understanding of power than one would arrive at if one explored, for example, the meanings with which people who identify as victims infuse that category. The state-centric notion of power, of course, is not foreign or invisible to people recognized as victims, some of whom choose to interact with state entities precisely because they seek such recognition and resources.

Power to effect change is full of promise. Many state officials felt the possibilities of being the state vis-à-vis people recognized as victims. Haunting, however, enters the picture again, at the moment at which it becomes apparent that the possibility unfolds on a different plane than its fulfilment. According to Berlant, 'Optimism is cruel when the object/scene that ignites a scene of possibility actually makes it impossible to attain the expansive transformation for which a person or a people risks striving.'[76] The existence of the institucionalidad represented possibility and, simultaneously, served as the explanation for the slowness of fulfilment. When asked what it means to have power within the institucionalidad, many interlocutors lamented the lack of it. Power was, apparently, always elsewhere.

'The problem is, we have no teeth [no tenemos dientes]', an official at the High Advisory for Human Rights said.[77] 'Other state institutions collaborate with us because we are nice. They like us. But it's not the same to be an adviser as it is to be a minister'. Explanations for the purported lack of power proliferated and varied. Power lies with ministries, not high advisories. Power lies with municipalities that interact with people who identify as victims in the day-to-day, not with centralized, national-level entities. Or power lies primarily with national-level entities that allocate budgets and write regulations, not with municipalities that 'just' implement them in regions framed as 'the periphery'. Power lies with elected officials and politicians, *and* politicians don't get as much done in a day as Daniela does in her little office full of ferns. Power lies with the law and the entities that craft it, contest it, and enforce it. Highlighting the deference to what Julieta Lemaitre calls 'legal fetishism',[78] a Victims' Unit senior official told me: 'I do what the Constitutional Court tells me. The Constitutional Court is my boss'.[79] Wherever the researcher

---

[76] Berlant, *Cruel Optimism*, p. 2.
[77] Interview with High Advisory for Human Rights official in Bogotá, January 2018.
[78] Julieta Lemaitre, 'Legal Fetishism: Law, Violence, and Social Movements in Colombia'. *Revista Juridica Universidad de Puerto Rico* 77 (2008): 331; Pellegrino, 'Between the Roll of Paper', p. 82.
[79] Interview with senior official at the Victims' Unit in Bogotá, October 2017.

goes looking for the materiality, rather than possibility, of power within the institucionalidad, she is unlikely to find it because power is limited or resides elsewhere. The ghost of state power haunts those who crave and deny it.

Some professionals speak back to and challenge this apparently spectral account of power in bureaucracies of victimhood. 'Stop following the court and embrace policymaking', a street-level bureaucrat at the Victims' Unit said, referring to the justifications his higher-ups offered for the slowness of action.[80] 'Assume your political mandate. Otherwise, what are you? An ATM [cajero] that pays out. You end up being a bank'. Accounts of origin stories, power, and politics are disputed accounts, and, as the next chapter elaborates, the contestations of state power and politics vis-à-vis victimhood do not only emerge from those who work outside or oppose 'the state'. 'The entire existence of this institucionalidad is due to the pressure and mobilization of social actors', a former state official said. 'These institutions were a response to demand'.[81]

The institucionalidad becomes one way 'the state' makes its presence known and felt in the lives of its professionals and the citizens who seek their attention. It represents both the possibility of power—to name subjectivities and endow them with rights, to create pathways for claims based on those rights, to allocate resources to the fulfilment of those rights—and the elusiveness, denial, and limits of that power. In this way, the existence of the institucionalidad evidences *and* obscures state action for those recognized as victims of the armed conflict; it simultaneously creates the possibility of action and the 'moral alibi for inaction'.[82]

In these ways, the institucionalidad on victimhood becomes part of the logic of what the anthropologist Valentina Pellegrino brilliantly terms 'complying incompliantly' [incumplir cumpliendo], 'a type of governmental response to a problem that it is responsible for solving'. Complying incompliantly 'consists of the government ostensibly *acting like* it is solving a problem without these actions *solving* anything, and yet having the response favourably evaluated'.[83] Complying incompliantly, with state responsibilities and legal obligations alike, is more than a strategy, device, or technique. It is not merely visible to critical researchers or state sceptics, but also obvious to many of the people who embody and enact the state. Like Pellegrino, 'I

---

[80] Interview with street-level bureaucrat at the Victims' Unit, July 2016.
[81] Interview with former state official in Bogotá, June 2018.
[82] Herzfeld, *The Social Production of Indifference*, p. 33.
[83] Pellegrino, 'Between the Roll of Paper', p. 80.

Figure 4.1 A partial view of a transitional justice bureaucrat's office. Written on the blackboard: 'I am sorry. Forgive Me. I love you. Thank you.'

hesitate to elucidate complying incompliantly as conscious intentionality, not to let state officials off the hook, but because this reduces the role of mediations and institutional arrangements that need further study'.[84]

Feeling Like a Good State

'I am sorry. Forgive me. I love you. Thank you'.[85] These were the words written on María Fernanda's whiteboard at the Ministry of Interior (figure 4.1). When I asked her about them, she said, 'They are the words you need to do the job well'.[86] 'Justice involves feelings', Sara Ahmed argues, which 'move us across the surfaces of the world, creating ripples in the intimate contours

---

[84] Pellegrino, 'Between the Roll of Paper', p. 82.
[85] Though María Fernanda did not explicitly make this connection, the phrase is associated with the Ho'oponopono, an ancient Hawaiian practice of forgiveness and reconciliation.
[86] Interview with Ministry of Interior official in Antioquia, March 2018.

of our lives'.[87] Feelings also reverberate across the intimate contours of the lives of justice professionals. When asked how they navigate 'being the state' in the eyes of people who identify as victims, bureaucrats express themselves in intensely affective terms. Feeling saturates the physical spaces of the institucionalidad, not just the narratives of the bureaucrats who constitute it.

Like power, feeling can reveal itself in the moments of its denial. 'Hopefully they like me, but I never cared that they love me', a senior official at the High Advisory for Victims responded, when asked about being the state in encounters with people who identify as victims.[88] 'I never cared that they love me', she repeated. The 'we' of the state splintered into a personal 'I' and an abstract 'they'. 'I'm not interested in that kind of politics', she concluded, leaving the kind of politics premised on love unspecified.[89]

This rhetorical distancing from the tone of one's relationships with claimants was easier for senior officials than for street- and mid-level bureaucrats who encountered people recognized as victims every day. For this latter group, a perceived sense of care not only *for* claimants appearing before the state, but also *from* them towards state officials became essential for sustaining the work. These warm relations with claimants had many names, with love, trust, respect, and care all appearing recurrently in these professionals' vernacular of victimhood. Crucially, whatever one called the nature of the relations, they emphasized the manifestation of feeling in actions, such as phoning or seeking the attention of a particular bureaucrat as opposed to others. 'I know that they like me, they trust me, some maybe even love me', a street-level bureaucrat at the Ministry of Justice told me.[90] When I asked how he knew, he laughed: 'Roxani, how do you ever know someone loves you?' I smiled and shrugged, conceding the point. He continued: 'They tell me, they call me, they say, 'Hey, can you help me with this?', and they know I always will. Or at least I try to'.

Bureaucrats of transitional justice were not simply content to narrate emotional proximity to those recognized as victims; they insisted on providing evidence in support of it. The evidence performs a certificatory function,

---

[87] Sara Ahmed, *The Cultural Politics of Emotion* (Edinburgh University Press, 2014), p. 202.

[88] Interview with senior official at the High Advisory for Victims in Bogotá, October 2018.

[89] I wish I had asked more about this at the time. Alas, I did not sufficiently start to pay attention to these politics of love and care in research until more recently. Q Manivannan, 'Imagining a Care Curriculum', KCL Feminist Perspectives, May 11, 2022, https://www.kcl.ac.uk/imagining-a-care-curriculum; Roxani Krystalli and Philipp Schulz, 'Taking Love and Care Seriously: An Emergent Research Agenda for Remaking Worlds in the Wake of Violence'. *International Studies Review* 24, no. 1 (2022): 1–25.

[90] Interview with Ministry of Justice official in Bogotá, November 2017.

wherein 'the victims' attest to the goodness of 'the state'—or at least, of specific officials within it. In this vision, 'the victims' implicitly become reliable witnesses of a high moral standing, and their judgment of 'the state' and its officials seems to carry a lot of weight. After I had observed a daylong meeting of a Mesa in Antioquia, Carmen, the state facilitator who had voted against the plebiscite asked me to accompany her for a coffee across the street. 'Ufff', she began, 'how do you think that went?' Before I had the chance to respond, she pulled up her cell phone, opened WhatsApp, and showed me her recent texts with elected victim representatives to that Mesa. 'Look! Ten messages from them, from just this morning. I'm the only one they trust. It's because I'm good to them'. I had seen this before: the phone with WhatsApp messages passed across the table as a plea for interpretation, with the recipient of messages hoping that they are a testament to a bond.

I sensed the urgency with which Carmen (and many professionals like her) wanted to be good—not just good at the job, but seen as good *to* those recognized as victims with whom she interacted.[91] The politics of victimhood structure not only ideas about good victims, but also expectations of what it means to be a good state official within the bureaucracy of victimhood.[92] Just as the bureaucrats' life histories and pathways into the profession varied, so did their ideas of goodness. For some, goodness was defined by opposition to an imagined, abstract 'average bureaucrat', the caricature of whom will be familiar to readers across contexts. 'I am not the standard state official [funcionario]', a professional at the High Advisory for Victims said.[93] 'In general, they just look at their notebooks and say, "These are my obligations, and that's it". . . . Or they are arrogant. This is how you give the state a bad name'. Professionals were aware that the name of the state depended on their conduct, and rhetorically distinguished themselves from those who marred it.

For other officials, goodness was evident in sustaining warm relations with those recognized as victims, in verbally and practically reaffirming affection,

---

[91] Ravecca and Dauphinee argue that the desire for goodness is some of what drives the attachments and pleas to innocence and denials of complicity in unequal power structures. In their words, 'The locus of that "good", and how it might appear, are the subject of philosophical, historical, political, and theological debates that have unfolded in deeply complicated and inevitably power-mediated ways. The trouble we find is how visions of the good become an unassailable and unquestionable fetish around which attachments to innocence orbit, thus becoming servile to the expressions of power that cohere in the ways we have described'. Ravecca and Dauphinee, 'What's Left for Critique?', p. 44.

[92] For similar reflections in a different context, see Heath Cabot's research on 'good police officers' working on asylum procedures in Greece. Heath Cabot, 'The Good Police Officer: Ambivalent Intimacies with the State in the Greek Asylum Procedure', in *The Anthropology of Police*, edited by Kevin Karpiak and William Garriott (Routledge, 2018).

[93] Interview with High Advisory for Victims official in Bogotá, May 2018.

trust, and an ongoing bond. For yet others, the 'good state official' was a rebel, who broke from the party line of 'the state' and resisted institutional norms in ways they perceived to favour those recognized as victims. 'You have to talk to my supervisor', an official on the gender team said.[94] 'She's a really good soul. She's not your standard son-of-a-bitch [hijoeputa] state official. She is a revolutionary, a rebel. She constantly pushes back, she breaks all the rules'. A logic of exception and distinction underpinned this yearning for goodness, as though proximity, in the sense of both emotional closeness and acts of solidarity, with people recognized as victims set some professionals apart. And, at the same time, there was a quiet hope that goodness was generalizable, that the goodness of particular officials can boil up, like steam off the nozzle of a kettle, and give a virtuous face to the state as a whole.[95]

These relational bonds—aspirational and present, narrated and evidenced—were another reminder that the existence of victims of the armed conflict, and the corresponding creation of 'institutionality', also make the state during transitions from violence. The closer 'the institutionality' can claim to stand to 'the victims', the stronger the image of the virtuous state becomes. In one of the offices of the registry team at the Victims' Unit, a calendar featured a smiling, dark-skinned woman, accompanied by the caption '8 million reasons to reconstruct the social fabric'.[96] 'We work for 8 million reasons', a different poster echoed at the Ministry of Justice, again featuring a darker-skinned woman and a man in a straw hat standing in tall grass (figure 4.2). The 'we' of the state incarnating during the-time-of-not-war-not-peace relies on victimhood, in all its racialized, gendered, and classed valances. 'For the victims, for the peace', read the Victims' Unit banners that officials dragged to the front of the room before many Mesa meetings. The posters named no actors and no actions. Naming the intended recipients and outcomes was the crucial vector for bringing, as the tagline announced, 'a new country' into being.

---

[94] Interview with state official in Bogotá, June 2018.
[95] I'm grateful for Burneyat's frame of the face of the state and Dávila's understanding of the virtuous state for helping me think about these nuances. Burnyeat, *The Face of Peace*; Dávila, 'The Land of Lawyers'.
[96] At the time, there were approximately eight million individuals recognized as victims of the armed conflict.

MAKING THE (GOOD) STATE   127

Figure 4.2 A banner displayed at a Victims' Unit event in 2018 reads, 'We work for eight million reasons', accompanied by photos of people presumed to be victims of the armed conflict. The logos 'all for a new country: peace, equality, education' and 'Victims' Unit' are visible at the top.

'It's Not Me, It's the State'

Narratives and practices of love and care coexist with those of hate and carelessness. Nearly every life story relating people's pathways into the bureaucracy contained a retelling of a formative moment in which professionals realized the ruptures and conflicts that would come with this role. Gabriela narrated an incident early in her tenure as a state official working on returns of forcibly displaced people to the areas from which they had fled. 'We were in Bolívar, in Montes de María, but something like this also happened in Chocó another time. We were there to talk about a program of collective reparation. We started talking to the community leaders, to explain to them the program and all that. And from one moment to another, they started to give us stick [darnos palo]. That the state is always corrupt, and this and that. And I thought 'yes, of course, everyone knows that this [corruption] happens, but we are here as the state with a legitimate interest in doing things for them'. We were there to serve them, to repair them,[97] in the end, which is our mandate. I felt very frustrated. I wanted to cry. So much hate'.[98]

A former official at the Victims' Unit who now works at an international organization said, 'That job at the Unit made me appreciate public officials. What I found with victims was that they hated me'.[99] How did she know this? 'They told me! Every chance they got'. A different official, whose partner worked within a state agency, said, 'I have been married to the bureaucracy of victims that you study. Let me tell you. Those first few months were difficult. My wife would come home and say, son of a bitch, they really hate me!'[100] These feelings became their own sort of haunting, spilling over from professional encounters and offices into the home, and remaining memorable for years.

State officials who had previously worked in NGOs or alongside victims' groups were particularly frustrated by tense encounters with people with whom they previously enjoyed constructive, even warm, relationships. This was a problem of temporality: the present shouted louder than the past. It was also a problem of location: In the eyes of those seeking state attention, who were often disappointed in the amount and quality of that attention, being a professional of a state bureaucracy in the present was more visible than any work from other institutional locations in the past. In an imagined conversation with her critics, one official said: 'I want to tell the victims, "I am on your side. I work for you. I have always been with you". But they don't see me that way. They see me and they only see the state'.[101] A mid-level official at the Ministry of Justice used similar language: 'I am their friend, I have

---

[97] In Spanish, 'reparar' is an active verb, referring both to the act of offering reparations in the context of transitional justice and to the act of mending (e.g., a broken object).
[98] Interview with former senior official in the bureaucracy of victimhood, August 2018.
[99] Interview with former Victims' Unit official in Bogotá, November 2017.
[100] Interview with state official in Bogotá, October 2017.
[101] Interview with state official in Bogotá, August 2016.

always been', he said, referring to (undifferentiated) victims. 'I came out of activism pure and hard [puro y duro]. But because I'm now the state, they see me as something other, something different. I have something of the institutionality in me. My past does not matter'.[102]

Having something of the institutionality in oneself becomes its own kind of haunting, with the institutionality framed as a pathogen that causes ills. The antidotes varied. Most state officials did not dispute the legitimacy of the anger among people who identified as victims. Instead, they attested to the hate and frustration being justifiable, and a product of being the state at a time of lacking public policy fulfilment. While professionals within bureaucracies interpreted goodness to stem primarily from personal actions and relationships and from proximity to people recognized as victims, they attributed hate to disillusionment with 'the state' writ large. 'I know they are not mad at us', one official said. 'The institutional offer for victims is not sufficient.... The victims know this, and they see us as their political enemy for being state officials'.[103]

This pattern recurred throughout my conversations with bureaucrats: goodness was imagined to be intensely personal and stemming from the behaviour of individual professionals; hate was directed 'at the state', framed as separate from the professionals who incarnated it. In his study of bureaucracy in Greece, Herzfeld found that 'people generally hold character responsible for their own successes and others' failures',[104] and attribute faults to 'bureaucracy as "the system", which . . . becomes an impersonal force on which all manner of individual and collective misfortunes may be blamed'.[105] In the Colombian context, professionals' proximity to victimhood, through personal experience or caring conduct, allowed for an image of 'the good state' to come into being, while distancing from bureaucratic authority shielded those same professionals from the ills and conflicts of being the state.

---

[102] Interview with mid-level official at the Ministry of Justice in Bogotá, January 2018. Victim-bureaucrats, by contrast, occupied a different position by virtue of their identification with the status of 'victim' and their simultaneous positioning within the state. For more on this, see Krystalli, 'Being Seen'.

[103] Interview with High Advisory for Victims official in Bogotá, June 2018.

[104] Herzfeld, *The Social Production of Indifference*, p. 135.

[105] Herzfeld, *The Social Production of Indifference*, p. 147. Javier Auyero finds a similar tendency to attribute all flaws to 'the system' and all virtues to personal qualities in his ethnography of the politics of waiting in Argentina. Javier Auyero, *Patients of the State: The Politics of Waiting in Argentina* (Duke University Press, 2012), pp. 115–16.

'Bureaucracy sucks the soul; bureaucracy is ethics in action', Lea posits. 'It stands in the way of freedom; it is freedom's insurance.... The oppositions express the anthropological challenge: How do we grapple with such a promiscuous concept?'[106] Tracing the life histories of bureaucrats with curiosity about their complex personhood, and exploring their professional trajectories into state entities of transitional justice, has shed light on the affective, relational nature of becoming, being, and being seen like the state during transitions from violence.

Revisiting the stories of transitional justice professionals through the hauntings they narrated and experienced was at times a dizzying exercise. I asked myself whether the 'disappointing state' was the more common material reality, with the 'good state' as its ghost. I realized, however, that attempting to pin down hauntings, to definitively identify a singular ghost, is premised on a relationship to truth, knowledge, and experience different from the one informing this inquiry on bureaucracies and the politics of victimhood. The power of haunting lies not in its singular determination, but in its interpretative ambiguities and multiplicity. Investigating the political as a question in a realm of hauntings requires remaining attentive to ghosts and surrendering to the aspects of political life that make themselves felt in ways that resist being pinned down. Ghosts are neither singular nor particularly clear. They make themselves felt by insisting on being seen, by demanding a reckoning. There are multiple ghosts, just as there are multiple 'states', and they all haunt through the longings they inspire, the desire for goodness, the pain of unfulfilled promise, the continuities and ruptures of convictions and loyalties.

What, precisely, haunts professionals in bureaucracies of victimhood? It is perhaps unsurprising that disappointment and the lack of fulfilment of promises of justice have a haunting effect. This chapter has illuminated that the promise of goodness can haunt too—especially when it remains mostly a promise. Bureaucrats are haunted by having to embody and work towards fulfilling a promise of peace and justice that felt real enough to draw them into 'the state', but whose fulfilment remains out of reach. The simultaneity of promise and disappointment, the possibility of justice in a present continuous of injustice, causes and sustains the haunting.

What bureaucrats describe as 'the ghost of the state' also haunts their relationships. The life histories of transitional justice professionals are

---

[106] Lea, 'Desiring Bureaucracy', p. 61.

populated not only by people who identify as victims, but also by a more intimate cast of characters: mothers who voted for Uribe, fathers who were assassinated, murdered cousins, frustrated spouses, friends from activist NGOs who no longer speak to those who embody the state with contaminated hands. For these professionals, 'becoming the state' came with a realignment of relationships. Where new and sometimes nourishing bonds formed, other relationships were haunted by a sense of betrayal, of carrying (and sometimes disappointing) the expectations of friends, family, and communities these professionals held dear. Though professionals can enter and exit 'the state', their affiliation with it has a lasting effect. The ghosts persist, and so does the haunting.

5
Victim Professionals and Professionalized Victims

The Land of Beautiful Papers

'Guava or arequipe?'[1] Carmen asked everyone walking through the door. She was setting up breakfast pastries and juice boxes for the attendees of a municipal Mesa meeting in Antioquia. In addition to Carmen, whose main task that day was to be the facilitator of the meeting, three officials from the Municipal Victims' Team, the National Victims' Unit, and the Public Ministry were also in attendance on behalf of state entities of transitional justice. Five minutes before the meeting was meant to begin, chairs were still being set up. The room was bare, except for a wall clock and a poster of a tree with hearts as its fruit. Beneath it, in block capital letters: "Mándanos la paz." Send us the peace.

As people trickled in, a state official circulated an attendance sheet with eight columns: Name, ID number, phone number, email, signature, time of arrival, time of departure, observations. When a blind man arrived, the Public Ministry official placed a pen in his fist and wrapped her hand around his, so he, too, could sign the attendance sheet. Right before the meeting began, a man I had not previously met sat next to me. 'Jairo, Unidad', he introduced himself, as though 'Victims' Unit' were his surname. He spent much of the meeting looking at my notebook, occasionally commenting on my handwriting or suggesting I correct the spelling of a place. In this setting, even the observers are observed.

---

[1] Arequipe is a caramelized milk that is popular in Colombia. It tastes like butterscotch or dulce de leche. An earlier version of parts of this chapter first appeared as a journal article in *PoLAR: Political and Legal Anthropology Review*'s 'Bureaucracy, Justice, and the State in a Post-Accord Colombia' series. Thank you to the editors and peer reviewers for their feedback. I have significantly revised and expanded parts of the article for publication in this book. Roxani Krystalli, 'Attendance Sheets and Bureaucracies of Victimhood in Colombia', *PoLAR: Political and Legal Anthropology Review* 10 (2020), https://polarjournal.org/2020/11/24/attendance-sheets-and-bureaucracies-of-victimhood-in-colombia/

Good Victims. Roxani Krystalli, Oxford University Press. © Oxford University Press 2024.
DOI: 10.1093/oso/9780197764534.003.0005

Another attendance sheet went around, asking people to check off boxes for the characteristics of the enfoque diferencial [differential approach] they represented. The differential approach was a cornerstone of the peace-and-justice policy in Colombia. Both predating and enshrined in the Victims' Law, it 'recognizes that there are populations with particular characteristics due to their age, gender, sexual orientation, and disability. For this reason, the forms of humanitarian assistance, attention, and integral reparation established in this Law must have such an approach'.[2] The premise was that these so-called differential characteristics affected people's experiences of the armed conflict and their navigation of the peace-and-justice systems in ways that state policies and practices ought to consider. The differential approach relied on the collection of disaggregated data through attendance sheets, like the one that landed in front of me at the Mesa.

The first time I was asked to fill out such a form, many of the acronyms were unfamiliar, but over time, I became fluent in them and in the choreography of attendance sheets. Some of the columns collected similar information to the attendance sheet that had circulated a few minutes earlier: name, phone number, email, signature. Most of the form, however, sought different data. In the language of the form, the major columns asked participants to indicate their age, whether they were pregnant mothers, their sex/gender, their social sector, and their ethnic group/cultural identity. Sub-columns provided options for each of these categories, and attendees had to tick off the one they thought most closely matched their experience. For example, the sex/gender category was broken down into sub-columns of women/men/other. The social sector category included sub-columns for rural community, person with disability, person who is a victim of the armed conflict, LGBTQI, person who lives on the street, person who exercises prostitution, and person deprived of liberty.[3] The ethnic group/cultural identity column included sub-columns for Afro-descendant populations; Gypsy and Roma groups; Indigenous community, and 'without ethnic affiliation'. I handed the attendance sheet to Jairo, but he nudged me to fill it out myself. 'Are you sure?' I whispered. 'I'm not a victim of the armed conflict or a state official'. 'Yes, yes, yes', he replied. 'We need to be judicious and document all the data', he reassured me. 'Write "woman" and pass it on (figure 5.1).'

---

[2] Law 1448 of 2011, Article 13. I critically engage with the approach at length in Chapter 6.
[3] All translations are my own and mirror the language of the form as closely as possible.

134　GOOD VICTIMS

	GESTIÓN DOCUMENTAL																	
	LISTADO DE ASISTENCIA Enfoque Diferencial Poblacional																	
		Población Objetivo																
		UPZ																
Edad	Sexo/genero			Sector Social							Grupo Étnico -Identidad Cultural							Teléfono
	M	H	O	CR	PCD	PVCA	LGBTIQ	PHCLL	PEP	PPL	MIG	Población Afrodescendiente			PRr	P-CI	SPE	
												CN	CP	PRZ				

Figure 5.1 A screenshot from an Excel document that offers a partial view of an attendance sheet reflecting the differential approach. This photo zooms in on the columns that correspond to age, sex/gender, social sector, and ethnic group/cultural identity, with their sub-columns listed in acronym form below.
Source: Alcaldía Mayor de Bogotá, Gestión Documental, Listado de Asistencia, July 2018.

At 9:40 a.m. Carmen called the meeting to order. 'Good morning, everyone', she said sternly. 'Good morning', the room echoed. 'Listen, I must say I am very disappointed. You all know that we must have attendance of at least 80 percent. That means arriving at 9:00 a.m. and staying at least—at least!—until 3:00 p.m. That is how you get the transportation subsidy'. She gestured vividly as she spoke. 'That is meant to be an incentive for your participation. If you stay for three hours, how can I categorize that as participation? Same problem when half the people don't come or leave early'.

Luz, one of the elected victim representatives to the Mesa, interjected. 'Carmen, today I have to leave the Mesa early to talk to the district attorney about a case of forced disappearance that my organization is handling'. 'That is fine', Carmen responded. 'That is a valid excuse'. Iris, a different elected victim representative who participated in multiple Mesas in this region, added: 'Carmen, I forgot to say that Marina could not be in this meeting today because they invited her to speak at an event about displacement at the University of Antioquia'. Carmen took a deep breath. 'Now, ladies and gentlemen, let's talk for a minute about valid excuses. You cannot just miss a Mesa meeting because there is another event you would like to attend. I, as Carmen, would like to go to plenty of events. For example, I would like to go to the museum today. But I have a Mesa to attend. It is not a valid excuse. That is not professional'.

As Carmen turned away from Iris to face the rest of the desks arranged in a semicircle, her tone and body language evoked that of a schoolteacher lecturing students about unexcused absences. 'If you cannot come to the meeting, you must send an email to the official who is the coordinator of the Mesa. For example, today, here, that is me. You must also send a copy to the victim coordinator of the Mesa. That is Jhon. The email must say, "I cannot attend because of a valid excuse". And then you tell us what the excuse is'. Carmen emphasized: 'Now, let me repeat. It must be an email, not a WhatsApp message. WhatsApp is not official. This is a matter of professionalization'. I was surprised by this, given that my own efforts to email bureaucrats as part of this research project had largely failed because most of my interlocutors were primarily reachable via WhatsApp.

'Carmen', Iris interjected again. 'The thing is that I have not had services [electricity, gas, water] in my house this month. I don't have internet. WhatsApp on my phone is all I have to communicate'. Carmen turned to face the rest of the room again. 'See? That is another valid excuse. Iris can WhatsApp. Everyone else, though, you must communicate your valid excuses by email. It's a professional issue'. On that note, she looked at the clock. Forty-five minutes of the day's Mesa meeting on victim participation in public policy had been consumed in this lecture on professional conduct.

This chapter critically engages with the expectations of professionalization that recurred in bureaucrats' encounters with people recognized as victims. A focus on professionalization highlights that it is not enough to simply *be* a victim; one must also *do* victimhood. Existing literature has powerfully demonstrated the labour involved in performing suffering in legible ways to secure initial recognition as a victim.[4] I show that the work of doing victimhood does not end when people have secured this recognition through the state's bureaucratic processes. Rather, people must do ongoing labour in accordance with particular scripts of professionalism to affirm and demonstrate themselves as subjects worthy of the state attention and resources to which the 'victim' label potentially grants access. Focusing on the legacies of transitional justice mechanisms, rather than the legacies of the violence

---

[4] Fredy Mora-Gámez, 'Reconocer a los reclamantes: Sobre el Registro Único de Víctimas en Colombia como ensamblado sociotécnico', *Im-Pertinente* 1, no. 1 (2013): 11–31; Mora-Gámez, 'Reparation Beyond Statehood'.

of the armed conflict, this chapter brings to the fore the labour, paperwork, vernaculars, and ways of being these programmes require and inspire.

Being a 'victim' in the eyes of the state—and, even more so, being a 'good victim'—requires constant work. This is the labour of presence, of attending meetings and signing forms, and of participation in state-facing spaces beyond mere presence, which involves holding the state accountable to its promises on behalf of others who identify as victims.[5] It is also the labour of narration involved in these spaces, the work of what Theidon calls 'talking trauma'.[6] Many of those who identify as victims also do the work of movement-building, as well as caring for others seeking recognition as victims and members of their broader communities.[7] Thinking of victimhood as work requires asking which work counts and gets counted, whose work is compensated or remains invisible, and what the stakes of counting, compensation, and visibility are. Framing victimhood as work also draws attention to who gets credit for doing it and invites curiosity about the forms of labour that are (il)legible as professional. As encounters between bureaucrats and those recognized as victims highlight, the labour of victimhood is *contested* work.

Narratives of professionalism invoke an ideal subject, a model professional. What kind of subject is the professional(ized) victim, and what work do the narratives and practices of professionalization do during transitions from violence? Speaking of professional*ization*, rather than only of professional*ism*, brings a process into focus. I am interested both in the politics of the 'victim' subject this process produces and in the mechanisms and labour by which this subject comes into being, becomes ideal(ized), or is contested.

The process of professionalization manifests in documents and indicators, in attendance sheets at meetings and expected or prescribed scripts of professional communication. 'Colombia is a ... vast paper-made state', Pellegrino has aptly argued, noting that 'the machinery of the state runs on paper by registering, preserving, and moving information for governing'.[8] Many of my interlocutors referred to Colombia as 'the land of beautiful papers'.[9]

---

[5] De Waardt and Weber, 'Beyond Victims' Mere Presence'.
[6] Theidon, *Intimate Enemies*, p. 33.
[7] For more on caregiving as work, see Leah Lakshmi Piepzna-Samarasinha, *Care Work: Dreaming Disability Justice* (Arsenal Pulp Press, 2018); Tronto, *Moral Boundaries*, p. 108; Virginia Held, *The Ethics of Care* (Oxford University Press, 2006); Silvia Federici, *Revolution at Point Zero: Housework, Reproduction, and Feminist Struggle* (PM Press, 2012).
[8] Pellegrino, 'Between the Roll of Paper', p. 79.
[9] I credit my friend Sarah Richardson, who was the first to draw my attention to this phrase.

Following the paperwork, as well as the encounters that reward or chastise (un)professional behaviour, can illuminate how notions of 'good victims' form and circulate.

It is seductively easy to assume that the 'victim' subject that results from bureaucratic encounters and professionalization expectations is not a political subject, that these processes have depoliticized victimhood and stripped it of its potential power. Indeed, this is a criticism advanced by some of my interlocutors across a range of relationships to the state and victimhood alike. 'I think it is a piece of crap [una porquería] that we expect victims to behave themselves, to say please and thank you in meetings', a street-level bureaucrat at the Municipal Victims Team in Medellín said.[10] According to its proponents, however, 'Technocracy offers the possibility of constructing mechanisms that are free from bias and that can depoliticize issues that are often viewed through political lenses'.[11] For some, this is a desirable depoliticization. 'Technocrats', the peacebuilding scholar Roger Mac Ginty states, 'would see their approach as being anodyne and free from the subjective pitfalls of value judgements'.[12] Following this argument, professionalization through paperwork and other instruments of technocracy may result in what James Ferguson call an 'anti-politics' of victimhood,[13] privileging measurable, indicator-led, 'solutions' over deeper and more contentious engagements with the political.

Though these critiques are salient in the Colombian context, I argue here that the process of professionalization also does political work. What do we find if we investigate the political as a question in the realm of attendance sheets and invocations for people recognized as victims to 'be professional?' Such an inquiry begins to illuminate the discrepancies in who can readily become legible as professional, by which standard, and with what effect. In the realm of the labour of victimhood, expectations of professionalism are distinct from respecting the expertise of people recognized as victims.[14] Exploring the political as a question draws attention to the ways in which professionalization becomes a ritual of verification.[15] What it verifies is not exclusively the labour of victimhood on the part of those recognized as

---

[10] Interview with Municipal Victims Team official in Medellín, February 2018.
[11] Roger Mac Ginty, 'Routine Peace: Technocracy and Peacebuilding', *Cooperation and Conflict* 47, no. 3 (2012): 291.
[12] Mac Ginty, 'Routine Peace', p. 291.
[13] Ferguson, *The Anti-politics Machine*.
[14] I am grateful to María Fernanda Olarte-Sierra for helping me draw out this point.
[15] Michael Power, *The Audit Society: Rituals of Verification* (Oxford University Press, 1999).

victims, but the work of professionals within state bureaucracies—and, by aspirational extension, the presence of 'the state' and fulfilment of its promises of justice during transitions from violence. In this way, professionalization produces not only a 'victim' subject, but also the 'state' during transitions from violence.

This argument does not imply that 'the state' uniformly places professionalization expectations on people recognized as victims, or that the latter reject those expectations entirely. I am particularly interested in the moments in which state officials and people who identify as victims alike demonstrate complex relationships to the professionalization script. 'People can act politically by strategically reproducing—rather than simply resisting—ideologies of language', the anthropologist E. Summerson Carr argues in her ethnographic study of addiction treatment in the United States.[16] Some of the political work of professionalization reveals itself in the moments in which people recognized as victims and bureaucrats alike 'flip the script' of professionalization, 'formally replicating prescribed ways of speaking about themselves and their problems without investing in the *content* of those scripts'.[17] Flipping the script creates possibilities for alliances and solidarities, for moments of agency to claim legibility as a particular kind of subject and to shape encounters between 'the state' and people who identify as victims during transitions from violence.

The Double Bind of Professionalization

Embracing the ubiquitous script of professionalism was not universally desirable or risk-free. On the contrary, people who identified as victims faced a double bind. On the one hand, acting professionally—which meant in accordance with the state's ideas and scripts of professionalism—was essential for being seen as a 'good victim', with all the benefits associated with that status. This need was legible to state officials pushing for victim professionalization in the first place. 'You may not believe me', a street-level bureaucrat in Antioquia told me, 'but I really want these victims to be taken seriously. And I know the state. I know how to move in it, make demands, make people take me seriously. I am trying to help them see that'.[18] In the modern universe

---
[16] Summerson Carr, *Scripting Addiction*, p. 19.
[17] Summerson Carr, *Scripting Addiction*, p. 3.
[18] Interview with a state liaison to a Mesa in Antioquia, March 2018.

of peacebuilding and transitional justice, professionalization is the currency of seriousness. On the other hand, professionalizing victimhood could lead to suspicion on the part of both state officials and others who identify as victims. 'The most important thing', a former senior official at the National Commission for Reparation and Reconciliation said, 'is to avoid converting victims into professional victims. They become installed in the condition of victim and expect permanent assistance from the state and society. The "professional victim syndrome" in Colombia is very dangerous'.[19]

The language of pathology, of syndromes and conditions, suggests that some see attachment to the category of 'victim' as an illness. Victimhood is more palatable as an ephemeral, passing state, rather than a longer-term basis of subjectivity and claim-making. This is, in part, an anxiety about time, about the future of victimhood, the expectations that victim claims generate, and the way those expectations haunt the state.[20] Alongside those concerns, critiques of victim professionalization stem from a sense that victimhood ought to emanate purely and naturally from the experience of having been victimized. Any additional labour to 'self-stage' as a 'victim',[21] attachment to the category, or fluency in the ways of being that this form of subjectivity enables, invites critics to question the authenticity of victim claims and their underlying experiences.

This is the paradox of professionalization: victimhood requires constant, contested work; at the same time, victimhood must emerge effortlessly, and professionalization undermines the credibility of people's suffering. This double bind will be familiar to feminists, and to people who have struggled to make their losses legible to those who disbelieve them.[22] Ultimately, this is a question of humanity—of whose humanity is immediately believable and whose takes work to convey. 'The human is an exclusive category through which particular kinds of care and solidarity are extended',[23] the sociologist Akwugo Emejulu writes, in close conversation with the work of the novelist and cultural theorist Sylvia Wynter. Connecting these reflections to her own experiences of race and racial hierarchy, Emejulu argues that 'to be outside the community of humans is to be at the mercy or the whims of those who do not consider you their equal and most likely do not consider you at all'.[24]

---

[19] Interview with former senior official at the National Commission for Reparation and Reconciliation in Bogotá, June 2018.
[20] Chapter 7 discusses these ideas about the future of victimhood.
[21] Utas, 'Victimcy', p. 403.
[22] Dina Nayeri, *Who Gets Believed?* (Harvill Secker, 2023).
[23] Akwugo Emejulu, *Fugitive Feminism* (Silver Press, 2022), p. 26.
[24] Emejulu, *Fugitive Feminism*, p. 27.

Discussions of victim professionalization, then, are not 'just' about the work of victimhood or the processes that render peacebuilding, transitional justice, and state-building technocratic. They are about the believable bases of humanity and about the contestations of who gets to be what kind of human in the wake of violence.

Follow the Attendance Sheet

The construction of professional(ized) victim subjectivity passes through paperwork. Just as encounters between bureaucrats and people who identify as victims make both the 'victim' subject and 'the state', so do the forms and documents that record those encounters. These records not only reflect, but also create ideas about professionalization. As the public policy scholar David Dery asserts, 'Through record keeping, a crucial control mechanism, organisations engage in the construction and privileging of views of the world that become the world'.[25]

Attendance sheets and the statistics that result from them are instruments of audit culture, the 'norms and social practices of assessment, through which accountability and "good practice" are demonstrated and made visible'.[26] Although it is particularly observable in Colombia, audit culture is a worldwide phenomenon.[27] Commenting on the transformation of NGO advocacy on transitional justice, Jelena Subotić finds that there has been 'a profound cultural shift from do-gooder volunteerism to professionalization, specialization, and bureaucratization, all of which have brought greater visibility and international credibility to these efforts'.[28] The credibility dimension is important, both because it represents a shift away from the idea that a desire to 'do good' is sufficient for working on peace and justice and because the

---

[25] David Dery, '"Papereality" and Learning in Bureaucratic Organizations', *Administration and Society* 29, no. 6 (1998): 678.
[26] Christian N. Vannier, 'Audit Culture and Grassroots Participation in Rural Haitian Development', *Political and Legal Anthropology Review* 33, no. 2 (2010): 283.
[27] 'The indicator is at the heart of the quantitative evaluation system', Pamina Firchow writes in her compelling book on measuring and evaluating peace differently. 'Growing interest in quantitative evaluation is apparent across sectors, including public health, education, and global governance. The growing impetus for data-informed policymaking is increasingly felt in the fields of international peacebuilding and related fields of development, human rights, and humanitarian intervention'. Pamina Firchow, *Reclaiming Everyday Peace* (Cambridge University Press, 2018), pp. 29, 37.
[28] Jelena Subotić, 'The Transformation of International Transitional Justice Advocacy', *International Journal of Transitional Justice* 6, no. 1 (2012): 118.

legitimacy of these peace and justice efforts requires demonstration through rituals of professionalization.

The professionalization of peace and justice work has consolidated a vernacular and set of practices, from key performance indicators to metrics that monitor and evaluate the effectiveness of projects. Having spilled over from the world of accounting and finance, audit culture is 'almost impossible to criticise in principle—after all, it advances values that academics generally hold dear, such as responsibility, openness about outcomes, and widening of access'.[29] Over time, 'This "businessification" of social, political and cultural organization and practice has become so commonplace that it may be regarded as "normal" and somehow an unremarkable part of the fabric'.[30] Feminist curiosity involves asking how practices come to appear unremarkable, and attempting to treat them as potentially surprising anew.

Though they appear to be inanimate objects made up of columns and checkmarks, attendance sheets are alive with feeling. State liaisons to Mesas tracked the documents with anxiety as they made their way around the room and filed them into folders with urgency as soon as meetings concluded. Over the course of a single Mesa meeting in February 2018, the attendance sheet had circulated six times. When asked to recall her first experience of facilitating a Mesa meeting, Ximena remembered the attendance sheets. 'The first time I showed up at a Mesa, it was terrible', she said. 'They attacked me'.[31] 'They', in this context, referred to the elected victim representatives to that Mesa. 'They wouldn't talk', she added. 'Or they would say, "The High Advisery for Victims doesn't do anything, so why are we here?" And they wouldn't sign the attendance form. I thought to myself "Oh god! Where did I put myself?" I was afraid that if I came back [to the office] without the attendance list, that would be it for me'.

Attendance sheets lent materiality to rituals through which the state did what McFee calls 'making a presence' [hacer presencia].[32] The act of making a presence was often more important than the substance or purpose of the presence itself, which at times remained a mystery to state officials. 'We're here to provide information and support today, and to *make an act of presence* [hacer un acto de presencia]', a street-level bureaucrat told McFee in

---

[29] Marilyn Strathern, *Audit Cultures* (Routledge, 2000), p. 2.
[30] Mac Ginty, 'Routine Peace', p. 296.
[31] Interview with High Advisory for Victims official in Bogotá, July 2018.
[32] Erin McFee, "Making a Presence': Reconciliation and the State in Colombia', *Political and Legal Anthropology Review* 10 (2020): n.p.

Caquetá in December 2015 at the Fair for Reconciliation, 'but what we do doesn't have any connection to reconciliation. They just told us to be here today; we don't know why'.[33] Similarly, at her first Mesa facilitation, Ximena understood that she had to return a completed attendance sheet to her office no matter what, even if the nuances of presence and participation had yet to fully reveal themselves.

Attendance sheets thus became rituals of verification, 'whose technical efficacy is less significant than their role in the production of organizational legitimacy'.[34] They verified not only the presence of people recognized as victims in a given space, but also, crucially, the presence of 'the state' itself. The latter hinged on the former; that is, demonstrating the presence of 'the state' and the fulfilment of its public policy towards victims required people recognized as victims to do the labour associated with presence, participation, and advocacy in state-facing spaces.

Neither the acts of making a presence nor the rituals that verify them end when a signed attendance sheet enters a bureaucrat's folder at the conclusion of a meeting. Following the attendance sheet on its onward journey through a world of data monitoring and analysis highlights its lasting effect on producing a particular idea of victimhood, state presence, and the professionalization script. Luisa was a data analyst at a Municipal Victims' Team in Medellín. While she was happy to speak with me, she was not sure if she could be helpful. 'I understand you work with victims', she said. 'But I don't work with victims, I work with data'.[35] In Luisa's understanding, data created by, about, and for people recognized as victims was fundamentally separate from the people themselves.

Luisa's job primarily consisted of managing a series of systems summarized in acronyms. Every quarter, she updated the FUT (Unique Territorial Form), a system that contains projections of the state's financial investments in programming for people recognized as victims. Every month, she also updated the RUSICST tool. She admitted that she did not remember what each letter of the acronym stood for,[36] but explained that the work consisted

---

[33] McFee, 'Making a Presence', n.p.
[34] Power, *The Audit Society*, p. 14.
[35] Interview with data analyst at the Municipal Victims' Team in Medellín, February 2018.
[36] Unified Report of the System of Information, Coordination and Territorial Monitoring of Public Policy for Victims of the Internal Armed Conflict [Reporte Unificado del Sistema de Información, Coordinación y Seguimiento Territorial de la política pública de víctimas del conflicto armado interno]. I must admit that, like Luisa, I have also had to look up this acronym every time I have written about it.

of monitoring the territorial dimensions of public policy for victims. Monitoring unfolded along several thematic lines, such as conflict dynamics, territorial articulation of public policy, adequacy of teams and spaces, and participation. 'Basically, it is about whether the [Victims'] Law is fulfilled or not', Luisa summarized.

To arrive at this determination of fulfilment, Luisa and her team sorted through the data that emerged from Mesa meetings and state events for people recognized as victims. 'There are lots of attachments to the RUSICST', Luisa explained. 'We have Excel sheets showing how many programs we ran and how many people came and how much money we spent. The attendance lists are really important to show participation and that the state is creating spaces for victims. We socialize this data with the Mesa regularly to fulfil the process laid out in the law. We also attach some more qualitative data, like meeting minutes and photos, but that can go in the appendices. The qualitative data isn't really required', she claimed. 'It's more the statistics that are required'.

The work and process of professionalization, and the ways they have been rendered unremarkable, become apparent in the fluency with which state officials repeat the script of 'articulation' and 'socialization' of the data. In February 2018, I observed a Mesa meeting during which the budget reporting on the state's investment in victim projects took place. Contrary to Luisa's language of 'socializing' the data, there was little sociality to the process, which mostly consisted of bureaucrats presenting final versions of spreadsheets for projects that had concluded years earlier. Andrés, a member of the Municipal Victims Team, stood in front of the room while his colleague attempted to get the projector to work. A third member of the team moved the 'For the victims, for the peace' banner out of the way, as it obstructed the view of the spreadsheet that would soon be projected onto the wall. The spreadsheet had six columns: Component [of Public Policy], Project, Objective, Indicators, Goals, 2016 Achievements. 'Let's start with returns and relocations', Andrés said. There were two projects in that municipality in 2016, with the objective of accompanying displaced families in the process of returning to their place of origin. The indicator was 'household returns' and the goal was to accompany 210 such processes. 'We achieved 253', Andrés said, 'and that means the state exceeded the goal that had been projected'.

Before Andrés could go on to the next indicator, Iris interjected. 'Where do you find out how big the universe of victims who want to return is? How do you pick this "210" number as your goal?' People recognized as victims are not merely passive recipients, audiences, and sources of indicators. They also contest their creation and circulation, whether by refusing to sign the attendance sheet or by resisting a state narrative about the story indicators tell.[37] Andrés looked at his colleagues, who shrugged and pointed at him. 'The thing is, it's actually the National Victims' Unit that has responsibility for the numbers', Andrés said hesitantly. 'The municipal teams are doing this out of solidarity. We know it's important to have numbers. Okay? Okay. Let's move on'. It was unclear if the stated solidarity was with people recognized as victims, or with the state project of data collection. The rest of the afternoon unfolded similarly, with state officials reading through the rows and columns. Every time a number required interpretation, the professionals responsible for 'socializing' the data admitted that they did not have context for how the indicators were crafted, deflecting that responsibility to another entity far away, whose representatives were not in the room.

The state professionals in these situations are not merely cogs in the machine of acronyms and indicators. They, too, expressed frustration at the obsession with numbers and forms, as well as skepticism about their own process of professionalization. 'Every so often, there are technical assistance sessions for state officials', Luisa said. 'They have been going on for four or five years and it's always the same orientation. It only goes so far'. She and her colleagues had created proposals on how to improve the system, but 'nothing more happens. They only care to show that the municipality complied'. 'They' is the impersonal, faceless state, imagined as separate from the care and commitment that Luisa narrated. 'We have really qualified people here', she lamented. 'We want to do more, to give, but the process is rigid, and we can't depart from it'. Once again, ghosts of 'the system' and 'the process' rear their head. An abstract, distant, rule-following 'they' constrains a compassionate, committed 'we'.

The statistics haunt and provide relief from haunting. Through attendance sheets and other instruments appended to a monthly report and uploaded to a database, 'victim participation' and 'state policy fulfillment' become part of 'the magic of numbers', creating 'certainty in spaces of great ambiguity'.[38] In a paper-made state, the magic of numbers is essential to constructing a form

---

[37] Similar instances at Mesas for displaced people have led Schouw Iversen to argue that Mesas in Colombia 'provided the displaced with opportunities for engaging in "confrontational collective action"'. Karen Schouw Iversen, 'Participation as Confrontation: Resistance within and outside the Mesas de Participación Established for IDPs in Colombia', *Journal of Refugee Studies* 35, no. 3 (2022): 1328.

[38] Merry, *The Seductions of Quantification*, p. 127.

of presence and supplying evidence of fulfilment of promises of justice. What rituals of verification leave unverified is analytically important to the story of evidence and indicators. Since 'the qualitative data isn't really required', as Luisa said, one is left wondering what 'victim participation' truly looks like, what 'fulfilment' means, and who is able to meaningfully enjoy them.

Contestations of Compensation

María José, the victims' association leader who was the elected coordinator of a Mesa in a peri-urban neighbourhood of Bogotá, called the second half of that day's meeting to order. Unlike other Mesas, the facilitation duties in this space fell to one of the elected victim representatives, rather than to a state official.[39] 'Dear companions', María José said with a big smile, 'after such a delicious lunch for all of us, except this girl [*gestures to the right*] who didn't eat enough and it worries me—please, at least have a refreshment!—we move on to the last item on today's agenda: our incentive payments'.

Incentive payments are a strategy for compensating some of the labour of victimhood. Being an elected representative to a Mesa entails mandatory attendance at several meetings each month, a burden that increases for those who are part of multiple Mesas (e.g., a local Mesa, a Mesa for Indigenous victims, an LGBTQI Mesa, and more). Many victim representatives to Mesas 'were feeling overwhelmed by the number and length of meetings', which 'took up half a day and consequently required people to take time off from their work and daily activities'.[40] Meetings unfold hours away from the neighbourhoods in which many elected victim representatives live, requiring hours on public transit. Participation in one space can therefore mean lost wages in another. The labour of victimhood can preclude other forms of (paid) labour, jeopardizing the livelihoods of people who were already precariously hovering near or below the poverty line.

In recognition of these dynamics, the Colombian state made provisions to offer compensatory incentives to victims of the armed conflict elected to

---

[39] This variation was common among Mesas and seemed to be attributable to the personal preferences of the various elected victim leaders, as well as their relationships to the state officials liaising with each Mesa.
[40] De Waardt and Weber, 'Beyond Victims' Mere Presence', p. 221.

participate in the Mesas.[41] In 2017–2018, when the observations I relate in this chapter took place, the incentives corresponded to 1.25 times the minimum daily wage, plus a transportation subsidy. At the time, this totalled 43,000 COP ($13.79) per person per meeting.[42] Language for referring to these financial amounts ranged from 'incentives' to 'subsidies' to 'compensatory support'. Most of my interlocutors within state agencies actively chose not to refer to these amounts as payments. Illustrating this attitude during a Mesa meeting she was facilitating in Antioquia, Carmen said: 'This is an incentive, it is not a payment. We are not paying you to be victims. To receive this subsidy, which is meant to help with transportation and other little things like that, you need to show up. You need to participate. You need to be professional'.

When the subject of incentives came up during the Mesa in Bogotá, Ximena, the High Advisory for Victims official who was the primary state liaison to that space, opened her notebook. 'We need to know who has received the incentives and who has not. This is for the period from January to April of this year'. Iván, a leader of a victims' NGO, opened his own notebook. 'With all due respect, I did the math. We are supposed to receive 1.25 times the minimum wage, according to Regulation 282. This means 39,000 COP per session, plus 4,400 COP for the transport. This means 43,662 COP per person per session'.[43] María José and Ximena nodded. Many victim representatives took notes while Iván spoke. 'For those of us in this Mesa, this means four sessions between January and April 2018, so we multiply that number by four. For people who have double participation in this Mesa and the national Mesa, they should count double. For those who participate in three spaces, triple'. Iván turned to face Ximena and the state officials who sat beside her. 'Now, I have a question because I think I may have made a mistake in my calculations. I heard we aren't being paid for January. But the High Adviser for Victims told us in another space that we will be paid for January, February, March, and April', he said, lifting a finger corresponding to each

---

[41] These compensatory incentives pertain specifically to labour that elected victim representatives to Mesas do as part of that role, and are separate from people's right to compensation as a fundamental pillar of reparations.

[42] I have collated this information from numerous policy documents, including Victims' Unit Resolution 01282 (November 2016), Resolution 0388 (2011), preceding Resolutions 0544 (2014) and 0622 (2015), Law 1448 (2011), and Decree 4802 (2011).

[43] At the time of this research, 39,000 COP corresponded to USD 12.36. The total amount of 43,662 corresponded to USD 13.84.

month. 'What's the truth? I ask respectfully that you give us a real data point that we can confront'.

'The real data point is the following', Ximena replied. 'On January 22, the session of this Mesa was informational only. There was no quorum. You only receive compensatory payment when there is quorum'. Teresa, another victim representative, disagreed. 'No, there was definitely quorum. After lunch, someone came and there was quorum'. Ximena replied: 'Let's look at the minutes. We don't need to fight. Let's look at the minutes'. She turned to an official from the municipality, who opened a big binder to pull out an attendance sheet from the January meeting. Teresa began to count signatures with her finger. 'Yes, there was quorum. Look at all these signatures!' 'Ah yes', Ximena responded, 'but you have to be there for at least 60 percent of the meeting for it to count as quorum.[44] I can't count your five minutes of being there as participation'.

María José, the victim representative facilitating the meeting, echoed Ximena's point. 'Dear companions', she said, 'according to the protocols and regulations, you have to be there for at least 60 percent of the meeting. You could have signed in, but if you are not there for the right percentage of the meeting, it doesn't count as quorum'. Iván opened his binder of laws, regulations, and decrees. 'Decree 672 applies here', he said, as he brought out a paper copy. 'I refer specifically to Article 6. There are no percentages in the decree. The law says nothing about percentages and participation'. Other victim representatives nodded around the table.

Ximena turned to face Iván. 'Do you really think I will not compensate someone if they came and sat here for three hours? Is that the kind of person you think I am?' In the back, a victim representative who had been quiet until that point spoke up. 'They pay congressmen just for raising their hand and saying "present"'. Laughter filled the back row. 'Let me be clear', Ximena said. 'We have no problem at all with you. But you all know that there are people at other Mesas who show up, sign, and leave. Allow me to repeat: this is not a problem we have with you here. But those people are why the regulations exist'. Waving the regulation in the air, Iván replied: "Doctora,[45] with all

---

[44] This was a different percentage than Carmen had cited as required at the Antioquia Mesa narrated earlier.

[45] The term 'doctor' is used to respectfully address others in Colombia. The term indicates seniority or respect, not necessarily conferred by the educational status associated with medical doctors or PhD holders.

due respect, the 672 doesn't say anything about informational sessions or percentages'.

Before Ximena could respond, Teresa addressed the state officials. 'Earlier, when we were talking to the municipality, the Public Ministry representatives got up and left. Nothing I said during that time was recorded in the minutes. You are not practising what you preach. If you don't respect the hours of this meeting, you shouldn't be compensated, just like the rest of us'. The state officials whispered amongst themselves in the corner, visibly taken aback. None of them spoke, however, and María José, the victims' representative and Mesa facilitator, was the next to take the floor.

> Teresa, I ask you and the rest of our companions to do me a favor. We are here for discussion, not discordance. I suggest, with all due respect, that we ought to express our gratitude to our state officials because they are doing a good job. I am in many Mesas, I talk to people all day. I am a leader of victims. You know this. I fight all day for us. I can tell you this: we are the only Mesa that has this kind of accompaniment from the state. We are here to construct public policy, not to see each other as enemies. So we need to learn to manage our emotions and impulses. Teresa, you are very aggressive. All of this is not Ximena's fault. She didn't do anything arbitrary. I remind everyone that we did not come to this space for the money, or for our interests.

Stillness hung over the room for a moment. A man who had not spoken at all that day was the next to comment. 'Of course, yes, you are right, María José. It's just that what I don't like are the delays in getting our payments'. Ximena jumped back into the discussion, facing the man. 'You are right. There are delays. This Mesa is the only compensated space in the whole country.[46] We are learning. It's madness at the Secretary of Housing, let me tell you. The women there stay at work until 8:00 or 9:00 p.m., looking at identity documents and attendance sheets. It's stressful. The number of victims is an incredible figure, an incredible madness [una figura y una locura increíble]. All of this has been a lesson for us. Definitely, things have to improve'.

---

[46] Over the course of the research, I did meet others who identify as victims in different areas who had received their incentive payments, suggesting Ximena had exaggerated. I still choose to include her remark here, both because she said it at the time and because it is essential to critically examine rumours and half-truths—what Lee Ann Fujii calls 'shades of truth and lies'—as narratives that tell a particular kind of story about transitions from violence. Fujii, 'Shades of Truth'.

With that, María José attempted to return to the agenda. 'Okay, how many have already received compensation? Remember, this is from January till April'. Two people in the room raised their hands. One person said she had not had the chance to look at her bank account. The rest were silent. 'I repeat: Who has already received and withdrawn their incentives? Please, look in your documents and your bank accounts. This is important. Iván, do you have Resolution 489 of 2017? I need to verify something'.

As Iván searched through his binder of laws and decrees, Carolina, a state official from the Public Ministry, reacted to Teresa's earlier comment that state officials still get paid even when they miss portions of meetings. 'This is a constant offering from us, of heart and of work', Carolina said, with tears in her eyes. 'We do it with love. They also pay us, but that does not mean this is not a labour of love. So we are really not in agreement with Teresa's attitude. It makes us look as though we are not complying. I clarify this not as Public Ministry, but as Carolina. We are not here to violate your rights or take anything away from you. We are here to serve you, not to tolerate your lack of respect'. Iván responded immediately. 'In the name of the Mesa, we ask for your forgiveness'. A chorus of other victim representatives said, 'Yes, yes', seconding Iván's plea. María José added: 'For this reason, Teresa, please: you have to manage your emotions'. Teresa remained silent.

'We all make mistakes'. Ximena concluded the discussion of this incident. 'Now, here is what we are going to do. I'm going to read your names and tell you how many sessions I have you down as having attended. If there is a mistake somewhere, including a mistake I made, we can clarify'. Bianca, another victim representative, asked: 'This is for January to April of this year, yes? What about last year?' 'Things should already be resolved for last year', Ximena responded. 'It's August 2018. People should have been paid for 2017 already'. Bianca shrugged and did not follow up on her question. 'Ximena, I have something to say', Ernesto, an elected representative of disabled victims, said. 'I am disabled. I have a chronic illness. You have me down for two sessions, when I attended four. You scold me when I do not come, and you do not pay me when I do. Is this rational?'

As Ernesto was finishing his sentence, six young girls in matching pink coats over school uniforms entered the room and sat in women's laps. 'Look, the norm is one thing', Ximena said. 'I, as a human being, am another. As a human, I want to pay you. But if you did not sign, what can I do? They ask me for the lists too. What can I show them if you did not sign? There are Mesas that are terrible. At least we pay you here. Now, please, let's finish this up. The children are arriving and people have to get home'.

The 'Good State' Here, the 'Unprofessional Victims' Elsewhere

Paperwork makes the professional; paperwork anchors professionalization. People recognized as victims not only come to know the norms and laws pertaining to their legal status and rights, but also carry paper copies with them, wave them around, take them in and out of binders in support of their case. The paperwork of victim professionalization has its own shorthand. Iván refers to 'the 672', as though the regulation were an old friend.[47] In engaging with papers that the state deems official and pertinent to victimhood, people recognized as victims demonstrate awareness of a particular script of professionalization, in which they become fluent and which they sometimes replicate, challenge, and flip.[48] People run their fingers over documents, count signatures, tally up numbers, ask for a real data point they can confront. They look through invoices and bank accounts; they compile and refer to counter-archives that exist in parallel to the state's folders and notebooks. These compilations, references, and invocations are attempts at mattering— at getting the labour of victimhood to be seen and compensated by those who have the power to confer that recognition and its associated resources.

In her excellent book *Paper Cadavers*, the historian Kirsten Weld paves the way for thinking about the duality of archival logics pertaining to the police archives in Guatemala.[49] Weld traces a logic of 'surveillance, social control, and ideological management' and a parallel logic of 'democratic opening, historical memory, and the pursuit of justice'.[50] In the context of Colombia and in bureaucrats' hands, paperwork provides a record of (their) work, fulfilment of public policy promises, and (state) presence. Papers also

---

[47] For more on the papers of victimhood, see Kate Cronin-Furman and Roxani Krystalli, 'The Things They Carry: Victims' Documentation of Forced Disappearance in Colombia and Sri Lanka', *European Journal of International Relations* 27, no. 1 (2020): 79–101.

[48] Importantly, the expectations to perform this script, and worries about what the script erases or justifies, are reasons why some people who identify as victims reject the Mesas as a space and do not run for election to be victim representatives.

[49] I have not directly relied on the frame of an archive in my own analysis (largely because this was not a dominant frame in my interlocutors' narratives), though it is possible to think of the various papers of victimhood as forming and constituting archives.

[50] Kirsten Weld, *Paper Cadavers* (Duke University Press, 2014), p. 6.

regulate and discipline, distinguishing between 'good victims', who may get rewarded for their behaviour in the future and unprofessional ones, who allegedly mar the collective reputation of those homogeneously imagined as victims.

These distinctions often involve pitting the people in a given space against others recognized as victims, located at an abstract 'elsewhere': at other Mesas, in other municipalities, dealing with different state liaisons, who are invariably framed as less compassionate or competent than the state official in this room. Those 'other victims' are framed as less diligent, 'arriving, signing in, and leaving', thus tainting the reputation of those recognized as victims writ large. This narrative implicitly places responsibility on people who identify as victims to protect the goodness of the category on the whole. State officials also claim that these 'other victims elsewhere' have received less attention in the form of timely subsidies. This communicates to people recognized as victims 'right here' that they should be grateful for *any* attention, rather than striving for what would feel meaningful or dignified to them. Echoing the sociologist Javier Auyero's ethnography of state bureaucracies in Argentina, 'The state tells its subjects, either implicitly or explicitly, 'wait, be patient, and you might benefit from my reluctant benevolence'.[51] The expectation of the performance of gratitude haunts people recognized as victims.[52] When they do not perform gratitude, they risk humiliation.[53]

In the hands of people recognized as victims, the same papers tell a different story—that often relies on the same sources and script. This is the story of holding a state to account by leveraging the promises it made through regulations. The instruments the state created to track fulfilment of its own promises, such as attendance sheets, simultaneously serve as records of *un*fulfilment, of labour on the part of people recognized as victims that is neither sufficiently acknowledged nor adequately compensated. It matters that the scripts people recognized as victims perform to advocate for their labour and its compensation are semi-public and state-facing, rather than insights shared privately at an interview. The nature of the Mesa space and the positioning of the people who inhabit it shape how people recognized as

---

[51] Auyero, *Patients of the State*, p. 15. I've also benefitted from thinking with Bourdieu, who argues that domination functions by 'making people wait . . . , delaying without destroying hope, . . . adjourning without totally disappointing'. Pierre Bourdieu, *Pascalian Meditations*, trans. Richard Nice (Stanford University Press, 2000), p. 228.
[52] Again, I am grateful to María Fernanda Olarte-Sierra for this language.
[53] Dina Nayeri, *The Ungrateful Refugee* (Canongate, 2019).

victims craft the script, ostensibly complying with the expectations of professionalism and fluency in normativity.[54]

According to Summerson Carr, script flipping is a 'kind of expertise', and script flippers are 'ethnographers of language in their own right, in that they constantly strive to decipher the conditions in which they speak so that they can linguistically maneuver within them'.[55] In the context of the labour of victimhood, flipping the script involves making references to legal, policy, and normative frameworks that govern that labour and its compensation, and then demanding that the state fulfill its own promises, as opposed to, for example, making a case for compensation based on broader moral principles of justice.

Shifting Sands of Solidarities

Adherence to and flipping of the script of professionalization opens people recognized as victims to criticism from others who also identify with the category. 'To be honest, I do not agree with the strategy we take as victims all the time', an elected victim representative to the Mesa that María José leads told me.[56] 'Look at María José, for example. She shows up in her suit and talks about the agenda and quorum and protocols and routes. And then she asks us to say thank you to the state! We are not here to do state politics. We have our own politics. When did we as victims convert into the state?' In adopting the professionalization script (even if only to flip it), people who identify as victims may displace their own vernacular and sense of politics in favour of being legible and likable to 'the state'. In the eyes of those who are skeptical, fearful, or critical of 'the state', people who identify as victims risk *becoming* the state by adhering to the professionalization script. This is professionalization as co-optation, which represents a rupture of the threads of solidarity among people who identify as victims. 'This is what the "victim participation" narrative does', a former state official told me.[57] 'It domesticates victims.

---

[54] De Waardt and Weber find something similar, remarking that 'in several meetings the Victims Unit not only made clear that other institutions were responsible for most of the reparation measures, pointing at their own limited responsibility, but also urged the communities to start "getting their house in order", know the Victims' Law and its protocols, and attend municipal meetings'. De Waardt and Weber, 'Beyond Victims' Mere Presence', pp. 221–22.
[55] Summerson Carr, *Scripting Addiction*, p. 19.
[56] Interview with elected victim representative to a peri-urban Mesa in greater Bogotá, August 2018.
[57] Interview with former state official in Bogotá, January 2018.

Best to domesticate them and make victims part of the establishment, so they can drop their opposition to the state. It is a perverse thing, isn't it?'

At the same time, both state officials and people recognized as victims break from what might presume to be 'party line' scripts in order to maintain a relationship with each other. Put differently, the professionalization script, its paperwork, and its attendant expectations are not only sustained by state officials and challenged by those recognized as victims. Both constituencies engage in a fragile, shifting dance of distancing themselves from where one might expect their loyalties to lie, and of invoking proximity to different sources of knowledge and expertise as vectors of authority. Overtures like Iván's apology to state officials 'in the name of the Mesa', Teresa's encouragement to fellow victim representatives to 'express our gratitude to state officials', Ximena's concessions about delays in processing payments, and bureaucrats' shifting self-narration from a state 'we' to a personal 'I' are the overtures that hold the Mesa together.

These overtures can be surprising. I was taken aback when María José chastised Teresa for 'not managing her emotions' when she had pointed out that the consequences for failing to be fully present or act professionally fell unequally on state officials and those recognized as victims. In sanctioning Teresa's behaviour, María José derived—and explicitly narrated—her credibility and authority from being 'a leader of victims', from her presence in many spaces of interaction between people recognized as victims and the state, and from the knowledge of the state and victimhood alike that she had accumulated through that positioning. When someone like María José says, 'We are the only Mesa that has this kind of accompaniment from the state', the room hears it differently than when that statement comes from the mouths of state officials.

These shifting allegiances and moments of castigation and forgiveness create possibilities for coaching, as well as for potential solidarity across social positionings. Professionals have coached claimants on the dynamics of legibility as particular kinds of subjects in a range of settings worldwide, from humanitarian aid to refugee asylum processes.[58] Coaching is an act of pulling back the curtain to reveal the vocabularies and strategies of self-presentation that are more likely to make people's claims believable in a

---

[58] Fassin and Rechtman, *The Empire of Trauma*; Ticktin, *Casualties of Care*; Lewis Turner, 'Syrian Refugee Men as Objects of Humanitarian Care', *International Feminist Journal of Politics* 21, no. 4 (2019): 595–616; Noelle Brigden, *The Migrant Passage* (Cornell University Press, 2018).

setting of contested personhood. 'This is why it is important to participate professionally', Carmen told the elected victim representatives and other state officials in the room at a Mesa meeting she was facilitating. 'We need to be able to present our work as the voice of the Mesa. If we do not have good participation, if we are not professional, then we cannot show representation, we cannot represent all the other victims who count on us'. The pronouns here include Carmen in the collective struggle of victim representation. She continued in a similar vein: 'We need to be able to make demands, not just go along with the agendas of academia and the institutionality. To do that, we need to set our own agendas, we need to show up, be involved, be professional'.

In this view, coaching as an act of solidarity is observable in the realignment of pronouns. According to Carmen, professionalism is a cornerstone of fulfilling the aims of collective victim representation and claim-making in front of the state. Coaching, however, is a double-edged sword, especially when the person who takes on that role makes assumptions about the goals of collective action and the best strategies for achieving them. In many ways, Carmen did not investigate the political as a question; she asserted it, and her 'political' was state-facing and required the performance of a script of professionalization. By contrast, 'For many activists, who viewed their activism as rooted in a radical vision of social transformation, efforts at professionalisation contradicted the underlying purpose of their work'.[59]

The Uses of Professionalization

The theater of the professionalization of victimhood is not a Greek tragedy, in which the audience knows something that the actors do not. Elected victim representatives to Mesas were keenly aware of the ironies of professionalization, whereby attendance sheets and other rituals of verification attested to the presence of 'the state', while those recognized as victims continued to do invisible and unpaid labour. 'We are very sad as victims when the institutions use us', María José, the Mesa coordinator from the preceding vignettes, told me in an interview.[60] I asked what made her feel used. 'They get lots of resources for attention to victims and they use it to pay state officials. They

---

[59] Tate, *Counting the Dead*, p. 136.
[60] Interview with elected victim representative to a peri-urban Mesa in greater Bogotá, August 2018.

earn lots, they live through victims. Do you understand me?' I nodded. 'Sometimes we feel they understand us too. But it's very difficult, my dear, when we feel abandoned, when we are hungry, and the state officials win money on our backs.[61] They use us to legalize their salaries and resources', she concluded.

The language of use recurred in conversations with elected victim representatives to different Mesas. Héctor, a human rights defender and victim of displacement and land dispossession in Usme, shared that 'the majority of the state officials live in the name of the institution of 'victim'. . . . They eat because we exist'.[62] Juan Pablo, an Afro-Colombian leader of a victims' group in Chocó, echoed that 'they use our voice to accredit themselves as ensuring victim participation'.[63] I asked who 'they' were. 'The state', Juan Pablo replied. 'They keep publishing books. "The victims this, the victims that". Books are great. But what we want are resources. We want them to work for victims, not write books about us. Instead, they throw the ball to us to do the work of the institucionalidad'. Juan Pablo paused, took a breath, and laughed: 'And then, on top of that, they tell us, "You did not arrive on time!"'

I visited Iris, the victim representative to the Antioquia Mesa who did not have electricity or running water, on the day she expected a utility company to come out and see if they could make a payment arrangement that would eventually result in reconnecting the water in her house. She elaborated on the dynamics of exploiting victim labour to prove state policy fulfilment.

> I have two meetings a day. Most of them don't pay for breakfast or lunch, except the Mesa, which always comes with refreshments.[64] You have to get to the meeting, spend all day there, only to schedule another meeting. Again, only the Mesa gives us back some of the money for all these meetings, but not every meeting counts. When the Mesa requires us to schedule another meeting or sub-committee meeting or separate 'extraordinary session', then there's no payment. And for what? For the Victims' Unit to stand in front of us and say, 'We served X number of victims this year' and claim credit for our work.'[65]

---

[61] The literal translation is evocatively biblical. María José had said 'a costillas de nosotros', which would literally translate to 'the state officials win money off our ribs'.
[62] Interview with human rights defender in Usme, June 2018.
[63] Interview with elected victim representative to a Mesa in Chocó, May 2018.
[64] One of Schouw Iversen's interviewees said: 'This system doesn't offer you anything but sweets and lies and refreshments'. Schouw Iversen, 'Participation as Confrontation', p. 1337.
[65] Interview with elected victim representative to a Mesa in Antioquia, March 2018.

The utility company never came that day. When I left Colombia months later, the lights were still off at Iris's house.

According to Sara Ahmed, 'The word *used*, when used to describe ourselves, tends to imply the injustice of being treated as an object, or as a means to someone else's end'.[66] Ahmed encourages readers to follow the word 'use' around and interrogate what she calls 'the uses of use',[67] which can illuminate ideas about life, death, politics, and power. What use is professionalization in the realm of victimhood, then? For people recognized as victims, professionalization can be useful when it supplies a register of legibility and a way of being that opens up possibilities for interlocution with 'the state'. The paperwork, shorthand of regulations, and manners of speech mark a shared terrain and vocabulary for discussion. Those same possibilities of interlocution, however, can splinter collective victim mobilization by alienating individuals and groups whose activism expressly opposes the state. Even if this alienation and splintering do not transpire, the process of professionalization itself requires work—the work of learning, filing, tracking, and counter-archiving. In a landscape in which people recognized as victims do not have services in their house, in a universe in which the word 'hunger' saturates their narratives, the double-edged labour of becoming professionalized places obligations on already suffering, exhausted subjects.

Professionalism is less ambiguously useful for the state. The vernacular and rituals of professionalization serve as a distancing mechanism from the pain, suffering, and radical demands for justice that underpin victimhood. It is telling that the vignettes from Mesas are littered with references to protocols and decrees, while hunger populates the interview transcripts. This distancing, according to the anthropologist Angélica Franco Gamboa, furthers the coloniality of knowledge about violence and justice.[68] The professionalized subject behaves herself, manages her emotions, refuses to complain or raise a voice, instead deferring to seemingly unemotional, quantified, or legalistic sources of 'expert knowledge'.[69] State institutions, in turn, instrumentalize the rituals of professionalization to justify the existence of the transitional justice infrastructure. The materiality, relationality,

---

[66] Sara Ahmed, *What's the Use?* (Duke University Press, 2019), p. 5.
[67] Ahmed, *What's the Use?*, p. 3.
[68] Angélica Franco Gamboa, 'Fronteras simbólicas entre expertos y víctimas de la guerra en Colombia', *Antípoda* 24 (2016): 49.
[69] Franco Gamboa, 'Fronteras simbólicas', p. 48.

and processes of professionalization function as evidence of 'the state', its work, and its program of justice.

The existence of paperwork, protocols, and professionals also facilitates the denial of the ghosts. Gaps, absences, and lacks are harder to point to than indicators and photos of meetings. The promises that remain unfulfilled, the illusion of justice, the incomplete and partial delivery of policies for those recognized as victims get flooded out of the frame by the papereality that takes centre stage.

Care Work

'Okay, everyone, last item! The day is almost over', Carmen said to the participants of the Mesa in Antioquia. She introduced Fernanda, a psychologist from a state agency. Carmen emphasized Fernanda's role was 'not to provide personal psychosocial support to individual victims, but instead to accompany the process'. 'I am here to provide psychosocial accompaniment', Fernanda repeated, albeit without elaborating on the meanings of these terms.

'Excuse me, Fernanda. Pardon me', Iris interrupted. 'Carmen, I do not understand why we have to do this. There is a whole periodic table of state officials who come, who go, who introduce themselves, present their work, and leave. That's very difficult for us. This is not 'psychological accompaniment', or whatever you call it. Accompaniment requires constancy'. Before Carmen could reply, Fernanda promised to keep her intervention quick—never mind that Iris had requested continuity of presence rather than speed.

Fernanda took an audible breath. 'Good afternoon again. I wanted to ask you all how you are doing, how you are feeling'. The room was unresponsive. Some victim representatives looked at their cell phones, some whispered among themselves. Every state official was looking at a cell phone. 'How is everybody feeling today?' Fernanda repeated. 'I have a headache', said a victims' association representative. 'Did you get it here or did you come with it?' Fernanda followed up. 'I got it here'. The reply ended this exchange.

'How do you feel?' Fernanda asked nobody in particular. Silence. 'I am interested in your feelings', she tried again. Iris, who had previously seemed skeptical about the exercise, spoke up. 'Tired, stressed, without solutions, worried'. 'In this space, or in all the spaces?' Fernanda asked. 'In all the spaces. It's the tiredness of labour and emotions [cansanso laboral y emocional]', Iris expanded. 'It is 4:00 p.m. I have been here since 9:00, left home at 6:00. I will go back to the neighbourhood, it will be 8:00 or 9:00 in the evening, and people will come looking for me. "Doña Iris, this thing happened". They see me as someone who can help. But I feel impotent when I have been working all day for victims and then I return home and more people ask for help and I cannot do anything'. 'Look at you again', Fernanda remarked, 'thinking of others!' Her demeanor brightened. 'For a few minutes, I do not want you to think about others. I want you to think only about yourselves'. More silence. 'What was the question again?' Luis asked, a full minute later. 'The question was: How do you feel?'

When Fernanda and I debriefed this exchange after the meeting, she expressed frustration that 'they won't give me anything. It's all one-word answers'. Ximena had expressed similar frustrations about her first-ever Mesa facilitation. Because, in the eyes of state officials, the 'good victim' in these spaces is chatty and responsive, withholding speech can be an effective strategy for people who want to shed light on the limits of meaningful 'victim participation' in state-facilitated spaces. Fernanda said, 'You've been here a lot. You see them too. Why do you think they're so silent with me?'

In the sociopolitical universe that people who identify as victims navigate, there is little separation between the concerns of the self and the concerns of others. The model of so-called psychosocial attention and accompaniment in conflict-affected settings focuses on the individual,[70] but the rigid division between individual and collective needs does not always resonate. Worse, it can come across as a state strategy for denying, erasing, or fracturing the politics of collectivity. When I shared this view with Fernanda, she did not find it surprising. She had a bachelor's degree in psychology, and though she was new to this particular role at the Mesa, she had previously worked in accompanying family members of the disappeared at exhumations, as well as in supporting displaced people in their return to their areas of origin. 'I do not think you are wrong, Roxani', she conceded. 'But I need to report on individuals in my assessments, not on collectives and their politics'.

Audit culture strikes again, highlighting the tensions of the labour of victimhood. State officials regularly reminded elected victim representatives

---

[70] As Theidon's research in Peru highlights, critiques of the individualism of psychosocial support interventions do not mean that people who identify as victims reject these approaches altogether. With reference to the category of 'traumado' (traumatized), Theidon writes: 'Although being "traumado" was introduced into these communities by external agents, over the years I did hear some Quechua speakers use the term. "Estar traumado" became part of local dynamics as people mobilized the category to different ends'. Theidon, *Intimate Enemies*, p. 29.

to Mesas that these were collective spaces and they were not to discuss individual cases of reparation, psychosocial needs, or bureaucratic impediments. 'A victim should participate in the public space, but in a selfless manner', the sociologists Sandra Ríos and Carolina Hormaza have similarly found in their own research on victim participation mechanisms in public policy in Colombia. 'A victim should be collective-oriented, meaning that they seek the benefit of the group; and they should be well versed in the norms and legal and technical aspects. . . . The dignified victim here is one who is not confrontational but collaborative, is well-spoken, and has no personal agenda'.[71] At the same time, nearly every monitoring mechanism collected and analysed data at the individual level, with checkboxes in columns that did not necessarily account for collectivities. Even the forms of accompaniment that spaces like the Mesa created privileged a narrative of thinking only about oneself, as Fernanda had encouraged Iris to do, which ran counter to the relations that enabled people to survive and navigate the bureaucracy of victimhood.

Sustaining and tending to those relations was part of the labour of victimhood. The work fell especially to leaders of victims' associations who had high visibility in both their communities and state-facing spaces. Tellingly, the language of labour recurred in their narratives of describing the relational work of care. 'Maybe what we need to do to get proper attention is to put the issue in labour terms [terminos laborales]', Juan David, a victim leader in the municipality of Rafael Uribe told me.[72] 'They should recognize our continued work. We keep putting it in terms of the "norm", reminding them of what the normativity says about recognition of victims and subsidies and reparations and I don't know what. But really, maybe we should put it in terms of work'.

Over the course of one week in March 2018, Iris left me daily WhatsApp voice messages about what she considered her work to be. Sometimes the labour of victimhood unfolded in the same language bureaucrats used to describe their own work in the Mesas. The vernacular of accompaniment and procedure forms reappeared, and Iris's fluency in it allowed others in her community the navigation of spaces and processes that might have felt impossible without her. 'Today I am accompanying a woman from the

---

[71] Sandra Ríos Oyola and Carolina Hormaza, 'The Role of Civil Servants in the Dignification of Victims in Meta, Colombia', *Third World Quarterly* 44, no. 4 (2023): 803.
[72] Interview with victim leader in Rafael Uribe, July 2018.

community to the Victims' Unit to file a procedure form because she has not heard anything for weeks', Iris said. That week, she dropped off food and checked on ill elders. She phoned state officials, whom she had gotten to know through her role at the Mesa, to ask them to connect people who identified as victims in her community to urgent medical care. 'This woman, Araceli, is pregnant and I am sure the baby is not well. It's a very sad story. . . . I won't bore you, precious. Anyway, I've been trying to reach the girl [muchacha] from the Secretariat of Health all day, but she won't answer my messages'.

Iris helped people less fluent in the paperwork of victimhood fill out documents and figure out where and how to submit them. She attended Mesas, reported back on the events at the Mesa at various community-level victim groups, debriefed the Mesas with other victim leaders. She listened to people's worries about safety, money, health, and justice. She soothed what she could and held what she couldn't. Though care work is work, and it is tiring, it is important not to frame it as 'an isolated, begrudgingly done task that is never a site of pleasure, joy, or community building'.[73] Iris's voice notes were often full of laughter, neighbourhood gossip, terms of endearment, and exclamations. These lively markers of enmeshed affection were as real as the suffering she witnessed and the fatigue she carried. And, alongside it all, Iris talked to me. 'Talking to you is political work', Juan David from Rafael Uribe reminded me.[74] 'Talking to people all day—victims, state officials, the public—that is political work. I talk to people about being displaced, about losing everything. Then I talk to people about the struggle [la lucha] to deal with all these entities . . . knocking on doors all day to see if people have all the forms they need, if they have medicine, if. They have services. That's political work'.

The work and the politics alike lie in protecting and sustaining what gives life and what might move closer to justice people who have experienced harms. The understanding of politics and work in these narratives differs from the imperatives of professionalization that demanded people recognized as victims show up early, stay for the whole meeting, email to account for excused absences, and participate eagerly in exercises. The labour of victimhood people like Iris and Juan David bring to light is still state-facing work at times, facilitated by the way some victim leaders have learned to navigate bureaucracy and by the relationships they have built with its

---
[73] Piepna-Samarasinha, *Care Work*, p. 46.
[74] Interview with victim leader in Rafael Uribe, July 2018.

professionals. However, it is not exclusively or primarily state-facing work. Doing this labour does not cement the project of consolidating the state and its presence during transitions from violence; on the contrary, it highlights the tenuousness, rather than constancy, of that state presence. This political work of victimhood draws attention to the moments of state abandonment.[75] Crucially, this is work that does not appear on attendance sheets. It does not make its way into acronymed databases, and its results do not get 'socialized' in meetings with the aim of reporting on the state's fulfilment of the public policy towards victims. This labour of victimhood does not make people eligible for subsidies or compensation. It counts and matters for survival and for struggles for justice, but it does not get counted.

The political labour of victimhood is gendered work. Though it sustains life and the relationships that foster it, it simultaneously drains the caregivers. 'I don't know many men who do the same kind of work I do, do you?' Iris asked me.[76] 'It's the women answering the phones and the doors. The whole world comes to the women so we can solve their problems'. She laughed as she uttered her next sentence. 'The men want to be elected to the Mesa, of course. They think they want to be leaders. But answer the door at 10:00 p.m. because a señora is newly displaced in the comuna and needs help? That's what they call Doña Iris for. It's the same patriarchy everywhere, even in the victims'. In being relational, caring, and justice-oriented, the labour of victimhood is not magically free of the inequalities and power imbalances that inflect other forms of work.

Male victim representatives do not dispute the gendered nature of the labour of victimhood. Luis, who is elected to the same Mesa as Iris, said that 'nobody wants to come to me at night to cry when they can go to Iris. The women are more affectionate, more tender at this kind of thing'.[77] In suggesting that tenderness naturally and effortlessly springs from the condition of femininity, this narrative, too, minimizes and essentializes the labour that care involves.

Doing this work can make people like Iris feel alone, despite being enmeshed in many relations of varying mutuality. She told me many times that it is not a coincidence that many female leaders of victims' associations are single. Shortly before the fieldwork for this project concluded, I decided

---

[75] Ballvé, *The Frontier Effect*, p. 8; Ramírez, *Between the Guerrillas*.
[76] Interview with elected victim representative to a Mesa in Antioquia, April 2018.
[77] Interview with elected victim representative to a Mesa in Antioquia, April 2018.

to ask her explicitly about it. Why are female victim group leaders single? Iris laughed. 'Ah, yes. Well, we have to start with the war. A lot of us lost husbands, boyfriends, and companions in the violence in one way or another, and we are continuing to lose them.'[78] I nodded. 'Now, after all this, some women chose to organize their lives as victim leaders. They met a companion, maybe they got married, maybe had a family again. They started to make a life [hacer su vida]. But then', Iris continued, 'when that man sees the dynamic that is the life of a female leader . . .' She trailed off and took a long pause. We sat together in the silence. 'When he sees that they knock on your door at ten, eleven at night, that they call you on the phone at any hour to solve whichever situation . . . well, that man becomes uncomfortable. That is how so many of us became single'. Then she started to count: 'Me, Luz, Marina, . . .' A roll call of care.

Revisiting the 'Good Victim'

Professionalization, and the labour on which it hinged or which it rendered invisible, constituted a particular kind of 'good victim'. 'Good victims' show up at the meeting on time and stay for the whole meeting every time. They do not complain, they do not critique, they do not ask for more money or timely payment, or even call it a payment at all. They do not raise their individual cases, but they help 'the state' track individual indicators. They wait, they listen, they do not raise their voices or interrupt. They manage their emotions, and discipline their companions when they fail to manage their own. They do the labour of victimhood; they learn the scripts and the choreography of meetings, the vernacular of laws and norms. They fill out attendance sheets, participate in exercises, and respond to questions—but as volunteers, not demanding support or recognition. They say, 'Thank you' to 'the state'. They are professional, but not too professional.

Juan David, who had encouraged me to think about victimhood in terms of work, also reminded me that 'this is not just about work, it is about dignity'.[79] The contestations around labour, compensation, and professionalization are undignifying for people who identify as victims, particularly when contrasted with the relative ease with which bureaucrats become legible as

---

[78] Interview with elected victim representative to a Mesa in Antioquia, August 2018.
[79] Interview with victim leader in Rafael Uribe, August 2018.

professionals, meaning that they can claim a salary and derive an identity and sense of purpose from their positioning vis-à-vis victimhood. 'You know the subsidies we receive for being part of the Mesa?' Juan David asked.[80] 'Well, as you know, I am part of the Mesa of Rafael Uribe. Most of us in that Mesa are Black.... Did you know, Roxani, that for us to receive our subsidy, we have to put our finger in an ink pad and then place the finger on the attendance list?' I shook my head no. 'We have to place the finger [colocar la huella]', he repeated.

> 'Imagine that.... The other day, I was in a meeting with the High Adviser for Victims, Gustavo.[81] Gustavo is a good man, I think. I wanted to say to him 'Gustavo, I, as a victim, receive about 40,000 COP per meeting. You get paid a liiiiitle [un poquiiiiiito] more than me every month, I think. Do you have to put your finger anywhere for your salary? Is this lack of trust in my 40,000 COP because I am Black? Because I am a victim? Or because I am poor?' Enrique Peñalosa, the mayor—he is being paid in millions. How many fingers does he have to place? Does he have to lie down on his back, with his spine in the ink, because there are just not enough fingers for the amount of money?'

[80] Interview with victim leader in Rafael Uribe, August 2018.
[81] This was Gustavo Quintero, who was the High Adviser for Victims, Peace, and Reconciliation at the time.

6
'Victim' as Distinction

Apertures of Violence

A queue formed outside the auditorium of Bogotá's Teatro Mexico an hour before the event began. Half an hour later, it snaked around the block. People had brought snacks to eat while they waited. Two men darted down the theatre steps to meet a woman in a suit, who had said into her walkie talkie moments earlier: 'They are here! They have arrived!'

They, in this case, were boxes of the latest report of the National Centre for Historical Memory (CNMH), titled *The War Inscribed in the Body: National Report on Sexual Violence in the Armed Conflict*.[1] One of the stated aims of CNMH is to 'contribute to the comprehensive reparation and to the right to truth' through 'the recovery, conservation, and dissemination of the plural memories of the victims, as well as the duty of memory of the state and all the perpetrators of violations that occurred in the context of the Colombian armed conflict'.[2] The 2011 Victims' Law formalized the creation of CNMH as a public institution in Colombia, and gave it administrative and financial autonomy.[3] This setup allowed CNMH to maintain relative intellectual and operative autonomy as well, despite links to the Colombian state.[4]

The report launching in November 2017 was one of seventeen such volumes that CNMH had produced that year, and one of hundreds since the 2011 Victims' Law that mandated the creation of the centre. These reports

---

[1] Centro Nacional de Memoria Histórica, *La guerra inscrita en el cuerpo* (Centro Nacional de Memoria Histórica, 2017).

[2] 'About Us', National Center for Historical Memory, http://www.centrodememoriahistorica.gov.co/en/about-the-national-center-about-the-national-center.

[3] For more on CNMH and the institutions that preceded it, see Juan Pablo Vera Lugo, 'Transitional Justice, Memory, and the Emergence of Legal Subjectivities in Colombia', in *A Sense of Justice: Legal Knowledge and Lived Experience in Latin America*, edited by Sandra Brunnegger and Karen Ann Faulk (Stanford University Press, 2016), pp. 25–49.

[4] Pilar Riaño-Alcalá and María Victoria Uribe, 'Constructing Memory amidst War: The Historical Memory Group of Colombia', *International Journal of Transitional Justice* 10, no. 1 (2016): 14. As Riaño-Alcalá and Uribe write, the questions of the CNMH's positioning vis-à-vis victims, armed actors, and the state presented various epistemological, ethical, and political dilemmas for the team members that supported its work.

populated the bookshelves of many offices I visited during this research. With their black spines and yellow lettering, and rarely numbering fewer than five hundred pages, the tomes mark the landscape of memory in a distinctive way, immediately recognizable to anyone familiar with their brand.

Both the language of branding and its artifacts were omnipresent during the Colombian transition. Recounting her formative years with the Office of the Ombudsman in Montes de María, Ximena, the High Advisory for Victims official introduced in earlier chapters, said: 'It was there that I learned the brand of war'.[5] I asked her what she meant by brand. 'A brand is like Coca-Cola', she laughed. 'I began to see, with my communications background, that war is a brand, something that must be sold. . . . A brand gave profitability to, well, obviously, those who make weapons. A brand provides profitability to the media with their stories. It's all brands'. While I absorbed Ximena's insights, she drew connections to the evolution of brands in transitional period. 'Today we start to see another brand', she said. 'The brand of "peace", the brand of "memory". It is a market—different market, of course, with different connotations, but in the end, everything is a market. When I go to companies with this job I have now and say to them, "We are going to do social responsibility through our victims project," "victims" becomes the brand'.[6]

In the moment, I found Ximena's framing uncomfortable. The discomfort betrayed my own naivety, my hope that the corporate language of branding was irrelevant to and incongruous with the experience of victimhood. The temptation to associate victimhood with a kind of purity and innocence, as though it can exist separately from neoliberal market logics, is strong, even for researchers who critique these frames and who endeavour to think beyond the binaries of the 'good victim' and the 'bad corporation'. Ximena reminded me that if scholars and practitioners are to take seriously that victimhood does not emanate passively from having suffered harm, that it takes work to both secure recognition as a 'victim' and to remain legible as *the right kind* of victim, then paying attention to branding is essential for shedding light on the aesthetic decisions, distinctions, and framing efforts that go into communicating about these experiences.

---

[5] Interview with High Advisory for Victims official in Bogotá, June 2018.
[6] For more on these politics of humanitarian branding, see Lisa Richey and Stefano Ponte, *Brand Aid: Shopping Well to Save the World* (University of Minnesota Press, 2011).

The launch of *The War Inscribed in the Body* was a lesson in the importance of aesthetics and curation. The event took place on a Tuesday evening in an auditorium of twelve hundred seats. Prior to entering the auditorium, guests received free notebooks with the hashtag #NoAcepto (#IDoNotAccept) on the cover. The hashtag made numerous appearances throughout the evening, as presenters encouraged audience members to tweet and 'use the hashtag #NoAcepto to show your rejection of sexual violence and your support for the victims'. Inside the auditorium, the first four rows were reserved for dignitaries from international organizations and senior officials of the Colombian government, who greeted each other with kisses as they arrived. There were also reserved seats in the front rows for people recognized as victims of the armed conflict who had been invited to be part of the event. As the rest of us waited for the event to begin, men carried boxes of the just-arrived report to the front of the room, where women spoke into headpieces with urgency as they arranged the volumes into stacks. A photographer took photos of the packed audience from the stage, as people stood and waved their lit cell phone screens around in an attempt to spot their friends. In the back, a paramedic stood in full emergency gear beside a stretcher. 'Please, dear guests, please!' An announcer interrupted the din of conversation. 'There are many people outside. If there is an available seat next to you, please let us know. We also know that it is hot in here and we will work to adjust the temperature'.

Moments later, the stage went dark. The din quieted. The formal proceedings of the event began with victims/survivors of sexual violence directly telling their own story.[7] This marked a departure from many other events at which a state official would usually begin by thanking sponsors and donors. By contrast, at this event, the voice of an unseen male announcer offstage introduced the first speaker as a 'victim participant'. She slowly emerged from the darker background to stand in the spotlight. 'This history is not mine', she began. 'It is not only one person's [story], it is all of ours'. She then recounted fragments of her memory of wartime rape.[8] 'I remember hands on my naked body. What I wanted more than anything was to have wings so I could fly. So I could fly where hands cannot touch me'. The speaker took a long pause. 'I

---

[7] I deliberately use both terms side by side here because they reflect the range of identification that various speakers used during this event. When others at the event made reference to the speakers, they commonly used the language of 'victims/survivors', unless noted otherwise in this vignette.

[8] Jenny Edkins has written extensively on the ways in which trauma disrupts the linearity both of memory itself and of storytelling about it. Edkins, *Trauma*.

hope that there will not be even one more statistic. Not one more figure [ni una cifra más]', she emphasized, referring to the statistics of violation. 'I hope that my story will convert into truth and justice for all'.

She walked off the stage to silence, as another woman walked on. Her testimony was in the Wayuu language, spoken by the Wayuu people in the Guajira peninsula of northeast Colombia.[9] There was no simultaneous interpretation or translation of her remarks. Given the resources and attention devoted to every other aspect of the event, this seemed like a deliberate choice, perhaps intended to allow the speaker to take the stage in her language—and to allow that language to fill the room. In the context of the colonial politics of language domination, among other forms of violence Indigenous groups have suffered, this moment was particularly poignant.[10] For the next three minutes, the audience sat in silence, watching a woman cry onstage in a language most Spanish speakers did not understand. A man appeared from backstage with a glass of water for the speaker. The moment allowed for a break in the tension, and applause filled the room. The speaker said, 'Thank you' in Spanish and walked off.

A few moments later, the director of the National Centre for Historical Memory, Gonzalo Sánchez, took the floor to deliver his own remarks.[11] He began by thanking people for their testimony, and by greeting the representatives of the United Nations, the High Advisory for Victims, the Victims' Unit, and the authors of the report (in that order). 'Sexual violence is not just an issue of the armed conflict', Sánchez said, opening the substantive portion of his speech. 'It is a matter of patriarchal norms'. This premise drew attention to what feminist scholars call the 'continuum of violence',[12] which is a way of making sense of the violence of war in the context of broader gendered harms, including those that people experience in alleged peacetime. This frame softens the temporal distinction between war and peace and brings wider patriarchal dynamics into focus, without underestimating that the

---

[9] For an excellent analysis of the politics of victimhood as pertaining to the Wayuu and other Indigenous communities, see Pablo Jaramillo, *Etnicidad y victimización* (Ediciones Uniandes, 2014).

[10] I have learned much from Pilar Riaño-Alcalá's beautiful reflections on storytelling, memory, and the Wayuu. Pilar Riaño-Alcalá, 'Stories That Claim: Justice Narratives and Testimonial Practices among the Wayuu', *Anthropological Quarterly* 93, no. 4 (2020): 589–623.

[11] He is cited by name here because this was a public event.

[12] Cynthia Cockburn, 'The Continuum of Violence: A Gender Perspective on War and Peace', in *Sites of Violence: Gender and Conflict Zones*, edited by Wenona Giles and Jennifer Hyndman (University of California Press, 2004); Annick T. R. Wibben, 'Everyday Security, Feminism, and the Continuum of Violence', *Journal of Global Security Studies* 5, no. 1 (2020): 115–21.

gendered violence of wartime can represent a rupture and a 'shattering experience of discontinuity'.[13]

Hearing Sánchez make this pronouncement filled me with hope. Being a 'gender person' meant I had attended many events on similar subjects in Colombia and elsewhere. Outside of explicitly feminist spaces and gatherings, I was more accustomed to the denial of sexual violence or to resistance to acknowledging patriarchy than I was to their explicit naming. No matter what critiques I would develop of the framing of violence and its nuances at this event and others like it, I sat in an auditorium of twelve hundred people who had filled a theatre on a weeknight to enthusiastically welcome a report documenting often silenced aspects of gendered violence. Years after the event, I still cannot quite imagine many places in which such a gathering, with such a corresponding degree of commitment and excitement about the urgency of the project, would be possible.

Despite the promising start, the rest of Sánchez's talk that evening focused on sexual violence in armed conflict, not on the broader patriarchal violence he had initially referenced. 'Sexual violence is part of the grammar of the conflict', he said, as he summarized the findings of the report regarding the perpetrators of this violence and the effects on the lives of victims/survivors. Even though he made brief references to masculinity and to sexual violence not being a female-only problem, Sánchez said, 'The bodies of women and girls are the site of war'. The rest of his remarks, as well as the rest of the speeches, echoed this sense of shifting apertures: widening for just a moment, enough to render patriarchy and a continuum of violence visible, only to shrink and zoom in more narrowly on wartime rape.

Seven speeches and an act of symbolic commemoration later, the event drew to a close. The host thanked the women for their bravery, and everyone else for attending, before announcing that 'the women who participated in the testimonies will now hand the report to you'. The women in the front rows stood to face the audience, holding stacks of the 547-page tomes in their hands. The audience gave them a standing ovation. With audience members still standing, the women made their way across the rows, handing out a copy of the bound book to each attendee. In the row in which I was seated, 'Thank you for your courage' was the most common response upon receipt.

---

[13] Margaret Urban Walker, 'Gender and Violence in Focus: A Background for Gender Justice in Reparations', in *The Gender of Reparations: Unsettling Sexual Hierarchies While Redressing Human Rights Violations*, edited by Ruth Rubio-Marín (Cambridge University Press, 2009), p. 24.

The shifting apertures for making sense of violence form the foundation of this chapter. Rather than analysing the well-documented hierarchies the status of 'victim' reflects and constructs among different people who embrace it,[14] the chapter focuses on how the category of 'victim of armed conflict' itself functions as a maker of hierarchy and creates distinctions and divisions among forms of violence, social movements, and even versions of one's own self. I show how the status of 'victim of armed conflict' marks and divides terrain between the violence of armed conflict and violence deemed 'other', as well as between the bureaucracy of transitional justice and the system people call 'ordinary justice'. These distinctions pertain not only to bureaucratic avenues and encounters, but also to socio-political mobilization around violence and the (re)making of the self and relationships in the wake of war.

This analysis complicates the understanding of political subjectivity and agency people exercise through claims of victimhood. Without discounting that, as I have argued throughout the book, victimhood can be a meaningful basis for political ways of being, actions, and relations, I now demonstrate that it also gives rise to *fractured* politics. Fractures invite us to attend to the break, to ask who or what is being splintered, how, and with what effect— to take seriously what hurts. I look at two sources of fractures: the armed conflict itself, and the differential approach incorporated into the peace and justice process.[15] The focus on the violence of the armed conflict potentially splinters social movements and hampers mobilization on different bases of violation or injustice. Conversely, the implementation of the differential approach creates hierarchies and contests among different aspects of one's own self. In practice, bureaucratic forms and encounters require people to choose between their womanhood and their ethnicity, or the sexuality and disability they simultaneously experience.

It may be possible to make sense of the decisions people make to be legible as particular kinds of subjects through the lens of strategic or affirmative essentialism. The logic of strategic or affirmative essentialism holds that people can make choices to rely on simplified or seemingly reductive presentations of the self, identity, and belonging for the sake of fulfilling specific political objectives[16]—in this case, becoming legible as particular kinds of victim

---

[14] Gabriel Gatti, *Un mundo de víctimas* (Anthropos, 2017); Berry, *War, Women, and Power*; Lawther, 'Let Me Tell You'; Chouliaraki, 'Victimhood'; Helms, *Innocence and Victimhood*; de Waardt, 'Naming and Shaming'; Golubović, 'One Day'; Barton Hronešová, 'The Uses of Victimhood'.
[15] For an analysis of the indicators pertaining to this approach, see Chapter 5.
[16] Helms, *Innocence and Victimhood*, p. 9; Utas, 'West-African Warscapes'.

subjects that merit differential attention. Gayatri Chakravorty Spivak's important work highlights that there can be 'strategic uses of positivist essentialism in a scrupulously visible political interest'.[17] Inspired by Spivak and by the ways I have witnessed people reclaim identities, statuses, and processes and infuse them with meaning, I am sceptical of accounts that claim that one intervention or another precludes the possibility of agency altogether.

At the same time, I argue that not every exercise of agency is affirming of life. The bureaucratization of the differential approach relies on a fixed imaginary of the victim subject, pinning it down to specific markers of identity, rather than allowing for victim subjects that 'exist in relation to others with whom they are in continuous negotiation over the meaning and value of life'.[18] The resulting view of victimhood is one that does not adequately allow for reckoning with the forms of power that bring this subject into being, or with the relationships that affirm, sustain, or contest the self in the world. In the production of legible victim subjectivity, 'a great deal of human dignity has to be left on the cutting room floor'.[19]

Scholars who draw attention to similar fractures and distinctions in different contexts have critiqued a perceived failure of transitional justice to address 'chronic structural violence and unequal social relations'.[20] This literature revolves around highlighting tensions between different forms, scales, and horizons of violence, contrasting 'slow violence' to 'event-based violence',[21] or structural to physical violence.[22] Unlike these important interventions, I have chosen not to label the distinctions that the status of 'victim of armed conflict' creates and reflects. Rather than classifying poverty or patriarchy as 'structural', 'systemic', 'chronic', or 'slow' violence, I follow the terms people use to describe their experience of different forms of harm and the distinctions among them. This is both because I am interested in the

---

[17] Gayatri Spivak, 'Subaltern Studies: Deconstructing Historiography?', in *The Spivak Reader*, edited by Donna Landry and Gerald MacLean (Routledge, 1996), p. 214.
[18] Erin Baines, "'Today, I Want to Speak Out the Truth': Victim Agency, Responsibility, and Transitional Justice", *International Political Sociology* 9, no. 4 (2015): 320.
[19] Enloe, *The Curious Feminist*, p. 22.
[20] Paul Gready and Simon Robins, 'From Transitional to Transformative Justice: A New Agenda for Practice', *International Journal of Transitional Justice* 8, no. 3 (2014): 342.
[21] Rob Nixon, *Slow Violence and the Environmentalism of the Poor* (Harvard University Press, 2011), p. 2.
[22] Jelke Boesten, *Sexual Violence during War and Peace: Gender, Power, and Post-conflict Justice in Peru* (Palgrave Macmillan, 2014); Dáire McGill, 'Different Violence, Different Justice? Taking Structural Violence Seriously in Post-conflict and Transitional Justice Processes', *State Crime Journal* 6, no. 1 (2017): 79–101; Zinaida Miller, 'Effects of Invisibility: In Search of the "Economic" in Transitional Justice', *International Journal of Transitional Justice* 2, no. 3 (2008): 266–91.

frames people rely on to make sense of their own experiences and because structural power dynamics cannot easily be divorced from their physical, material, and relational manifestations.

Some of the research in this area is oriented at calling for transformative justice, which Paul Gready and Simon Robins define as 'transformative change that emphasizes local agency and resources, the prioritisation of process rather than preconceived outcomes and the challenging of unequal and intersecting power relations and structures of exclusion at both the local and the global level'.[23] Proponents of transformative justice hope that such an approach would address some of the hierarchies, distinctions, and fractures narrated in this chapter.[24] My approach in this chapter is not normative. Instead, I empirically demonstrate the effects of the divisions that result from the category of 'victim of armed conflict' and show what people have at stake when they call for eliminating or preserving those divisions. In other words, through tracing the relational and material effects of how a legal category and socio-political status delineates the world, I shed light on what makes the project of transformation so challenging in the bureaucratic universe of the politics of victimhood.

As the research evolved, my persistent question became: If this is the 'success' of the professionalization model described in the previous chapter, what is the loss? Who or what do people feel they can(not) be and do because of the limits and possibilities of being 'victims of the armed conflict'? What world of solidarity, politics, and justice do people imagine might have been possible if it were not for the distinctions that the category of 'victim of armed conflict' makes in a universe of harms? What is the loss—what hurts?—when people consider broadening the category beyond the remit of the armed conflict?

In the closing lines of Tomas Tranströmer's prose poem 'The Blue House', the speaker declares: 'I am grateful for this life! And yet I miss the alternatives. All sketches wish to be real'.[25] The poem concludes: 'We do not actually know it, but we sense it: our life has a sister vessel which plies an entirely different route'. This chapter highlights the distinctions between different routes of

---

[23] Gready and Robins, 'From Transitional to Transformative', p. 340.
[24] Wendy Lambourne, 'Transitional Justice and Peacebuilding after Mass Violence', *International Journal of Transitional Justice* 3, no. 1(2009): 28–48; Kamari Clarke, *Fictions of Justice* (Cambridge University Press, 2009); Rodrigo Uprimny and Diana Guzmán, 'En búsqueda de un concepto transformador y participativo para las reparaciones en contextos transicionales', *International Law* 17 (2010): 232–86.
[25] Tomas Tranströmer, *The Blue House*, translated by Göran Malmqvist (Thunder City Press, 1987).

violence and justice, while seeking to shed light on the loss people feel when they cannot travel on the sister vessels that might have been.

The Carousel of Gendered (In)justice

The launch of the report on *The War Inscribed in the Body* was emblematic of a script about gender-based violence in war. Between 2013 and 2018, I attended seven public events commemorating and documenting wartime gender-based violence in Colombia. Nearly every such event opened with an acknowledgement of patriarchal norms that extended beyond the armed conflict. Sexual violence was 'just one example of the patriarchal logics of both peace and war'.[26] Speakers would then usually clarify that gender-based violence consists of 'more than just rape'.[27] That said, rape would almost always be framed as 'the most forgotten and most silenced form of violence'.[28] Event organizers commonly expressed gratitude for women's testimonies. The power of testimony itself was a key component of this script, with speakers emphasizing that 'we are putting intimate pain in the public space to break the social silence'.[29] The implied theory of change rested on an assumption that visibility would lead to different attitudes, that public pain could be transformative both for those who narrated it and for those who bore witness.

Speakers would then underscore that every perpetrator in the armed conflict, from guerrillas to paramilitaries and from state armed forces to criminal groups, used sexual violence 'as a weapon and strategy of war', which is language that has recurred in settings beyond Colombia as well.[30] While speakers would state that sexual violence has been used against men, and while they would sometimes make reference to 'diverse sexual identities', their examples and discussion of archetypal or 'emblematic cases' overwhelmingly

---

[26] Field diary, *La guerra inscrita en el cuerpo*, Bogotá, November 2017. This language is also reflected in the final report of the Truth Commission, which makes repeated references to patriarchy, patriarchal logics, and patriarchal power dynamics that go beyond the strict context of the war itself.
[27] Field diary, *Voces de Vida* event, Bogotá, December 2017.
[28] Field diary, *Memorias con Enfoque de Género* event, Bogotá, January 2018.
[29] Field diary, Truth Commission Meeting with Victims' Associations in Antioquia, March 2018.
[30] Maria Eriksson Baaz and Maria Stern, *Sexual Violence as a Weapon of War? Perceptions, Prescriptions, Problems in the Congo and Beyond* (Zed Books, 2013); Milli Lake, *Strong NGOs and Weak States: Pursuing Gender Justice in the Democratic Republic of Congo and South Africa* (Cambridge University Press, 2018). For the limits of the 'rape as a weapon of war' script, and the experiences it forecloses, see Doris Buss, 'Rethinking "Rape as a Weapon of War"', *Feminist Legal Studies* 17, no. 2 (2009): 145–63.

focused on female victim/survivors and on forms of heterosexual violence. Finally, these speeches typically closed by highlighting the multiple identities of victim/survivors. This would take the form of stressing that people ought to view them as 'women of not only pain, but above all, of dignity',[31] or as 'women of courage', 'women of strength'.[32] The implication is that victimization in the context of the armed conflict ought not be totalizing, that victim identity ought not obscure other senses of self or ways of being in the world.

The success of a script depends on its recognizability. The narrative above was familiar to people who identified as victims, bureaucrats who worked with them, and activists who worked on preventing and responding to gender-based violence. When I sat beside them in the audience of one public event or another, they would pinch me, wink across the room, or mouth the words to 'weapon and strategy of war' as though it were a hymn we all knew how to sing. There was an authorized and prescribed way of speaking about gender-based violence in the Colombian armed conflict, and producers and audiences of this script alike demonstrated their fluency in it. In many ways, the recognizability of this script is a success—one that is largely due to the hard work of feminist scholars and activists who have persistently conveyed that rape is not inevitable in armed conflict or separate from the other logics of violence.[33] I became curious about the work this script did in the context of the politics of victimhood.

Alicia trained as a lawyer, worked for a few years with the Victims' Unit on gender issues in what she called 'the Colombian periphery', and most recently worked in a civil society organization with a mandate to respond to gender-based violence across the Colombian territory. She left the NGO world due to what she described as immense burnout, the effects of which she felt at the time of our meeting. She described herself as 'a reformed and recovering NGO worker', with that identity shaping her sense of self and work more than her previous affiliation with the state bureaucracy of transitional justice. 'NGOs have their own form of institucionalidad', Alicia told me.[34] 'They must constantly produce, they always have to look for money.

---

[31] Field diary, *La guerra inscrita en el cuerpo* event, Bogotá, November 2017.
[32] Field diary, *De las cenizas al fuego de la palabra* event, Medellín, March 2018; field diary, Truth Commission meeting with victims' associations in Antioquia, March 2018.
[33] Dara Kay Cohen, *Rape during Civil War* (Cornell University Press, 2016); Elisabeth Jean Wood, 'Rape as a Practice of War: Toward a Typology of Political Violence', *Politics & Society* 46, no. 4 (2018): 513–37.
[34] Interview with former state official in Bogotá, January 2018.

Our agenda was concentrated on the war, which means that other agendas, such as reproductive health or intimate partner violence were put to the side'.

In her own analysis of similar dynamics in the Democratic Republic of Congo, the feminist scholar Milli Lake found that 'when social services designed to redress historical imbalances are offered exclusively to victims of particular harms, other forms of victimhood are necessarily sidelined'.[35] The sidelining was heartbreaking, not only for those who experienced it, but also for those who enforced it. Alicia recalled that, during her days of working with the Victims' Unit, women would come to fairs and 'technical assistance days' that different bureaucratic entities would organize.[36] 'There would always be a woman who would approach us, whispering and looking around her', Alicia remembered.[37] 'She would say her husband was violent, that he mistreated her or abused her. We tried to do our best. We would ask when this happened, to try to establish if it was in the context of the armed conflict, or if her husband was a combatant, or anything that could maybe hook this woman to the kind of assistance we could offer'. I nodded in recognition, having also observed the behaviours Alicia was describing. 'Usually, though', she lamented, 'it was just another woman with a violent husband in a violent, patriarchal society. This is not what the Victims' Unit was created for'. Alicia made a sound through her lips, as though mimicking a flood of water. 'Whoooosh!' We sat together in the sadness.

The distinction between gender-based violence in the context of the armed conflict and 'other' violence that was part of broader social dynamics affected state entities and NGOs alike. 'The emphasis on the armed conflict was a real source of tension and rupture, not just in our NGO, but everywhere in civil society', Monica, a different NGO worker and former state official, told me.[38] 'Some of us thought that, as an organization, we were actually displacing feminist issues that were not related to the conflict—issues like abortion, political quotas for women in parliament, or other violence that was "not related to the conflict"', she continued, making quotes in the air to indicate relations to the conflict were less straightforward than the phrase suggested. Organizational principles or personal values were rarely the obstacles to including those issues in the mandate of work. 'We needed to keep a close relationship to those

---

[35] Lake, *Strong NGOs*, p. 223.
[36] For more on the model of the 'fair' for peace, justice, or reconciliation, see McFee, 'Making a Presence'.
[37] Interview with former state official in Bogotá, January 2018.
[38] Interview with former state official in Bogotá, February 2018.

issues, some of us thought', Monica shared. 'It was in the name and mission of our NGO to work with women and their concerns, after all. But then our colleagues rightly said: Do we have the capacity to represent every woman's case? Do we have lawyers? Do we have resources?'

Gender-based violence in the context of the armed conflict came with different—and, crucially, better resourced—funding streams, workplans, international support, visibility, dedicated staff, protocols, and routes, within and beyond the state bureaucracy of transitional justice. This is the reality that prompted a senior state official to state, 'If "victim" is your first name, "of the armed conflict" is your surname'.[39] The armed conflict became the delimiting suffix that directed attention and resources. In conversations and events, the script became víctimas, en el marco del conflicto armado—victims, in the context of the armed conflict. The armed conflict distinguishes among forms of violence that coexist in the same societies and communities, and sometimes cohabitate in the same body.

'I remember these women would call the office', Alicia recalled, referring to her days of working with a women's NGO.[40] 'They were raped in the barrio, or their husband would mistreat them, and unfortunately, because of our mandate, we couldn't help them directly. They weren't the victims we could work with.'[41] There were still avenues of assistance and justice-seeking available to the women who were not, in Alicia's words, the victims the organization could work with. 'We told them to call the Secretariat for Women's Affairs or a few of the other NGOs. But we knew that's not enough. Those entities do not have the same resources. Those issues are not of the same priority, sadly'. The professionals who made and enforced these distinctions often took care to clarify that, in their eyes, the distinctions were not meaningful, did not hold, or should not exist. A senior official at the Ministry of Justice told me that 'for me, they are equally victims. The only thing that is distinct is the route'.[42] She continued: 'The theme of "which victim is a victim" is very

---

[39] Interview with senior state official in Medellín, March 2018.
[40] Interview with former state official in Bogotá, January 2018.
[41] In her incisive analysis of a similar phenomenon in Bosnia and Rwanda, Marie Berry concludes that such divisions ultimately 'fracture the women's movement. Whereas during the war women had come together to form small, informal self-help organization[s] . . . , in the aftermath, many of these organizations became specialized—they were exclusively for rape victims, widows, survivors of concentration camps, and so forth. Not only did these specialized groups ignore women who did not fit cleanly into a particular one, they also pitted 'rape survivor' groups against widows, concentration camp survivors, and returnees in competition for donor funds, leading to infighting, a lack of trust, and limited opportunities for collaboration'. Berry, *War, Women, and Power*, p. 190.
[42] Interview with senior official at the Ministry of Justice in Bogotá, November 2017.

complicated. What I hate the most is that it is another excuse for the carousel: what you are looking for is not here, go elsewhere. Go to this Ministry or that entity. Your problem does not correspond to my mandate'. The official sighed. 'This isn't justice. It's a carousel, and it's a cultural theme of living in Colombia during this time'.

In the carousel of justice, the promise of transitional justice feels shinier and more hopeful than the system of 'ordinary justice', even if both are prone to hauntings, partial fulfilments, and disappointments. Transitional justice looms extraordinary, especially when it comes with adjectives of international praise, logos, swag, sponsorships of foreign donors, and dedicated routes. By contrast, 'ordinary justice' feels like the familiar injustice, like the ordinary disappointment of closed doors, deferrals, and delays. Illustrating these dynamics, Monica told me: 'If you are dealing with a girl who is twelve or thirteen years old, and she becomes pregnant because of sexual violence in the armed conflict, you send her to the hospital so they can carry out a voluntary interruption of the pregnancy'.[43] Monica was deliberate about using that language, rather than the terminology of abortion. Abortion in Colombia had been severely restricted at the time of our conversation. It was only in 2006 that the Constitutional Court lifted what had been until then a total ban on abortions to decriminalize it in limited circumstances, such as when the 'life or health of the pregnant woman is threatened, when a doctor certifies that the foetus has an abnormality incompatible with life, and when a pregnancy results from an incident of rape or incest that has been duly reported to the authorities'.[44]

In the immediate post-accord period, both abortion restrictions and negative societal attitudes towards abortion restricted access to reproductive choice. 'If it's sexual violence in the context of the armed conflict, it's a different thing', Monica said.[45] 'Despite the difficulties this issue may carry with it, if you say that the woman was a victim of the armed conflict, the

---

[43] Interview with former state official in Bogotá, February 2018.

[44] Elena Prada, Susheela Singh, Lisa Remez, and Cristina Villareal, 'Unintended Pregnancy and Induced Abortion in Colombia' (Guttmacher Institute, 2011), p. 5. In 2022, and in response to the persistent work of Colombian civil society and activist groups working on gender issues, feminist causes, and reproductive health, the Constitutional Court legalized abortion during the first twenty-four weeks of pregnancy. This led Mariana Ardila, the managing attorney for the rights group Women's Link Worldwide in Colombia, to declare that 'Colombia now is the country with the most progressive abortion laws in Latin America and the Caribbean'. John Otis, 'Abortion Laws in Colombia Are Now among the Most Liberal in the Americas', *National Public Radio*, July 13, 2022, https://www.npr.org/sections/goatsandsoda/2022/05/10/1097570784/colombia-legalized-abortions-for-the-first-24-weeks-of-pregnancy-a-backlash-ensu.

[45] Interview with former state official in Bogotá, February 2018.

interruption of the pregnancy can be, shall we say, dealt with. It's more acceptable'. Monica was not just referring to laws and regulations; she was referring to social reception and to meaningful life options, to the attitudes a person might expect to encounter when she sought help. 'Now', she clarified, 'if you are a girl of twelve or thirteen years of age and you go to the health centre in the neighbourhood, maybe with your mum, and she tells them, "The thing is, her boyfriend raped her and she needs to interrupt the pregnancy", they might not think it is such a grave issue. Accessing that interruption is much more difficult'. Monica concluded: 'The thing with the armed conflict is that it's very complicated, and, in a perverse way, it opens some doors'.

This is a delicate point and it is important to be clear: no form of violence is easy to experience; no claim of victimhood comes lightly. The designation of 'victim of armed conflict' does not magically open up a world of instant remedy. Across social positionings, from bureaucracies of transitional justice to feminist NGOs and victims' associations, my interlocutors were clear-eyed about the challenges that people who identify as victims face in accessing the justice options, remedy, and reparations to which the category of 'victim of armed conflict' entitles them. Alongside victimhood in the context of armed conflict, however, there exist a range of gendered harms, violations, and experiences that are relegated to an understaffed and under-resourced universe of 'ordinary' state bureaucracy, civil society, and activism. The armed conflict becomes a sorting mechanism, marking the terrain of attention, claims, and resources. The violence of the armed conflict is rendered 'extraordinary'; the justice in its wake transitional. In a world in which harms made ordinary coexist with those rendered and labelled exceptional,[46] the distinctions unveil and deepen a fractured world of hurt.

A Fight among the Poor

Scholarship that calls for the localization of peacebuilding, humanitarian action, and transitional justice hopes to offer an alternative way for addressing the relationship between different harms, forms of violence, and justice options.[47] That scholarship proceeds from the premise that distinctions and

---

[46] Das, *Life and Words*.
[47] Rosalind Shaw, Lars Waldorf, and Pierre Hazan, eds., *Localising Transitional Justice: Interventions and Priorities after Mass Violence* (Stanford University Press, 2010); Alexander Hinton, ed., *Transitional Justice: Global Mechanisms and Local Realities after Genocide and Mass Violence* (Rutgers University Press, 2010); Roger Mac Ginty and Oliver Richmond, 'The Local Turn in Peace

hierarchies are born from the constitutive features of bureaucracies and from a 'top-down' approach to justice. 'Local forms of justice are commended for being closer to the victims', Adam Kochanski writes in his compelling synthesis of recent localization literature.[48] I am, as ever, left wondering: Which victims? 'The local'—which is as heterogeneous as 'the victims' and as prone to singular imagination too—is not necessarily more inclusive of a wider range of harms in more meaningful ways. In the specific context of the politics of victimhood, people who identify as victims may be just as invested in preserving the distinctions in policies, practices, and life options as other actors in the ecosystem of justice. Eliminating the distinctions on which justice relies is not universally desirable.

Two hours into an eight-hour Mesa meeting in Antioquia in 2018, a Victims' Unit official stood to make an announcement. 'I am afraid we must displace ourselves', he said. 'The thing is, this is the only room in the building with video-conference facilities and another institutional team needs to use them. We hope you understand'. Iris, the elected victim representative introduced in Chapter 5, smiled: 'The victims always understand, sir!' As we made our way out the door, people joked about the official's reliance on the language of displacement to make his announcement. 'Do you think this counts as massive displacement?' one of the elected victim representatives asked, with a laugh. The vernacular of victimhood spilled out of bureaucratic forms and into encounters, supplying humour and ways of navigating the carousel of justice.

As we situated ourselves in the new conference room, an attendance sheet made its way around the table, and two state officials struggled to turn on the projector. Blue light gave way to the familiar logo: 'Everyone for a new country'. 'Okay, okay, okay', Andrés said, in an obvious rush. He pulled up a spreadsheet, which was as familiar as the logo announcing a new country. In that day's meeting, the task was for the state to 'socialize' the results on education programming for victims of the armed conflict. The familiar choreography unfolded: a state official would read from the Excel sheet row by row, indicator by indicator. 'Component: Education. The projects are about

---

Building: A Critical Agenda for Peace', *Third World Quarterly* 34, no. 5 (2013): 763–83; Firchow, *Reclaiming Everyday Peace*.

[48] Adam Kochanski, 'The "Local Turn" in Transitional Justice: Curb the Enthusiasm', *International Studies Review* 22, no. 1 (2020): 30.

inclusion in the school system. The indicator is how many new students were included'.

Iris raised her hand. 'Excuse me. You need to tell us how many people there are in the municipality, not just how many you attended to, otherwise it's meaningless. And one more question, pardon me. How many of those services were specifically for victims of the armed conflict?' Andrés hesitated. 'Iris, unfortunately, we don't have that number for this specific indicator'. Iris was visibly frustrated with that answer. 'They are putting us all in the same bag' [nos están metiendo en la misma bolsa], she said. 'When we speak about services for victims of the armed conflict, we need to not all be swimming in the same bag as everybody else. This is chaos and confusion'. Other elected victim representatives around the room nodded in agreement, with one clapping his hand on the surface of the desk to indicate his approval of Iris's remarks. 'There are voices that want to advance themselves by saying that they work on victims' issues or that they provide services for victims. But that's not fair to the victims!' Before Andrés could respond, the official from the Public Ministry announced we were overtime for this session already. Lunch was getting cold. A new country would have to wait another day.

'Reparations are intended not only to provide something of concrete use and fitting value', the feminist scholar of transitional justice Margaret Urban Walker argues, 'but, in doing so, to "say" something definitively to victims and their society about why this performance *is owed specifically to victims as a matter of justice*'.[49] Echoing Iris's concerns, Walker worries that 'development, reconstruction or redistribution initiatives that are not directed or addressed specifically to victims will fail precisely to send the message that victims specifically are due repair in response to their particular injuries as a matter of justice'.[50] For these reasons, Walker encourages scholars to understand 'what is at stake in moving the focus away from the needs and dignity of the individual victim'.[51] I turned to Iris with this question.

After the Mesa meeting concluded for the day, I had a coffee with Iris across the street while we waited for her bus. 'You had said in the meeting that you did not want to be "all in the same bag"', I mentioned.[52] 'What is the

---

[49] Margaret Urban Walker, 'Transformative Reparations? A Critical Look at a Current Trend in Thinking about Gender-Just Reparations', *International Journal of Transitional Justice* 10, no. 1 (2016): 119, emphasis mine.
[50] Walker, 'Transformative Reparations?', p. 120.
[51] Walker, 'Transformative Reparations?', p. 115.
[52] Unlike more structured interviews with Iris cited elsewhere in the book, this informal conversation is reconstructed from detailed fieldnotes.

bag? What does this mean?' 'Okay, here is the thing', Iris replied. 'We have spent our entire lives trying not to all be put in the same bag, all the victims in the same bag. And now we are all put in the same bag, not only with other victims, but also with the general population, with all of Colombia's poor [todos los pobres de Colombia]'. I asked Iris specifically why this was a problem. 'It is against the law', she said. 'The Constitutional Court had said from the start that the victims need special, differential attention and that within the universe of victims, there also has to be differential attention, for example to women, Afro-Colombians, the disabled, the LGBT, and what have you. But, instead, we are all in the same bag', she repeated. 'Yes', I acknowledged. 'And I understand that this bothers you because it is a violation of law and policy related to victims. Is that it?' 'Yes, that's how it is', Iris confirmed. 'But also, to be a victim in certain corners, in certain areas, means to be very stigmatized. People are suspicious of you, they target you'. She put her hand over her mouth to whisper conspiratorially. 'Ooooh, I wonder what she did to deserve what happened to her', she said, mimicking the suspicion and stigma she and others had experienced. 'We have fought so hard. We have taken so many risks. But then you ask the municipality, 'And how many of these programs were for victims?' And they don't know what to tell you. They say their public policy is for victims, or that the victims are at the centre of the peace. But then ... where are we?'

By all indicators, Iris had lived in conditions of poverty her whole life. Through her activism, work, and care, she strove to mitigate the effects of poverty on various community members. And at the same time, she vociferously articulated a vision of the status of 'victim' as distinct from that of 'the poor'. She understood victimhood as separate from poverty, resulting from different harms (even if the living conditions overlapped), carrying different social connotations and stigmas, and, crucially, opening up different justice options. Iris was enmeshed in relations of care and solidarity—but those relations, too, had their boundaries. In this context, heeding the caution 'not to romanticize the local'[53] means letting go of the expectation of total and unquestionable solidarity among all vulnerable people. Being recognized as a 'victim of the armed conflict' does not make one always and immediately charitable towards all forms of harm. Watching Iris expressly articulate the boundaries of solidarity at the Mesa and in other spaces is also an invitation to think about where we—scholars, practitioners, readers—expect collective,

---

[53] Gready and Robins, 'From Transitional to Transformative', p. 349.

unbounded compassion to emerge from, and what duties and weights those expectations place on already tired shoulders.

Bureaucrats of transitional justice encountered the distinctions between people recognized as victims of the armed conflict and 'the historically poor' [pobres históricos] regularly. 'A big issue for those of us who work in major cities is the tension between the 'historically poor' and victims of the armed conflict', a senior official at the High Advisory for Victims told me.[54] 'Not all victims are poor. Not all the poor are victims. But poor victims are the most poor among the poor'. That official remarked that the gap between poor victims of the armed conflict and other poor populations in Colombia who were not recognized as victims was 'an enormous gash'.

Interpreting the sources of these tensions, Álvaro, a victim leader elected to a different Mesa than Iris, offered that ' "victim" is a way to direct social resources for certain categories'.[55] That is why bureaucrats, NGO professionals, and people who identify as victims alike remain fiercely protective of the boundaries of the category. As a state official at the Ministry of Justice said, in a country of limited resources and limitless needs, ' "Victim" is a calling card for a state that may otherwise not pick up the phone'.[56]

In the continuities of violence and vulnerability that many people have experienced in Colombia, the harms of the armed conflict also represent a rupture—one that the category of 'victim of the armed conflict' is designed to acknowledge and repair. It may be fruitful to return to one of the orienting questions for this chapter: What is the loss? What hurts when people contemplate broadening the category? People who identify as victims have mobilized, often at great personal cost and in the face of significant risks, to secure recognition and to access the rights and resources to which they are entitled. Many of these people do not dispute the necessity of expanding social protections, welfare, or development programs to address a universe of overlapping needs. They do not, however, think that this ought to be the work of people recognized as victims of the armed conflict or work done in the name of victimhood. For this group of people, the distinctions between vulnerabilities, statuses, and the resources attached to them are meaningful and worthy of preservation. Otherwise, people who identify as victims feel like they do the work of the state, justify the existence of a state bureaucracy

---

[54] Interview with senior official at the High Advisory for Victims in Bogotá, May 2018.
[55] Interview with elected victim representative to a Mesa, March 2018.
[56] Interview with Ministry of Justice official, December 2017.

of justice, but do not actually experience the promises of justice that these mechanisms ought to deliver.

The under-resourcing of the state's enormous transitional justice program only deepens people's protectiveness over the boundaries of the 'victim' category. Colombia's transitional justice scheme was designed with a much smaller number of victims in mind than the universe that came forward to seek recognition as such.[57] 'The Victims' Law was originally destined for four million victims', Senator Juan Manuel Gallán said, presiding over a meeting of the Congressional Monitoring Committee for the implementation of the Victims' Law. 'With the number of victims in it now, this has put an institutional weight on the law that has made it hard to respond'. Starting in 2017, a year before his term as the Colombian president would come to an end, Juan Manuel Santos started to manage expectations on victim reparation: 'There are no resources to offer reparation to all victims at the same time. This will take time. Maybe the most urgent, the most in need, and then we go from there. . . . The truly incredible thing is that there are eight million victims in the Victims' Registry. That is a lot of victims. A lot of victims. That is a monumental challenge'.[58]

Colombia's history of racialized classism has also shaped the distinctions between victims of the armed conflict and other poor or vulnerable groups. 'In this country, we are still classist and racist—and racist in our classism', a Colombian employee at a large international organization with a transitional justice mandate, said.[59] 'Once you arrive at a particular point in life, you don't notice class any more. But do not forget: Colombia is very feudalistic and stratified. This is very important for understanding how people view victims'. On the one hand, people who identify as victims must differentiate themselves from the 'historically poor' in order to access resources specifically designated for victims. On the other hand, they still need to perform need in legible ways so as not to deviate from others' expectations of victim behaviour[60]—all the while not appearing too needy or too well-off, lest they undermine the perceived authenticity of their claim to

---

[57] Rettberg, 'Ley de víctimas'.
[58] 'Santos: No hay recursos para reparar todas las víctimas al mismo tiempo: Santos | Nacional | Caracol Radio', *Caracol*, August 18, 2017, https://caracol.com.co/radio/2017/08/14/nacional/1502735685_067139.html.
[59] Interview with representative of an international organization working on transitional justice in Bogotá, January 2018.
[60] 'Victims who do not conform to received ideas [about victimhood] are barred from receiving the benefits bestowed on those considered legitimate sufferers'. Rudling, 'I'm Not That Chained Up', p. 423.

victimhood.[61] These intricate performances of socioeconomic class require simultaneous assimilation into imaginations of vulnerability and distinction from poverty.

'Poverty makes people uncomfortable here', a state official working on the registry team told me.[62] 'This is a fundamental feature of the Colombian soul'. A different official echoed: 'I can imagine that if the category of "victim" did not exist, some people would say, "These are poor, illiterate campesinos. Why do we have to give them anything?" The label "victim" allowed people to mobilize under a different flag'.[63] The implication here is clear: For poor people who had suffered violence in the context of the armed conflict, the category of 'victim' allowed for a form of claim-making, mobilization, and way of being in the world that the condition of poverty had not previously enabled.

The scholar of international development Ananya Roy has written that 'the issue is how and why at particular historical moments, poverty becomes sharply visible and serves as a lightning rod for social action and change'.[64] In the case of Colombia, victimhood on the basis of violations suffered in the armed conflict became the lightning rod for action, mobilizing responses that poverty, on its own, did not. 'For those who are vulnerable but not victims of the conflict, the idea of "the victim" created a world of privilege', a National Center for Historical Memory official explained.[65] 'There is a segment of society that resents the victims. They see victims as privileged. The frontier between "victim" and "poor" has become very complicated in a society with so many shortages in all directions'. The result was

---

[61] On this point, Camila, a victim leader in Sumapaz whose husband was forcibly disappeared in the early 2000s, told me:

> My neighbors at the time said to me when I was about to apply for the housing benefit for victims. 'Look, be careful. This law has certain requirements. You are always nicely put together, your little house [casita] looks beautiful. They may misunderstand your needs'. . . . One day this young girl [niña] came for the house visit as part of the assessment process this entity had. She was from the Victims' Unit, or from Family Well-Being, or maybe the Secretariat of Health, I don't remember, to tell you the truth. So she told me: 'Señora Camila, forgive me for what I am about to say to you. When you get ready to go to the appointments, please don't paint your nails. Don't go dressed in this way. With your appearance, they will give you nothing'. I said to that niña: 'You don't need to ask for forgiveness. But you need to tell me: What am I supposed to do? Am I supposed to hide the fridge?'

[62] Interview with registry team official in Bogotá, June 2018.
[63] Interview with a representative of an international organization working on transitional justice, January 2018.
[64] Ananya Roy, *Poverty Capital* (Routledge, 2010), p. 6.
[65] Interview with National Centre for Historical Memory official in Bogotá, January 2018.

what one feminist NGO leader called 'a fight among the poor'. She went on: 'People attached themselves to the victim label to access rights. You know why? Because there are no other rights in Colombia. No real rights for the poor. So what the Victims' Law did is that it established poor people of the first, second, and third order [pobres de la primera, segunda, y tercera categoría]'.[66]

The 'fight among the poor' has revealed and created multiple fractures. For people who suffered gendered harms in a context that was similarly separate from the conflict or who experienced vulnerabilities that resulted from a life of deprivation, the loss and hurt stem from exclusion from the 'victim' category. These are people left looking longingly from the other side of the glass. For some of them, the system of 'ordinary justice' may create options, but these avenues appear less promising than the mechanisms, attention, and resources that the bureaucracy of transitional justice can direct. Like the state bureaucracy of transitional justice, civil society organizations, NGOs, and victims' groups also organize along the fault lines of the armed conflict, replicating and reinforcing hierarchies and distinctions among harms. For many actors in that universe, these are *necessary* distinctions that are not only produced by institutional mandates and funding mechanisms, but also fittingly acknowledge the particularities of conflict-related harms.

For people who identify as victims, some of the labour of victimhood is geared at making those particularities visible and guarding against their dilution. In so doing, they challenge a vision of unquestioned solidarity among all vulnerable groups. Hierarchies and distinctions are not only created by 'the state'; people who identify as victims also participate in their preservation. These contestations make the weight of the labour of victimhood heavier to carry, as people who identify as victims navigate the stigma and indignity of their victimization, the overstretched and under-resourced bureaucracy and its disappointments, and the resentment of others whose losses are not as readily legible to bureaucracies of justice.

All the while, the carousel of justice keeps spinning. People try to imagine, repair, and reconstruct selves, relationships, and communities in the wake of war. That project, too, is fraught with distinctions.

---

[66] Interview with Municipal Victims' Team official in Antioquia, February 2018.

Markers of Difference

In an attempt not to put 'all victims in the same bag', as Iris had said, the Colombian peace and justice system has adopted a differential approach. 'Asking about the differential approach in a specific way', Dora Ines Munévar Munévar, Nicolás Torres and Ángela Patricia Martínez argue, 'necessarily implies asking about its uses and abuses among those who work institutionally and territorially with said approach for the rights of certain social groups or populations'.[67] An inquiry into how the differential approach became bureaucratized reveals the ways transitional justice processes can result in the fragmentation of the self.

Like many aspects of transitional justice in Colombia, the differential approach pre-dated the Havana peace accords and has received much international praise.[68] Both the meanings of the approach and its translations into English vary, even within the same official document.[69] Echoing the anthropologist Juan Felipe Hoyos, I treat the differential approach 'as a legal-political principle, as a public policy guideline, and as a field of dispute between the actors who converge in its implementation'.[70]

'There is confusion, even among us, on what the differential approach means', a state official said.[71] 'If someone is Afro-Colombian and a woman and she arrives in Medellín as a displaced person from Chocó, which aspect do we deal with first?' The processes, documents, and convening mechanisms of the state bureaucracy of transitional justice were designed to address some of these factors in isolation, not in tandem. Not all spaces, forms, and procedures were equally well developed; in fact, state officials broadly agreed that the gender dimension had received more attention and that both capacities and procedures to address other dimensions of the approach were lacking. A former Victims' Unit official admitted that these

---

[67] Dora Inés Munévar Munévar, Nicolás Torres Rodríguez, and Ángela Patricia Martínez Sánchez, 'Provocaciones sentipensadas desde Colombia para cuestionar el "enfoque diferencial"', *Mundos Plurales-Revista Latinoamericana de Políticas y Acción Pública* 8, no. 2 (2021): 22.

[68] Astrid Jamar, 'The Exclusivity of Inclusion: Global Construction of Vulnerable and Apolitical Victimhood in Peace Agreements', *International Journal of Transitional Justice* 15, no. 2 (2021): 284–308.

[69] There is even variation in the official translation of the Colombian peace accord, which refers to a 'differential approach' and an 'equity-based approach'. Sara Koopman, 'Building an Inclusive Peace Is an Uneven Socio-spatial Process: Colombia's Differential Approach', *Political Geography* 83 (2020): 4.

[70] Juan Felipe Hoyos García, '"El desplome de lo igual es irreversible": La emergencia del enfoque diferencial étnico en Colombia', *Revista Colombiana de Antropología* 59, no. 1 (2023): 111.

[71] Interview with Municipal Victims' Team official in Medellín, February 2018.

realities were frustrating for the bureaucrats who had to implement the approach. 'The approach does not pretend to create categories that delimit with absolute certainty the plan of action of the state', he said.[72] 'We used to say to our supervisors, "Tell me, please, how to translate the approach into action towards the victims?" And we would hear, "There is no capacity to tell you as the state".'

State institutions—or, sometimes, teams within the same institution—had different processes for making sense of difference. The effect on people who sought state attention was dizzying. 'On Monday, I am Afro-Colombian. On Tuesday, I am a woman. On Wednesday, I am a lesbian', a victim leader in Antioquia said.[73] Though the approach rightly aims to offer tailored attention to different groups with potentially different needs, it can lead to the creation of a hierarchy among identities within the same person, to a splintering of oneself into parts to become a legible subject of assistance. That splintering has material, emotional, and relational costs, as it enhances the bureaucratic burden on people who need to expend time and resources to visit separate offices, interact with different teams, learn to navigate different bureaucratic universes with different expectations, fill out different forms, and perform their 'differential' nature for different audiences.

'The problem is not with the approach itself', a state official on a gender team said.[74] 'The approach is clear: It is intended to recognize different forms of conflict effects. The problem is how the institucionalidad implemented it. It created a competition or annihilation of other subjectivities and identities. You especially see this when people have to pick which aspect of their identity to use to seek protection. Are you Afro-Colombian? A woman? Disabled? You cannot be all three. If you are all three, nobody can attend to you'. This official underscored that the victim subject in transitional justice is necessarily a fragmented subject, as the current mechanisms for addressing difference are not conducive to making sense of an integrated wholeness.[75]

The survival of people who identify as victims in a bureaucratic universe depends in part on identifying possibilities for action. Over time, they come

---

[72] Interview with former Victims' Unit official in Medellín, March 2018.
[73] Interview with victim leader in Antioquia, March 2018.
[74] Interview with state official on a gender team in Bogotá, May 2018.
[75] María Martin de Almagro develops a similar critique of the Women, Peace, and Security agenda and its production of the 'woman participant' in ways that isolate dynamics of gender, race, and class. Martin de Almagro, 'Producing Participants'. See also Toni Haastrup and Jamie Hagen, 'Racial hierarchies of knowledge production in the Women, Peace and Security agenda,' *Critical Studies on Security* 9 (no. 1): 27–30.

to know which teams are more competent, which state officials are likely to act compassionately, and which processes are worthy of the investment of time and effort. There are moments of agency available to people when they learn to read the landscape of the bureaucracy, diagnose where they are likely to find assistance, and fashion themselves as the right kind of subject by highlighting aspects of their identity while sidelining others. I posit, however, that these flashes of agency offer limited possibilities of freedom—in part because they preclude the freedom of being a whole self. Erin Baines powerfully conceptualizes 'political agency as the actions, words, or gestures that contest one's status as a person or nonperson within the web of human relationships that makes life meaningful'.[76] Violence fractures the self and reconfigures social relations. The transitional justice system set up to repair those harms, however, continues to rely on and produce a fractured self.

The effects of this self-segmentation transcend the individual to shape the universe of socio-political mobilization. 'The victims are islands in Colombia', a UN official working on what he described as the 'victims' portfolio' said.[77] 'Each of them went their own way, the displaced, the disappeared, the women, the Afro-Colombians. Some built bridges, but most victims and their organizations started to think through the perspective of their modality of victimization'. These comments echo the findings of the feminist scholar Marie Berry in Rwanda and Bosnia, 'competition for resources either from the state or from international actors has led to infighting and a lack of trust, . . . has limited opportunities for collaboration, and caused groups to privilege the identities thought to bring about the most funding'.[78] The category of 'victim of the armed conflict', coupled with the segmented implementation of the differential approach, has complicated the project of wholeness for selves and movements alike.

The vernacular of victimhood reflects some of the ways in which wholeness was out of reach. The language of 'modalities of violence', or of 'victimizing acts' [hechos victimizantes], recurred in official spaces, as well as people's self-descriptions. 'We are all here, each with our own act', Iris said before a Mesa meeting began. It is through acts and modalities that it becomes real and material in the lives of people; it is through the language of harms that the hurts begin to become visible. Thinking and acting only or

---

[76] Baines, 'Today, I Want to Speak', p. 317.
[77] Interview with UN official working on victims' portfolio in Medellín, March 2018.
[78] Berry, *War, Women, and Power*, p. 191.

primarily through the frame of 'victimizing acts' and individual modalities, however, can obscure both the potential for solidarities and the workings of relational power. 'Focusing on singular acts of extraordinary violence', Baines convincingly argues, 'lifts these events outside of the historical and social context that gives violence its form'.[79] As several critics of the differential approach in Colombia have stated, the approach is at its most compelling not when it reproduces an essentialized understanding of harm in which women or Afro-Colombians are always already vulnerable, but when it prompts curiosity about people's dynamic situatedness in relation to harms.[80] In practice, this would mean investigating how gendered, racialized, and classed dynamics of power affect the production of different victim subjectivities, as well as the vulnerabilities and possibilities of agency that come into view through different subject-positions and webs of relation.

This view of the differential approach is much closer to an understanding of the concept and practice of intersectionality as pertaining not to fixed individual identity, but to ever shifting power relations.[81] As the feminist geographer Sara Koopman notes, 'The term intersectionality was rarely used at the time by feminists in Colombia, though there have been debates in the movement about difference'.[82] Many professionals and organizations attempted to *do* intersectional work in practice, or identified the challenges in attempting to do such work, even if they did not use the language.[83] 'It would be a lot easier if the gender team also had training on how to deal with dimensions of ethnicity', a professional tasked with implementing the differential approach told me.[84] An official working on the data and indicators teams echoed that the forms ought to reflect more than one dimension, not least because that would make the navigation of the bureaucratic universe easier for people who identified as victims. The pitfalls of focusing on relatively fixed identities in isolation, as opposed to analysing intersecting power relations, were obvious to many of the people tasked with implementing the differential approach through bureaucracy.

---

[79] Baines, 'Today, I Want to Speak', p. 317.
[80] Hoyos, 'El desplome', p. 114.
[81] Patricia Hill Collins and Sirma Bilge, *Intersectionality* (John Wiley & Sons, 2016), p. 1.
[82] Koopman, 'Building an Inclusive Peace', p. 8.
[83] Samuel Ritholtz, José Fernando Serrano-Amaya, Jamie Hagen, and Melanie Judge, 'En construcción: Hacia una teoría y praxis de la construcción de la paz queer/cuir', *Revista de Estudios Sociales* 83, no. 1 (2023): 3–22; Angela Lederach, 'Youth Provoking Peace: An Intersectional Approach to Territorial Peacebuilding in Colombia', *Peacebuilding* 8, no. 2 (2020): 198–217.
[84] Interview with state official in Bogotá, July 2018.

A historical overview of the origins of the differential approach suggests that this relational frame was once more visible than current bureaucratic iterations might indicate. The feminist anthropologist Donny Meertens articulated an early version of what became the differential approach in a UNHCR report on displacement in Colombia in 2002.[85] Meertens's conception 'proceeded relationally: it did not take women's intrinsic conditions for granted, but rather analysed the links between events and the situations in which women were inserted'.[86] In so doing, Hoyos argues that Meertens's articulation 'established another type of relationship between the subjects of politics and the state, as well as the place of the differential approach as an interface between both'.[87] However, as the language of victimizing acts, modalities of violence, indicators, processes, and routes proliferated in Colombia, the differential focus 'skewed towards the reproduction of spurious essentialisms and binary ideals', eventually framing people as 'foreigners', 'others', and 'subalterns'.[88]

Towards a Seed-Sowing Theory and Praxis of Justice

I have been, and sometimes still work as, a gender practitioner, of the kind who would have to design or implement an approach just like the one I am critiquing. It is approximately at this point in the critique that the practitioner part of myself—a whole self, even if occasionally also made up of islands and fragments—becomes uncomfortable and sighs in frustration. I picture my practitioner colleagues, within and beyond state bureaucracies, within and beyond Colombia, reading these words and shaking their heads. I picture them telling me that they know all of this; after all, in the preceding pages, several of my practitioner colleagues within and outside state bureaucracies were the ones who articulated the dynamics that this critique is based on.

I share these colleagues' frustration. In the projects of dismantling patriarchy or working towards justice, one must begin somewhere. All beginnings are partial, humble, and flawed. In that spirit, it is possible to interpret and welcome the differential approach as a beginning, as an intervention that

---

[85] Donny Meertens, 'Colombia: Internally Displaced Persons and the Conditions for Socioeconomic Reintegration' (United Nations High Commission for Refugees, 2002).
[86] Hoyos, 'El desplome', p. 117.
[87] Hoyos, 'El desplome', p. 117.
[88] Munévar Munévar et al., 'Provocaciones sentipensadas', pp. 10–11.

may not go far enough when it comes to addressing power or seeing the self as full of multiplicities and relationalities, but which still sows important seeds for how to pay differential attention to subjects and harms in peace and justice processes. It is also possible to imagine the 'sister vessel' of justice in practical terms: to picture a form that allows people to narrate multiple facets of their experiences, to document multiple ways of being situated in relation to power and harms. It is possible to envision a team of transitional justice professionals who have the mandate, training, and resources to attend to that multiplicity within one's experience, rather than redirecting parts of a self to another office across town.

Both my academic research and my years as a practitioner have nudged me towards a seed-sowing theory of justice and social change. Sowing seeds, like other acts of gardening, requires living across temporal horizons, with feet rooted in the present and an imagination towards what might emerge and thrive in the future. Building theory through learning from seed is a call for acknowledging the possibilities of politics and justice alike across different horizons of time. As the next chapter illuminates, shifting apertures of time enable people to consider hope and heartache, to hold loss and potential in the same embrace.

As a seed for the future, both in Colombia and in other settings reckoning with the wake of armed conflict and mass violence, Colombia's approach to the category of 'victim of the armed conflict', as well as its development of a differential approach to peace and justice, can hold much promise. If the purpose of critique is not merely to tear down and to find flaw, but also to rebuild worlds, the Colombian peace-and-justice process has given critics, practitioners, activists, scholars, and rebuilders of all stripes many fruitful materials with which to remake a universe of justice.

For people currently mired in bureaucracies of victimhood, however, who experience the ways in which the category of 'victim of armed conflict' marks terrain, functions as a distinction between harms, and sometimes requires people to segment aspects of themselves in order to be legible as subjects of justice, the limits of rigid categories and bureaucratic processes are acutely felt. These are not people who can be consoled by longer horizons of time. They are alive now and seek justice with urgency in the present.

The 'sister vessel' of justice that might have been, the alternative model that might have allowed for a more meaningful, relational conception of politics and agency alike, looks different for differently positioned subjects. For some of the historically poor populations in Colombia who do not have recognition as 'victims of the armed conflict', expanding social services to address their needs is both necessary and desirable. For the bureaucrats tasked with delimiting need and directing resources, the expansion of social services is daunting, especially in an environment in which resources to provide reparations to those recognized as victims are already insufficient. And for some of the people who identify as victims of the armed conflict, the potential expansion of the 'victim' category to include harms not related to the violence of the conflict itself represents a further loss, and a violation of the state's promise and duties towards those it recognized as victims.

One of my orienting questions for the chapter was 'Who or what do people feel they can(not) be and do because of the limits and possibilities of being (particular kinds of) "victims of the armed conflict"?' In addition to asking what the losses are when fractures in selves and movements become apparent, we might also ask: How do people tend to what hurts? The political does not only reveal itself in injury and fragmentation, but also in the remaking. The final chapter of the book centres these questions by examining where and how people find wholeness in the realm of victimhood.

7
The Future of Victimhood

Fashions and Fads

'Would you like a flower for your jacket?' The municipal employee who handed me a forget-me-not sticker was clad in them herself. Her T-shirt featured a printed forget-me-not, with the hashtag #NoMeOlvides (#DoNotForgetMe) written on top of it. The emblem of the city of Bogotá and the slogan 'Bogotá, better for everyone' were printed on the bottom. On the left, above the hashtag, she had pinned an additional forget-me-not; on the right, she had affixed a sticker like the one she was offering me. In this instance, memory was a uniform. 'Take one, please', she said, pressing the sticker into my hand. 'Actually, take many. I must give them out', she insisted, filling my fist with flowers. I thanked her, stuck a flower to my own lapel, stuffed the rest of them into my bag, and walked in the direction of the coffins.

In April 2018, in the centre of Bogotá's Plaza Bolívar, where street vendors typically sold bread for tourists to feed the pigeons, human rights defenders had arranged coffins in concentric circles (figure 7.1). Each black coffin had a white cross painted onto it. People left carnations in the middle of the crosses and scribbled messages in coloured chalk around them. 'We are not numbers. We are people. Fathers, mothers, sons, brothers', one message read. Below it: 'Mother Earth is also a victim. When will they repair her?' On the next coffin: 'Enough with the corruption. It is killing us. Peace is a right. Do not kill us'. And on the one beside that: 'We demand peace! Uribe, do not kill any more. No more dead victims and social leaders'.[1]

There was a noticeable contrast between these messages and the laminated banners hanging from Liévano Palace in the west corner of the plaza, on the facade of the building that housed some of the offices of the High Advisory for Victims. As the banners announced, it was April 9, designated by the

---

[1] This commemorative event took place during the presidency of Juan Manuel Santos. However, many activists decried the continued influence of former president Álvaro Uribe on politics and the effect of his incendiary rhetoric on the lives of human rights defenders.

Figure 7.1 On the National Day of Memory and Solidarity with Victims of the Armed Conflict in 2018, victims' associations organized coffins in concentric circles in Bogotá's Plaza Bolívar to protest attacks against human rights defenders and the slowness of the government's fulfilment of the promises of the peace accord. Flowers rested on each coffin, and messages were scribbled in chalk to draw attention to the ongoing justice needs of people who identified as victims and their communities.

Victims' Law of 2011 as the annual National Day of Memory and Solidarity with Victims of the Armed Conflict. While the official branding focused on symbolic flowers and hashtags, the commemorations that human rights defenders led consisted of denouncements and demands that the state fulfil its public policy towards those it recognized as victims. The messages written on the coffins and on posters around them also drew attention to social inequalities and injustices that pre-dated the armed conflict and lasted beyond the peace accord. In a banner laid beside the coffins, one of the groups of victims elected to a Mesa in Bogotá had written, 'Peace with hunger and without social justice is an illusion'.

In a different corner of the plaza, human rights defenders had laid out a large map of Colombia, onto which they were pinning the names of social leaders and victims of the armed conflict who had been assassinated in each region since the signing of the peace accord. On the bottom right-hand corner of the map that the human rights defenders had rolled out, in the area reserved for legends, there was a handwritten message in all caps: 'This is the work of the Nobel Peace Prize'.

This was the second Victims' Day since the signing of the peace accord between the Colombian government and the FARC, and the seventh since the legal establishment of this occasion. Evident in the human rights defenders' commemoration strategies was a refusal to relegate memory to the past. The past provides fodder for memory, but the acts of meaning-making and claim-making continue in the present and inform imaginations of the future. Human rights defenders realigned the tenses, rejecting the treatment of victimhood as a historical occurrence and grounding violence in the present.

Meanwhile, those involved in bureaucracies of victimhood shared with me their anxiety about the future. 'Once someone has the shirt of "victim" on, it becomes installed as a paralyzing category', said one former state official.[2] 'They put on the suit of a victim [traje de víctima] and do not want to take it off', an NGO director echoed.[3] And in a conversation about the future of victim status, a former senior official of the Victims' Unit who contributed to the design of Colombia's transitional justice policy commented: 'What I am interested in is this: How and when will you take off the dress of being a victim [vestido de víctima]?'[4]

The fear in these narratives is that victimhood is a permanent uniform. In the words of one state official, 'Victim is a status with only one door: entry. There is not a single exit'.[5] This worry about the future of the victim category prompted many implementers of transitional justice programs to argue that it was time to 'pass from the condition of victim to another state',[6] 'to transition from being victims to being political subjects'.[7] Among people who identified as victims, however, temporal anxieties about the future

---

[2] Interview with former state official in Bogotá, January 2018.
[3] Interview with NGO director in Medellín, March 2018.
[4] Interview with former senior official at the Victims' Unit in Bogotá, January 2018. The reliance on the language of fashion to describe victimhood is not specific to Colombia. For a similar discussion of 'development fashions' and transitional justice in Peru, see Mijke de Waardt and Eva Willems, 'Recipients versus Participants: Politics of Aid and Victim Representation in Transitional Justice Practices in Peru', *Human Rights Quarterly* 44, no. 2 (2022): 339–63.
[5] Interview with street-level bureaucrat at the Municipal Victims' Team in Medellín, February 2018.
[6] Field diary observations from the meeting of the Congressional Commission on Monitoring the Implementation of Victims' Law, May 2018.
[7] Interview with senior state official in Victims' Unit, May 2018.

of the category were oriented in a different direction—also expressed in clothing metaphors. 'We know that victims are fashionable [de moda] now', one victim leader in Antioquia told me. 'But what happens to us when the world no longer looks to Colombia as a referent for transitional justice?'[8] The clothing metaphors in these narratives are both apt and limited. Like fashion, victimhood constructs selves. It invites performances and requires audiences who confer statuses on subjects. However, while people can selectively engage with the label and performance of 'victim' in the way that one can take clothes on and off, the harms that initially make one eligible for this status are less easy to shed. The effects of violence are more lasting than a change of outfit would suggest.

Anxieties expressed in terms of fashion are, fundamentally, anxieties about time. This chapter looks towards the future of the victim category by asking: What are the implications of insisting on transitioning away from a victim identity and asking people to leave claims of victimhood in the past, while violence is ongoing and public policy fulfilment for people recognized as victims is incomplete? How do different actors imagine the future of victimhood, and how do these framings of past, present, and future shape politics, relationships, and claim-making?

Ideas about 'good victims' reflect contests over the resonance of identities and statuses across different time horizons. In one story about the future of victimhood, many state officials and programs suggest that 'good victims' are the economically responsible ones, whose livelihoods do not depend on the expectation of state assistance, but instead stem from self-reliant entrepreneurship and notions of productivity. These narratives shift the responsibility of overcoming harm onto the individuals who experienced it, deflecting attention away from the duty of the state to deliver on its transitional justice promises. Many of these narratives about the future reflect an aspiration for those who identify as victims to develop a sense of citizenship and a practice of politics that is *not* based on victimhood. According to this story, the 'good victim' of the future is, in fact, the one who chooses not to identify as a victim at all.

At the same time, among both some state officials and people who identify as victims, there is resistance to the projected aspiration to leave victimhood behind. This resistance underscores the power and political salience of victim status not only in times of immediate transition from armed

---

[8] Interview with victim leader in Antioquia, March 2018.

conflict, but also as a basis for longer-term relationships, claim-making, and understandings of citizenship. In this second story, ideas about expressly political subjectivities, rather than about entrepreneurship and productivity, are at the core of enacting the present and imagining the future. Rather than treating the past, present, and future as fully distinct temporal phases that one can linearly travel through, this story frames time more fluidly. Violence, victimhood, and the political subjectivities they bring to bear blur the tenses; they link the past, present, and future, shaping people's memories, imaginations, and claims.

These temporal horizons do not only pertain to the lives of individuals. Anxieties about the (good) victim of the future are, at their heart, also anxieties about the centrality of the bureaucracy of victimhood for the present and future of the Colombian state. What is at stake here is how 'a country of victims' ages over time.[9] Contests over the future of victimhood also bring to light competing imaginations and anxieties about how the state establishes its presence, and how bureaucracies of victimhood shape state-citizen relations during transitions from violence.

Pain, Power, Politics, and Time

The end of victimhood raises different questions than the end of armed conflict. In one sense, both are fraught, contestable endings. They raise questions about how to address what Rob Nixon calls the 'temporal overspill' of violence: the violence that persists after a peace accord is signed, the victims that are made after a conflict has allegedly ended.[10] Feminist scholars have long been curious about what ends with a formal peace process,[11] questioning proclamations of a 'post-conflict' that exists primarily on paper and not necessarily in the embodied reality of everyday life for people affected by violence.

---

[9] The phrase 'a country of victims' is from an interview with a Ministry of Justice official in November 2018, which I discuss in greater detail later in this chapter. The phrase also appeared in the Truth Commission final report.

[10] Nixon, *Slow Violence*, p. 8.

[11] Fionnuala ní Aoláin, 'Women, Security, and the Patriarchy of Internationalized Transitional Justice', *Human Rights Quarterly* (2009): 1055–85; Annick Wibben, Catia Cecilia Confortini, Sanam Roohi, Sarai B. Aharoni, Leena Vastapuu, and Tiina Vaittinen, 'Collective Discussion: Piecing-Up Feminist Peace Research', *International Political Sociology* 13, no. 1 (2019): 86–107.

Pinning down the end of violence—like identifying a definitive start of the armed conflict—is a complicated endeavour. However, an inquiry into the end of victimization is not synonymous with an exploration of the future of victimhood.[12] My primary interest here is in the shifting resonance, performance, and reliance on the status of 'victim' over time. This focus on the future and evolution of victimhood complements existing work on the 'birth of victims as political actors'.[13] How does the victim subject age? What are the growing pains, milestones, and aspirations associated with victimhood as a long-term basis of subjectivity? What kind of subject is the imagined 'post-victim' subject, and what fears and aspirations do different actors attach to this form of subjectivity? 'If we do not scrutinize time', Elizabeth Cohen argues in her reflections on the political value of time, 'it can seem like it stands outside of law, politics, and social facts'.[14] This chapter illustrates how people's imaginations of and relationships to the 'victim' category—and the claims and mobilizations on the basis of it—evolve with time.

In the context of this chapter, what Kimberly Hutchings calls 'the inter-subjective time of politics'[15] refers to how transitional justice bureaucrats and people who identify as victims experience and make sense of the past, present, and, especially, the future of victimhood. Imaginations of the future are not 'unified, universal, and singular';[16] they vary in the ways that people's memories of violence and recollections of the past also do.[17] This analysis is gratefully indebted to queer scholarship on time, which urges humans 'to think and feel our way backward, forward, or sideways in time',[18] therefore challenging expectations of linearity or unidirectional progress, and defying a neat separation between past, present, and future.

The anxiety about the limits of a future premised on victimhood is not exclusive to transitional justice bureaucrats or to Colombia. It also extends

---

[12] In this approach, I echo the sociologist Laura Acosta: 'Becoming a victim not only depends on unfortunate experiences of victimisation, but also on the common understanding of the validity of the claim "I am a victim" in a given situation. This means that, at different times and places, different people may identify as a "victim". It may also be the case that individuals change their self-definitions depending on the situation they find themselves in'. Acosta, 'Victimhood Dissociation', p. 680.
[13] Rettberg, 'Victims of the Colombian Armed Conflict'.
[14] Elizabeth Cohen, *The Political Value of Time* (Cambridge University Press, 2018), p. 10.
[15] Kimberly Hutchings, *Time and World Politics* (Manchester University Press, 2008), p. 4.
[16] Chamon, 'Turning Temporal', p. 406.
[17] For fascinating reflections on time in the discipline of international relations, see Rahul Rao, *Out of Time: The Queer Politics of Postcoloniality* (Oxford University Press, 2020); Paulo Chamon, 'Turning Temporal: A Discourse of Time in IR', *Millennium* 46, no. 3 (2018): 396–420; Katharina Hunfeld, 'The Coloniality of Time in the Global Justice Debate: De-centring Western Linear Temporality', *Journal of Global Ethics* 18, no. 1 (2022): 100–117.
[18] Rao, *Out of Time*, p. 17.

to scholars of violence, who offer different imaginations of what the future of such scholarship ought to be. According to Joel Robbins, 'The subject living in pain, in poverty or under conditions of violence or oppression now very often stands at the centre of anthropological work'.[19] Robbins proposes reorienting scholarship towards an 'anthropology of the good', whose 'more modest aim is to explore the different ways people organise their personal and collective lives in order to foster what they think of as good, and to study what it is like to live at least some of the time in light of such a project'.[20] Such a study would depart from 'the genre of crisis'[21] to inquire about hope, change, empathy, and care.[22]

These calls to take hope seriously are not a denial or erasure of suffering. Robbins himself acknowledges that 'the point of developing this new kind of anthropology would not be to displace the anthropology of suffering', but to 'help realise . . . the promise suffering slot anthropology always at least implicitly makes: that there must be better ways to live than the ones it documents'.[23] I propose here that, even though studies of the future, the good, and the hopeful sometimes frame their origins in opposition to the study of suffering, these inquiries can exist alongside and inform one another. Seeing these bodies of work as potentially in conversation is important because such an attitude more accurately reflects the coexistence of hope and suffering, of harm and aspiration, in the lives of people who have experienced loss.

Scholars have sometimes relied on the language of 'turns' to describe the shifting fashions of where and how we orient our attention: the 'local turn',[24] the 'everyday turn',[25] 'the reflexivity turn'.[26] There are enough turns to make one dizzy. 'Turns' may make certain imaginations, practices, and relationships possible. At the same time, I am troubled by what it means to turn away. Intervening in people's lives to ask about harm, violence, politics,

---

[19] Joel Robbins, 'Beyond the Suffering Subject: Toward an Anthropology of the Good', *Journal of the Royal Anthropological Institute* 19, no. 3 (2013): 448.
[20] Robbins, 'Beyond the Suffering Subject', p. 457.
[21] Berlant, *Cruel Optimism*, p. 7.
[22] Krystalli and Schulz, 'Taking Love and Care Seriously'.
[23] Robbins, 'Beyond the Suffering Subject', p. 458.
[24] Thania Paffenholz, 'Unpacking the Local Turn in Peacebuilding: A Critical Assessment towards an Agenda for Future Research', *Third World Quarterly* 36, no. 5 (2015): 857–74; Mac Ginty and Richmond, 'The Local Turn'.
[25] Maria-Adriana Deiana, Milena Komarova, and Cathal McCall, 'Cross-Border Cooperation as Conflict Transformation: Promises and Limitations in EU Peacebuilding', *Geopolitics* 24, no. 3 (2019): 529–40; Roger Mac Ginty, *Everyday Peace: How So-Called Ordinary People Can Disrupt Violent Conflict* (Oxford University Press, 2021).
[26] Inanna Hamati-Ataya, 'Reflectivity, Reflexivity, Reflexivism: IR's 'Reflexive Turn'—and Beyond', *European Journal of International Relations* 19, no. 4 (2013): 669–94.

and the worlds these rupture and bring into being requires, in the words of Donna Haraway, 'staying with the trouble'.[27] I am sympathetic to the need to evolve with the questions we ask,[28] and, like Robbins, I am drawn—emotionally, politically, analytically—to inquiries about hope, love, and care. I suggest, however, that we do not need to leave violence or victimhood 'behind' in order to seek goodness elsewhere, at new sites, with new questions and interlocutors. By examining how bureaucrats of transitional justice and people who identify as victims imagine the future, I sow the seeds of an ethic and methodology of alongside-ness, holding room for hope in a present of loss, for joy against a backdrop of suffering, for goodness and violence to coexist across all tenses.

This reframing also invites scholars and practitioners of transitional justice, peacebuilding, and political violence to think about the relationship between time, violence, and politics differently. I argue for seeing politics *in* and *through* victimhood, not merely after it. I highlight the ways in which claim-making based on victimhood does not necessarily foreclose political futures, or ideas about agency, citizenship, and hope, but may, in fact, enable them. As a result, narratives of needing to move away from victimhood may not always have the liberating effect they intend. Instead, they may erase or deny—rather than augment—the agency they claim to foment.

A Country of Victims

Though the banners in Plaza Bolívar on Victims' Day rightly insisted that 'the victims are not a number', the anxiety of numbers permeates Colombian imaginations about the future of the victim category. This anxiety bears kinship to the haunting reliance on the magic of indicators, attendance sheets, and other ways of making the transitional justice processes of the state knowable and material.[29] At nearly every event I attended as part of my research, representatives of state entities or international organizations would refer to 'the figures' [las cifras]. Sometimes they brought PowerPoint slides or printouts of charts; other times, they would recite numbers from memory.

---

[27] Donna Haraway, *Staying with the Trouble: Making Kin in the Chthulucene* (Duke University Press, 2016).
[28] I have discussed some of the ways in which I have evolved with—and sometimes out of—my research in the reply to comments published alongside Krystalli, 'Being Seen'.
[29] I discuss this at length in Chapter 5.

For some, this was a reluctant recitation. 'We are always repeating these figures in so many spaces, but oh well, let's go', the Technical Director of Reparations at the Victims' Unit said, with apparent resignation, at an event on reparation policy fulfilment. She proceeded to tell the audience how many Colombians had successfully registered as victims of the armed conflict. Others framed the numbers as a necessary component of telling a credible story about policies for those the state recognized as victims. In his presentation at a congressional monitoring event on the implementation of the Victims' Law, the director of the Victims' Unit said: 'I know we said in a previous panel that the victims are not a number. They are, of course, more than a number. But we have to look at the numbers. We have to demonstrate how many victims there are in the registry today and how many we have managed to reach'.

On that day, the director sounded hopeful about the story numbers could tell about policy fulfilment. In both public events and research interviews, many state officials expressed satisfaction about having successfully registered a large number of victims across a diverse array of identities, locations, and harms suffered. They frequently referred to the Harvard-led evaluation of the Victims' Unit, which had praised the Colombian reparations program for being among the more progressive in the world, in terms of both its conceptualization of eligible victims and its registration scheme.[30] The Harvard evaluation became shorthand in many conversations, with my interlocutors saying, 'You know the Harvard report, I assume', and then carrying on, as though their point had already been made. The seal of Harvard transferred the credibility of an elite university in Cambridge, Massachusetts, to the transitional justice process headquartered in Bogotá.

However, the same expansive registration system that sometimes fostered pride and often elicited praise more commonly triggered anxiety among those who had to implement the transitional justice program. A Victims' Unit official whose role was to work on the victims' registry said, 'Every time I look at the home page on my computer, my head hurts. Uffff!'[31] This official was referring to the counters that the Victims' Unit features on the front page of its website. One of the counters lists the number of people who have successfully completed the state's registration process as victims of the armed conflict. The Victims' Unit refers to this number as 'historically registered

---

[30] Sikkink et al., 'Evaluation of Comprehensive Reparations'. I discuss the evaluation in Chapters 1 and 2.

[31] Interview with registry team official in Bogotá, December 2018.

victims'. As of March 2023, there were over nine million such people in Colombia.[32] This means that the Colombian state officially recognizes approximately one in six Colombians as a victim of the armed conflict. Reflecting on the magnitude of these numbers, a Ministry of Justice senior official told me: 'We will be a country of victims.'[33]

For many state officials, the numbers were a source of simultaneous pride and worry. These emotions stemmed from the same source. The fact that Colombia's transitional justice program was so extensive and comprehensive led to much international praise, as well as a sense of satisfaction among the people who worked on it. Yet the expectations that this program created among the vast universe of people recognized as victims were a constant source of stress for professionals whose job it was to fulfil this promise—not all of whom had the resources to do so, or the agency to direct and allocate those resources. The numbers hold promise; the numbers haunt.

People who identified as victims had their own anxieties about the numbers. One indicator recurred as the source of worry among them: the number of people recognized as victims who had not yet received compensation as part of the reparations program. As the UN Basic Principles and Guidelines on the Right to a Remedy and Reparation underscore, compensation is one of the five forms of reparation, which also include restitution, rehabilitation, satisfaction, and guarantees of non-repetition.[34] In the Colombian case, those eligible for compensation include people recognized as victims of nine types of conflict-related crimes,[35] and the compensation ranges from ten to forty times the minimum monthly wage, depending on the nature of the harm.

Placing the importance of compensation in the wider context of both the transitional justice program and the politics of victimhood is a delicate task.

---

[32] Unidad para la atención y reparación integral a las víctimas, home page, https://www.unidadvictimas.gov.co.

[33] Interview with senior official at the Ministry of Justice, November 2018. As noted earlier, the Truth Commission final report also included the phrase 'a country of victims'.

[34] Basic Principles, 'Guidelines on the Right to a Remedy and Reparation for Victims of Gross Violations of International Human Rights Law and Serious Violations of International Humanitarian Law', General Assembly Resolution 60 (2006).

[35] These are (a) homicide; (b) forced disappearance; (c) kidnapping; (d) personal injuries that generated permanent disability; (e) personal injuries that generated inability to work; (f) illicit recruitment of youth and adolescents; (g) crimes against sexual liberty and integrity, including children and adolescents born as a consequence of sexual violation in the context of armed conflict; (h) torture, and cruel, inhumane, or degrading treatment; (i) forced displacement. Unidad para la atención y reparación integral a las víctimas, 'Indemnización', accessed August 1, 2022, https://www.unidadvictimas.gov.co/es/indemnizacion/8920.

On the one hand, it is important to not reduce justice to financial compensation, and to highlight the complex and conflicting feelings that many who identify as victims have towards compensation for the harms they suffered. These feelings range from relief at the possibility of addressing some of the socioeconomic hardship caused by the armed conflict to a sense that compensation represents 'blood money' and, therefore, accepting it compromises the struggle for justice.[36] On the other hand, for many of those who identify as victims, it is impossible to speak of or imagine the future of victimhood while the state promise of compensation remains largely unfulfilled.

Unlike the counter on the Victims' Unit home page, the number of people who have received compensation is less readily available. One of the most comprehensive sources that sheds some light on this issue is the annual report of the Commission for Monitoring of the Implementation of Victims' Law.[37] While this report is publicly available, it is neither displayed on the front page of the Victims' Unit website nor as easy to find as other statistical information about people recognized as victims of the armed conflict. In the hierarchy of statistics about violence, some numbers are harder to locate and display than others.

As of 2021, only 12 percent of people recognized as victims of the armed conflict had received compensation in the ten years since the passage of the Victims' Law.[38] The report reiterates that compensation is only one of the measures of reparation, and that people who are recognized as victims have access to various other measures of individual, collective, symbolic, or material reparation, ranging from psychosocial support to professional training. Yet the authors conclude that, at the current rate, 'by 2031, a quarter of the victims will be compensated and the rest would have to wait up to sixty more years to receive resources.'[39] By this account, if the horizons of transitional

---

[36] Some communities, such as the Peace Community of San José de Apartadó, have even made it a core principle that 'members should not accept any reparations, a highly unusual precedent in Colombia'. Gwen Burnyeat, *Chocolate, Politics and Peace-Building* (Palgrave Macmillan, 2018), p. 160.

[37] Comisión de Seguimiento, 'Octavo Informe'. Each year, the report lists the activities that various entities organized to fulfil the promises of the Victims' Law, aggregates the implementation indicators between 2011 and the present day, and looks towards the future to see what additional resources are necessary to ensure fulfilment of the transitional justice program. The latest report, published in August 2021, enumerates 195 tables, twenty graphs, and eight additional figures, and amounts to a total of 480 pages of text. Rather than naming specific authors, the report lists the staff at each of the three state entities responsible for the monitoring of the implementation of the Victims' Law, as well as the three Mesa representatives of victims who participated in this process.

[38] Comisión de Seguimiento, 'Octavo Informe', p. 243.

[39] Comisión de Seguimiento, 'Octavo Informe', p. 265.

justice are partly defined by public policy fulfilment towards those the state recognizes as victims, then Colombia is looking at a long future of victimhood.

In the crafting of stories about bureaucracies of victimhood and the fulfilment of promises, sequencing matters. The authors of the monitoring report start telling the story of the implementation of the Victims' Law through numbers that emphasize financial investment. The national government of Colombia invested 135.5 billion COP into the reparation program between 2012 and 2021.[40] Based on current spending projections, existing data on the numbers of people recognized as victims, and the rate of public policy fulfilment, the commission estimates that the 142.1 billion COP that is allocated to the fulfilment of the Victims' Law in the next decade 'continues to be insufficient'. The estimated value of necessary services for fulfilment of the Colombian transitional justice program is closer to 328.3 billion COP.[41] 'It all makes me very anxious, to tell you the truth', a Ministry of Interior official admitted in response to these realities. 'We opened our mouth this much, we didn't measure the consequences, and now the problem is how to bring things back—first because people don't trust us, and second because the level of reparation is very low. This is a dynamic that the state created'.[42]

Cast in this light, being 'a country of victims' is not only a reflection of the magnitude of violence during the armed conflict, but also an ongoing reminder of the pending promises of public policy fulfilment on the part of the state. Not only did the state play a part in the bureaucratic creation of the 'victim' subject, but also its program of transitional justice endowed that category with hope: of reparation, of access to resources, of attention. Sources of hope can quickly turn into sources of disappointment. In this context, it became increasingly urgent for state officials to manage expectations of state assistance, and to promote visions of the future that are not premised on a victim identity. As the next vignette illustrates, this process of expectation management was one of 'remaking subjects in the aftermath of war'.[43]

---

[40] Comisión de Seguimiento, 'Octavo Informe', p. 11.
[41] Comisión de Seguimiento, 'Octavo Informe', p. 31.
[42] Interview with Ministry of Interior official in Bogotá, January 2018.
[43] Emma Shaw Crane and Catalina Vallejo, 'Remaking Subjects in the Aftermath of War: Colombia's Postconflict', *Social Science Research Council* (blog), July 31, 2018, https://items.ssrc.org/from-our-fellows/remaking-subjects-in-the-aftermath-of-war-capitalism-personhood-and-colombias-postconflict/.

The Productive Victim

Remaking subjects in the aftermath of war requires (re)naming them. 'Are you here for "The Victims in the Post-Conflict"?' I asked a group of people congregating outside the Emerald Salon in a Bogotá hotel. A victims' association leader turned to face me. 'Yes, we are. But the post-conflict hasn't arrived yet'.

'The Victims in the Post-Conflict' was a day-long forum that took place in December 2017, a year after the signing of the peace accord between the Colombian government and the FARC. A weekly magazine dedicated to socio-political commentary and analysis had organized the event in tandem with the Victims' Unit in Bogotá. The panels brought together state officials from various entities enacting public policy for people recognized as victims of the armed conflict, as well as leaders of victims' associations, academics, representatives of international organizations, and private sector businesses. When I showed proof of identification to complete my registration, a security guard handed me a badge with my name printed against a faded map of Colombia, as well as a notebook with the name and date of the event on the cover. In December 2017, the 'post-conflict' may not have been an embodied reality for many in Colombia; yet, it also appeared real enough to print on notebook covers.

The third panel of the day was titled Productive Opportunities and Employability of the Victims. It featured an economist working as an academic at one of Bogotá's private universities, a senior leader of the association of hotels and tourism in Colombia, and a senior official at an international retail company with offices in Colombia. This panel composition was different from that of the earlier events on non-violence, reconciliation, and reparation, which had drawn together a mix of victims' associations leaders, human rights defenders, and representatives of state entities.

The moderator, who was affiliated with the magazine organizing the day's events, introduced the panel. 'Victims need to be able to be sustainable in the future: not only to overcome the condition of victim, but also to advance their personal projects', she began. The language of 'personal projects', 'productive projects', or 'life projects' has proliferated in Colombia. The legal origins of this phrasing can be traced to the 2011 Victims' Law.[44] The 'life

---

[44] Article 134 of the Victims' Law of 2011 reads: 'The national government, through the Administrative Unit for Attention to and Reparation of Victims [Victims' Unit], will implement a program of accompaniment to promote an adequate investment of the resources that victims receive

project' is an example of a term with legal origins that became part of the vernacular of victimhood. 'Life project' sounds expansive enough to encompass a range of aspirations. However, in practice, the term primarily referred to economic activities aimed at income generation. As the sociologist Catalina Vallejo writes in her powerful study of life projects in Colombian reparation initiatives, 'Beneficiaries are encouraged to adopt practices that will allow them to be disciplined with money, become income generators, and ultimately be responsible for their own recovery'.[45]

Manuela, an international organization consultant, was tasked with implementing life project development programs in partnership with the Victims' Unit, aimed at women who had experienced sexual violence in the armed conflict. 'Basically, the life project reflects the concern of the [Victims'] Unit that women take advantage of [aprovechar] the money they get through the compensation route of reparation', Manuela said. 'Of course, it's not just the money that's important. But it's important to invest it, to not waste it, to have something productive come out of it'.[46]

This concern with productivity, and with the appropriate investment of the compensation that some were eligible to receive as part of reparations, was a key theme of the final panel at 'The Victims in the Post-Conflict'. The first panellist, an economist primarily working within academia, acknowledged the context of the discussion by noting that it is difficult 'to put this issue in such cold terms, cold figures and statistics, after all the stories we heard from victims this morning'. She also cautioned that 'we cannot speak about poverty and economic projects for victims without talking about mental health and the effects of the war on the decision-making of those victimized'. Further, she recognized the resistance that those who identify as victims sometimes have against state-sponsored training for 'productive projects' that do not resonate with their own ideas about their life. 'We know that not all victims want to open a hair salon', she said, prompting laughter among many in the audience.[47]

---

as administrative reparation with the purpose of reconstructing their life project, principally oriented towards: 1. Technical or professional education for the victims or their children. 2. The creation or strengthening of productive enterprises or productive assets. 3. Acquisition or improvement of new or used housing. 4. Acquisition of rural properties'. Law 1448 of 2011. Catalina Vallejo notes that the language of life projects also appears in judgments of the Interamerican Course of Human Rights. Vallejo, 'Pricing Suffering', p. 137.

[45] Vallejo, 'Pricing Suffering', pp. 138–39.
[46] Interview with international organization 'gender consultant' in Bogotá, February 2018.
[47] This comment echoes the findings of Cronin-Furman et al., who suggest that development program implementers often offer conflict-affected individuals the opportunity to learn how to sew or

Despite this important framing, however, the rest of the panel focused narrowly on ways in which entrepreneurship could help those recognized as victims overcome the condition of victimhood. Like the 'life project', the language of 'condition' was part of the vernacular of victimhood. As Daniel, another international organization official implementing state training programs on life projects, told me: 'Our trainings always begin by communicating that to be a victim is not bad [el ser víctima no es malo]. It does not mean you did anything wrong. It is a condition'. Daniel kept nodding reassuringly as he spoke: 'We are not going to erase this condition. We are going to build something from this condition. It is about how to manage it, about how to put things in another place [poner las cosas en otro lugar]. The focus is not on the violation, but on what will happen in the future'.

In the context of 'The Victims in the Post-Conflict', victimhood was framed as a condition that one ought to overcome. This aspirational overcoming would allegedly happen through the economic mechanisms of production and consumption. The representative of the hotelier and tourism alliance of Colombia illustrated this logic. He had brought with him tapestries and artisanal bags that a victims' group had woven in Mampuján. In 2000, paramilitaries forcibly displaced over three hundred people from Mampuján and committed a massacre that received extensive attention both within Colombia and in international media. 'The beautiful things that victims make with their own hands are on sale in all our hotels', the panellist said. 'My dream is to make Mampuján a destination of communitarian tourism. People want to come and get to know the community and what it survived', he continued.

The representative from the international retail conglomerate then referred to jars of marmalade that victims of the armed conflict had made and said: 'People are wondering how they can contribute, how they can help the victims. The victims are helping themselves, making all these things and obtaining some resources. One way we can help them is to consume these wonderful products—marmalades, sweets, soaps, artisanal goods—that we can find in hotels and shops'.

During the question-and-answer session that followed, a Victims' Unit official seated in the audience raised her hand to speak: 'Look at the occupational and professional productivity of the victims! I must commend

style hair without fully engaging with these individuals' needs or preferences. Kate Cronin-Furman, Nimmi Gowrinathan, and Rafia Zakaria, 'Emissaries of Empowerment' (The Colin Powell School for Civic and Global Leadership, City College of New York, 2017).

these panellists and all the victims for their productive projects'. She paused, seemingly for applause that never came, and then continued: 'Some of these victims, we know, have twenty or thirty diplomas from trainings. They are learning a lot. And we, as the [Victims'] Unit, are empowering communities to be better recipients of state efforts to develop life projects'.

The officials in the audience, recognizable by the institutional lanyards around their necks, nodded along. The final question went to a man in the second row. He said: 'This is very interesting, thank you, and good afternoon to all of you. I just wanted to share that I am a victim of an armed group and I have not been part of these productive projects. I have not received anything, no help, no assistance. I would like help with resources. What do I do?'

The woman from the Victims' Unit who had made the earlier comment about productive livelihoods took the microphone and directed the man to the 'special zones for economic socialization of the post-conflict', where he could find lots of resources on employment opportunities, trainings, and businesses supporting victims. With that, the moderator announced that time was up. There were sandwiches and coffee in the hotel lobby.

Benevolent States, (Un)grateful Victims

Sitting in the audience of 'The Victims in the Post-Conflict', my initial reaction was one of discomfort. The idea of transforming a site of violence into a tourist destination may have been well intentioned, but it also had the potential to be another instance of 'slum tourism' or conflict voyeurism.[48] It also seemingly ran counter to the purported theory of change. It is difficult to imagine how people would 'overcome' their condition of victimhood if they had to confront the gaze of others who came to visit a community on account of it having been affected by war. The tourist gaze locks people into a present continuous of violence, rather than moving them towards the future to which many transitional justice professionals aspired.

---

[48] 'Slum tourism involves transforming poverty, squalor and violence into a tourism product. Drawing on both altruism and voyeurism, this form of tourism is a complex phenomenon that raises various questions concerning power, inequality, and subjectivity'. Eveline Dürr and Rivke Jaffe, 'Theorizing Slum Tourism: Performing, Negotiating and Transforming Inequality', *Revista Europea de Estudios Latinoamericanos y del Caribe / European Review of Latin American and Caribbean Studies*, no. 93 (2012): 113. Debbie Lisle has powerfully examined how the separation of imagined sites of tourism from sites of war constructs dichotomies between a safe here/now and a dangerous there/then. Debbie Lisle, 'Consuming Danger: Reimagining the War/Tourism Divide', *Alternatives* 25, no. 1 (2000): 91–116.

Anxieties about asistencialismo, which imperfectly translates to 'welfarism', fuelled the 'productive project' approach. Much of the literature on this subject defines asistencialismo through its mechanisms or effects. 'When reparation projects obey an asistencialista logic', Villa et al. argue, 'they generate in people a begging place, dependence, and disempowerment; there is a waste of resources and a permanent demand to institutions and officials, in many cases, without assuming duties or responsibilities'.[49] A High Advisory for Victims official echoed this view: 'When people talk about asistencialismo, they talk about the attitude of thinking that victims were given everything and that they live by asking for subsidies'.[50] A Victims' Unit official further illustrated the logic of asistencialismo. 'It is important to tell you that not all victims are asistencialistas', she clarified. 'Some of them are, though. They are the ones who take advantage or won't move forward. They want us [the state] to gift them things. This attitude must be changed. It's a bad spirit to always want to be assisted, to always demand, to always want more.[51]

Productive projects are intended to interrupt or prevent those outcomes. 'Interventions based on income generation or employability', Ximena Castro-Sardi and Juliana Olano explain, 'centred their efforts on empowering victims through inserting them into the world of work, thereby hoping to . . . provide them with economic resources that permit them to migrate from the welfare logic'.[52] A defining feature of asistencialismo is not only the provision of assistance on the part of the state, but the perceived reliance on it on the part of those recognized as victims, coupled with the recipients' resistance to moving to a new phase or relationship that is not predicated on this continued provision. 'They don't want to stop being victims! What do we do about that? How do we make sure they understand they need to stop being victims? I don't have answers to that', an international organization official told me.[53] Another official elaborated on her frustrations with this approach: 'You want to spend all this holy life as a victim and the government

---

[49] Juan David Villa Gómez, Daniela Barrera Machado, Laura Arroyave Pizarro, and Yirley Montoya Betancur, 'Acción con daño: Del asistencialismo a la construcción social de la víctima. Mirada a procesos de reparación e intervención psicosocial en Colombia', *Universitas Psychologica* 16, no. 3 (2017): 10.

[50] Interview with High Advisory for Victims official in Bogotá, June 2018.

[51] Interview with Victims' Unit official in Medellín, March 2018.

[52] Ximena Castro-Sardi and Juliana Olano, 'Reparación y escucha del sujeto-víctima: Discursos y prácticas en la intervención psicosocial con víctimas del conflicto armado en Colombia', *Revista Colombiana de Ciencias Sociales* 9, no. 1 (2018): 86.

[53] Interview with international organization representative in Bogotá, August 2017.

has to keep subsiding everything, giving you money? No. You have to search, you have to do, you have to move forward. This is how I see the situation. . . . There are many, yes, yes, many victims of the armed conflict who have moved forward, who have not stayed behind. . . . But there are others who want to continue with the same line of waiting for "a little help, please". As the official wrapped up this thought, she put a hand out, imitating a beggar.[54]

'Forward' and 'behind' contain value judgments. These labels reinforce an understanding of what Jenny Edkins calls 'linear time', relying on ideas of unidirectional progress.[55] The ideal relationship to assistance in these narratives is one whereby those recognized as victims receive assistance from the state, gratefully acknowledge it, and promptly move on. Moving on, or 'forward', also implies leaving victimhood, as well as the associations and claims based on it, behind. As Vallejo concludes, 'This desired moment of independence is only possible when victims redirect their attention from a past filled with loss and political violence to a promising future replete with victims-cum-entrepreneurs'.[56]

This imagined future of victimhood hinges on a particular kind of entrepreneurship. Many state programs implicitly or explicitly advance a view of 'overcoming' victimhood that relies on a transactional logic of production and consumption. The suggestion that purchasing marmalade, for instance, can help conflict-affected individuals 'overcome' the condition of victimhood places the responsibility of overcoming on those who suffered harm, who are urged to become productive citizens, and onto the general public, who are urged to buy goods to support this endeavour. Senator Juan Manuel Galán, the president of the Commission for the Monitoring of the Implementation of the Victims Law, relied on what he considered to be a positive framing of victim entrepreneurship to challenge the narrative of asistencialismo: 'The victims are not a kind of burden that has been put on society', he said in his remarks at one of the meetings of the commission. 'No, no. We are not subsidizing them. Through productive projects, we show that they are owners of their destiny. They can provide for their families, for their lives. Victims are not subjects of asistencialismo. With their experience,

---

[54] Interview with state official in Medellín, March 2018.

[55] Jenny Edkins, 'Remembering Relationality: Trauma Time and Politics', in *Memory, Trauma and World Politics: Reflections on the Relationship between Past and Present*, edited by Duncan Bell (Palgrave Macmillan, 2006), pp. 99–115. See also Jenny Edkins, 'Temporality, Politics and Performance: Missing, Displaced, Disappeared', in *The Grammar of Politics and Performance*, edited by Shirin Rai and Janelle Reinelt (Routledge, 2014), pp. 134–47.

[56] Vallejo, 'Pricing Suffering', p. 137.

with their education, with their entrepreneurship, they can contribute to the territories'.

There is value to challenging the myth of the 'greedy' or 'ungrateful victim' who has allegedly become a burden on state and society, particularly when this defence comes from a high-profile senator. However, Galán's remarks also reflect the transactional assumptions underpinning encounters in transitional justice schemes. People recognized as victims are expected to produce, to be entrepreneurial, to 'contribute to the territories'. In other words, through their labour, they need to show themselves to be worthy of state investment. This is a view of reparations fundamentally different from that articulated in the international norms that have shaped approaches to transitional justice. The Basic Principles and Guidelines for Remedy and Reparation frame reparation as a right, and as a form of redress for violations and harms suffered in the context of an armed conflict—and crucially not as state investment in development, or as a transaction that creates future obligations on the part of recipients towards state and society. Simply put: people recognized as victims of armed conflict have a right to reparation that does not depend on earning or deserving assistance through their own entrepreneurship or productivity.

Not all entrepreneurial initiatives on the part of those recognized as victims are equally well received by state officials. 'There are victims who see their role as a business, who convert the label of 'victim' into a business. They become mafias of public space', one state official said.[57] 'There is a logic of consumerism, a logic of the market, that has affected how people approach reparations', Fernanda, the psychologist supporting programs for victims of the armed conflict introduced in Chapter 5, claimed. 'For some, being a victim becomes the life project'.[58]

Herein lies the irony of the charge of asistencialismo in the context of the politics of victimhood. Victim entrepreneurship is encouraged—so long as the status of 'victim' is not the commodity or currency in question in the political economy of transition from violence. Life projects are desirable—but only insofar as those arise from outside or beyond the realm of victimhood. The 'good victim' in this context is self-reliant, resourceful, entrepreneurial, and economically responsible. In fact, the 'good victims' of the future are not victims at all, because they have graduated to a new state beyond the realm of victimhood.

---

[57] Interview with state official in Bogotá, June 2018.
[58] Interview with Victims' Unit psychologist in Medellín, March 2018.

In this script, there are implicitly permissible and impermissible exercises of agency. Those recognized as victims are allowed, and even encouraged, to exercise agency towards managing what is framed as the investment of the state. However, if people recognized as victims exercise agency in the direction of demanding more (or more timely) resources from the state, pointing out the limits or flaws of the reparations program, choosing to direct their reparations in ways that resonate more with them than the prescribed 'life projects' approach, or resisting the state narrative of benevolence, they are more likely to be labelled ungrateful and judged for their relationship to both victimhood and the state. In most of these narratives, the role of the violators is conveniently left out of the story, as is the question of state responsibility for delivering transitional justice.[59]

In fact, to the extent that the state appears in this story, it is primarily as a benefactor. The goal, one of the officials at the 'Victims in the Post-Conflict' event had said, was 'empowering communities to be better recipients of state efforts to develop life projects'. The vision of the state that comes into being through these accounts is one of a benevolent actor, a version of what Tate calls 'the aspirational state', 'the state as an ideal form: caring, responsive, generous, and abundant, rather than distant, repressive, and extortive.'[60] As a High Advisory for the Post-Conflict official told me, 'There's very much an attitude of "Be grateful we're at least giving you this. I'm giving you this because I'm the state—I'm the good guy".'[61]

Once again, the stories of victimhood and statehood come together. The future of victimhood contains not only imaginations of the 'good victim', but also of the 'good state'. The good state provides, cares, invests—all of which are verbs, aspirations, and imaginations that become possible *through* the bureaucracy of victimhood. In a 'country of victims', however, the line is thin between the massive bureaucracy of victimhood establishing the presence of the (good, benevolent) state and fuelling the disappointment of unfulfilled promises of justice. When state officials feel the urgency of partial fulfilment or the infeasible magnitude of the promise, a corresponding urgency is observable to transform into a country of whatever lies beyond 'victims'.

In many ways, there are parallels between the fears and anxieties surrounding the future of victimhood and the concerns about aid or welfare

---

[59] In some cases, the violator *was* the state.
[60] Tate, 'The Aspirational State', p. 236.
[61] Interview with the High Advisory for the Post-Conflict official in Bogotá, January 2018.

dependency outside the context of armed conflict. The feminist scholars Nancy Fraser and Linda Gordon point out that 'dependency is an ideological term' and, further, that 'naming ... problems ... as dependency tends to make them appear to be individual problems, as much moral or psychological as economic'.[62] Importantly, however, feminist scholars are not the only ones who develop critiques of asistencialismo. State officials also expressed their reservations, highlighting the polyphony and fractiousness of the state during transitions from violence. As one such official concluded: 'I detest those state officials who view victims as "something to maintain", as someone dependent on the state, as non-entrepreneurial, non-fighting, or victims as people accustomed to subsidy and paternalism. I say to that, false! You cannot speak of asistencialismo without providing assistance'.[63]

Expecting people who identify as victims to move 'forward', leaving their identification with victimhood behind, ignores the fact that many have not yet experienced the justice the state promised and to which they are legally entitled. This official was not alone in criticizing life project interventions. 'The "life project" is crap', a Victims' Unit official told me. 'We tell people, "Peace is in your hearts" and "You can achieve what you want" and "You shouldn't be asistencialista". Of course you should be asistencialista if you're hungry!'[64] A different state official echoed: 'Living off the label "victim" is a question of survival, not of defrauding the state'.[65]

Framing victim behaviour as a form of asistencialismo can erase state complicity in generating expectations of assistance and attention in the first place. 'We talk about asistencialismo and forget that the concept has a bit of the institucionalidad inside it', a senior official said.[66] A different official elaborated on this point: 'The Victims' Law is a very transactional law. For a big percentage of victims, compensation is their main or only interest. It is not their fault. The law created this expectation, this dynamic of "I'm a victim, now give me a house". . . . The law promised victims much, but gave them little. I tell my team all the time: we cannot judge victims for asking for things'.[67]

---

[62] Nancy Fraser and Linda Gordon, 'A Genealogy of Dependency: Tracing a Keyword of the U.S. Welfare State', *Signs* 19, no. 2 (1994): 311.
[63] Interview with official at the High Advisory for Victims in Bogotá, June 2018.
[64] Interview with former state official in Bogotá, February 2018.
[65] Interview with state official at the Victims' Unit in Bogotá, January 2018.
[66] Interview with official at the Municipal Victims' Team in Medellín, February 2018.
[67] Interview with a senior team leader at the High Advisory for Victims in Bogotá, May 2018.

Political Subjects: Being and Becoming

Researching the future of victimhood requires being attuned to hope when it surfaces, including the spontaneous surges of it in moments of not asking directly about it or not expecting to encounter it. This is hope as a practice, not an imposition; hope as a chosen orientation, not an expectation. The hope that I, like Rebecca Solnit, am interested in 'is about broad perspectives with specific possibilities, ones that invite or demand that we act. It's . . . not a sunny everything-is-getting-better narrative. . . . You could call it an account of complexities and uncertainties, with openings'.[68]

Like other emotions and practices oriented towards the future, hope, too, is liable to co-optation. It is possible to summarize the story of this chapter until this point as a story of hope: the hope on the part of some state officials that Colombia will be more than (or something other than) 'a country of victims', the hope that some of those who now identify as victims will leave that identity behind, the hope that economic interventions and 'productive projects' will move people beyond victimhood. The critical geographer Gavin Brown calls these aspirations 'neoliberal social hope',[69] concerned with motion towards progress. This type of hope rests on assumptions of linear recovery and of (primarily economic) interventions that work. The people this kind of hope brings into view are ones who outgrow identities assumed to be passive, such as 'victim', in favour of a future full of agency, which manifests in entrepreneurship, self-reliance, and few(er) expectations of assistance.

Another vision of hope runs parallel to that story. The seeds of this hope are sown in the present, rather than being oriented primarily towards the future, and the sources of this hope can be traced to people's imaginations and enactments of political subjectivities, as opposed to being rooted in economic interventions or transactions between 'the state' and 'the victims'. Crucially, these subjectivities are best understood in the plural, through the frame of what my interlocutors call 'political subjects' [sujetos politicos].

Rather than waiting for a political education or 'capacity-building' to descend into their lives from the state or other interveners in the future, my interlocutors who identified as victims already understood themselves as political subjects. Through their labour and words, they both showed and told

---

[68] Rebecca Solnit, *Hope in the Dark* (Haymarket Books, 2016), pp. xii–xiv.
[69] Gavin Brown, 'The Revolt of Aspirations: Contesting Neoliberal Social Hope', *ACME* 12, no. 3 (2013): 419–30.

me what this meant to them, and how it oriented their visions towards the future. My conversation with Juan David, the victims' leader in the municipality of Rafael Uribe introduced in earlier chapters, illustrates themes that echo conversations with others who identify as victims. I said, 'There is a term that I have heard a lot in my research. It is the idea of the "political subject". Does this speak to you? What does it mean to be a political subject?'[70] 'Yes, yes, the political subject', Juan David said. 'There are many things to say here. First of all, many victims haven't understood that we are political subjects regardless of what they recognize or they give us'. I paused to ask who 'they' are in this case. 'The state', Juan David said. 'Some victims think that the state made us political subjects by recognizing us as victims. The [Victims'] Law, by calling me a victim, has given me the possibility to enter certain spaces and make claims. But it did not make me a political subject. That is one important thing to say. Now, many people in this country conflate being a political subject with the militant politics of XYZ organization'. I asked, 'When you say organization, do you mean political parties? Or do you mean militant politics like those of armed groups?' 'Both', Juan David replied. 'Many confuse being political with being a formal political movement, so that they can elect us and we can have certain positions. That is what some people mean when they say "political subjects". You can probably understand why some want this for the victims, and why some think that is very unattractive'.

'But for others, like me, like many others', Juan David continued, 'political work is rebellious work. For many state officials, rebellion is a dirty word. For many victims too, because of the conflict. But for many of us, rebellion is a proud word. It gives us energy. It describes what it means to do politics [hacer política]'. And what does it mean to do politics? 'It means to claim, demand, argue, propose, and organize. It means to exist publicly, to be in conversation. This is political activity, even unconsciously. "Political subject" requires a collective understanding, not individual leadership. You cannot be a Messiah. This is not one person's work'.

Others who identify as victims have described political subjects similarly. 'To be a political subject is to be in the fight [la lucha]', Iris told me. When I asked her what 'the fight' was, she said: 'Uyyyy, friend, the fight is to survive, to make sure others survive. Justice is the fight'.[71] The language of 'the fight' or 'the struggle' illuminates the contentious work of victimhood. As Iris

---

[70] Interview with victim leader in Rafael Uribe, August 2018.
[71] Interview with elected victim representative to a Mesa in Antioquia, August 2018.

reminded me, however, there is also joy and hope in doing political work, to 'being in the political with others', as Berlant put it.[72] 'We aren't sad, poor little victims, waiting for the state', Iris said.[73] 'We dance, gossip, share food and cigarettes. After all these years in the fight, I have learned that you have to live with hope'. When I asked Iris to fill in the rest of that sentence—hope for what?—she said: 'Hope that things will improve. They will improve through our political work'. Hope and political work bridge the past, present, and future. They allow for imaginations of the future to form while also clearly recognizing the violence of the past, its continuities, echoes, and effects in the present, and the ways these arcs shape the future.

This understanding of politics and political work acknowledges that war not only destroys senses of self and politics, but also generates them. For some of those who identify as victims, the process of advocating on behalf of themselves and others was itself politicizing. As Juan David told me in a separate conversation, 'For some of us, being a victim allowed a political project to be born. The violence was a school and everything we had to do to get ourselves registered [as victims] radicalized us. . . . So, especially for those people, to tell them to remove the label of victim, . . . that is the opposite of recognizing them as political subjects'.[74] In this context, state pressure to leave the identification as a 'victim' behind is likely to have a disenfranchising effect. As one state official also acknowledged, 'You cannot take away the category of "victim" from people who fought for it without erasing the responsibility of the state or denying people their politics'.[75]

The political subjectivities in these narratives also challenge individual framings of victimhood and the future. Interlocutors who identified as victims spoke of being in the fight in the collective 'we': Estamos en la lucha. We are in the fight. This fight involves *doing* politics, not merely *being* political. This work of politics does not necessarily originate or primarily unfold in institutions of official, formal power. If, as Iris had said, being in the fight for justice involves doing the work of staying alive and ensuring others survive in an unjust world, then the domain of politics is daily life itself.

Many interlocutors within state agencies also used the language of 'political subjects', but their framing of political subjectivity and its sources was fundamentally different. 'They need to stop being victims, start being survivors,

---

[72] Berlant, *Cruel Optimism*, p. 260.
[73] Interview with elected victim representative to a Mesa in Antioquia, August 2018.
[74] Interview with victim leader in Rafael Uribe, August 2018.
[75] Interview with National Center for Historical Memory official in Bogotá, January 2018.

and then transition into political subjects and citizens of Colombia. This is important, we are pushing it', Daniela told me. I asked Daniela why transitional justice professionals are pushing for this future beyond victimhood. 'It is important for victims' mental health', she said. In my conversations with Daniela and other state officials, 'mental health' became shorthand that justified all manner of interventions.

'We need to convert "victim" to something positive: a more active subject and citizen, a subject more prone to negotiation, more of a subject of politics', a different international organization representative echoed.[76] From the stage of 'The Victims in the Post-Conflict' event discussed earlier, a Victims' Unit representative said: 'The actions of reparation ought to accompany Colombians who suffered in the war to return to feeling like citizens, like part of this country, to become political subjects'. The paternalistic, benevolent state rears its head again in these narratives, asserting knowledge of what 'the victims' would consider healthy, rather than allowing people who identify as victims to practice the diverse, multi-vocal, and heterogeneous acts of agency that might determine what a healthy relationship to victimhood, citizenship, and the state can look like.

Similarly to narratives of asistencialismo, these narratives frame citizenship and political subjectivity as states of being that lie beyond and after victimhood. In this story, victimhood negates political subjectivity and evacuates citizenship. For many implementers of transitional justice programs, it was the logic of asistencialismo that rendered it difficult to see people who identified as victims as full political subjects. 'To be a political subject does not mean only accessing the benefits of the government', Daniela argued. 'It also means that you fulfil your duties, that you participate in the political arena as a citizen. I have seen families overcome vulnerability and still claim to be victims'. She continued: 'We need to become transparent. We need to leave the informal world behind and become formalized. I see families who are victims, with kids in university, doing well, and they still don't want to show the government their income so they don't lose their benefits. Their history of victimization is their history. It will always be theirs. But to relive it and use it to access things means you are not part of society. You are not a full citizen'.[77]

---

[76] Interview with international organization representative in Bogotá, January 2018.
[77] Interview with international organization representative in Bogotá, January 2018.

Sebastián, an official at the High Advisory for Victims, echoed this understanding of asistencialismo as invalidating the political content of the victim category: 'Our reparations model in this country does not have political content', he told me.[78] When I asked what it means to have political content and why the reparations model allegedly lacks it, he replied: 'Our model is basically asistencialista. It is a model that reflects Colombian society: clientelist, asistencialista, living on subsidies. For some victims, this is a way of life: they are looking for a subsidy. "Let's see what they give us this year"'. Sebastián paused, then went on: 'Culturally, we have constructed a very clientelist society and the institucionalidad established its reparations program like that too. That is not what it means to be a political subject'.

According to these views, economic self-sufficiency is a necessary condition for political subjectivity. Reliance on state assistance is perceived to diminish the political content of one's being and claim to citizenship. But this makes politics a privilege of the relatively wealthy, as opposed to a practice, a set of actions, and a way of being also available to the poor, the vulnerable, and the violated. This understanding of politics also makes the state the arbiter of it, conferring the status of 'the political' upon others, and contesting others' claims of politics when those claims don't match—or directly challenge—state understandings.

Lifelong attachment to some statuses is more permissible than others. There are echoes between the pressure to leave the status of 'victim' behind and the expectation that combatants in non-state armed groups 'demobilize' and sever ties to those whom they knew as their comrades as part of their transition to civilian life.[79] Meanwhile, former members of state armed forces get to claim veteran status for life. Yet when some of my interlocutors who identify as victims say, 'I am a victim for life',[80] many state officials meet that pronouncement with fear and bristling. The claims of people who have violently opposed the state or who make demands of it as a result of violation are perhaps less threatening in the eyes of the state when they are ephemeral, when both the victim subject and the former combatant are seen as transitional, rather than as generating long-lasting subjectivities and ideas about citizenship and politics.

---

[78] Interview with mid-level High Advisory for Victims official in Bogotá, May 2018.
[79] Roxani Krystalli, 'Engage with Former Combatants as Interlocutors for Peace, Not Only as Authorities on Violence', in *Feminist Solutions for Ending War*, edited by Megan MacKenzie and Nicole Wegner (Pluto Press, 2021), pp. 152–65.
[80] Interview with victim organization leader in Antioquia, March 2018.

I attempted to point out some of these tensions to my interlocutors. When I asked Sebastián why he thought of becoming a political subject as an aspirational, future state for those who identify as victims, as opposed to a description of the present, he said: 'Very few victims understand themselves as political subjects. The majority of victims are not organized or close to the state'.[81] In his view, contrary to what Juan David had articulated earlier, it was formal organization that was legible and proximate to a state that made people political. An official at a different state entity echoed that view: 'The majority of victims are not politicized. They are not part of a party. There is no victims' movement'.[82] While, as I also argue in Chapter 6, there is evidence to support the claim that the universe of victimhood is splintered, the political does not always or exclusively dwell in formal movements and organizations that are legible to 'the state'.

There are cracks to this story too. Some transitional justice professionals vehemently disagreed with the discourse of victims needing to transition into political subjects. "To pass from being a victim to being a citizen' is one of the most horrible things I have heard in my life', an international organization official told me. 'Being a victim does not impede citizenship'.[83] A former official at the National Centre for Historical Memory agreed: 'The victim is much more of a political subject than any hybrid human being that results from a state workshop or training'.[84]

If the debate about asistencialismo was partly a contest over phrasal verbs—getting over pain, moving forward with 'life projects', or leaving the victim category behind—the discussion on political subjectivity illuminates the tensions that arise from contrasting verbs. For many officials anxious about the future of the victim category, a political subject is something that those who identify as victims must *become*, or into which they ought to convert, pass, transit, graduate, and transform. The process of becoming often requires both shedding an attachment to victimhood and participating in capacity-building through mechanisms of the state, international organizations, or others these actors see as knowledgeable authorities. By contrast, for many of those who identify as victims, and for their allies within the bureaucracy of victimhood, a political subject is a description of who they currently *are* and of the work they do. For some, this occurred itself *through* the

---

[81] Interview with mid-level High Advisory for Victims official in Bogotá, May 2018.
[82] Interview with state official in Bogotá, January 2018.
[83] Interview with international organization representative in Medellín, March 2018.
[84] Interview with former National Center for Historical Memory official in Bogotá, February 2018.

mobilization and claim-making associated with 'victim' status; for others, it pre-dated it. For some, the practice of politics manifests in interactions with the state itself or with organized victim movements; for others, these practices unfold in domains that are less official or less legible as formally political. For nearly all, political subjectivity is not an aspirational future state that will reveal itself after a person has 'overcome' the condition of 'victim'.

'I Don't Feel Like a Victim' and Other Stories of Transformation

When I arrived at the San Ignacio building in Medellín, a man was spreading rose petals on the stage. The occasion was the launch of a book co-authored by twenty-one women who identified as victims and survivors of the Colombian armed conflict.[85] The book was called *Flight of the Phoenix: From the Ashes to the Fire of the Word*.[86] The bookmarks that attendees at the launch received as gifts featured a phoenix with fountain pens drawn on its tail. A message was printed on the bottom: Sanar, Renacer, Escribir. Heal, be reborn, write.

The book that launched in March 2018 was the product of a partnership between Colombian NGOs in the Antioquia region, the National Centre for Historical Memory, the international development non-profit ACDI/VOCA, and the United States Agency for International Development. During my fieldwork, I encountered various book projects that followed a similar approach. With funding from international organizations and support from the Colombian government, NGOs would convene conflict-affected individuals to reflect on their life stories, document them, and share them with the Colombian public in the form of a book. Over the course of fifteen months, I attended three such book launches, corresponding to books with titles like *Souls That Write: Memories and Hope*.[87] I also observed part of a cycle of training workshops, in which state officials attempted to facilitate the process of writing these books with people who identified as victims. The books, and the processes by which they came into being, offer direct windows into how

---

[85] I use survivor language here alongside 'victim' because this is how the event was framed.
[86] Organización de Mujeres Víctimas Ave Fénix y diversas autoras, *El vuelo del fénix* [The flight of the phoenix] (Centro Nacional de Memoria Histórica; Corporación Ayuda Humanitaria; ACDI/VOCA; USAID Colombia, 2017).
[87] *Almas que escriben: Memorias y esperanza* [Souls That Write: Memories and Hope] (Alcaldía Mayor de Bogotá, 2018).

people author the self, interpret the harms they suffered, make sense of the past, and imagine the future.

In the introduction to these books, project facilitators summarize the theory of change: 'The idea is to construct the memory of the victims and, at the same time, heal our pain', writes Lina María Palacio Lemos in the opening pages of *Flight of the Phoenix*.[88] A project facilitator for a different book project echoed this attitude in an interview: 'My interest in writing is to help people remember, and heal themselves'.[89] And as a third facilitator for another creative writing project announced to women recognized as victims of the armed conflict participating in a writing workshop in Usme, 'We have gathered here today to remember, to write, and to heal'. In all these programs, healing through memory emerged consistently as the aspirational outcome, with writing as the stated intervention that links the past and present to that future aspiration. 'Healing' itself remained undefined.

As I browsed the banners of the sponsors in the still empty room before the *Flight of the Phoenix* book launch, the trail of rose petals grew, stretching from the table onstage to the front row. There were rose petals sprinkled on top of the stack of books, and carnations placed beside the bookmarks. Heads of calla lilies on the mosaic tiles pointed towards the hallway. One event staff member yelled to another to bring the hydrangeas. She then arranged them around the authors' black-and-white portraits that were lined on the floor against a wall, with lit candles surrounding them. This setup was at once funereal and celebratory. The rituals of mourning, resistance, and celebration echoed one another.

As people filtered into the room, a video played in the background. 'We are women who do not want them to write our history without us', one of the authors featured in the video declared. She did not specify who 'they' are, but it was clear that the imagined writers of history were different from the women who were gathering on the stage. As the video played on loop, images of women reading in a garden or by a lake were interspersed with quotes by famous authors. The video gathered together an unexpected cast of characters: The Uruguayan author Eduardo Galeano's words 'Wars lie' faded out to make room for Ayn Rand's 'Only I can free my mind'. The video

---

[88] Palacio Lemos, *El vuelo del fénix*, p. 18. Because the book is publicly available, I preserve the identification (by first name, full name, or pseudonym) that the project facilitators and participants used in the published version of the book.

[89] Interview with writing program facilitator for conflict-affected individuals in Bogotá, November 2017.

closed by featuring words in two columns, reflecting dyads of aspirational transformation. In the column on the left: pain, war, doubt, stigma. On the right: hope, peace, trust, truth. 'We hope with our words to transmute hate to forgiveness', one of the women said in the voice-over. The invitation to 'heal, be reborn, write' flashed across the screen one last time.

'Thanks to the National Centre for Historical Memory and USAID, the wounds that a brave group of women victims suffered are closing in a slow way, through the written word', one of the organizers said, as the music from the video faded out. Before she could finish her remarks, however, loud salsa music spilled into the room from the plaza outside. We should close the windows, some people said, while others complained that it was simply too hot for that. Both the music and the discussion about it were more audible than the remarks from the stage. Eventually, the ACDI/VOCA representative holding the microphone acknowledged the noise. 'We are competing with the party outside, but the words of the valiant women are keeping us here. This is a story of metamorphosis: of transformation of pain into words'.

Admittedly, I had brought my own impatience into the room that day. Observing the event, I wondered why pain had to transform into anything at all, why it could not remain in the world as pain. How much of the pressure to 'overcome' victimhood, to leave claims to the status of 'victim' in the past in favour of moving towards a 'post-victim' future, potentially stems from a collective discomfort with the persistence and omnipresence of grief? I am asking these questions near the end of a book about the politics of victimhood in Colombia, but they find resonance in other corners too. I am writing these sentences at the not-quite-end of a global pandemic that has seen many express an impatience to 'return to normal', to declare the 'post-pandemic' here already, while illness persist and collective grief remains largely unaddressed.

The recurrent references to transformation can be read as a heavy-handed metaphor that echoed the phoenix branding of this event. Equally, it may be easy to conclude that the transformation narrative merely served the purposes of event sponsors and organizers. The story of metamorphosis hinges on a tidy, linear path from war to peace, from pain to words. Yet it is important to notice the ways in which people who identified as victims and survivors also embraced this script.

'I feel saved and happy', Mary Luz began. When she took the microphone, she was introduced as an author whose work appeared in the book, rather than as a victim or a survivor. In fact, in her own telling, victimhood belonged in the past. 'I was once a victim, but not any more. I don't feel like a victim.

I feel like a woman', she said. Rousing applause momentarily drowned out the sounds of salsa. The other authors who spoke that evening reinforced this message. 'Through writing I was able to liberate what I was previously not capable of naming', one of them said. 'With psychosocial support, memory was converted into a tool to denounce and make visible [acts of violence]. Memory was converted into strength'. A third participant echoed: 'Through writing I saw that I didn't have to stay in the past. I saw that I could move forward. Everything that happened in this painful life . . . everything that happened, all the pain . . .' At this point, she took a long pause. 'I don't have to stay there. I am a very courageous woman who can move forward. I am not a victim. This process has allowed people who suffered harms to rename themselves.' The last participant to speak before the question-and-answer session with the audience restated this theme of leaving the victim label behind in favour of identities that resonated more: 'I am proud. Why am I proud? I don't feel like a victim. I feel like an empowered person'.

Some of the women's remarks explicitly acknowledged the institutional framework that underpinned both the book production and the testimonies at the event associated with it. In the words of Mary Luz: 'The Victims' Unit here took us by the hand since our birth as a collective [of women writers]. The Unit has been a pillar of support for the victims of Medellín. We must thank them'. She raised one hand towards the audience to indicate a cue for applause. 'Yes, yes, please', she continued, as the applause came, 'they deserve our applause. Dear National Center for Historical Memory: You have all my affection. You are a tree that gives good fruit. USAID and ACDI/VOCA also deposited their trust in us. Without your support, we couldn't have done it. My biggest gratitude is reserved for the other women here. This book is their child too. All my love to you, women. All my love'. More applause filled the room.

The institutional actors that Mary Luz named were not just sponsors; they were audiences for victim performances. Performance here carries a double meaning. It encompasses both the performativity of victimhood in the sense of the iterative embodied and narrative practices that produce certain effects,[90] and the theatrical notion of performance as a presentation to an audience. One must be a particular kind of victim in order to have her story

---

[90] Judith Butler, 'Performative Acts and Gender Constitution: An Essay in Phenomenology and Feminist Theory', in *Performing Feminisms: Feminist Critical Theory and Theatre*, edited by Sue-Ellen Case (Johns Hopkins University Press, 1990), pp. 270–82.

included in a book published by state-affiliated entities, or to be handed the microphone on stage.

One may argue that the donors and implementers of projects for conflict-affected individuals play a critical role in defining the permissible public performances of victimhood. As Iris told me in many conversations, 'If you are a restless [inquieta] victim like me, and you say things as they are, the state stigmatizes you and casts you aside, at least when it comes to the public face of victims' issues'.[91] Some state officials agree that this is a problematic dynamic. 'I don't like that we expect victims to "behave", to be nice and polite on stage all the time at these things', one state official told me after having sat in the audience of a tense event on victim reparations.[92]

Against this backdrop, it is understandable to be sceptical about the public moments in which people who formerly identified as victims now embrace the 'transformation' arc (with all its religious undertones of being saved and reborn). Listening to Mary Luz proclaim her affection for different state entities, I asked myself whether she had a meaningful choice to be anything *other* than a paradigmatic once-a-victim-but-no-more. Yet I hesitate to dismiss these public performances as mere acts of puppeteering, wherein the state or international organizations pull the strings and those who identify as victims produce a desirable script on demand. Such a dismissal risks minimizing the agency of people who identified as victims to co-opt or outright challenge the narrative expectations that others project onto them. Further, it overstates the intentionality and control that the state, international donors, and NGO event organizers can meaningfully exercise over others' performances of victimhood. For these reasons, I treat performances of victimhood and its rejection as both sincere *and* strategic, at once reflecting truths about people's self-identification and considerations regarding the usefulness and salience of the frame of victimhood in a given setting.

If victimhood itself allows for practices of politics and for notions of political subjectivities, then it follows that researchers must also remain attuned to the politics that emerge through the rejection of the victim label. Such an investigation acknowledges that there is no single pathway to politics or

---

[91] Interview with victim leader in Medellín, March 2018.
[92] Interview with Victims' Unit official in Bogotá, December 2017. These considerations also extend to researchers' entanglements with state officials and those who identify as victims. At numerous points during my fieldwork, state officials would suggest that I speak to someone 'because he's a charismatic victim' or that I take caution in interviewing someone else 'because she is very radical'. These comments are a form of data. The adjectives that state officials attach to those who identify as victims can tell stories about the politics, performances, and hierarchies of victimhood.

singular understanding of 'the political', and takes up the invitation to 'engage with our informants' own ideas about what might and might not count as political'.[93] What would it mean, then, to take seriously people's narratives about wanting to leave their victim identity in the past?

The books in which conflict-affected individuals tell their stories in their own terms illuminate answers to this question. I reread *Flight of the Phoenix* and *Souls That Write*, the books that emerged from the writing workshops for people recognized as victims, with an eye towards how the writers use the future tense.[94] This approach recognizes the authority of people affected by violence in defining and narrating their own experience. The root of the word 'authority', referring to validity or credibility, is the word 'author', referring to a writer. I am curious about how researchers might understand the future of victimhood differently if we treat the writing of those affected by it as a primary source.

Many of the texts in these books are first-person accounts of harms the writers suffered during the armed conflict. Others, like María Lucely Durango's 'Birthday Card to Juan in the Sky', are letters to family members who were killed or disappeared. The illustrations in both books echo the themes of rebirth and transformation. The page numbers in *Souls That Write* are enclosed in a seedling. Plants at various phases of development appear in *Flight of the Phoenix* as well. A fern frond grows out of a heart chamber. A bench grows roots. In one of the opening pages, before a text addressed to a baby born of wartime rape, a woman's body is depicted as though it were made of leaves. A fetus is in her uterus and a bird of paradise is perched on her breast. Flowers sprout from fountain pens, caterpillars turn to butterflies. These images defy the separation of 'the human' and 'the natural' and resist a literal depiction of war, focusing instead on what grows, flies, and is built or written in its wake.

---

[93] Curtis and Spencer, 'Anthropology and the Political', p. 169.

[94] I have selected these two books because they were published during the time of my fieldwork and I was able to interview facilitators and program implementers associated with their production. *Flight of the Phoenix* drew together female victims and survivors of the conflict in the region of Antioquia, while *Souls That Write* emerged from a program implemented in Bogotá, drawing together individuals of all genders from the greater region of Cundinamarca. The participants in the *Flight of the Phoenix* workshops had experienced harm in the context of the armed conflict, while *Souls That Write* was also open to those who identified as former combatants of non-state armed groups or members of the state armed forces. Because many of the people whose stories are included in the books had been displaced, both books reflect a range of experiences, conflict-related harms, and coping strategies across a wide spectrum of identities and locations in Colombia.

The past is also present in these pages. 'Today I am a young woman of seventeen years of age, and writing this letter has been the hardest thing I have done in my life. This is my story'.[95] This is how a woman by the pseudonym of Andrea begins narrating how her mother was assassinated in front of her and her siblings. In Andrea's life, this event was followed by multiple incidents of sexual abuse that she experienced both in the context of the armed conflict and in the hands of acquaintances. Neither Andrea nor the other storytellers in *Flight of the Phoenix* shy away from detailed descriptions of the violence they have experienced. In narrating these details, some writers claim to seek freedom from a past that had grabbed hold of them. 'From now on, I will not save anything that causes me pain; I am going to take out everything that I have kept stored inside me', Laura Palacio wrote.[96] This approach to facing the future through storytelling is not a denial of violence, but an attempted release from the grip of its memory.

Few writers spoke of 'overcoming' as such, but many articulated a vision of moving adelante: forward. What propels people forward, however, is not a resolute break from the past, but a sense of duty and responsibility towards it. 'Despite the Pain, I Must Continue', Luz Marina Hache Contreras titled her essay, addressed in the second person to her disappeared companion.[97] 'Your life must be more than the empty room in which you have left your fingerprint and the air of your absence'. Like Luz Marina, many of the writers in these collections write letters to their dead or disappeared loved ones, reassuring them that they have managed to cope and build a future. 'I want you to know that, no matter the circumstances, I have been able to go forward', Roberto Carlos Fuentes del Toro writes, addressing his sister.[98] In this sense, 'forward' is a path to honouring the dead and the missing through insisting on the persistence of life—a full life, a vivacious life—in the present.

Survival, in this context, looks less like a triumphant graduation than like exhaustion. In a text titled 'Tired', Rosalba Mariaca likens herself to a plant, 'whose roots desire fresh soil; that is how I feel, tired, cornered in a world without an exit'.[99] The facilitators of the writing workshops I interviewed all

---

[95] Andrea (no surname recorded), 'Stop', in Organización de Mujeres Víctimas Ave Fénix y diversas autoras, *El vuelo del fénix*, p. 89.
[96] Laura Palacio, 'Who Am I?', in Organización de Mujeres Víctimas Ave Fénix y diversas autoras, *El vuelo del fénix*, p. 30.
[97] Luz Marina Hache Contreras, 'Despite the Pain, I Must Continue', in *Almas que escriben*, p. 97.
[98] Roberto Carlos Fuentes del Toro, 'Thank You, María Patricia', *Almas que escriben*, p. 120.
[99] Rosalba Mariaca, 'Tired', in Organización de Mujeres Víctimas Ave Fénix y diversas autoras, *El vuelo del fénix*, p. 69.

noted the 'fatigue of being a victim' [el cansancio de ser víctima].[100] This is the fatigue of not only having been victimized, but also having to continuously perform victimhood. 'They have to wear the dress of a victim in all their struggles. The hardest thing was to teach them to find and speak in a different voice', one of the facilitators told me, once again echoing the clothing metaphors of victimhood.[101] She continued:

> I had to massage the words out of them sometimes. I told this one woman, 'where is the daughter's voice? You are a daughter!' Sometimes all their experience in how to be a victim in public spaces gets in the way of their authentic voice. They forget what does it mean to say 'I'. Not 'I, the victim', but 'I, the person'. They tell me this themselves: 'I had forgotten my own voice. I had the voice I had to have for my struggle as a victim'.

Narrating, embodying, and performing victimhood can be totalizing, all-consuming, and exhausting—even when it can simultaneously feel energizing or necessary, or when it fuels forms of agency, solidarity, and community. In this sense, the vision of the future that emerges from these writing interventions and their outputs is one that enables other selves to come to light.

'I write without exuberance about an act that does not define me and which belongs to my body like an unloved scar', Natylem Gómez Martínez said in the conclusion of her essay about gendered violence.[102] The other selves that emerge alongside the injured one have not necessarily transcended suffering, nor are they 'beyond victimhood'. Rather, they make every effort to no longer be entirely submerged in it. In the words of Lina María Palacio Lemos, 'We want to show that we are much more than victims of the armed conflict and our stories away from the war have value too'.[103]

This idea of not being defined entirely by violence recurs in both collections, as writers refer to themselves as husbands, wives, sons, daughters, activists, students, or women of peace. 'Writing permits people to rename themselves',

---

[100] Interview with facilitator of writing workshop for conflict-affected individuals in Bogotá, November 2017.
[101] Interview with facilitator of writing workshop for conflict-affected individuals in Bogotá, November 2017.
[102] Natylem Gómez Martínez, 'Obsession with Memory', in Organización de Mujeres Víctimas Ave Fénix y diversas autoras, *El vuelo del fénix*, p. 117.
[103] Palacio Lemos, *El vuelo del fénix*, p. 19.

THE FUTURE OF VICTIMHOOD   227

one workshop facilitator said.[104] Creating pockets in which people can live with a variety of self-identifications—alongside, outside, or beyond the label of 'victim'—can hold the promise of wholeness, of freedom.

The kind of freedom that the writers in these collections describe or aspire to is similar to the freedom that state officials hope people who identify as victims can find if they shed the label of 'victim'. Yet when people are pushed to leave victimhood behind, they often resist. This is because the freedom these writers narrate comes from within, from the agency of *deciding*—rather than being told—whether and how to relate to victimhood. It is the freedom of permission, not imposition. For some, hope is found in living as a political subject, understood through the many layers of meaning I have highlighted in these pages. 'Hope engenders political vocabularies', said the writer John Berger.[105] I have shown here that political vocabularies also engender hope.

They 'dream of a different country',[106] of a Colombia in peace, of truth and justice, of activism premised on love. Some of the dreams are wishful. 'I would like to be a fairy so I could disappear these sentiments and plant love in the hearts of all of humanity', María Lucely Durango wrote.[107] Other dreams are concrete and not pegged to conflict or peace, to justice or activism. They include wanting to travel the world, to go to university. 'I want to be much happier than I have been until now', Laura Palacio wrote. 'I am going to study everything I want and learn much from life. I am in this world to do grand things'.[108]

---

[104] Interview with facilitator of writing workshop for conflict-affected individuals in Bogotá, November 2017.
[105] John Berger, *Confabulations* (Penguin, 2016).
[106] María Lucely Durango, 'Invisible Frontier', in Organización de Mujeres Víctimas Ave Fénix y diversas autoras, *El vuelo del fénix*, p. 51.
[107] María Lucely Durango, 'Invisible Frontier', p. 51.
[108] Laura Palacio, 'Who Am I?', pp. 30–31.

Bibliography

Acosta, Laura. 'Victimhood Dissociation and Conflict Resolution: Evidence from the Colombian Peace Plebiscite'. *Theory and Society* 50, no. 4 (2021): 679–714.

'Agreement on Victims of the Conflict: Comprehensive System of Truth, Justice, Reparation, and Non-Repetition'. Alto Comisionado para La Paz, 2016. https://www.peaceagreements.org/wgenerateAgreementPDF/1547.

Ahmed, Sara. *The Cultural Politics of Emotion*. Edinburgh University Press, 2014.

Ahmed, Sara. *Living a Feminist Life*. Duke University Press, 2017.

Ahmed, Sara. *What's the Use? On the Uses of Use*. Duke University Press, 2019.

Almas que escriben: Memorias y esperanza. Alcaldía Mayor de Bogotá, 2018.

Anderson, Kjell, and Erin Jessee, eds. *Researching Perpetrators of Genocide*. University of Wisconsin Press, 2020.

Andrés Díaz, Fabio. 'Colombia Elects a Conservative Who Promises to "Correct" Its Peace Accord'. *The Conversation*. June 2017. http://theconversation.com/colombia-elects-a-conservative-who-promises-to-correct-its-peace-accord-98273.

Aparicio, Juan Ricardo. *Rumores, residuos y Estado en 'la major esquina de Sudamérica'*. Ediciones Uniandes, 2015.

Aretxaga, Begoña. 'Maddening States'. *Annual Review of Anthropology* 32, no. 1 (2003): 393–410.

Arjona, Ana. *Rebelocracy: Social Order in the Colombian Civil War*. Cambridge University Press, 2016.

Autesserre, Severine. *Peaceland*. Cambridge University Press, 2014.

Auyero, Javier. *Patients of the State: The Politics of Waiting in Argentina*. Duke University Press, 2012.

Babül, Elif. *Bureaucratic Intimacies: Translating Human Rights in Turkey*. Stanford University Press, 2017.

Baines, Erin. *Buried in the Heart: Women, Complex Victimhood and the War in Northern Uganda*. Cambridge University Press, 2017.

Baines, Erin. '"Today, I Want to Speak Out the Truth": Victim Agency, Responsibility, and Transitional Justice'. *International Political Sociology* 9, no. 4 (2015): 316–32.

Ballvé, Teo. *The Frontier Effect: State Formation and Violence in Colombia*. Cornell University Press, 2020.

Barokka, Khairani. 'The Case against Italicizing "Foreign" Words'. *Catapult*. February 11, 2020. https://catapult.co/stories/column-the-case-against-italicizing-foreign-words-khairani-barokka.

Barton Hronešová, Jessie. 'The Uses of Victimhood as a Hegemonic Meta-narrative in Eastern Europe'. *Journal of Contemporary European Studies* 2022: 1–17.

Berents, Helen. 'Hashtagging Girlhood: #IamMalala, #BringBackOurGirls and Gendering Representations of Global Politics'. *International Feminist Journal of Politics* 18, no. 4 (2016): 513–27.

Berlant, Lauren. *Cruel Optimism*. Duke University Press, 2011.

Berry, Marie. *War, Women, and Power: From Violence to Mobilization in Rwanda and Bosnia-Herzegovina*. Cambridge University Press, 2018.
Berry, Marie, and Trishna Rana. 'What Prevents Peace? Women and Peacebuilding in Bosnia and Nepal'. *Peace and Change* 44, no. 3 (2019): 321–49.
Bhadra-Heintz, John. *A Tyranny against Itself: Intimate Partner Violence on the Margins of Bogotá*. University of Pennsylvania Press, 2022.
Björkdahl, Annika, Oliver Richmond, and Stephanie Kappler. 'The Field in the Age of Intervention: Power, Legitimacy, Authority vs the "local"'. *Millennium* 44, no. 1 (2015): 23–44.
Bleiker, Roland. 'Forget IR Theory'. *Alternatives* 22, no 1 (1997): 57–85.
Bliesemann de Guevara, Berit, and Morten Boas. *Doing Fieldwork in Areas of International Intervention: A Guide to Research in Violent and Closed Contexts*. Bristol University Press, 2021.
Boesten, Jelke. *Sexual Violence during War and Peace: Gender, Power, and Post-conflict Justice in Peru*. Palgrave Macmillan, 2014.
Borda Guzmán, Sandra. 'La administración de Álvaro Uribe y su política exterior en materia de derechos humanos: De la negación a la contención estratégica'. *Análisis Político* 25, no. 75 (2012): 111–37.
Bourdieu, Pierre. *Pascalian Meditations*. Translated by Richard Nice. Stanford University Press, 2000.
Bourdieu, Pierre. 'Rethinking the State: Genesis and Structure of the Bureaucratic Field'. In *State/Culture: State-Formation after the Cultural Turn*, edited by George Steinmetz, pp. 53–75. Cornell University Press, 1999.
Bouvier, Virginia. 'Gender and the Role of Women in Colombia's Peace Process'. UN Women and US Institute of Peace, 2016. https://www.usip.org/sites/default/files/Gender-and-the-Role-of-Women-in-Colombia-s-Peace-Process-English.pdf.
Boyle, Kaitlin, and Kimberly Rogers. 'Beyond the Rape "Victim"-"Survivor" Binary: How Race, Gender, and Identity Processes Interact to Shape Distress'. *Sociological Forum* 35, no. 2 (2020): 323–45.
Brett, Roddy. 'The Role of the Victims' Delegations in the Santos-FARC Peace Talks'. In *The Politics of Victimhood in Post-conflict Societies*, edited by Vincent Druliolle and Roddy Brett, pp. 267–99. Palgrave Macmillan, 2018.
Brett, Roddy. *La voz de las víctimas en la negociación: Sistematización de una experiencia*. United Nations Development Program, 2017.
Brett, Roddy. 'Victim-Centred Peacemaking: The Colombian Experience'. *Journal of Intervention and Statebuilding* 16, no. 4 (2022): 475–97.
Brigden, Noelle. *The Migrant Passage*. Cornell University Press, 2018.
Brigden, Noelle, and Anita Gohdes. 'Transparency Intersections in Studying Violence: The Politics and Ethics of Data Access across Methodological Boundaries'. *International Studies Review* 22, no. 2 (2020): 250–67.
Brown, Gavin. 'The Revolt of Aspirations: Contesting Neoliberal Social Hope'. *ACME: An International Journal for Critical Geographies* 12, no. 3 (2013): 419–30.
Brown, Wendy. 'Wounded Attachments'. *Political Theory* 21, no. 3 (1993): 390–410.
Buchely, Lina. *Activismo burocrático: La construcción cotidiana del principio de legalidad*. Ediciones Uniandes, 2015.
Burnyeat, Gwen. *Chocolate, Politics and Peace-Building*. Palgrave Macmillan, 2018.
Burnyeat, Gwen. *The Face of Peace: Government Pedagogy amid Disinformation in Colombia*. University of Chicago Press, 2022.

Buss, Doris. 'Rethinking "Rape as a Weapon of War"'. *Feminist Legal Studies* 17, no. 2 (2009): 145–63.
Butler, Judith. *Frames of War: When Is Life Grievable?* Verso Books, 2016.
Butler, Judith. 'Performative Acts and Gender Constitution: An Essay in Phenomenology and Feminist Theory'. In *Performing Feminisms: Feminist Critical Theory and Theatre*, edited by Sue-Ellen Case, pp. 270–82. Johns Hopkins University Press, 1990.
Cabot, Heath. 'The Good Police Officer: Ambivalent Intimacies with the State in the Greek Asylum Procedure'. In *The Anthropology of Police*, edited by Kevin Karpiak and William Garriott, pp. 209–29. Routledge, 2018.
Calhoun, Craig. 'A World of Emergencies: Fear, Intervention, and the Limits of Cosmopolitan Order'. *Canadian Review of Sociology / Revue Canadienne de Sociologie* 41, no. 4 (2004): 373–95.
Castillejo Cuéllar, Alejandro. 'Unraveling Silence: Violence, Memory and the Limits of Anthropology's Craft'. *Dialectical Anthropology* 29, no. 2 (2005): 159–80.
Castro-Sardi, Ximena, and Cristian Erazo. 'Sufrimiento y agencia política: Pesquisa sobre la condición de víctima en Bojayá, Colombia'. *Athenea Digital* 19, no. 1 (2019): 1–22.
Castro-Sardi, Ximena, and Juliana Olano. 'Reparación y escucha del sujeto-víctima: Discursos y prácticas en la intervención psicosocial con víctimas del conflicto armado en Colombia'. *Revista Colombiana de Ciencias Sociales* 9, no. 1 (2018): 85–108.
Centro Nacional de Memoria Histórica. *La guerra inscrita en el cuerpo*. CNMH, 2017.
Centro Nacional de Memoria Histórica. *Paramilitarismo: Balance de la contribución del Centro Nacional de Memoria Histórica al esclarecimiento histórico*. CNMH, 2018.
Cerwonka, Allaine, and Liisa H. Malkki. *Improvising Theory: Process and Temporality in Ethnographic Fieldwork*. University of Chicago Press, 2007.
Céspedes-Báez, Lina. 'En los confines de lo posible: Inclusion del enfoque de genero en el acuerdo de La Habana'. In *Utopía u oportunidad fallida: Analisis critico del acuerdo de paz*, edited by Lina Céspedes-Baéz and Enrique Prieto-Rios, pp. 295–98. Editorial Universidad del Rosario, 2017.
Céspedes-Báez, Lina. 'Gender Panic and the Failure of a Peace Agreement'. *American Journal of International* Law 110 (2016): 183–87.
Chadwick, Rachelle. 'The question of feminist critique'. *Feminist Theory* (2023).
Chamon, Paulo. 'Turning Temporal: A Discourse of Time in IR'. *Millennium* 46, no. 3 (2018): 396–420.
Chouliaraki, Lilie. 'Victimhood: The Affective Politics of Vulnerability'. *European Journal of Cultural Studies* 24, no. 1 (2021): 10–27.
Clarke, Kamari Maxine. *Fictions of Justice: The International Criminal Court and the Challenge of Legal Pluralism in Sub-Saharan Africa*. Cambridge University Press, 2009.
Clifford, James, and George Marcus, eds. *Writing Culture: The Poetics and Politics of Ethnography*. University of California Press, 1986.
Cockburn, Cynthia. 'The Continuum of Violence: A Gender Perspective on War and Peace'. In *Sites of Violence: Gender and Conflict Zones*, edited by Wenona Giles and Jennifer Hyndman, pp. 24–44. University of California Press, 2004.
Cohen, Dara Kay. *Rape during Civil War*. Cornell University Press, 2016.
Cohen, Elizabeth. *The Political Value of Time*. Cambridge University Press, 2018.
Cohn, Carol. *Women and Wars*. Polity Press, 2013.
Cole, Alyson. *The Cult of True Victimhood*. Stanford University Press, 2006.
Collins, Patricia Hill, and Sirma Bilge. *Intersectionality*. John Wiley & Sons, 2016.

'Colombian Voters Reject Farc Peace Deal'. *BBC News*. October 3, 2016. https://www.bbc.com/news/world-latin-america-37537252.

Comisión de la Verdad (CEV). *Hay futuro, si hay verdad: Informe final de la Comisión para el Esclarecimiento de la Verdad, la Convivencia y la No Repetición*. CEV, 2022.

Comisión de Seguimiento y Monitoreo a la Implementación de la Ley 1448 de 2011. *Noveno informe de seguimiento al Congreso de la República, 2021–2022*. Contraloría General de la República, 2022.

Comisión de Seguimiento y Monitoreo a la Implementación de la Ley 1448 de 2011. *Octavo informe de seguimiento al Congreso de la República 2020–2021*. Contraloría General de la República, 2021.

Comisión de Seguimiento y Monitoreo a la Implementación de la Ley 1448 de 2011. *Quinto informe de seguimiento al Congreso de la República 2017–2018*. Contraloría General de la República, 2018.

Comisión Histórica del Conflicto y sus Víctimas. *Contribución al entendimiento del conflicto armado en Colombia*. Ediciones desde Abajo, 2015.

'Comisiones de Seguimiento a La Ley de Víctimas y Decretos Leyes Étnicos Alertan Sobre Aumento de Nuevos Hechos de Violencia y Precisan Que Se Requiere $115,9 Billones Para Reparar a Las Víctimas'. Contraloría General de la Republica, August 2019.

Conley, Bridget. 'Who Is the Subject of Atrocities Prevention?' *Global Responsibility to Protect* 6, no. 4 (2014): 430–52.

Cooper, Davina. *Feeling Like a State: Desire, Denial, and the Recasting of Authority*. Duke University Press, 2019.

Counter, Max. 'Producing Victimhood: Landmines, Reparations, and Law in Colombia'. *Antipode* 50, no. 1 (2018): 122–41.

Crane, Emma, and Catalina Vallejo. 'Remaking Subjects in the Aftermath of War: Colombia's Postconflict'. *Social Science Research Council* (blog). July 31, 2018. https://items.ssrc.org/from-our-fellows/remaking-subjects-in-the-aftermath-of-war-capitalism-personhood-and-colombias-postconflict/

Cronin-Furman, Kate, Nimmi Gowrinathan, and Rafia Zakaria. 'Emissaries of Empowerment'. Colin Powell School for Civic and Global Leadership and City College of New York, 2017. https://www.ccny.cuny.edu/colinpowellschool/emissaries-empowerment

Cronin-Furman, Kate, and Roxani Krystalli. 'The Things They Carry: Victims' Documentation of Forced Disappearance in Colombia and Sri Lanka'. *European Journal of International Relations* 27, no. 1 (2020): 79–101.

Cronin-Furman, Kate, and Milli Lake. 'Ethics Abroad: Fieldwork in Fragile and Violent Contexts'. *PS: Political Science & Politics* 51, no. 3 (2018): 607–14.

Curtis, Jennifer, and Jonathan Spencer. 'Anthropology and the Political'. In *The Sage Handbook of Social Anthropology*, edited by John Gledhill and Richard Fardon, pp. 168–82. Sage, 2012.

Das, Veena. *Life and Words: Violence and the Descent into the Ordinary*. University of California Press, 2006.

Das, Veena, and Deborah Poole, eds. *Anthropology in the Margins of the State*. School of American Research, 2004.

Dávila Sáenz, Juana. 'A Land of Lawyers, Experts, and 'Men without Land': The Politics of Land Restitution and the Techno-Legal Production of 'Dispossessed People' in Colombia'. PhD dissertation: Harvard University, 2017.

'Declaración de Principios Para la Discusión del Punto 5 de La Agenda: "Víctimas" - Comunicado Conjunto'. Alto Comisionado para la Paz. June 7, 2014.

Deiana, Maria-Adriana, Milena Komarova, and Cathal McCall. 'Cross-Border Cooperation as Conflict Transformation: Promises and Limitations in EU Peacebuilding'. *Geopolitics* 24, no. 3 (2019): 529–40.

Dery, David. '"Papereality" and Learning in Bureaucratic Organizations'. *Administration & Society* 29, no. 6 (1998): 677–89.

De Waardt, Mijke. 'Naming and Shaming Victims: The Semantics of Victimhood'. *International Journal of Transitional Justice* 10, no. 3 (2016): 432–50.

De Waardt, Mijke, and Sanne Weber. 'Beyond Victims' Mere Presence: An Empirical Analysis of Victim Participation in Transitional Justice in Colombia'. *Journal of Human Rights Practice* 11, no. 1 (2019): 209–28.

De Waardt, Mijke, and Eva Willems. 'Recipients versus Participants: Politics of Aid and Victim Representation in Transitional Justice Practices in Peru'. *Human Rights Quarterly* 44, no. 2 (2022): 339–63.

DiFruscia, Kim Turcot. 'Listening to Voices: An Interview with Veena Das'. *Altérités* 7, no. 1 (2010): 136–45.

Doty, Roxanne Lynn. 'Foreign Policy as Social Construction: A Post-positivist Analysis of US Counterinsurgency Policy in the Philippines'. *International Studies Quarterly* 37, no. 3 (1993): 297–320.

Druliolle, Vincent, and Roddy Brett, eds. *The Politics of Victimhood in Post-conflict Societies*. Palgrave Macmillan, 2018.

Dunn, Jennifer. '"Victims" and "Survivors": Emerging Vocabularies of Motive for "Battered Women Who Stay"'. *Sociological Inquiry* 75, no. 1 (2005): 1–30.

Duriesmith, David. 'Negative Space and the Feminist Act of Citation'. In *Rethinking Silence, Voice, and Agency in Contested Gendered Terrains*, edited by Jane Parpart and Swati Parashar, pp. 66–77. Routledge, 2018.

Dürr, Eveline, and Rivke Jaffe. 'Theorizing Slum Tourism: Performing, Negotiating and Transforming Inequality'. *European Review of Latin American and Caribbean Studies / Revista Europea de Estudios Latinoamericanos y del Caribe*, no. 93 (2012): 113–23.

Echavarría Álvarez, Josefina, Mateo Gómez Vásquez, Brenda Forero Linares, Mariana Balen Giancola, Miyerlandy Cabanzo Valencia, Elise Ditta, et al. 'Five Years after the Signing of the Colombian Final Agreement: Reflections from Implementation Monitoring'. Kroc Institute for International Peace Studies / Keough School of Global Affairs, 2022. https://keough.nd.edu/five-years-after-the-signing-of-the-colombian-final-agreement-reflections-from-implementation-monitoring/

Edkins, Jenny. 'Remembering Relationality: Trauma Time and Politics'. In *Memory, Trauma and World Politics: Reflections on the Relationship between Past and Present*, edited by Duncan Bell, pp. 99–115. Palgrave Macmillan, 2006.

Edkins, Jenny. 'Temporality, Politics and Performance: Missing, Displaced, Disappeared'. In *The Grammar of Politics and Performance*, edited by Shirin Rai and Janelle Reinelt, pp. 134–47. Routledge, 2014.

Edkins, Jenny. *Trauma and the Memory of Politics*. Cambridge University Press, 2003.

Ellard-Gray, Amy, Nicole Jeffrey, Melisa Choubak, and Sara Crann. 'Finding the Hidden Participant: Solutions for Recruiting Hidden, Hard-to-Reach, and Vulnerable Populations'. *International Journal of Qualitative Methods* 14, no. 5 (2015): 1–10.

Emejulu, Akwugo. *Fugitive Feminism*. Silver Press, 2022.

England, Kim. 'Getting Personal: Reflexivity, Positionality, and Feminist Research'. *Professional Geographer* 46, no. 1 (1994): 80–89.
Enloe, Cynthia. *The Curious Feminist*. University of California Press, 2004.
Enloe, Cynthia. *Seriously! Investigating Crashes and Crises as Though Women Mattered*. University of California Press, 2013.
Enns, Diane. *The Violence of Victimhood*. Penn State University Press, 2012.
Eriksson Baaz, Maria, and Maria Stern. *Sexual Violence as a Weapon of War? Perceptions, Prescriptions, Problems in the Congo and Beyond*. Zed Books, 2013.
Eroukhmanoff, Clara, and Alister Wedderburn. 'Introduction: Constructing and Contesting Victimhood in Global Politics'. *Polity* 54, no. 3 (2022): 841–48.
'"Este es el gobierno de la vida, de la paz, y así será recordado": Presidente Petro'. Presidencia de la República. August 7, 2022. https://petro.presidencia.gov.co/prensa/Paginas/Este-es-el-Gobierno-de-la-vida-de-la-paz-y-asi-sera-recordado-Presiden-220807.aspx.
Fassin, Didier. *At the Heart of the State: The Moral World of Institutions*. Pluto Press, 2015.
Fassin, Didier. 'Heart of Humaneness: The Moral Economy of Humanitarian Intervention'. In *Contemporary States of Emergency*, edited by Didier Fassin and Mariella Pandolfi, pp. 269–94. Zone Books, 2010.
Fassin, Didier, and Richard Rechtman. *The Empire of Trauma: An Inquiry into the Condition of Victimhood*. Princeton University Press, 2009.
Fattal, Alex. 'Violence and Killings Haven't Stopped in Colombia Despite Landmark Peace Deal'. *The Conversation*. February 2019. http://theconversation.com/violence-and-killings-havent-stopped-in-colombia-despite-landmark-peace-deal-111232.
Federici, Silvia. *Revolution at Point Zero: Housework, Reproduction, and Feminist Struggle*. PM Press, 2012.
Felbab-Brown, Vanda. 'Death by Bad Implementation? The Duque Administration and Colombia's Peace Deal(s). Brookings, 2018. https://www.brookings.edu/blog/order-from-chaos/2018/07/24/death-by-bad-implementation-the-duque-administration-and-colombias-peace-deals/.
Ferguson, James. *The Anti-politics Machine: 'Development', Depoliticization and Bureaucratic Power in Lesotho*. Cambridge University Press, 1990.
Firchow, Pamina. *Reclaiming Everyday Peace: Local Voices in Measurement and Evaluation after War*. Cambridge University Press, 2018.
Forero Angel, Ana María. *El coronel no tiene quien le escuche*. Ediciones Uniandes, 2017.
Franco Gamboa, Angélica. 'Daño y reconstrucción de la cotidianidad en covíctimas y sobrevivientes de minas antipersonal en Colombia'. *Nómadas* 38 (2013): 115–31.
Franco Gamboa, Angélica. 'Fronteras simbólicas entre expertos y víctimas de la guerra en Colombia'. *Antípoda* 24 (2016): 35–53.
Fraser, Nancy, and Linda Gordon. 'A Genealogy of Dependency: Tracing a Keyword of the US Welfare State'. *Signs* 19, no. 2 (1994): 309–36.
Fujii, Lee Ann. 'Shades of Truth and Lies: Interpreting Testimonies of War and Violence'. *Journal of Peace Research* 47, no. 2 (2010): 231–41.
García-Godos, Jemima. 'Victims in Focus'. *International Journal of Transitional Justice* 10, no. 2 (2016): 350–58.
García-Godos, Jemima, and Knut Andreas O. Lid. 'Transitional Justice and Victims' Rights before the End of a Conflict: The Unusual Case of Colombia'. *Journal of Latin American Studies* 42, no. 3 (2010): 487–516.

García-Godos, Jemima, and Henrik Wiig. 'Ideals and Realities of Restitution: The Colombian Land Restitution Programme'. *Journal of Human Rights Practice* 10, no. 1 (2018): 40–57.

García-González, Andrea. 'Desde el conflicto: Epistemología y política en las etnografías feministas'. *Antípoda: Revista de Antropología y Arqueología* 35, no. 1 (2019): 3–21.

García-González, Andrea, Elona Marjory Hoover, Athanasia Francis, Kayla Rush, and Ana María Forero Angel. 'When Discomfort Enters Our Skin: Five Feminists in Conversation'. *Feminist Anthropology* 3, no. 1 (2022): 151–69.

Gatti, Gabriel. *Un mundo de víctimas*. Anthropos, 2017.

Gaviria Betancur, Paula, and Laura Gil Savastano. *La agenda de las víctimas en el Congreso 2007–2009: Aprendizajes para la incidencia desde la sociedad civil*. Fundación Social, 2010.

Georgi, Richard. 'Peace through the Lens of Human Rights: Mapping Spaces of Peace in the Advocacy of Colombian Human Rights Defenders'. *Political Geography* 99 (2022).

Gharib Seif, Sarah. 'Beyond the "Jihadi Bride": Interrogating the Colonial, Racialised, and Gendered Narratives of Women Who Joined IS'. PhD thesis: University of St Andrews, forthcoming.

Golubović, Jelena. '"One Day I Will Tell This to My Daughter": Serb Women, Silence, and the Politics of Victimhood in Sarajevo'. *Anthropological Quarterly* 92, no. 4 (2019): 1173–99.

Gomez-Suarez, Andrei. *El triunfo del no: La paradoja emocional detrás del plebiscite*. Icono, 2016.

Gordon, Avery. *Ghostly Matters: Haunting and the Sociological Imagination*. University of Minnesota Press, 2007.

Gready, Paul, and Simon Robins. 'From Transitional to Transformative Justice: A New Agenda for Practice'. *International Journal of Transitional Justice* 8, no. 3 (2014): 339–61.

Guerra, Sebastian, and Steve Hege. 'Colombia's New Administration Raises Hopes for 'Total Peace''. United States Institute of Peace. July 12, 2022. https://www.usip.org/publications/2022/07/colombias-new-administration-raises-hopes-total-peace

Gupta, Akhil. *Red Tape: Bureaucracy, Structural Violence, and Poverty in India*. Duke University Press, 2012.

Gutiérrez-Sanín, Francisco, and Elisabeth Jean Wood. 'What Should We Mean by "Pattern of Political Violence"? Repertoire, Targeting, Frequency, and Technique'. *Perspectives on Politics* 15, no. 1 (2017): 20–41.

Haastrup, Toni, and Jamie J. Hagen. 'Racial hierarchies of knowledge production in the Women, Peace and Security agenda'. *Critical Studies on Security* 9, no. 1 (2021): 27–30.

Haesbaert, Rogerio. 'Del cuerpo-territorio al territorio-cuerpo (de la tierra): Contribuciones decoloniales. ' *Cultura y Representaciones Sociales* 15, no. 29 (2020): 267–301.

Haiven, Max, and Alex Khasnabish. *The Radical Imagination: Social Movement Research in the Age of Austerity*. Zed Books, 2014.

Hamati-Ataya, Inanna. 'Reflectivity, Reflexivity, Reflexivism: IR's "Reflexive Turn"—and Beyond'. *European Journal of International Relations* 19, no. 4 (2013): 669–94.

Hanson, Heather, and Rogers Romero Penna. 'The Failure of Colombia's "Democratic Security"'. *NACLA Report on the Americas* 38, no. 6 (2005): 22–24.

Haraway, Donna. 'Situated Knowledges: The Science Question in Feminism and the Privilege of Partial Perspective'. *Feminist Studies* 14, no. 3 (1988): 575–99.

Haraway, Donna. *Staying with the Trouble: Making Kin in the Chthulucene*. Duke University Press, 2016.

Harding, Sandra. 'Is There a Feminist Method?' In *Feminism and Methodology: Social Science Issues*, edited by Sandra Harding, pp. 456–64. Indiana University Press, 1989.

Harding, Susan. 'Representing Fundamentalism: The Problem of the Repugnant Cultural Other'. *Social Research* 58, no. 2 (1991): 373–93.

Haspeslagh, Sophie. *Proscribing Peace: How Listing Armed Groups as Terrorists Hurts Negotiations*. Manchester University Press, 2021.

Held, Virginia. *The Ethics of Care*. Oxford University Press, 2006.

Helms, Elissa. *Innocence and Victimhood: Gender, Nation, and Women's Activism in Postwar Bosnia-Herzegovina*. University of Wisconsin Press, 2013.

Hemmings, Clare. *Why Stories Matter: The Political Grammar of Feminist Theory*. Duke University Press, 2011.

Hemmings, Clare, and Amal Treacher Kabesh. 'The Feminist Subject of Agency: Recognition and Affect in Encounters with "the Other"'. In *Gender, Agency, and Coercion*, edited by Sumi Madhok, Anne Phillips, and Kalpana Wilson, pp. 29–46. Palgrave Macmillan, 2013.

Henry, Nicola. 'The Fixation on Wartime Rape: Feminist Critique and International Criminal Law'. *Social & Legal Studies* 23, no. 1 (2014): 93–111.

Herbolzheimer, Kristian. 'Innovations in the Colombian Peace Process'. Noref / Norwegian Peacebuilding Resource Center, 2016. https://www.c-r.org/resource/innovations-colombian-peace-process

Herrera, Martha Cecilia, and Carol Pertuz Bedoya. 'Narrativas femeninas del conflicto armado y la violencia política en Colombia: Contar para rehacerse'. *Revista de Estudios Sociales* 53 (2015): 150–62.

Herzfeld, Michael. *The Social Production of Indifference: Exploring the Symbolic Roots of Western Bureaucracy*. Routledge, 1992.

hooks, bell. *Feminist Theory: From Margin to Center*. 3rd ed. Routledge, 2014.

hooks, bell. *Teaching to Transgress*. Routledge, 1994.

Hoyos García, and Juan Felipe. '"El desplome de lo igual es irreversible": La emergencia del enfoque diferencial étnico en Colombia'. *Revista Colombiana de Antropología* 59, no. 1 (2023): 107–32.

Hunfeld, Katharina. 'The Coloniality of Time in the Global Justice Debate: De-centring Western Linear Temporality'. *Journal of Global Ethics* 18, no. 1 (2022): 100–117.

Hutchings, Kimberly. *Time and World Politics*. Manchester University Press, 2008.

Inayatullah, Naeem. 'If Only You Could See What I Have Seen with Your Eyes: Staging an Encounter between Social Science And literature'. 2001. https://citeseerx.ist.psu.edu/viewdoc/download?doi=10.1.1.602.1126&rep=rep1&type=pdf.

Indepaz. 'Desafío a la paz total'. November 2022. https://indepaz.org.co/wp-content/uploads/2022/11/INFORME_GRUPOS_FINAL_NOV28.pdf.

Jacoby, Tami Amanda. 'A Theory of Victimhood: Politics, Conflict and the Construction of Victim-Based Identity'. *Millennium* 43, no. 2 (2015): 511–30.

Jamar, Astrid. 'The Exclusivity of Inclusion: Global Construction of Vulnerable and Apolitical Victimhood in Peace Agreements'. *International Journal of Transitional Justice* 15, no. 2 (2021): 284–308.

James, Erica. *Democratic Insecurities: Violence, Trauma, and Intervention in Haiti*. University of California Press, 2010.

Jaramillo, Pablo. *Etnicidad y victimización*. Ediciones Uniandes, 2014.

Jauregui, Beatrice. 'Intimacy: Personal Policing, Ethnographic Kinship, and Critical Empathy'. In *Writing the World of Policing: The Difference Ethnography Makes*, edited by Didier Fassin, pp. 62–90. University of Chicago Press, 2017.

Jimeno, Myriam. 'Lenguaje, subjetividad y experiencias de violencia'. *Antípoda* 5 (2007): 169–90.

Kaplan, Oliver. *Resisting War: How Communities Protect Themselves*. Cambridge University Press, 2017.

Kaplan, Oliver, and Enzo Nussio. 'Explaining Recidivism of Ex-Combatants in Colombia'. *Journal of Conflict Resolution* 62, no. 1 (2018): 64–93.

Karl, Robert. *Forgotten Peace: Reform, Violence, and the Making of Contemporary Colombia*. University of California Press, 2017.

Kinsella, Helen. *The Image before the Weapon: A Critical History of the Distinction between Combatant and Civilian*. Cornell University Press, 2011.

Kleinman, Arthur, Veena Das, and Margaret Lock, eds. *Social Suffering*. University of California Press, 1997.

Knott, Eleanor. 'Beyond the Field: Ethics after Fieldwork in Politically Dynamic Contexts'. *Perspectives on Politics* 17, no. 1 (2019): 140–53.

Kochanski, Adam. 'The "Local Turn" in Transitional Justice: Curb the Enthusiasm'. *International Studies Review* 22, no. 1 (2020): 26–50.

Koopman, Sara. 'Building an Inclusive Peace Is an Uneven Socio-spatial Process: Colombia's Differential Approach'. *Political Geography* 83 (2020): 1–11.

Koopman, Sara. 'Making Space for Peace: International Protective Accompaniment in Colombia'. In *Geographies of Peace*, edited by Nick Megoran and Philippa William, pp. 109–30. IB Tauris, 2014.

Kreft, Anne-Kathrin, and Philipp Schulz. 'Political Agency, Victimhood, and Gender in Contexts of Armed Conflict: Moving beyond Dichotomies'. *International Studies Quarterly* 66, no. 2 (2022): 1–11.

Krystalli, Roxani. 'Attendance Sheets and Bureaucracies of Victimhood in Colombia'. *PoLAR: Political and Legal Anthropology Review* 10 (2020). https://polarjournal.org/2020/11/24/attendance-sheets-and-bureaucracies-of-victimhood-in-colombia/.

Krystalli, Roxani. 'Being Seen Like a State: Transitional Justice Bureaucrats and Victimhood in Colombia'. *Current Anthropology* 64, no. 2 (2023): 128–46.

Krystalli, Roxani. 'Engage with Former Combatants as Interlocutors for Peace, Not Only as Authorities on Violence'. In *Feminist Solutions for Ending War*, edited by Megan MacKenzie and Nicole Wegner, pp. 152–65. Pluto Press, 2021.

Krystalli, Roxani. 'Feminist Methodology'. In *Gender Matters in Global Politics: A Feminist Introduction to International Relations*, 3rd ed., edited by Laura J. Shepherd and Caitlin Hamilton, pp. 34–46. Routledge, 2022.

Krystalli, Roxani. 'Narrating Victimhood: Dilemmas and (In)dignities'. *International Feminist Journal of Politics* 23, no. 1 (2021): 125–46.

Krystalli, Roxani. 'Of Loss and Light: Teaching in the Time of Grief'. *Journal of Narrative Politics* 8, no. 1 (2021): 41–44.

Krystalli, Roxani. 'When Humans Become Data'. In *The Companion to Peace and Conflict Fieldwork*, edited by Roger Mac Ginty, Roddy Brett, and Birte Vogel, pp. 35–46. Palgrave Macmillan, 2020.

Krystalli, Roxani, and Cynthia Enloe. 'Doing Feminism: A Conversation between Cynthia Enloe and Roxani Krystalli'. *International Feminist Journal of Politics* 22, no. 2 (2020): 289–98.

Krystalli, Roxani, Elizabeth Hoffecker, Kendra Leith, and Kim Wilson. 'Taking the Research Experience Seriously: A Framework for Reflexive Applied Research in Development'. *Global Studies Quarterly* 3, no. 1 (2021): 1–10.

Krystalli, Roxani, and Philipp Schulz. 'Taking Love and Care Seriously: An Emergent Research Agenda for Remaking Worlds in the Wake of Violence'. *International Studies Review* 24, no. 1 (2022): 1–25.

Lake, Milli May. *Strong NGOs and Weak States: Pursuing Gender Justice in the Democratic Republic of Congo and South Africa*. Cambridge University Press, 2018.

Lambourne, Wendy. 'Transitional Justice and Peacebuilding after Mass Violence'. *International Journal of Transitional Justice* 3, no. 1 (2009): 28–48.

Laplante, Lisa, and Kimberly Theidon. 'Transitional Justice in Times of Conflict: Colombia's Ley de Justicia y Paz'. *Michigan Journal of International Law* 28 (2006): 50–106.

Law, John. *After Method: Mess in Social Science Research*. Routledge, 2014.

Lawther, Cheryl. 'Haunting and Transitional Justice: On Lives, Landscapes and Unresolved Pasts'. *International Review of Victimology* 27, no. 1 (2021): 3–22.

Lea, Tess. 'Desiring Bureaucracy'. *Annual Review of Anthropology* 50 (2021): 59–74.

Lederach, Angela. ' "The Campesino Was Born for the Campo": A Multispecies Approach to Territorial Peace in Colombia'. *American Anthropologist* 119, no. 4 (2017): 589–602.

Lederach, Angela. ' "Each Word Is Powerful": Writing and the Ethics of Representation'. In *The Companion to Peace and Conflict Fieldwork*, edited by Roger Mac Ginty, Roddy Brett, and Birte Vogel, pp. 455–70. Palgrave Macmillan, 2020.

Lederach, Angela. *Feel the Grass Grow: Ecologies of Slow Peace in Colombia*. Stanford University Press, 2023.

Lederach, Angela. 'Youth Provoking Peace: An Intersectional Approach to Territorial Peacebuilding in Colombia'. *Peacebuilding* 8, no. 2 (2020): 198–217.

Lemaitre, Julieta. *El estado siempre llega tarde*. Siglo XXI Editores, 2019.

Lemaitre, Julieta. 'Legal Fetishism: Law, Violence, and Social Movements in Colombia'. *Revista Juridica Universidad de Puerto Rico* 77 (2008): 331–44.

Lewis, Chloé, Alfred Banga, Ghislain Cimanuka, Jean de Dieu Hategekimana, Milli Lake, and Rachael Pierotti. 'Walking the Line: Brokering Humanitarian Identities in Conflict Research'. *Civil Wars* 21, no. 2 (2019): 200–227.

Linke, Uli. 'Contact zones: Rethinking the Sensual Life of the State'. *Anthropological Theory* 6, no. 2 (2006): 205–25.

Lipsky, Michael. *Street Level Bureaucracy: Dilemmas of the Individual in Public Services*. Russell Sage Foundation, 1980.

Lisle, Debbie. 'Consuming Danger: Reimagining the War/Tourism Divide'. *Alternatives* 25, no. 1 (2000): 91–116.

Londoño Ortiz, Ana María. 'Más del 80% de víctimas de la violencia en Colombia esperan ser reparadas'. *RCN Radio*. February 5, 2019. https://www.rcnradio.com/colombia/mas-del-80-de-victimas-de-la-violencia-en-colombia-esperan-ser-reparadas

Mac Ginty, Roger. *Everyday Peace: How So-Called Ordinary People Can Disrupt Violent Conflict*. Oxford University Press, 2021.

Mac Ginty, Roger. 'Routine Peace: Technocracy and Peacebuilding'. *Cooperation and Conflict* 47, no. 3 (2012): 287–308.

Mac Ginty, Roger, and Oliver P. Richmond. 'The Local Turn in Peace Building: A Critical Agenda for Peace'. *Third World Quarterly* 34, no. 5 (2013): 763–83.

Madhok, Sumi. *Rethinking Agency: Developmentalism, Gender and Rights*. Routledge, 2013.

Madhok, Sumi, Anne Phillips, and Kalpana Wilson, eds. *Gender, Agency, and Coercion*. Palgrave Macmillan, 2013.
Madlingozi, Tshepo. 'On Transitional Justice Entrepreneurs and the Production of Victims'. *Journal of Human Rights Practice* 2, no. 2 (2010): 208–28.
Malejacq, Romain, and Dipali Mukhopadhyay. 'The "Tribal Politics" of Field Research: A Reflection on Power and Partiality in 21st Century Warzones'. *Perspectives on Politics* 14, no. 4 (2016): 1011–28.
el-Malik, Shiera. 'A Letter to Baba'. *Review of International Studies* 49, no. 4 (2023): 539–46.
Malkki, Liisa. *Purity and Exile: Violence, Memory, and National Cosmology among Hutu Refugees in Tanzania*. University of Chicago Press, 1995.
Mallon, Florencia. 'The Promise and Dilemma of Subaltern Studies: Perspectives from Latin American History'. *American Historical Review* 99, no. 5 (1994): 1491–515.
Manetto, Francesco. 'Iván Duque advierte de que cambiara los acuerdos de paz sin romperlos'. *El País*. June 19, 2018. https://elpais.com/internacional/2018/06/18/colombia/1529351991_715042.html.
Manivannan, Q. 'Imagining a Care Curriculum'. *KCL Feminist Perspectives* (blog). May 11, 2022. https://www.kcl.ac.uk/imagining-a-care-curriculum.
Marcos, Ana. 'Los estratos en Colombia: Eres el lugar en el que vives'. *El País*. April 22, 2018. https://elpais.com/internacional/2018/04/20/colombia/1524176587_818282.html.
Martín de Almagro, María. 'Producing Participants: Gender, Race, Class, and Women, Peace and Security'. *Global Society* 32, no. 4 (2018): 395–414.
Massey, Dorreen. *Space, Place and Gender*. John Wiley & Sons, 2013.
Mazurana, Dyan, Karen Jabobsen, and Lesley Gale, eds. *Research Methods in Conflict Settings: A View from Below*. Cambridge University Press, 2013.
McFee, Erin. 'An Ambivalent Peace: Mistrust, Reconciliation, and the Intervention Encounter in Colombia'. PhD dissertation: University of Chicago, 2019.
McFee, Erin. '"Making a Presence": Reconciliation and the State in Colombia'. *Political and Legal Anthropology Review* 10 (2020). https://polarjournal.org/2020/11/24/making-a-presence-reconciliation-and-the-state-in-colombia/.
McGill, Dáire. 'Different Violence, Different Justice? Taking Structural Violence Seriously in Post-conflict and Transitional Justice Processes'. *State Crime Journal* 6, no. 1 (2017): 79–101.
Meertens, Donny. 'Colombia: Internally Displaced Persons and the Conditions for Socioeconomic Reintegration'. United Nations High Commission for Refugees, 2002.
Meier, Anna A. 'The idea of terror: Institutional reproduction in government responses to political violence'. *International Studies Quarterly* 64, no. 3 (2020): 499–509.
Meister, Robert. 'Human Rights and the Politics of Victimhood'. *Ethics & International Affairs* 16, no. 2 (2002): 91–108.
Merriman, Dani. 'Contentious Bodies: The Place, Race, and Gender of Victimhood in Colombia'. *Transforming Anthropology* 28, no. 1 (2020): 24–40.
Merry, Sally. *The Seductions of Quantification*. University of Chicago Press, 2016.
Meyers, Diana. 'Two Victim Paradigms and the Problem of "Impure" Victims'. *Humanity* 2, no. 2 (2011): 255–75.
Miller, Zinaida. 'Effects of Invisibility: In Search of the "Economic" in Transitional Justice'. *International Journal of Transitional Justice* 2, no. 3 (2008): 266–91.

Misión de Verificación de las Naciones Unidas en Colombia. 'Informe trimestral del Secretario General'. December 26, 2022. https://colombia.unmissions.org/sites/defa ult/files/infografia_informe_enero_2023.pdf.

Mora-Gámez, Fredy. 'Reconocer a los reclamantes: Sobre el Registro Único de Víctimas en Colombia como ensamblado sociotécnico'. *Im-Pertinente* 1, no. 1 (2013): 11-31.

Mora-Gámez, Fredy. 'Reparation beyond Statehood; Assembling Rights Restitution in Post-conflict Colombia'. PhD dissertation: University of Leicester, 2016.

Motta, Sara. *Liminal Subjects: Weaving (Our) Liberation*. Rowman & Littlefield, 2018.

Mukhopadhyay, Dipali. *Warlords, Strongman Governors, and the State in Afghanistan*. Cambridge University Press, 2014.

Munévar Munévar, Dora Inés, Nicolás Torres Rodríguez, and Ángela Patricia Martínez Sánchez. 'Provocaciones sentipensadas desde Colombia para cuestionar el "enfoque diferencial"'. *Mundos Plurales: Revista Latinoamericana de Políticas y Acción Pública* 8, no. 2 (2021): 9-34.

Myrttinen, Henri. 'Stabilising or Challenging Patriarchy? Sketches of Selected 'New' Political Masculinities'. *Men and Masculinities* 22, no. 3 (2019): 563-81.

Myrttinen, Henri, and Subhiya Mastonshoeva. 'From Remote Control to Collaboration: Conducting NGO Research at a Distance in Tajikistan'. *Civil Wars* 21, no. 2 (2019): 228-48.

Nader, Laura. 'Up the Anthropologist: Perspectives Gained from Studying Up'. Distributed by ERIC Clearinghouse (1972): 1-28.

Nayeri, Dina. *The Ungrateful Refugee*. Canongate, 2019.

Nayeri, Dina. *Who Gets Believed? When the Truth Isn't Enough*. Harvill Secker, 2023.

Nelson, Diane. *Who Counts? The Mathematics of Death and Life after Genocide*. Duke University Press, 2015.

Ní Aoláin, Fionnuala. 'Exploring a Feminist Theory of Harm in the Context of Conflicted and Post-conflict Societies Emerging Paradigms of Rationality'. *Queen's Law Journal* 35, no. 1 (2009): 219-44.

Ní Aoláin, Fionnuala. 'Women, Security, and the Patriarchy of Internationalized Transitional Justice'. *Human Rights Quarterly* 31 (2009): 1055-85.

Nixon, Rob. *Slow Violence and the Environmentalism of the Poor*. Harvard University Press, 2011.

Nordstrom, Carolyn. *A Different Kind of War Story*. University of Pennsylvania Press, 1997.

Nordstrom, Carolyn. *Shadows of War*. University of California Press, 2004.

Nuijten, Monique. 'Between Fear and Fantasy: Governmentality and the Working of Power in Mexico'. *Critique of Anthropology* 24, no. 2 (2004): 209-30.

Office of the High Commissioner for Peace in Colombia. 'El tiempo de las víctimas'. June 9, 2014. https://www.funcionpublica.gov.co/eva/admon/files/empresas/ZW1wcmV zYV83Ng==/archivos/1462299931_1c28b3e9306b3b7e4820233b2b2c4bf8.pdf.

Olarte-Sierra, María Fernanda. 'On Bodies and Our Own Bodies: Care and Vulnerability When Teaching about Death and Loss'. *Curare Journal of Medical Anthropology* 46, no. 1 (2023): 106-12.

Olarte-Sierra, María Fernanda, Gina Urazan Razzini, David Garces, and Sergio Rodríguez Vitta. 'Forensic Tales: Embodied Peace and Violence in Colombian (Post) Armed Conflict'. *Trajectoria* 4, no. 1 (2023): 1-16.

Olufemi, Lola. *Feminism Interrupted: Disrupting Power*. Pluto Press, 2020.

Oquendo, Catalina. 'Los exsecuestrados de las FARC que buscan llegar al Congreso de Colombia'. *El País*. January 31, 2022. https://elpais.com/internacional/2022-01-31/los-exsecuestrados-de-las-farc-que-buscan-llegar-al-congreso-de-colombia.html

Organización de Mujeres Víctimas Ave Fénix y diversas autoras. *El vuelo del fénix*. Centro Centro Nacional de Memoria Histórica; Corporación Ayuda Humanitaria; ACDI/VOCA; USAID Colombia, 2017.

Orozco, Iván. 'Reflexiones impertinentes: Sobre la memoria y el olvido, sobre el castigo y la clemencia'. In *Entre el perdón y el paredón*, edited by Angelika Rettberg, pp. 54–71. Idrc, 2005.

Otis, John. 'Abortion Laws in Colombia Are Now among the Most Liberal in the Americas'. *National Public Radio*. July 13, 2022. https://www.npr.org/sections/goatsandsoda/2022/05/10/1097570784/colombia-legalized-abortions-for-the-first-24-weeks-of-pregnancy-a-backlash-ensu

Pachirat, Timothy. *Among Wolves: Ethnography and the Immersive Study of Power*. Routledge, 2018.

Pachirat, Timothy. 'The Tyranny of Light'. *Qualitative & Multi-method Research* 13, no. 1 (2015): 2–64.

Paffenholz, Thania. 'Unpacking the Local Turn in Peacebuilding: A Critical Assessment towards an Agenda for Future Research'. *Third World Quarterly* 36, no. 5 (2015): 857–74.

Parkinson, Sarah Elizabeth, and Elisabeth Jean Wood. 'Transparency in Intensive Research on Violence: Ethical Dilemmas and Unforeseen Consequences'. *Qualitative & Multi-Method Research* 13, no. 1 (2015): 2–64.

Parpart, Jane, and Swati Parashar, eds. *Rethinking Silence, Voice and Agency in Contested Gendered Terrains: Beyond the Binary*. Routledge, 2018.

Pellegrino, Valentina. 'Between the Roll of Paper and the Role of Paper: Governmental Documentation as a Mechanism for Complying Incompliantly'. *PoLAR: Political and Legal Anthropology Review* 45, no. 1 (2022): 77–93.

Pérez Fernández, Federico. 'Laboratorios de reconstrucción urbana: Hacia una antropología de la política urbana en Colombia'. *Antípoda* 10 (2010): 51–84.

Pham, Phuong, Patrick Vinck, Bridget Marchesi, Doug Johnson, Peter Dixon, and Kathryn Sikkink. 'Evaluating Transitional Justice: The Role of Multi-level Mixed Methods Datasets and the Colombia Reparation Program for War Victims'. *Transitional Justice Review* 1, no. 4 (2016): 1–35.

Piepzna-Samarasinha, Leah Lakshmi. *Care Work: Dreaming Disability Justice*. Arsenal Pulp Press, 2018.

Pillay, Navi. 'Colombia puede convertirse en un ejemplo global al escuchar a las víctimas'. *La Semana*. August 14, 2014. https://www.semana.com/opinion/articulo/colombia-puede-convertirse-en-un-ejemplo-global-al-escuchar-las-victimas/399178-3/.

Pizarro, Eduardo. *Cambiar el futuro*. Debate, 2017.

Power, Michael. *The Audit Society: Rituals of Verification*. Oxford University Press, 1999.

Prada, Elena, Susheela Singh, Lisa Remez, and Cristina Villareal. 'Unintended Pregnancy and Induced Abortion in Colombia'. Guttmacher Institute, 2011.

Puig de la Bellacasa, María. *Matters of Care: Speculative Ethics in More Than Human Worlds*. University of Minnesota Press, 2017.

Puig de la Bellacasa, María. ' "Nothing Comes without Its World": Thinking with Care'. *Sociological Review* 60, no. 2 (2012): 197–216.

Ramírez, María Clemencia. *Between the Guerrillas and the State: The Cocalero Movement, Citizenship, and Identity in the Colombian Amazon*. Duke University Press, 2011.

Ramírez, María Clemencia. 'The Idea of the State in Colombia: An Analysis from the Periphery'. In *State Theory and Andean Politics,* edited by Christopher Krupa and David Nugent, pp. 35–55. University of Pennsylvania Press, 2015.

Ramírez, Sebastián. 'Making Home in War: An Ethnography on Reparations and Horizons in the Eve of Peace in Colombia'. PhD dissertation: Princeton University, 2019.

Rao, Rahul. *Out of Time: The Queer Politics of Postcoloniality.* Oxford University Press, 2020.

Ravecca, Paulo. *The Politics of Political Science: Rewriting Latin American Experiences.* Routledge, 2019.

Ravecca, Paulo, and Elizabeth Dauphinee. 'Narrative and the Possibilities for Scholarship'. *International Political Sociology* 12, no. 2 (2018): 125–38.

Ravecca, Paulo, and Elizabeth Dauphinee. 'What Is Left for Critique? On the Perils of Innocence in Neoliberal Times'. *Las Torres de Lucca: Revista Internacional de Filosofía Política* 11, no. 1 (2022): 37–49.

Reddy, Deepa. 'Caught! The Predicaments of Ethnography in Collaboration'. In *Fieldwork Is Not What It Used to Be: Learning Anthropology's Method in a Time of Transition,* edited by James Faubion and George Marcus, pp. 89–112. Cornell University Press, 2009.

'Remarks by UN Women Executive Director Phumzile Mlambo-Ngcuka at the Peace Talks Table with the Government of Colombia and FARC-EP in Havana'. UN Women. July 2016. https://www.unwomen.org/news/stories/2016/7/speech-by-executive-director-in-cuba.

Rettberg, Angelika, ed. *Entre el perdón y el paredón.* Ediciones Uniandes, 2005.

Rettberg, Angelika. 'Ley de víctimas en Colombia: Un balance'. *Revista de Estudios Sociales* 54 (2015): 185–88.

Rettberg, Angelika. 'Victims of the Colombian Armed Conflict: The Birth of a Political Actor'. In *Colombia's Political Economy at the Outset of the 21st Century: From Uribe to Santos and Beyond,* edited by Bruce Bagley and Jonathan Friedman, pp. 111–40. Lexington Books, 2015.

Riaño-Alcalá, Pilar. 'Stories That Claim: Justice Narratives and Testimonial Practices among the Wayuu'. *Anthropological Quarterly* 93, no. 4 (2020): 589–623.

Riaño Alcalá, Pilar, and María Victoria Uribe. 'Constructing Memory amidst War: The Historical Memory Group of Colombia'. *International Journal of Transitional Justice* 10, no. 1 (2016): 6–24.

Rich, Adrienne. 'Notes Towards a Politics of Location'. In *Feminist Postcolonial Theory: A Reader,* edited by Reina Lewis and Sara Mills, pp. 29–42. Edinburgh University Press, 2003.

Richey, Lisa, and Stefano Ponte. *Brand Aid: Shopping Well to Save the World.* University of Minnesota Press, 2011.

Ricoeur, Paul. *Figuring the Sacred: Religion, Narrative, and Imagination.* Edited by Mark I. Wallace. Translated by David Pellauer. Fortress Press, 1995.

Rieff, David. *In Praise of Forgetting: Historical Memory and Its Ironies.* Yale University Press, 2016.

Ríos Oyola, Sandra, and Carolina Hormaza. 'The Role of Civil Servants in the Dignification of Victims in Meta, Colombia'. *Third World Quarterly* 44, no. 4 (2023): 795–813.

Ritholtz, Samuel, José Fernando Serrano-Amaya, Jamie Hagen, and Melanie Judge. 'En construcción: Hacia una teoría y praxis de la construcción de la paz queer/cuir'. *Revista de Estudios Sociales* 83, no. 1 (2023): 3–22.

Rivas, Jairo. 'Official Victims' Registries: A Tool for the Recognition of Human Rights Violations'. *Journal of Human Rights Practice* 8, no. 1 (2016): 116–27.

Robbins, Joel. 'Beyond the Suffering Subject: Toward an Anthropology of the Good'. *Journal of the Royal Anthropological Institute* 19, no. 3 (2013): 447–62.

Robins, Simon. 'Failing Victims'. *Human Rights and International Legal Discourse* 11 (2017): 41–58.

Rodríguez, Carolina. '¿Conflicto armado interno en Colombia? Más allá de la guerra de las palabras'. *Magistro* 4, no. 7 (2010): 111–25.

Rodríguez Castro, Laura. *Decolonial Feminisms, Power, and Place: Sentipensando with Rural Women in Colombia*. Palgrave Macmillan, 2021.

Rodríguez Castro, Laura. '"We Are Not Poor Things": Territorio Cuerpo-Tierra and Colombian Women's Organised Struggles'. *Feminist Theory* 22, no. 3 (2021): 339–59.

Rodríguez Idárraga, Nicolás. 'La naturalización de la violencia: Damnificados, Víctimas y desarrollo en la segunda mitad del siglo XX colombiano'. PhD Dissertation: University of Montreal, 2017.

Romero, Mauricio. *Paramilitares y autodefensas: 1982–2003*. Temas de Hoy, 2003.

Ross, Fiona. 'On Having Voice and Being Heard: Some After-Effects of Testifying before the South African Truth and Reconciliation Commission'. *Anthropological Theory* 3, no. 3 (2003): 325–41.

Roy, Ananya. *Poverty Capital: Microfinance and the Making of Development*. Routledge, 2010.

Rudling, Adriana. '"I'm Not That Chained-Up Little Person": Four Paragons of Victimhood in Transitional Justice Discourse'. *Human Rights Quarterly* 41, no. 2 (2019): 421–40.

Rudling, Adriana. 'What's inside the Box? Mapping Agency and Conflict within Victims' Organisations'. *International Journal of Transitional Justice* 13, no. 3 (2019): 458–77.

Saeed, Huma. 'Victims and Victimhood: Individuals of Inaction or Active Agents of Change? Reflections on Fieldwork in Afghanistan'. *International Journal of Transitional Justice* 10, no. 1 (2016): 168–78.

Sáenz Cabezas, Marya Hinira. *La paz en primera plena*. Universidad Nacional de Colombia, 2017.

Safford, Frank, and Marco Palacios. *Colombia: Fragmented Land, Divided Society*. Latin American Histories, 2002.

Sánchez, Gonzalo. 'La Violencia in Colombia: New Research, New Questions'. *Hispanic American Historical Review* 65, no. 4 (1985): 789–807.

Sánchez León, Nelson Camilo. 'El momento de las víctimas en La Habana'. Dejusticia. June 16, 2014. https://www.dejusticia.org/column/el-momento-de-las-victimas-en-la-habana/.

Sandvik, Kristin, and Julieta Lemaitre. 'From IDPs to Victims in Colombia: A Bottom-Up Reading of Law in Post-conflict Transitions'. In *International Law and Post-conflict Reconstruction Policy*, edited by Matthew Saul and James Sweeney, pp. 251–71. Routledge, 2015.

'Santos: No hay recursos para reparar todas las víctimas al mismo tiempo: Santos | Nacional | Caracol Radio'. *Caracol*. August 18, 2017. https://caracol.com.co/radio/2017/08/14/nacional/1502735685_067139.html.

'Santos: "Recibo este premio Nobel en nombre de las millones de víctimas del conflicto en Colombia"'. *BBC News Mundo*. October 7, 2016. https://www.bbc.com/mundo/noticias-america-latina-37586193.

Schouw Iversen, Karen. 'Participation as Confrontation: Resistance within and outside the Mesas de Participación Established for IDPs in Colombia'. *Journal of Refugee Studies* 35, no. 3 (2022): 1327–43.
Schulz, Philipp. *Male Survivors of Wartime Sexual Violence: Perspectives from Northern Uganda*. University of California Press, 2020.
Scott, James. *Seeing Like a State: How Certain Schemes to Improve the Human Condition Have Failed*. Yale University Press, 1998.
Secor, Anna. 'Between Longing and Despair: State, Space, and Subjectivity in Turkey'. *Environment and Planning D: Society and Space* 25, no. 1 (2007): 33–52.
Serje, Margarita. *El revés de la nación*. Ediciones Uniandes, 2011.
Sharpe, Christina. *In the Wake: On Blackness and Being*. Duke University Press, 2016.
Shaw, Rosalind, Lars Waldorf, and Pierre Hazan, eds. *Localizing Transitional Justice: Interventions and Priorities after Mass Violence*. Stanford University Press, 2010.
Shepherd, Laura. *Gender, UN Peacebuilding, and the Politics of Space: Locating Legitimacy*. Oxford University Press, 2017.
Shepherd, Laura. *Narrating Women, Peace, and Security*. Oxford University Press, 2021.
Shepherd, Laura. 'Research as Gendered Intervention: Feminist Research Ethics and the Self in the Research Encounter'. *Crítica Contemporánea Revista de Teoría Política* 6 (2017): 1–15.
Sikkink, Kathryn, Phuong N. Pham, Douglas A. Johnson, Peter J. Dixon, Bridget Marchesi, and Patrick Vinck. 'An Evaluation of Comprehensive Reparations Measures in Colombia: Accomplishments and Challenges'. Carr Center for Human Rights Policy and Harvard Humanitarian Initiative, 2015.
Simpson, Audra. 'On Ethnographic Refusal: Indigeneity, "Voice" and Colonial Citizenship'. *Junctures* 9 (2007): 67–80.
Solnit, Rebecca. *Hope in the Dark*. Haymarket Books, 2016.
Special Report of the Kroc Institute and the International Accompaniment Component, UN Women, Women's International Democratic Federation, and Sweden on the Monitoring of the Gender Perspective of the Implementation of the Colombian Peace Accord. Kroc Institute, 2018. https://kroc.nd.edu/assets/297624/181113_gender_report_final.pdf.
Spivak, Gayatri. 'Subaltern Studies: Deconstructing Historiography?' In *The Spivak Reader*, edited by Donna Landry and Gerald MacLean, pp. 270–304. Routledge, 1996.
Stauffer, Jill. *Ethical Loneliness: The Injustice of Not Being Heard*. Columbia University Press, 2015.
Steele, Abbey. *Democracy and Displacement in Colombia's Civil War*. Cornell University Press, 2017.
Strathern, Marilyn. *Audit Cultures: Anthropological Studies in Accountability, Ethics, and the Academy*. Routledge, 2000.
Subotić, Jelena. 'The Transformation of International Transitional Justice Advocacy'. *International Journal of Transitional Justice* 6, no. 1 (2012): 106–25.
Summers, Nicole. 'Colombia's Victims' Law: Transitional Justice in a Time of Violent Conflict?' *Harvard Human Rights Journal* 25, no. 1 (2012): 219–35.
Summerson Carr, E. *Scripting Addiction: The Politics of Therapeutic Talk and American Sobriety*. Princeton University Press, 2010.
Sylvester, Christine. *War as Experience: Contributions from International Relations and Feminist Analysis*. Routledge, 2013.

Tapia Navarro, Nadia. 'The Category of Victim 'from Below': The Case of the Movement of Victims of State Crimes (MOVICE) in Colombia'. *Human Rights Review* 20 (2019): 289–312.

Tate, Winifred. 'The Aspirational State: State Effects in Putumayo'. In *State Theory and Andean Politics*, edited by Christopher Krupa and David Nugent, pp. 289–314. University of Pennsylvania Press, 2015.

Tate, Winifred. *Counting the Dead: The Culture and Politics of Human Rights Activism in Colombia*. University of California Press, 2007.

Tate, Winifred. *Drugs, Thugs, and Diplomats: US Policymaking in Colombia*. Stanford University Press, 2015.

Thaler, Kai. 'Reflexivity and Temporality in Researching Violent Settings: Problems with the Replicability and Transparency Regime'. *Geopolitics* 27, no. 1 (2019): 1–27.

Theidon, Kimberly. *Intimate Enemies: Violence and Reconciliation in Peru*. University of Pennsylvania Press, 2012.

Ticktin, Miriam. *Casualties of Care: Immigration and the Politics of Humanitarianism in France*. University of California Press, 2011.

Ticktin, Miriam. 'A World without Innocence'. *American Ethnologist* 44, no. 4 (2017): 577–90.

Transken, Si. 'Poetically Teaching/Doing the Profession of Social Work as a Joyful Undisciplined Discipline Jumper and Genre Jumper'. *Critical Social Work* 3, no. 1 (2002), https://ojs.uwindsor.ca/index.php/csw/article/view/5646.

Tranströmer, Tomas. *The Blue House*. Translated by Göran Malmqvist. Thunder City Press, 1987.

Tripathi, Shambhawi. 'But Where Is the Magic? Emotional-Relational Humans and Their Untold Stories in International Relations'. *Millennium* 51, no. 1 (2023): 157–83.

Tronto, Joan. *Moral Boundaries: A Political Argument for an Ethic of Care*. Routledge, 1993.

Trouillot, Michel-Rolph. 'Anthropology and the Savage Slot: The Poetics and Politics of Otherness'. In *Global Transformations*, edited by Michel-Rolph Trouillot, pp. 7–28. Palgrave Macmillan, 2003.

Tsing, Anna. *The Mushroom at the End of the World: On the Possibility of Life in Capitalist Ruins*. Princeton University Press, 2015.

Tuck, Eve. 'Suspending Damage: A Letter to Communities'. *Harvard Educational Review* 79, no. 3 (2009): 409–28.

Tuck, Eve, and K. Wayne Yang. 'Decolonization Is Not a Metaphor'. *Decolonization: Indigeneity, Education and Society* 1, no. 1 (2012): 1–40.

Turner, Lewis. 'Syrian Refugee Men as Objects of Humanitarian Care'. *International Feminist Journal of Politics* 21, no. 4 (2019): 595–616.

Ulmer, Jasmine Brooke. 'Pivots and Pirouettes: Carefully Turning Traditions'. *Qualitative Inquiry* 26, no. 5 (2020): 454–57.

Unidad para la atención y reparación integral a las víctimas. https://www.unidadvictimas.gov.co.

Uprimny, Rodrigo, and Diana Guzmán-Rodríguez. 'En búsqueda de un concepto transformador y participativo para las reparaciones en contextos transicionales'. *International Law* 17 (2010): 232–86.

Uprimny, Rodrigo, and María Paula Saffon. 'Usos y abusos de la justicia transicional en Colombia'. *Anuario de Derechos Humanos*, no. 4 (2008): 165–95.

Uribe, María Victoria, and Juan Felipe Urueña. *Miedo al pueblo: Representaciones y autorrepreentaciones de las FARC*. Editorial Universidad del Rosario, 2019.

Utas, Mats. 'West-African Warscapes: Victimcy, Girlfriending, Soldiering: Tactic Agency in a Young Woman's Social Navigation of the Liberian War Zone'. *Anthropological Quarterly* 78, no. 2 (2005): 403–30.
Vallejo, Catalina. 'Pricing Suffering: Compensation for Human Rights Violation in Colombia and Peru'. PhD dissertation: University of Virginia, 2019.
Vandermaas-Peeler, Alex, Jelena Subotić, and Michael Barnett. 'Constructing Victims: Suffering and Status in Modern World Order'. *Review of International Studies* 2022: 1–19.
Vannier, Christian. 'Audit Culture and Grassroots Participation in Rural Haitian Development'. *PoLAR: Political and Legal Anthropology Review* 33, no. 2 (2010): 282–305.
Vera Lugo, Juan Pablo. 'Burocracias humanitarias en Colombia: Conocimiento técnico y disputas políticas en la implementación de la Ley de Víctimas y Restitución de Tierras'. *Revista de Estudios Sociales* 81 (2022): 21–37.
Vera Lugo, Juan Pablo. 'The Humanitarian State: Bureaucracy and Social Policy in Colombia'. PhD dissertation: Rutgers University, 2017.
Vera Lugo, Juan Pablo. 'Transitional Justice, Memory, and the Emergence of Legal Subjectivities in Colombia'. In *A Sense of Justice: Legal Knowledge and Lived Experience in Latin America*, edited by Sandra Brunnegger and Karen Ann Faulk, pp. 25–50. Stanford University Press, 2016.
'Víctimas serán las protagonistas: Duque—Colombia'. *ReliefWeb*. November 2018. https://reliefweb.int/report/colombia/v-ctimas-ser-n-las-protagonistas-duque.
Vidal-López, Roberto. *Derecho global y desplazamiento interno: Creación, uso y desaparición del desplazamiento forzado por la violencia en el derecho contemporáneo*. Pontificia Universidad Javeriana, 2007.
Villa Gómez, Juan David, Daniela Barrera Machado, Laura Arroyave Pizarro, and Yirley Montoya Betancur. 'Acción con daño: Del asistencialismo a la construcción social de la víctima. Mirada a procesos de reparación e intervención psicosocial en Colombia'. *Universitas Psychologica* 16, no. 3 (2017): 264–76.
Walker, Margaret Urban. 'Gender and Violence in Focus: A Background for Gender Justice in Reparations'. In *The Gender of Reparations: Unsettling Sexual Hierarchies While Redressing Human Rights Violations*, edited by Ruth Rubio-Marín, pp. 18–62. Cambridge University Press, 2009.
Walker, Margaret Urban. 'Transformative Reparations? A Critical Look at a Current Trend in Thinking about Gender-Just Reparations'. *International Journal of Transitional Justice* 10, no. 1 (2016): 108–25.
Wedeen, Lisa. 'Ethnography As Interpretive Enterprise'. In *Political Ethnography: What Immersion Contributes to the Study of Power*, edited by Edward Schatz, pp. 75–94. University of Chicago Press, 2009.
Weld, Kirsten. *Paper Cadavers: The Archives of Dictatorship in Guatemala*. Duke University Press, 2014.
Wibben, Annick. 'Everyday Security, Feminism, and the Continuum of Violence'. *Journal of Global Security Studies* 5, no. 1 (2020): 115–21.
Wibben, Annick. *Researching War: Feminist Methods, Ethics and Politics*. Routledge, 2016.
Wibben, Annick, Catia Cecilia Confortini, Sanam Roohi, Sarai B. Aharoni, Leena Vastapuu, and Tiina Vaittinen. 'Collective Discussion: Piecing-Up Feminist Peace Research'. *International Political Sociology* 13, no. 1 (2019): 86–107.

Wood, Elisabeth Jean. 'Rape as a Practice of War: Toward a Typology of Political Violence'. *Politics & Society* 46, no. 4 (2018): 513–37.

Wu, Joyce. '"Doing Good and Feeling Good": How Narratives in Development Stymie Gender Equality in Organisations'. *Third World Quarterly* 43, no. 3 (2022): 634–50.

Young, Kevin. 'Ledge'. Academy of American Poets. April 28, 2023. https://poets.org/poem/ledge.

Zalewski, Marysia. 'Distracted Reflections on the Production, Narration, and Refusal of Feminist Knowledge in International Relations'. In *Feminist Methodologies for International Relations*, edited by Brooke Ackerly, Maria Stern, and Jacqui True, pp. 42–61. Cambridge University Press, 2006.

Zeiderman, Austin. *Endangered City: The Politics of Security and Risk in Bogotá*. Duke University Press, 2016.

Zulver, Julia. *High-Risk Feminism in Colombia*. Rutgers University Press, 2022.

Index

For the benefit of digital users, indexed terms that span two pages (e.g., 52–53) may, on occasion, appear on only one of those pages.

Note: Figures are indicated by *f* following the page number

abortion restrictions, 176–77
activism. *See* feminism/feminist activism
agency
   feminist theorization of, 19
   political agency, 169, 186–87
   survivor and, 19–20
   victimhood intersection with, 19
Ahmed, Sara, 25, 26–27, 99, 123–24, 156
alongsideness, 24, 34, 58–59, 92, 105, 128–29, 198–99, 226–27
anonymity in victimhood research, 89–92
anti-ending, 31–32
anti-politics, 26, 137
Aretxaga, Begoña, 6–7
asistencialismo (welfarism), 207–12, 216–19
attendance sheets, 140–45
Auyero, Javier, 151

Baines, Erin, 19
Ban Ki-moon, 61
Basic Principles and Guidelines for Remedy and Reparation, 210
being the state, 102–7, 108, 109, 116, 121, 123–24, 129
Berlant, Lauren, 104–5
Berry, Marie, 187
Brett, Roddy, 46, 48–49
Brown, Wendy, 12
Buchely, Lina, 15–16
bureaucracies/bureaucrats of victimhood activism, 15–16
   being the state, 102–7, 108, 109, 116, 121, 123–24, 129
   counting and narrating harms, 39–43
   feelings in, 123–26

fictional beginnings, 33–35
ghosts in, 30–31, 106–7, 117, 118–23, 130–31, 144, 157
good state and, 102–7, 109–18, 123–31
hauntings in, 106–7, 109, 117, 121, 128–31, 144–45, 176
independence from colonial rule, 35–36
institutional framework and, 66–68
internal armed conflict, 61–62
introduction to, 4–8, 30–31, 102–7
La Violencia, 36, 37–39
life stories, 107–9
longings in, 102, 106, 117, 130
peace agreements, 43–56
peacebuilding, 36, 43–49
post-accord peace, 34, 52–54, 176–77
transitional justice, 34–35, 50, 51–52, 55–56, 59–60, 102–7, 109–18, 123*f*, 127–31
unlikely bureaucrat, 117
victim-centred peacemaking, 43–49
victim identity markers and, 170
businessification, 141. *See also* victim professionalization

capacity-building, 73, 111, 213–14, 218–19
care work, 157–62
Carr, E. Summerson, 138, 152
Castro-Sardi, Ximena, 110–12, 117, 141–42, 146–50, 153, 158, 165, 208–9
Centre Democratic Party, 54–55
Centre for Thought and Follow-up to the Peace Dialogue of the National University, 46
Cerwonka, Allaine, 5
civil society actors, 44, 45–46, 90

claim-making, 2, 12, 15, 19, 21–22, 139, 154, 183, 194, 195–96, 199, 218–19
Cold War, 37–38
Colombian Congress, 58
Colombian Constitutional Court, 51–52, 54, 58–59, 121–22
Commission for Monitoring of the Implementation of Victims' Law, 202, 209–10
Commission for the Clarification of Truth, Coexistence and Non-Repetition (Truth Commission), 21, 22, 38, 39–43, 46, 50, 70–71, 102–7
complex personhood, 98, 108–9, 130
Comprehensive System of Truth, Justice, Reparation, and Non-Repetition, 50
conflict voyeurism, 207
Conley, Bridget, 17
Contreras, Luz Marina Hache, 225
critique, 23–24, 26–27, 60, 93–98, 137–38, 139, 165, 170–71, 189–90, 211–12
Cuban Revolution, 37–38
cultural identity, 133, 134*f*
Curtis, Jennifer, 11–12

damnificados, 56–57
Das, Veena, 11, 20–21, 88–89
data
   acronyms in databases, 160–61
   articulation of, 142–44
   disaggregated, 133
   real data point, 146–47, 150
   socialization of, 143
   synthesis efforts, 39–41, 50, 64–65
De Roux, Francisco, 103–4
Dery, David, 140
DiFruscia, Kim Turcot, 11
disciplines (academic), 24, 27–28
dis-identification, 28–29
doing gender, 25
doing politics, 214–15
Doty, Roxanne Lynn, 17
Duque, Iván, 54–56, 68
Durango, María Lucely, 224, 227

Edkins, Jenny, 209
ELN. *See* National Liberation Army
Emejulu, Akwugo, 139–40

Enloe, Cynthia, 26
Episcopal Conference of the Catholic Church, 46
EPL. *See* Popular Liberation Army
era of the victims, 1–2, 13–14, 20–21
ethics. *See* narratives/storytelling in ethics of victimhood

FARC. *See* Revolutionary Armed Forces of Colombia
Fassin, Didier, 107–8
feelings in bureaucracies of victimhood, 123–26
feminism/feminist activism
   in global politics, 113
   methodologies, 14
   origin stories, 1–3
   on victimhood, 18, 24–30
   victim professionalization and, 141
feminist curiosity, 26–28, 107–8, 141
Ferguson, James, 137
Flight of the Phoenix: From the Ashes to the Fire of the Word, 219–27
Forero, Ana María, 93
fractured politics, 169
Fraser, Nancy, 211–12
Fund for Victims' Reparation, 66–67
FUT (Unique Territorial Form), 142–43
future of victimhood
   armed conflict and violence, 196–99
   asistencialismo (welfarism) and, 207–12, 216–19
   fashions and fads, 192–96
   hope as practice, 213–19
   introduction to, 31–32
   number of victims and, 199–203
   reparations and, 200–5, 208, 210–11, 216–17, 223
   transitional justice, 194–95, 197–203, 207, 210–11, 215–18, 219–27
   victim entrepreneurship, 14–15, 195–96, 206, 209–10, 213
   'The Victims in the Post-Conflict,' 204–7

Gaitán, Jorge Eliécer, 36–37
Galán, Juan Manuel, 209–10
Galeano, Eduardo, 220–21
gender analysis, 3, 25, 72

INDEX 251

gender-based violence. *See also* sexual violence
  future of victimhood, 226
  introduction to, 31
  overview of, 167–68, 172–77
  politics of victimhood research, 72–78
  poverty and, 177–84
  transitional justice and, 169, 170–71, 173–74, 175–87, 189–90
gender relations, 25
ghosts in bureaucracies of victimhood, 30–31, 106–7, 117, 118–23, 130–31, 144, 157
Golubović, Jelena, 22, 97
good state, 7, 30–31, 102–7, 109–18, 123–31
Gordon, Avery, 98, 106–7
Gordon, Linda, 211–12
Gready, Paul, 171
group identity, 133, 134f
Grupo de Memoria Historica, 114–15. *See also* National Centre for Historical Memory
guerrillas, 37–39, 41–42, 43–44, 56, 62, 115–16, 172–73
Gupta, Akhil, 81

Haraway, Donna, 198–99
haunting, 106–7, 109, 117, 121, 128–31, 144–45, 176
Havana peace talks, 1–2, 22, 50–52, 185
hierarchies of victimhood, 2, 95–96, 98
High Advisory for Human Rights, 121–22, 124, 125
hope, 213–19
Hormaza, Carolina, 158–59
Human Rights Data Analysis Group, 40–41
Hutchings, Kimberly, 197

Inayatullah, Naeem, 13–14, 71
innocence, 28–29, 97, 98, 165. *See also* purity
institutionality (institucionalidad), 94, 118–23, 126, 128–29, 153–54
interdisciplinarity, 7, 26–27, 28–29, 31–32, 107–8
internal armed conflict, 61–62

international humanitarian law, 41, 51, 62–63
international organizations
  displaced persons and, 57–58
  era of the victims, 1–2
  future of victimhood, 199, 204, 205, 206, 208–9, 216, 218–20, 223
  living ethics and, 70–71, 72–73, 78, 79, 85
  victim distinction, 166, 182–83
international relations (IR), academic discipline of, 25, 28–29

Jacoby, Tami Amanda, 9
Jaramillo, Sergio, 1–2
joy, 25, 84, 101, 160, 198–99, 214–15
Judgement T-025 (2004), 58–59
justice. *See also* transitional justice
  ordinary, 169, 176–77, 184
  peace-and-justice systems, 56, 76–78, 133, 190
  seed-sowing theory of, 189–91

kinship, 24, 27–30, 199
Kreft, Anne-Kathrin, 18–19
Kroc Institute for International Peace Studies, 53–54

labour of victimhood, 15, 26–27, 31, 136, 137–38, 145, 150, 152, 158–62, 184
Lake, Milli, 174
language of victimhood, 16–20, 56, 189, 198–99, See also vernacular of victimhood
Laplante, Lisa, 59
La Violencia, 36, 37–39
Law of Justice and Peace, 59–60, 62–66
Law of Victims and Land Restitution
  bureaucracies of victimhood in Colombia, 34–35, 61–68
  congressional monitoring, 200
  future of victimhood, 199–203
  institutional framework from, 66–68
  internal armed conflict and, 61–62
  Mesas and, 86–88
  public policy creation and, 87
  transitional justice and, 182
  victims, defined under, 62–66
  'The Victims in the Post-Conflict,' 204–7

Lea, Tess, 104
Lederach, Angela, 91, 99–100
LGBTQI individuals, 45, 133, 145
longings in bureaucracies of victimhood, 102, 106, 117, 130

Mac Ginty, Roger, 137
making a presence (hacer presencia), 141–42
Malkki, Liisa, 5
Mallon, Florencia, 15–16, 98
Mariaca, Rosalba, 225–26
Márquez, Francia, 56
Márquez, Gabriel García, 102–3
Martinez, Natylem Gomez, 226
massacres, 41, 113, 206
Meertens, Donny, 189
Merry, Sally, 39, 116
Mesas (Mesas de Participación Efectiva de Víctimas), 86–88, 90, 94–95, 124–25, 132–38, 140–45
    Forums for Victims' Participation (Mesas de Participación de Víctimas), 66
Meyers, Diana, 18–19
Mlambo-Ngcuka, Phumzile, 52
Municipal Victims' Team in Medellín, 81, 137, 142

Nader, Laura, 4
narcotrafficking, 38–39, 41
narratives/storytelling in ethics of victimhood
    afterlives of, 82–85
    anonymity and, 89–92
    encounters and inquiries, 78–82
    gendered violence, 72–78
    introduction to, 69–72
    loyalty to interlocutors, 93–98
    main interlocutors, 85–89
    Mesas and, 86–88
    methodology of alongsideness, 24, 34, 58–59, 92, 105, 128–29, 198–99, 226–27
    origin stories, 1–3
    politics of victimhood research, 92–93
    remaining dilemmas, 101
    theory of victimhood, 99–100
    transitional justice, 73–78, 76f, 77f, 85–86, 94
    victimization narrative/story, 92–93
National Centre for Historical Memory (CNMH), 33, 164–68, 183–84, 218, 219–20, 221
National Commission for Reparation and Reconciliation, 138–39
National Day of Memory and Solidarity with Victims of the Armed Conflict, 192–94, 193f
National Liberation Army (ELN), 37–38, 43–44, 56
Nelson, Diane, 39–40
19th of April Movement (M-19), 37–38
Nixon, Rob, 196

Office of the High Advisory for Victims, Peace, and Reconciliation in Bogotá, 81
Office of the High Commissioner for Peace, 61
Olano, Juliana, 208–9
Olufemi, Lola, 26
ordinary justice, 169, 176–77, 184
Orozco, Iván, 62

Pachirat, Timothy, 2
Palacio, Laura, 225, 227
Palacio Lemos, Lina María, 220, 226
Paper Cadavers (Weld), 150–51
paramilitarism, 38, 60
paramilitary groups, 38–39, 42, 43–44, 56, 59
passivity, 18–19
peace accords, 54–56, 62, 73, 82
peace agreements, 43–56
peace-and-justice systems, 56, 76–78, 133, 190
peacebuilding, 12, 36, 43–49
peace talks, 1–2, 22, 43–49, 50, 52, 56
Pellegrino, Valentina, 122–23, 136–37
Petro, Gustavo, 56
Pillay, Navi, 46
Pizzaro, Eduardo, 33
plebiscite, 51–52, 124–25
política, defined, 11
political agency, 169, 186–87

political subject/subjectivities
    agency and, 169, 186–87
    being and becoming, 213–19, 223–24, 227
    introduction to, 9
    transition from victimhood, 194–96
    victim subject as, 10–13, 14–15, 17, 19, 137
political work, 15, 90, 137–38, 160–61, 214–15
politics of victimhood. *See also* bureaucracies/bureaucrats of victimhood
    doing politics, 214–15
    fractured politics, 169
    introduction to, 3–7, 8–9, 10, 20–21, 22–23, 25–26, 30–32
    questions and aims, 13–14
    stories about, 14–16
Popular Liberation Army (EPL), 37–38, 115–16
post-accord peace, 34, 52–54, 176–77
poverty and victimhood, 177–84
professionals/professionalization. *See* bureaucracies/bureaucrats of victimhood; victim professionalization
purity, 29, 79–80, 88, 97, 98, 105, 114, 165. *See also* innocence

rape. *See* sexual violence
Ravecca, Paulo, 14
refugee asylum, 153–54
registration process, 62–66
reparation
    bureaucracies of victimhood, 33, 39–40, 51, 52, 55–56, 59–61, 64–68
    future of victimhood, 200–5, 208, 210–11, 216–17, 223
    good state and, 127–28
    narratives of victimhood, 70–71, 79, 87
    politics of victimhood, 9–10, 14–15, 21–22
    transitional justice and, 179
    victim professionalization and, 133, 138–39, 158–59
research, defined, 70. *See also* narratives/storytelling in ethics of victimhood
Rettberg, Angelika, 67–68
Revolutionary Armed Forces of Colombia (FARC), 37–38, 43–45, 50–52, 53, 62

Ríos, Sandra, 158–59
rituals of verification, 44, 137–38, 142, 144–45, 154–55
Robbins, Joel, 197–98
Robins, Simon, 171
Rodríguez Castro, Laura, 99–100
Rodríguez Idárraga, Nicolás, 56–57
Roy, Ananya, 183–84
Rudling, Adriana, 110–11
RUSICST tool, 142–43

Sánchez, Gonzalo, 167–68
Santos, Juan Manuel, 52, 54, 61, 110
Schulz, Philipp, 18–19
Secor, Anna, 102
seed-sowing theory of justice, 189–91
self-stage, 16–17, 139
sexual violence, 31, 164–77. *See also* gender-based violence
Shepherd, Laura, 28, 85
Single Registry of Victims, 64–65
slum tourism, 207
socio-political mobilization, 31, 56–58, 169, 187
Special Administrative Unit for Attention and Comprehensive Reparation of Victims (Victims' Unit), 62–68, 84, 109–18, 128, 132, 173–74, 178
Special Jurisdiction for Peace (JEP), 21, 40–41, 51
Special Unit for the Search of Missing Persons, 50–51
Spencer, Jonathan, 11–12
Spivak, Gayatri Chakravorty, 169–70
state
    being the state, 102–7, 108, 109, 116, 121, 123–24, 129
    good state, 7, 30–31, 102–7, 109–18, 123–31
    policy fulfillment, 144–45
    victimhood and, 102–7, 108, 109, 116, 121, 123–24, 129
storytelling. *See* narratives/storytelling in ethics of victimhood
studying up, 4, 5, 6
Subotić, Jelena, 140–41
suffering slot, 12, 198
survival, 19–20

Tapia Navarro, Nadia, 49, 60
terrorism, 61–62
Theidon, Kimberly, 59, 93
theorein, defined, 70
theory of victimhood, 99–100
Thousand Days' War (1899–1902), 35
Ticktin, Miriam, 97
transitional justice
  bureaucracies of victimhood in Colombia, 34–35, 50, 51–52, 55–56, 59–60, 102–7, 109–18, 123f, 127–31
  differential approach, 185–89
  future of victimhood, 194–95, 197–203, 207, 210–11, 215–18, 219–27
  gender-based violence and, 169, 170–71, 173–74, 175–87, 189–90
  hierarchies and legacies, 8–10
  introduction to, 2, 3–7, 8–10, 12, 19, 22–24, 26–27, 29–31
  politics of victimhood research, 73–78, 76f, 77f, 85–86, 94
  poverty and, 177–84
  seed-sowing theory of justice, 189–91
  victim professionalization and, 132, 135–36, 138–41, 156–57
trauma, 7, 9–10, 74–75, 136
Truth Commission. *See* Commission for the Clarification of Truth, Coexistence and Non-Repetition
Tsing, Anna Lowenhaupt, 31–32, 107–8
Tuck, Eve, 28–29
turns, language of, 198–99

UN Basic Principles and Guidelines on the Right to a Remedy and Reparation, 201
United Nations, 46
United States Agency for International Development, 219–20
UN Verification Mission in Colombia, 53
Uribe, Álvaro, 54–55, 61
Uribe, María Victoria, 114–15
US-Colombian relations, 38

vernacular of victimhood, 118, 124, 178, 187–88, 204–6, See also language of victimhood
victim, legal definition, 62–66
victim-based identity, 9
victim-bureaucrat, 112, 117
victim-centred peacemaking, 43–49
victim entrepreneurship, 14–15, 195–96, 206, 209–10, 213
victimhood. *See also* bureaucracies/bureaucrats of victimhood; future of victimhood
  anonymity in research, 89–92
  context and stakes in investigation of, 20–24
  era of the victims, 1–2, 13–14, 20–21
  feminism on, 18, 24–30
  hierarchies of, 2, 95–96, 98
  language of, 16–20, 56, 189, 198–99
  origin stories, 1–3
  overview of, 30–32
  particular kind, 22, 222–23
  theory of, 99–100
  trouble-making victims, 9
victim identity, 45, 98, 172–73, 195, 203, 219–27
victimization, 16–17, 41–42, 47, 62–63, 65, 67–68, 79–80, 92, 104, 112, 172–73, 184, 187, 197, 216
victimization narrative/story. *See* narratives/storytelling in ethics of victimhood
victimizing acts (hechos victimizantes), 41, 46, 67, 187–88, 189
victim participation, 22–23, 48, 135, 144–45, 152–53, 155, 158–59, 166–67
victim professionalization. *See also* bureaucracies/bureaucrats of victimhood
  attendance sheets, 140–45
  care work, 157–62
  compensation strategy, 145–50
  double bind of, 138–40
  good victim and, 162–63
  introduction to, 31, 132–38
  paper work, 150–52, 160
  solidarity in, 152–54
  uses of, 154–57
victims' associations, 40–41, 45–46, 47, 70–71, 74, 78, 95, 102, 113, 159, 161–62, 177, 193f, 204
'The Victims in the Post-Conflict,' 204–7, 211, 216

Victims' Law. *See* Law of Victims and Land Restitution
victims of armed conflict, 169, 170–71, 177, 190–91
Victims' Registry (Registro Único de Víctimas), 9–10, 64–65, 66–67, 182, 200–1
victims' team, 4–5, 81, 116–17, 132, 142
Victims' Unit. *See* Special Administrative Unit for Attention and Comprehensive Reparation of Victims

Waardt, Mijke de, 16–17, 22–23

The War Inscribed in the Body: National Report on Sexual Violence in the Armed Conflict (CNMH), 164–66, 172
Weber, Sanne, 22–23
Weld, Kirsten, 150–51
welfarism. *See* asistencialismo
well-behaved victims, 9, 98
Wynter, Sylvia, 139–40

Yang, K. Wayne, 28–29
Young, Kevin, 83

The manufacturer's authorised representative in the EU for product safety is Oxford
University Press España S.A. of El Parque Empresarial San Fernando de Henares,
Avenida de Castilla, 2 – 28830 Madrid (www.oup.es/en or product.safety@oup.com).
OUP España S.A. also acts as importer into Spain of products made by the manufacturer.

Printed in the USA/Agawam, MA
March 28, 2025

885041.007